WEST

ASSEMBLY

CARL R. TRUEMAN
Series Editor

The WESTMINSTER ASSEMBLY

READING ITS THEOLOGY IN HISTORICAL CONTEXT

ROBERT LETHAM

PUBLISHING

P.O. BOX 817 • PHILLIPSBURG • NEW JERSEY 08865-0817

Printed in the United States of America

Library of Congress Cataloging-in-Publication Data

Letham, Robert.
The Westminster Assembly : reading its theology in historical context / Robert Letham.
    p. cm. — (The Westminster Assembly and the Reformed faith)
Includes bibliographical references and indexes.
ISBN 978-0-87552-612-6 (pbk.)
1. Westminster Assembly (1643-1652) 2. Theology, Doctrinal—History—17th century. 3. Church history—17th century. 4. Presbyterian Church—Doctrines. 5. Reformed Church—Doctrines. 6. Westminster Confession of Faith. I. Title.
BX9053.L48 2009
230'.52—dc22
        2009026674

In memoriam
Philip Edgcumbe Hughes (1915-1990)
Anglicanus ecclesiasticus
Doctor eminentissimus seminarii Presbyterianii
Theologus Calvinianus
Scholasticus Reformationis ac Novi Testamenti
Consiliarius doctissimus
In impositione manuum cum presbyterio ordinatione mea participavit,
et sic in successionem apostolorum meo loculum donavit!

You are at this time as a citty set upon a mountaine; the eyes of E[ngland], S[cotland], I[reland] & of all reformed churches are upon you; a delight to this meeting [?]; a desire & fervent expectation. And the eyes of papists, Arminians, &c. are all upon you, & howsoever they may seeme to dispise the day of small things, yet they behould this Assembly with great feare and astonishment.

—ALEXANDER HENDERSON, in a speech at the Westminster Assembly, 15 November 1643 (Van Dixhoorn, 3:311.)

If it were practicable, it would be interesting to contemplate the Assembly more at length in its historical setting and relations;—to pass in review its vital connections with the antecedent developments of British Protestantism from the age of Henry VIII, and also with much of the civil history of Britain during the hundred years preceding its convocation;—to call to mind also the diversified movements of the developing Protestantism of the continent during this period, and study the amazing revolution in belief and experience which occurred throughout northern Europe between the age of Luther and Calvin and the memorable day when the Assembly held its opening session in the beautiful Chapel of Henry VIII. It would also be interesting, if we could contemplate the Assembly in its living connections with the other great Christian Councils from the era of Nicaea and Constantinople down to the memorable Council of Trent,—if we could compare its doctrinal products more specifically with those of others in that illustrious series, and estimate comprehensively its relative bearings upon the subsequent theology and faith of Christendom. Such comparative studies, if they did not stir us to special and reverent admiration, would at least make manifest to us the emptiness of much of the derogatory criticism which in earlier and in later times has been heaped upon that memorable body. It would also demonstrate the fact that, if indeed the Westminster divines were not individually notable, as unfriendly critics have alleged, the Assembly itself was great,—great in the magnitude and elevation of its aims, great in the specific work which it accomplished, and great in the influence it has exerted, and is still exerting, alike upon the religious beliefs and upon the moral activities of millions who in various lands speak the English tongue.

—EDWARD D. MORRIS, *Theology of the Westminster Symbols*

Contents

Series Introduction

The last two decades have witnessed a revolution in the way in which scholars have come to understand the nature and development of Reformed theology in the sixteenth and seventeenth centuries. It was in this context, and to further this scholarly revolution, that Westminster Theological Seminary in Philadelphia established the Craig Center for the Study of the Westminster Standards in 2002. The Center provides a forum for promoting scholarly study of the history and theology of the Westminster Assembly, the various documents that it produced, and the way in which these documents have been received and used over the years.

As part of this project, the Craig Center has joined forces with P&R Publishing Company to commission a series of books, including monographs and collections of essays, that reflect this agenda. Each volume stands within the trajectories set by this new scholarship and takes seriously the theological content of Reformed orthodoxy, while not naively divorcing that content from its historical or ecclesiastical context. Yet in doing this, these books do not become simply examples of antiquarianism or historicism. In fact, our desire is that this approach will free the past from the shackles and constraints of the agendas of the present day and thus allow voices from history to speak meaningfully to the world of today. It is thus the hope of the Craig Committee that both church and academy will benefit from this series for many years to come.

Carl R. Trueman
Chair of the Craig Committee

Acknowledgments

It is a particularly happy task to acknowledge help received from a variety of sources. My grateful thanks are due in more ways than one to Dr. Chad Van Dixhoorn. First of all, his research on the Assembly minutes has paved the way for a greatly enhanced appreciation of the Assembly in both its historical and its theological dimensions. Second, he has generously given of his time to examine some of the early chapters on the historical background to the Assembly. The Rev. R. Sherman Isbell of Fairfax, Virginia, has also looked at significant sections and made many pertinent comments. Dr. Robert B. Strimple, president and professor of systematic theology, emeritus, Westminster Seminary California, has read through a number of lengthy draft chapters and made some valuable suggestions. Even more than that, his course on the Westminster Confession at Westminster Theological Seminary, Philadelphia, in the fall of 1974, in his days on the faculty there, first stimulated my interest in the Assembly. This book has been much improved by the contribution of these scholars, and it goes without saying that any remaining defects cannot be charged to their account. None of them has seen the full text; that alone should tell the reader that I take responsibility for the contents of the book. Additionally, Dr. Robert Norris, senior minister of Fourth Presbyterian Church, Bethesda, Maryland, kindly granted me access to his University of St. Andrews Ph.D. thesis, "The Thirty-Nine Articles at the Westminster Assembly." I also thank Tony Lane, professor of historical theology and director of research, London School of Theology, for permission to quote him on Calvin—on whom he is one of the world's leading authorities—at a significant point in the introduction, relating to Calvin's attitude to the Book of Common Prayer.

I am appreciative of the encouragement of the publishers. Allan Fisher, when he was at P&R, urged me to complete this book *post haste*. My delay in working on this book, and instead completing another one first, was due to the need to await the arrival of a copy of Chad Van Dixhoorn's transcription of the minutes. Marvin Padgett, who succeeded Allan Fisher, has been patient in the face of delays while I moved back to the United Kingdom. Carl Trueman, director of the Craig Center for the Study of the Westminster Standards, has encouraged me in the work. Thanks are due to P&R team members Thom Notaro, Barbara Lerch, Jim Scott, and Eric Anest for their help. I am grateful too for the help of Dr. James Dennison, academic dean and professor of church history and biblical theology at Northwest Theological Seminary, Lynnwood, Washington, for refining the Latin in the dedication.

I have used the resources of a number of libraries. The Montgomery Library, Westminster Theological Seminary, Philadelphia, is first on the list, and I am glad to record once again my gratitude to Grace Mullen for her attentiveness to my bibliographic needs, especially in the provision at an early stage of a copy of Dr. Van Dixhoorn's thesis. Access to Early English Books Online (EEBO) via the libraries of Westminster Seminary and latterly the University of Wales (Lampeter) has been indispensable. The amount of time this resource has saved is incalculable. The facilities of Cambridge University Library, including the Rare Books Room, have also been of immense help. I have also used the British Library, London.

I am grateful to the Presbytery of Philadelphia, the Orthodox Presbyterian Church, for its invitation to deliver a lecture at its November 2003 meeting. My work was about to begin in earnest, but it had not yet taken proper shape. However, the exercise helped to focus my thinking at that critical early stage. Members of the Christian Studies Forum, Emmanuel Orthodox Presbyterian Church, Wilmington, Delaware, where I was senior minister for over seventeen years, listened patiently to my thoughts on the Assembly and its historical background. The session and congregation of Emmanuel provided study leave and a generous line item in the annual budget for research; some of this book, especially the historical excursus on the development of the doctrine of the imputation of Adam's sin, was undertaken on these occasions at the Bodleian Library, Oxford, and the Library of Congress, Washington, D.C. I also thank the members of the research studies seminar at Wales Evangelical School of Theology, and Dr. Eryl Davies, its leader, for enabling me to present a summary of my research.

Last but not least, I am continually grateful to my wife, Joan, for her love and support throughout this and other writing projects.

> Almightye and euerlastyng God, geue unto us the increase of faythe, hope, and charitie: and that we may obteine that whiche thou doest promise; make us to loue that whiche thou dost commaunde, through Jesus Christe our Lorde. (Collect for the fourteenth Sunday after Trinity, the Boke of Common Prayer and Administracion of the Sacramentes, and other Rites and Ceremonies in the Churche of England. Londini: In officina Edvvardi Whytchurche, 1552)

Abbreviations

Aldis, *Scotland*	Harry G. Aldis, *A List of Books printed in Scotland before 1700: including those printed furth of the realm for Scottish booksellers with brief notes on the printers and stationers* (Edinburgh: National Library of Scotland, 1970)
Annotations	Certain Learned Divines, *Annotations upon all the books of the Old and New Testament, wherein the text is explained, doubts resolved, Scriptures parallelled and various readings observed by the joynt-labour of certain learned Divines, thereunto appointed, and therein employed, as is expressed in the Preface* (London: John Legatt and John Raworth, 1645) [Wing D2063]
CD	Karl Barth, *Church Dogmatics* (ed. G. W. Bromiley and T. F. Torrance; 14 vols.; Edinburgh: T. & T. Clark, 1956–77)
CTJ	*Calvin Theological Journal*
EQ	*Evangelical Quarterly*
Institutes	John Calvin, *Institutes of the Christian Religion*
JBS	*Journal of British Studies*
JETS	*Journal of the Evangelical Theological Society*
LC	Larger Catechism
PRRD	Richard A. Muller, *Post-Reformation Reformed Dogmatics: The Rise and Development of Reformed Orthodoxy, ca. 1520 to ca. 1725* (2nd ed. of vols. 1–2; 4 vols.; Grand Rapids: Baker, 2003)
RRR	*Reformation and Renaissance Review*
RTJ	*Reformed Theological Journal*

SBET	*Scottish Bulletin of Evangelical Theology*
SCJ	*Sixteenth Century Journal*
SJT	*Scottish Journal of Theology*
STC	*Short-Title Catalogue of Books printed in England, Scotland, & Ireland and of English Books printed abroad, 1475–1640* (London: Bibliographical Society, 1926)
TrRHS	*Transactions of the Royal Historical Society*
Van Dixhoorn	Chad B. Van Dixhoorn, "Reforming the Reformation: Theological Debate at the Westminster Assembly 1643–1652" (7 vols.; Ph.D. thesis, Cambridge University, 2004)
WCF	Westminster Confession of Faith
Wing	Donald Wing, *Short-Title Catalogue of Books printed in England, Scotland, Ireland, Wales and British America, and of English Books printed in other countries, 1641–1700* (New York: Index South, 1945)
WTJ	*The Westminster Theological Journal*

References to the Assembly Minutes

References to the transcribed minutes of the Assembly are to Chad B. Van Dixhoorn's Ph.D. thesis ("Reforming the Reformation," Cambridge, 2004), with volume and page numbers. However, this will shortly be superseded by the publication of a multivolume work containing the minutes and all extant papers and correspondence of the Assembly and its members. Therefore, so that the record can be followed up, regardless of the source, I refer in the body of the text to the Assembly session number and the date when the discussion took place. This is set out in the format S540 F 21.11.45, where S540 stands for session 540, F indicates the day of the week (Friday), and 21.11.45 is the calendar date (day.month.year). Since the Julian calendar was in operation, for dates from 1 January to 25 March I have retained the old year number, but put the modern number in parentheses: S582 F 2.2.45(46). Normally, plenary sessions of the Assembly were held in the morning. For days when there were both morning and afternoon sessions, the designation is followed by "am" or "pm."

Introduction

The Westminster Assembly (1643–52) was held during the English Civil Wars, a time of immense turbulence and upheaval. It was a landmark event. Theologically, it produced the most expansive confessional documents in the Reformed churches, even in Protestantism in general. Historically, it is of great significance in understanding this seminal period in English history. Recent historical scholarship has brought back to center stage the recognition that religion was the largest single factor in these wars. The Assembly was at the heart of the questions of the day; it had a vital place in English history at that decisive time.

The Assembly's debates concerned both church government and theology. Until recently, scholarship on the Assembly was preoccupied with ecclesiology. The divines were commonly denominated by their convictions on church polity—Presbyterians, Independents, and Episcopalians. This was a focus that reached its apex in the work of Robert S. Paul.[1] Most scholarly work on the Assembly was conducted by Scottish or American Presbyterians, focusing in the main on angles of interest to their particular constituencies, whereas the body was an English one, with representation from Wales as well. The Scottish commissioners who appeared on the scene later contributed significantly to the debates, but were not members of the Assembly as such and did not take part in the voting.

The recent work of Chad Van Dixhoorn, in his seven-volume Cambridge University Ph.D. thesis, his other writings, and the forthcoming multivolume critical edition of the Assembly minutes, together with

1. R. S. Paul, *Assembly of the Lord: Politics and Religion in the Westminster Assembly* (Edinburgh: T. & T. Clark, 1983).

1

all other extant papers and correspondence of the Assembly and its members, has changed the perception of Westminster. The rigorously scientific transcription of the minutes—hitherto in virtual hieroglyphics, decipherable only by highly specialized paleographers—will alone be an overwhelming advance. These are not the same as minutes of meetings today. They are more than merely a record of motions passed and actions taken. They include records of debates and the names of the participants, besides details of other Assembly business, including its interactions with Parliament. At the same time, their coverage of debate is spotty. The scribe, Adoniram Byfield, showed great interest in some debates and little in others. Moreover, as time went on, the reporting of discussion grew less extensive, as initial enthusiasm flagged. Some of this unevenness will be reflected in what follows; there will be a disproportionate concentration on some issues rather than others. However, in this we will, to an extent, be reflecting the interests at the time of the Assembly, rather than our own interests, and that is exactly what this book tries to do. Again, it is sometimes difficult to interpret exactly what was said in debates, as frequently the summaries are more than a little cryptic. Notwithstanding, Van Dixhoorn has enlarged our knowledge of the debates greatly and has corrected glaring inaccuracies in the previously available minutes. Additionally, his research has unearthed a large, hitherto unpublished section of the journal kept by John Lightfoot, an important member of the Assembly. This will fill in previous gaps in the record. This research will bring about a sea change in the understanding of the Assembly, from both theological and historical perspectives. Theological factors will press to the foreground as never before. In this light, the time is opportune for a concerted examination of the theology of the Assembly in its theological and historical contexts.

In the following chapters, there are a number of excursuses in which I examine in detail the background either to discussions at the Assembly or to statements in the confessional documents. These place these debates in the context of the development of doctrine. The church's understanding of theology increases over the years. Disputes sharpen theological thinking and lead to expanded or corrected formulations. In order to know what the Assembly thought and what it meant, we need to consider it in its place in the ongoing flow of the history of theology, not from a vantage point in the distant future. It is a constant temptation for theologians to read back into an earlier time the more developed teaching that came later. In this way, they assume that the earlier age knew and taught the selfsame formulas that were worked out only through the passage of time or in the light of later debate. It is as if an author in the twenty-sixth century considered that we in our time were knowledgeable about, and consciously addressed, the issues of the twenty-third century. Not even the most farsighted visionary could be expected to do that. This is the problem of *anachronism*. Many who write on the Westminster Assembly fall into this trap.[2] These problems arise by neglecting the development of doctrine. While the revelation of God remains firm, human understanding of it grows. The church progresses in its grasp of biblical truth and its theological entailments. In this sense, we need to maintain a hold on history. The expression of theological truth that we now have is the result of a process of conflict, struggle, debate, and refinement. *These excursuses go into great detail. If you are not inclined to examine the issues in such a way, you may be best advised to skip them.*

I cannot emphasize too strongly that this is *not* a discussion of the theology of the Westminster Assembly as amended by North American Presbyterianism from the eighteenth century onwards. It seeks to locate the confessional documents in their historical context. In this respect, for example, the American notion of the separation of church and state is irrelevant, for the Assembly assumed that the two were connected. Moreover, the Assembly existed as a servant of Parliament, no less. Nor is this book an exposition of the Confession of Faith as such. I make an attempt to understand the theology of the Assembly as a whole, from the range of its doctrinal pronouncements of which the Confession is but one element, albeit a central and vital one. I try also to avoid the temptation to describe the theology of certain key members of the Assembly and then present that as the theology of the Assembly itself. The divines were varied in outlook within a generic Calvinism, and the debates demonstrate such diversity that the views of any one individual or group cannot be taken as representative of

---

2. On this and other such fallacies, see Q. Skinner, "Meaning and Understanding in the History of Ideas," in *Visions of Politics*, vol. 1: *On Method* (Cambridge: Cambridge University Press, 2002), 57–89.

the whole in any particular matter unless there is clear evidence to support it. In any case, the groups within the Assembly fluctuated from issue to issue. Nor is the book an attempt to use the Assembly as a springboard from which to address questions of today. It tries to consider Westminster in the light of its own time. This is another danger that bedevils readings from the past; the desire for contemporary relevance often drives an author to mine the past for ammunition for present-day conflicts.

For the same reason, *I do not intend what follows as an exposition of my own theology*. It is impossible to remove oneself entirely from the picture, but I have made a determined attempt to restrict myself to an exposition of the Assembly's theology as I understand the text of its documents and the record of its debates to reveal it to be. Some years ago, Thomas Oden stated in his preface to *The Word of Life*, the second volume of his systematic theology: "The only promise I try to make to my readers, however inadequately carried out, is that of *unoriginality*. . . . Nothing of my own, that would have my initials stamped upon it, is important in this discussion."[3] Much earlier, John Calvin had written that for the interpreter of Scripture "it is almost his only task to unfold the mind of the writer whom he has undertaken to expound."[4] This is the aim of this book. I am sure it will be fulfilled imperfectly, but it is the task I have set myself.

At the same time, this is not to say that my theology in principle differs from that of the Assembly. Naturally, much water has flowed under the bridge since the 1640s, and we live in very different conditions and face quite distinct theological challenges. I have been quite prepared to criticize the Assembly at certain points and indicate its weaknesses where I believe they are evident. However, the more closely I have examined the Assembly's documents, and considered the record of debate in the minutes, the greater my appreciation for its work has become. Allowing for the passage of time, and for developments the

3. T. C. Oden, *The Word of Life* (vol. 2 of *Systematic Theology*; New York: Harper & Row, 1989), xvi.

4. John Calvin, dedication to Symon Grynaeus, in his commentary on Romans, 1540, in *Calvin's Commentaries: The Epistles of Paul the Apostle to the Romans and to the Thessalonians* (ed. D. W. Torrance and T. F. Torrance; Grand Rapids: Eerdmans, 1973), 1.

Assembly could not have foreseen, I quite happily regard its theology as coinciding with mine.

Many earlier commentators tended to use the Westminster Confession of Faith as a springboard for a discussion of their own theology. This is true of popular manuals, but it is also the case with more serious ones. For example, at one notable point, A. A. Hodge describes, not the theology of the Confession, but the later Princeton theology. In considering the statement in WCF 6 that the sin of *our first parents* is imputed to their posterity since they are *the root of all mankind*, he writes of the sin of *Adam* being imputed since God constituted him *the federal head of the race*. His point may be true, and it can be argued from the rest of the Westminster documents, but it is not what chapter 6 is saying. Hodge ignores the confessional statement at this point and presents his own position. Moreover, in the same chapter he expounds the idea that Adam was under probation in the garden and would have been confirmed in blessedness if he had obeyed. Whatever its merits, and however it can be established as representing the theology of the Assembly, this idea is not present in the text he is attempting to explain.[5]

Often, unguarded polemics have disfigured discussions of Westminster. William M. Hetherington, writing in 1843 of the failure of attempts to bring about wider reform on the accession of Elizabeth I, refers to "the admixture of human inventions in the worship of God, so that the Church of England was thenceforth to remain, like one of her own grand cathedrals, a stately mass of petrified religion."[6] Yet this church produced William Perkins, William Ames, John Owen, Thomas Goodwin, and the host of Puritan preachers and divines—to say nothing of the multitude who followed, such as John Newton, William Wilberforce, Lord Shaftesbury, Charles Simeon, Henry Martyn, J. C. Ryle, John Stott, and J. I. Packer—a stately, petrified mass indeed! It was precisely this "stately mass of petrified religion" that was represented at the Assembly at Westminster, about which Hetherington writes. If the Assembly was so significant, then the church that

5. A. A. Hodge, *The Confession of Faith: A Handbook of Christian Doctrine Expounding the Westminster Confession* (repr., London: Banner of Truth, 1961), 109–15.

6. W. M. Hetherington, *History of the Westminster Assembly of Divines* (repr., Edmonton: Still Waters Revival Books, 1993), 35.

produced it could hardly be termed "petrified." At the same time, Hetherington passes over in silence the contribution of John Knox to undermining the cause of reform in England by his ill-advised and intemperate outburst in *The First Blast of the Trumpet against the Monstrous Regiment of Women.* This screed more than anything else turned Elizabeth against the Genevan exiles, even though it was not directed specifically at her. Moreover, Hetherington dredges up a misreading of Calvin in which he is purported to dismiss the liturgy of the Church of England in the reign of Edward VI as containing "popish dregs."[7] If there were any authentic evidence that Calvin had said this, it would have been unearthed and would be widely cited by those writing on the English Reformation.[8]

Hetherington also passes over the debates on the Thirty-Nine Articles at the Assembly on the grounds that they are of little interest to his Scottish readership. That may be so, but that document was clearly of interest *to the Assembly.* This is a particularly clear instance of the bias of the author precluding him from a properly contextual reading of the material. The Westminster Assembly was first and foremost an *English* body. That many of its interpreters have demonstrated little interest in the English context diminishes their capacity to be reliable guides of its documents.

Some such writings show a lack of rigor in the reading of the Westminster Confession and Catechisms. Among the notable exceptions are those of B. B. Warfield[9]—what a pity he was able to consider only part of the Assembly's work—and Edward Morris.[10] Alexander Mitchell's book on the Assembly is also valuable.[11] Robert Shaw's exposition of the Confession is useful.[12]

---

7. Ibid., 30–35.

8. I am indebted to Tony Lane for this observation, which I cite in his own words with his express permission.

9. B. B. Warfield, *The Westminster Assembly and Its Work* (New York: Oxford University Press, 1934).

10. E. D. Morris, *Westminster Symbols: A Commentary Historical, Doctrinal, Practical, on the Confession of Faith and Catechisms and the Related Formularies of the Presbyterian Churches* (Columbus: Champlin, 1900).

11. A. F. Mitchell, *The Westminster Assembly: Its History and Standards: Being the Baird Lectures for 1882* (Philadelphia: Presbyterian Board of Publication and Sabbath-School Work, 1897).

12. R. Shaw, *Exposition of the Westminster Confession of Faith* (repr., Fearn: Christian Focus, 2003).

Popular expositions of the Confession and the Larger Catechism, while of use for the purpose for which they were intended, are even more prone to distort or ignore large tracts of the Assembly's theology in favor of dealing with issues of the author's own time. Even J. G. Vos, in his welcome exposition of the Larger Catechism, points to the second commandment as prohibiting the Religious Bodies Law passed by the Japanese government during World War II, which forbade free assembly for Christian worship. This is a correct application of the second commandment in the spirit of the Assembly, although not a discussion of the Larger Catechism as such. However, in the same breath, he includes as a breach of the commandment "chewing gum during divine worship."[13]

I attempt in the following pages to locate the Assembly in the variety of its contexts—the often neglected English context, the context of the Reformed churches of the sixteenth and seventeenth centuries, and the context of the great tradition of the church. By focusing on the Assembly in context and refraining from addressing contemporary concerns, I expect that its theology may appear in greater relief and so be able to address contemporary concerns better than if they were intruded anachronistically into the text.

Many denominations claim the Westminster Confession and Catechisms as their secondary standards, under the supreme authority of Scripture. In the United States, this is frequently in an altered version, changed to account for civil constitutional developments to which the Westminster divines were strangers. Moreover, there were at Westminster a number of matters with which many contemporary Presbyterians may disagree. The relative prominence given by the divines to "the light of nature," the high view of the sacraments, and the wider flexibility and tolerance for differences of opinion on the decrees of God are three matters that immediately spring to mind. A close study of these documents raises questions as to exactly how they function today in the church. Moreover, the idea of subscription to the Westminster Confession and Catechisms as understood—in varying ways—in American Presbyterianism was alien to the seventeenth

---

13. J. G. Vos, *The Westminster Larger Catechism: A Commentary* (ed. G. I. Williamson; Phillipsburg, NJ: P&R, 2002), 298. I do not defend chewing gum during divine worship, having never had the slightest desire to chew gum in *any* situation!

century. When denominations in practice adhere to their own interpretation of the Assembly's theology and, indeed, add other elements
unknown to the divines, inevitable questions follow. I cannot and do
not address these matters here.

Inevitably, this book can present only a partial picture. One of the
constraints of writing is that the result must be kept to a manageable
size or it will not be read. A book of much over 400 pages cannot readily be assigned for a seminary class. The price of relative compactness
is incompleteness. However, in the Van Dixhoorn set we will have a
resource that will provide many opportunities for scholars to probe
further. It is my hope that this volume will encourage others to do so.
It is intended as a guide along the pathway that will lead to further
discovery and understanding. I also hope that there will dawn a widespread recognition that the theology of the Westminster Assembly, for
all its weaknesses, has much to contribute to the future of the Christian
church. Any body of theologians that considers that our chief purpose
is, in union and communion with Christ, to glorify God and enjoy
him forever, is right at the heart of the Christian faith.

PART 1

THE HISTORICAL CONTEXT

1

From Henry VIII to the First Civil War

Behind the Westminster Assembly lies the convoluted history of the English church in the preceding century, in large measure dominated by the religious and ecclesiastical policies of successive monarchs. The Assembly was an *English* body, and the English context must be grasped to understand it. Yet, due to its failure to effect change in England, its interpreters have largely been from elsewhere—predominantly Scotland or North America—and the English background has often been neglected. We begin our story at the Reformation.

Henry VIII (1509–47)

During the reign of Henry VIII, the church in England broke away from Rome. The immediate cause was Henry's unsuccessful attempt to secure papal approval for his divorce from his first wife, Catherine of Aragon. Henry believed, on the grounds of Leviticus 18:16 and 20:21, that his failure to produce a male heir was due to his having married his brother's widow. Thomas Cranmer, before he was archbishop, was dispatched to Europe to argue Henry's case, but the pope refused to grant an annulment.[1] In response, Henry forced

1. D. MacCulloch, *Thomas Cranmer: A Life* (New Haven: Yale University Press, 1996), 39–78.

11

through Parliament the Act in Restraint of Appeals (1533), effectively ending the papacy's legal jurisdiction over the English church by preventing appeals to Rome. Further, the Act of Succession (1534) protected Henry's subsequent marriage to Anne Boleyn, in open defiance of the pope. Later that year, the Act of Supremacy gave to the king the right "to visit, repress, redress, reform, order, correct, restrain and amend all such errors, heresies . . . and enormities . . . which by any manner spiritual authority or jurisdiction ought or may be lawfully reformed."[2] Henry was now the supreme head of the Church of England, under Christ. He had placed the Church of England under royal, not papal, control. By this time, the ideas of Martin Luther had been gaining headway.[3] In the following years, a gradual reform movement took place, largely Erasmian, guided with immense care and caution by Henry's chancellor, Thomas Cromwell, and by Thomas Cranmer. Cranmer became archbishop of Canterbury and had as his ultimate aim the alignment of the Church of England with the Reformed churches on the continent.[4]

Edward VI (1547–53)

Edward, a definite Protestant, became king at the age of 9, and died at 16. He was guided by the lord protector, Edward Seymour, duke of Somerset (ca. 1500–1552), who shared Calvin's theology, and then, after Somerset's fall from grace and execution, by John Dudley, duke of Northumberland (1504?–53). Leading Reformers from the continent were called to strategic appointments to promote reform— Martin Bucer of Strasbourg (who had a profound influence on Calvin) to Cambridge, where he died in 1551, and the Italian, Pietro Martire Vermigli, also from Strasbourg, to Oxford. These two contributed the foundations for generations of theologians and preachers at both

2. Ibid., 95–105.
3. See C. R. Trueman, *Luther's Legacy: Salvation and the English Reformers, 1525–1556* (Oxford: Clarendon Press, 1994).
4. See G. W. Bernard, *The King's Reformation: Henry VIII and the Remaking of the English Church* (New Haven: Yale University Press, 2005), for a provocative reassessment of Henry's religious policies. Bernard argues that Henry deliberately, consistently, and ruthlessly subjected the church to his authority, to the exclusion of all powers outside England and in the face of almost exclusive passivity within.

schools, committed to a theology in line with that of Calvin.[5] Cranmer drew up the Forty-Two Articles, which provided the basis for the Thirty-Nine Articles later. His prayer books of 1549 and 1552 were masterpieces of eclectic liturgical and literary craftsmanship. Cranmer wanted the Church of England to conform to the continental Reformed churches. Moreover, the Privy Council, with royal support, authorized the Polish Reformed exile, John à Lasco, superintendent of the foreign churches in England, to provide for the refugee churches a constitution that could, in the fullness of time, serve as a model for a fully Reformed Church of England.[6] However, the project ended suddenly when Edward died.

Mary (1553–58)

Mary succeeded Edward, and the pendulum swung violently toward Rome. She recalled to England Cardinal Reginald Pole who, exiled due to his opposition to the royal supremacy, was arguably the most gifted Englishman of his generation and had failed by one vote to become pope. She made Pole archbishop of Canterbury in place of Cranmer, who was imprisoned, but for a variety of reasons he was not enthroned until 1556. Thousands of theologians and ministers fled to the continent—to Frankfurt, Zurich, and Geneva. Many others were burnt at the stake, including bishops John Hooper (Gloucester and Worcester), Hugh Latimer (ex-Worcester), Nicholas Ridley (London), and eventually Cranmer himself. It seemed inevitable that the English church would again be reunited with Rome and the Reformation undone. However, in one night both Mary and Pole died from natural causes. The nightmare was over.

Elizabeth I (1558–1603)

Elizabeth, the daughter of Anne Boleyn, Henry VIII's second wife, was firmly Protestant. The monarch's role in the church was renamed

5. R. S. Clark and J. R. Beeke, "Ursinus, Oxford, and the Westminster Divines," in *The Westminster Confession into the 21st Century* (ed. J. L. Duncan III; 2 vols.; Fearn: Mentor, 2003–5), 2:1–32.
6. Mitchell, *Westminster Assembly*, 26–27.

as supreme governor, rather than supreme head. The exiles flocked home. Unfortunately, John Knox—who had been in exile at Frankfurt and latterly Geneva, with Calvin and Beza—undid much with his infamous *First Blast of the Trumpet Against the Monstrous Regiment of Women*, a stinging attack on female monarchs, aimed principally at Queen Mary, but with a sideways glance at Mary, Queen of Scots, both of whom were actively hostile to the Reformation. He also espoused the right to resist rulers who acted contrary to God's law. Not surprisingly, Elizabeth took offense—

> Heaven has no rage like love to hatred turned,
> Nor hell a fury, like a woman scorned.
>> William Congreve (1670–1729),
>> *The Mourning Bride*, III:viii

Despite Calvin's own horror at Knox's inflammatory hotheadedness, Elizabeth was alienated from the Genevan exiles, and few of them attained high office during her reign.[7] The Act of Settlement (1559) established the Church of England somewhere around the point of the 1552 Prayer Book, during the latter part of Edward's reign. However, it laid down savage penalties for departing from the prescribed liturgy. This imposed liturgy created problems for many. While the Act of Supremacy (1559) restored the crown's authority over the church, the Act of Uniformity granted Elizabeth the right to add such rites and ceremonies as she should judge to be for the glory of God and the good of religion. While the returned exiles who came to episcopal office privately sympathized with those from Geneva, they failed to secure any concessions to placate them.

7. Only Edmund Grindall, an unsuccessful archbishop of Canterbury (1575–83), reached episcopal office of those who had spent their exile in Geneva, although Thomas Sampson was offered Norwich, but declined it, and William Whittingham became dean of Durham. In contrast, many of the Zurich exiles achieved episcopal preferment: Thomas Bentham (Coventry and Lichfield), Robert Horn (Winchester), John Jewell (Salisbury), John Parkhurst (Norwich), James Pilkington (Durham), Edwin Sandys (archbishop of York), and John Aylmer (London). Additionally, many Zurich exiles received other high offices: Robert Beaumont (vice-chancellor of Cambridge University), William Cole (dean of Lincoln), Laurence Humphrey (dean of Winchester), Roger Kelke (archdeacon of Stowe), Thomas Lever (canon of Durham), John Mullins (archdeacon of London), Francis Russell (earl of Bedford), Thomas Spencer (archdeacon of Chichester), and Michael Reniger (archdeacon of Winchester). See D. J. Keep, "Henry Bullinger and the Elizabethan Church" (Ph.D. thesis, University of Sheffield, 1970), 52.

Draconian penalties were prescribed for any who diverged from the Prayer Book, although these were rarely, if ever, enforced. Moreover, at first considerable latitude was granted to those who balked at the requirements. They were permitted to use their metrical Psalter before and after prayers and sermons, the Geneva Bible was printed and distributed, and prayers and the confession in the Form of Prayers, which they had used in exile, were often appended to the Psalter and used in the pulpit, though not at the reading-desk, from where the prescribed prayers were made. Only from around 1564 was rigid uniformity required.[8] The underlying problem was that the Elizabethan Settlement, while Protestant, was still tied to a medieval church structure that continued to enforce the canon law from times under Roman jurisdiction, unless it contradicted the royal authority.[9]

When tighter control was implemented by the establishment, a nascent Presbyterian movement emerged in the 1570s and 1580s, with separate and private preaching (or "prophesying"). However, it was soon forced underground and many of its leaders, notably Thomas Cartwright, were driven into exile. To the establishment, it posed a threat since it appeared to set up an alternative church within the church, thus jeopardizing the unity and cohesion of both church and nation.[10] Indeed, it was estimated by some, and reported by Mitchell, that at one point up to one-third of the clergy of England were under suspension, with attendant destitution and penury, while their congregations were as a result deprived of the ministry of the Word and sacraments.[11] Yet English Presbyterianism was not destroyed, as has generally been thought. That it was alive and well in the early 1640s

8. Mitchell, *Westminster Assembly*, 47.

9. N. Jones, "Elizabethan Settlement," in *Oxford Encyclopedia of the Reformation* (ed. H. J. Hillerbrand; Oxford: Oxford University Press, 1996), 2:38.

10. See, e.g., Thomas Rogers, *The faith, doctrine, and religion professed & protected in the Realme of England, and Dominions of the same: expressed in 39 Articles concordablie agreed upon by the Reverend Bishops, and Clergie of this Kingdome, at two severall meetings, or Convocations of theirs, in the yeare of our Lord, 1562, and 1604: The said Articles analised into propositions, and the propositions prooved to be agreeable both to the written Word of God, and to the extant Confessions of all the neighbour Churches, Christianlie Reformed* ([Cambridge:] Iohn Legatt, Printer to the Vniversitie of Cambridge, 1607) [STC (2nd ed.) 21228], preface. Rogers was chaplain to the then archbishop of Canterbury, Richard Bancroft. In the preface, he stresses the agreement on doctrine with the Puritans, whom he calls "the Brethren," but in great detail disparages their insistence on further reformation of church ceremonies and discipline.

11. Mitchell, *Westminster Assembly*, 58–60.

15

is well known; it could hardly have been killed off, only miraculously to experience a sudden resurrection at a later date. In fact, it maintained itself subtly and undercover from 1590 to 1640. Polly Ha, using previously unexamined papers, has challenged the thesis that Presbyterianism was extinguished from England after its formal suppression in 1592.[12] She has shown that it continued, its advocates making a concerted effort to prove the compatibility of their ecclesiology with the monarchy. In turn, emergent Congregationalism set out its position in contrast with both Episcopacy and Presbyterianism; its differences with Presbyterianism extended to matters within the congregations as well as those on a wider basis. Citing John Morrill, Ha describes English ecclesiology in the early seventeenth century as "a curdled mix."[13]

The accepted historical orthodoxy has, until recently, pitted Anglicans against Puritans. More latterly, the antagonists were described as Calvinists and Arminians. The constitutional and ecclesiastical issues were regarded as separate from the theological, the Civil War being precipitated by the former, with religious matters, while significant, being of lesser impact. In recent years, this picture has been increasingly abandoned. The real situation was more complex than the simplifications of historians imply. The tendency to reduce the past to a readily comprehensible pattern is tempting but profoundly anachronistic, as Quentin Skinner argues.[14]

Indeed, as Mitchell observes, "the points of difference between the Puritans and those who fail to be distinguished from them in the Reformed Church of England seem at first to be few in number, and of minor importance."[15] In terms of doctrine, article 6 of the Thirty-Nine Articles stressed the sufficiency of Scripture for salvation, one of the key issues at stake: "Holy Scripture containeth all things necessary to salvation: so that whatsoever is not read therein, nor may be proved thereby, is not to be required of any man, that it should be believed as an article of the Faith, or be thought requisite or neces-

12. P. Ha, "English Presbyterianism c. 1590–1640" (Ph.D. thesis, Cambridge University, 2006), iv and passim.
13. Ibid., 255.
14. Skinner, "Meaning and Understanding."
15. Mitchell, *Westminster Assembly*, 3–4.

sary to salvation." Mitchell indicates that "it was the Anglo-Catholic party which, as it developed, first broke up the doctrinal harmony of the Reformed Church, and drifted farther and farther from the standpoint of its early leaders." Again, "the only expression at variance with the principle of Puritanism in the Articles of the Church was the first clause of the XXth Article, asserting the power of the Church to decree rites and ceremonies. This clause was not present in the corresponding article as framed in the time of Edward VI; and the Puritans strenuously contended it had been foisted in, somewhat inconsiderately, in the time of Queen Elizabeth."[16] Mitchell has support from Thomas Rogers, who in 1607 affirmed that the English clergy were at one in their support for the Thirty-Nine Articles as a confession in conformity with the other Reformed confessions.[17] The disputes focused in the main on unlawful rites that had been abused in an idolatrous and superstitious way, not to matters indifferent, which the article allows.[18] The Lambeth Articles (1595), produced under the oversight of the archbishop of Canterbury, John Whitgift, are proof positive of the doctrinal consensus; they resolved the proto-Arminian controversy at Cambridge by asserting without ambiguity the doctrine of the perseverance of the saints.[19] I will refer again in chapter 3 to this substantial doctrinal agreement. Meanwhile, when Elizabeth died unmarried and childless, the Tudor line ended and the Stuarts took the throne—the Welsh replaced by the Scots.

James I (1603–25) (James VI of Scotland)

The crowns of England and Scotland were united in 1603. James was raised a Presbyterian, but showed little inclination to promote Presbyterian church government or to meet the demands of the Puritans. He resisted the power of presbyteries in Scotland. In England, his

16. Ibid., 4–5.

17. Thomas Rogers, *The English creede, consenting with the true, auncient, catholique, and apostolique Church in al the points, and articles of religion, which everie Christian is to knowe and beleeve that would be saved* (London: Iohn VVindet [first part] and Robert Walde-grave [second part] for Andrew Maunsel, 1585, 1587) [STC 21226.5], preface, 2–3.

18. Mitchell, *Westminster Assembly*, 5.

19. H. Porter, *Reformation and Reaction in Tudor Cambridge* (Cambridge: University Press, 1958).

17

antipathy was evident by his reaction to the Millenary Petition, signed by several hundred ministers, requesting relief from their deprivations. In response, he called the Hampton Court Conference of 1604, at which he peremptorily dismissed many of their leading claims. Virtually the only concession James made was his agreement to authorize a new translation of the Bible. Indeed, he soon followed with a proclamation requiring strict conformity to the order of the Church. At the conference itself, James had threatened, "I will make them conform, or else I will harry them out of the land, or else do worse, hang them."[20] However, the Canons of 1604 merely reasserted the crown's right to rule the church, which was not a matter of controversy. The detailed provisions of these canons were, in any case, not enforced until the 1630s.[21] Fortunately too, George Abbot was soon to become archbishop of Canterbury—a thoroughgoing Calvinist with a more irenic spirit than Richard Bancroft, his predecessor. Abbot was able to secure royal authorization of Ussher's Irish Articles in 1615 and to arrange for a delegation to be sent to the Synod of Dort in 1618–19. Both of these achievements supported the establishment of Reformed doctrine outside England.

The chief point at issue for the Puritans was whether the church has the right to bind consciences with anything other than the declarations of the Bible. Mitchell puts the matter well when he says that the Puritans "claimed to restrict the authority of the church within narrower limits than their opponents, and to reclaim for liberty a larger province than they [their opponents] were disposed to allow her."[22] For the Puritans, worship and church polity—as well as matters of salvation—were to be drawn from the teaching of Scripture, either expressed or implicit.[23] For

---

20. Mitchell, *Westminster Assembly*, 72.

21. See G. Bray, ed., *The Anglican Canons 1529–1947* (Church of England Record Society, 6; Woodbridge: Boydell Press, 1998), 258–453, esp. 263ff.

22. Mitchell, *Westminster Assembly*, 63.

23. Contrary to N. Atkinson, *Richard Hooker and the Authority of Scripture, Tradition and Reason: Reformed Theologian of the Church of England?* (Carlisle: Paternoster, 1997), the Puritans did not require express statements of Scripture for every action, whether in the church or in everyday life. As we shall see, the prevalent doctrine of Scripture referred "the whole counsel of God" *both* to express biblical statements *and* to that which can be deduced from Scripture—not only to the *ipsissima verba*, but also to "the sense of Scripture." Atkinson, referring to Thomas Cartwright only indirectly, then argues that "the Puritans" required explicit statements of Scripture for "exact and precise details over the minutiae of everyday life" (88), claims that they "alone with their Bibles" disdained the past teaching of the church (106–7),

their opponents, the ancient practice of the church and the customs of the nation were of comparable authority. Moreover, their opponents developed a theory that the constitution of the Church of England was by divine right—*ius divinum*—and so to question it was more than an error; it was outright heresy.[24] However, while there was inevitably a range of opinion among conservative English Protestants, the differences at that time can be overstated; what they held in common was far greater. So much is evident in the British delegation to Dort, composed of self-conscious opponents of Arminius of varying stripes, all Calvinists, appointed by the king to represent the Church.[25] As Anthony Milton points out, some—he refers particularly to Julian Davies[26]—present too unified a view of "Jacobean Anglicanism" and ignore the strength of anti-Puritan sentiment,[27] yet the Church was not split into two simple factions; Hooker was only *apparently* in conflict with the Puritans, and he was treated with respect in Calvinist circles.[28] Whereas Whig and Marxist historians reduced the matter to a simplistic division between conservative Anglicans and radical Puritans,[29] more recent historians have highlighted a broader and more complex range of views.[30]

Charles I (1625–49)

Charles I, James's son, lacked the more solid theological upbringing of his father and also his political skills. Gwatkin's pithy summary

---

and lumps Cartwright together with Muntzer (122). All this is claimed without the support of a single primary source.

24. Mitchell, *Westminster Assembly*, 65.

25. A. Milton, ed., *The British Delegation and the Synod of Dort (1618–1619)* (Church of England Record Society, 13; [Woodbridge:] Boydell Press, 2005), *in passim*.

26. J. Davies, *The Caroline Captivity of the Church: Charles I and the Remoulding of Anglicanism 1625–1641* (Oxford: Clarendon Press, 1992).

27. A. Milton, *Catholic and Reformed: The Roman and Protestant Churches in English Protestant Thought 1600–1640* (Cambridge: Cambridge University Press, 1995), 531–32.

28. Milton, *Catholic and Reformed*, 532–33.

29. E.g., C. Hill, *Society and Puritanism in Pre-Revolutionary England* (London: Secker and Warburg, 1964).

30. See, among those cited elsewhere, N. Tyacke, *Anti-Calvinists: The Rise of English Arminianism, c. 1590–1640* (Oxford: Oxford University Press, 1987); D. Como, "Puritans, Predestination and the Construction of 'Orthodoxy' in Early Seventeenth Century England," in *Conformity and Orthodoxy in the English Church, c. 1500–1642* (ed. P. Lake and M. Questier; Woodbridge: Boydell Press, 2000), 64–87.

19

is telling; James I, he says, had "a genius for getting into difficulties," but "not without a certain shrewdness in stopping just short of catastrophe. If he steered the ship straight for the rocks, he left his son to wreck it."[31] Soon after his accession in 1625, Charles married Princess Henrietta Maria of France, who insisted on practicing the Roman rite with her own priests attendant. This foreshadowed trouble. In Antonia Fraser's words, there was "the smell of incense in high places."[32] Charles was overtly sympathetic toward the high-church party. He soon began to appoint militant high churchmen to senior positions, notably William Laud to Canterbury in 1633, Matthew Wren to Norwich and Ely, William Piers to Bath and Wells, and Samuel Harsnett and then Richard Niele to York. This changed the situation, for the high-church group was "unquestionably a minority."[33] Tension rose to fever pitch. Fears of popery, in the form of a political conjunction of France and Spain, created "electric currents of violence and hostility."[34] One contemporary remarked on "the pulse of the nation beating high towards liberty."[35]

As David Como indicates, the appointment of Laud upset the Calvinist consensus of the Church of England. It was an effective *coup d'église* and, due to the linkage with the state, a *coup d'état* as well.[36] Up to 1630, the Church of England was dominated by Calvinists—the British delegation at the Synod of Dort consisted of solidly Anglican senior churchmen. Under Charles, such people were sidelined, high churchmen were promoted, and the active persecution of Calvinists was begun. A classic example is the case of Samuel Harsnett (1561–1631). In 1594, he was severely rebuked by the archbishop of Canterbury, John Whitgift, for an attack on particular grace. As late as 1624, the House of Commons accused

31. Cited by M. Ashley, *England in the Seventeenth Century* (London: Penguin, 1967), 56.
32. A. Fraser, *Cromwell: The Lord Protector* (New York: Dell, 1973), 54.
33. Ashley, *England in the Seventeenth Century*, 70.
34. Fraser, *Cromwell*, 49.
35. Ibid., 55. If doctrine was not an issue before the emergence of Laud, there were problems with the royal supremacy, which came to the surface as the former pressures mounted. These were not questions of ideology, for which the English have never had a taste, but of practical politics, whether of church or state. To categorize the issues simply in terms of the divine right of kings or the divine right of church government, or the like, is a misunderstanding, as we shall note shortly.
36. D. Como, *Blown by the Spirit: Puritanism and the Emergence of an Antinomian Underground in Pre–Civil War England* (Stanford: Stanford University Press, 2004), 75.

him of popery. Yet in 1628 Charles appointed him archbishop of York, the second-highest church benefice. The following year, Harsnett condemned the mild semi-Calvinist John Davenant's sermon preached before the king, on the grounds of a brief reference to election. Later that year, on Harsnett's recommendation, Charles I issued instructions regulating and curbing preaching. Not only vigorous Calvinists were now under attack, but also those whom Moore terms "English hypothetical universalists."[37] It was a sea change in the theological balance of power, effected within three years of Charles's accession, so swift a coup was it. As early as June 1626, Archbishop Ussher was protesting against the new religious policies in a sermon to the king. In October, Laud was secretly promised Canterbury on the departure of Abbot. In 1628, Charles, by a royal declaration, silenced the controversy over predestination that had rumbled on since Richard Montagu was accused of Arminianism in 1624; Calvinist academics at Oxford and Cambridge were required to rein in their teaching. Later that year, Laud, as bishop of London, put an end to Calvinist preaching at St. Paul's Cross, hitherto a bastion of Puritan ministry, and Montagu was made bishop of Chichester. Soon Laud would be elevated to Canterbury, having only recently condemned the Calvinist Lambeth Articles (1595), drawn up under Archbishop Whitgift.[38]

This change was clearly against the doctrine of the Church of England as expounded by the Thirty-Nine Articles, as presented in Cranmer's Book of Common Prayer, and as taught carefully by Richard Hooker (who was in broad agreement with Calvin) in his *Lawes of Ecclesiastical Polity*.[39] The Reformed character of the Church of England was universally understood. Laud, who was thought to be an Arminian in theology (although this is disputable), had as his express purpose the severance of connections between the Church of England and the

37. J. D. Moore, *English Hypothetical Universalism: John Preston and the Softening of Reformed Theology* (Grand Rapids: Eerdmans, 2007), 229.

38. N. Tyacke, "Anglican Attitudes: Some Recent Writings on English Religious History, from the Reformation to the Civil War," *JBS* 35 (1996): 154–56.

39. On Hooker, note Atkinson, *Richard Hooker*; W. T. Kirby, *Richard Hooker's Doctrine of the Royal Supremacy* (Leiden: E. J. Brill, 1990); B. D. Spinks, *Two Faces of Elizabethan Anglican Theology: Sacraments and Salvation in the Thought of William Perkins and Richard Hooker* (Lanham, MD: Scarecrow Press, 1999).

nonepiscopal Reformed churches of the continent.[40] He sought, by a form of "almost judicial legalism,"[41] to implement James's threat to harry the Puritans out of the land.

All groups in the Church were in the process of change and development at this time, but Laud and his friends made a deliberate attempt to divide the Calvinist camp, isolating the more Puritan element from those of softer and more flexible principles. However, this policy would eventually backfire, as it generated fears of a popish plot. Such concerns appeared justified by Charles's marriage to Henrietta of Spain and the continued hostilities and carnage caused by the Thirty Years' War on the continent. Behind it lay the folk memory of the attack and defeat of the Spanish Armada in 1588 and the Gunpowder Plot of 1605, which had intended to blow up Parliament. That the Laudian changes raised the temperature on the other side is obvious, and it was further fueled by an upsurge of millenarian speculation. Joseph Mede's *Clavis Apocalyptica*, published in 1627, proved popular not only in England but in Europe too. Despite Mede's Arminianism, future members of the Westminster Assembly, such as William Twisse, Thomas Goodwin, and Jeremiah Burroughs, all spoke highly of it.[42] This was part of an eruption of eschatological expectation that accompanied a ferment of fears, spurred by the belief that the church of Christ was in a state of apostasy signaling a final battle with the Antichrist.[43]

The Laudians, for their part, feared that the idea that the pope was the Antichrist would undermine the doctrine of the apostolic succession of bishops, and that the Calvinists' strongly held doctrine of predestination sidelined the sacraments. Moreover, the Calvinists'

40. See J. R. Green, *Short History of the English People* (New York: Harper, 1877), 499–502, cited by Warfield, *Westminster Assembly*, 5.

41. Davies, *Caroline Captivity*, 66.

42. J. Jue, "The Active Obedience of Christ and the Theology of the Westminster Standards: A Historical Investigation," in *Justified in Christ: God's Plan for Us in Justification* (ed. K. S. Oliphint; Fearn: Mentor, 2007), 104–5.

43. See P. Toon, ed., *Puritans, the Millennium and the Future of Israel* (Cambridge: James Clarke, 1970); B. W. Ball, *A Great Expectation: Eschatological Thought in English Protestantism to 1660* (Leiden: E. J. Brill, 1975); R. Bauckham, *Tudor Apocalypse: Sixteenth Century Apocalypticism, Millenarianism, and the English Reformation* (Oxford: Sutton Courtenay Press, 1978); K. R. Firth, *The Apocalyptic Tradition in Reformation Britain, 1530–1643* (Oxford: Oxford University Press, 1979); I. Backus, *Reformation Readings of the Apocalypse: Geneva, Zurich, and Wittenberg* (Oxford: Oxford University Press, 2000).

continued interaction with continental Reformed churches, and deference to their leading theologians, was essentially subversive, since those churches were nonepiscopal. Episcopacy, the sacraments, the ritual—these were the things that the Laudians held dear and which the Calvinists, it was argued, were threatening.[44] In pursuance of these objectives, Laud required absolute submission to the king, extending to acceptance of every detail of church ritual. He introduced genuflecting, called the communion table an altar, and banned all publications that called the pope the Antichrist.[45] The climax came with Convocation's issuance of the Canons of 1640, to which we shall give attention shortly.

Charles's encouragement of the doctrine of the divine right of kings was in contrast with the landmark declarations of Thomas Bracton almost four centuries earlier. He used the prerogative powers of the crown—undefined powers to act on behalf of the nation, without recourse to Parliament—to an unprecedented extent. In support, Sir Robert Berkeley, the judge prosecuting John Hampden for nonpayment of ship-money, asserted, "Rex is Lex . . . for he is *lex loquens*, a living, speaking, and acting law." According to this theory, the king is above the law and has the right to determine law. However, four hundred years earlier the great medieval jurist, Henry de Bracton (d. 1268) had laid down the reverse, that the king is *sub legem*, answerable to the law and ultimately to Christ, who appointed him. In his groundbreaking and seminal work, *De legibus et consuetudinibus Angliae*, in which he systematized the laws of England, Bracton stated that the king was himself under the law "since law makes the king. Therefore let the king render to the law what the law has rendered to the king . . . for there is no king where will rules and not the law."[46] Furthermore, "As long as he does justice the king is the vicar of the eternal king, but he is the devil's minister when he deviates into injustice. He is a

44. See Milton, *Catholic and Reformed*, 319, 534–46, although Milton sets up a false antithesis. The Calvinist doctrine of the Church of England held the preaching of the Word, the sacraments, and public worship together under the authority of the Bible. Moreover, there is no evidence that before the Laudian hijacking of the Church there was any significant threat to the episcopal nature of the Church of England from mainstream Calvinist opinion.

45. Ibid., 120, 494–503.

46. *Bracton on the Laws and Customs of England* (trans. S. E. Thorne; 4 vols.; Cambridge, MA: Harvard University Press, 1968–77), 2:33.

king as long as he rules well, a tyrant when he oppresses by violent domination the people entrusted to his care. Therefore let him temper his rule by law."[47]

Charles needed the House of Commons to approve taxes for his wars, but wanted the Commons for little else. So he suspended it from 1629 to 1640. Then in 1640 the Scots rebelled against his attempt in 1637 to impose Episcopacy, a policy they found both ecclesiastically and nationally unacceptable. It had provoked the signing of the National Covenant in 1638 and now led to open warfare. Charles needed Parliament again. Parliament (largely Presbyterian) had a range of constitutional grievances, which it pursued with varying degrees of hesitancy, but the continued attempt of king and archbishop to subvert the church aroused its ire unstoppably.[48]

Events in England came to a head early in 1640, when Convocation enacted a series of canons asserting the divine right of kings to rule both in civil society and the church.[49] In many cases, Convocation was usurping the long-established rights of Parliament, and doing so in support of highly contentious ecclesiastical policy. For instance, "every parson, vicar, curate, or preacher, upon some Sunday in every quarter . . . at morning prayer, shall in the place where he serves, treatably and audibly read these explanations of the regal power," including the declaration that "the most high and sacred order of kings is of divine right, being the ordinance of God himself, founded in the prime laws of nature, and clearly established by express texts both of the Old and New Testaments." This entailed power over "all persons of what rank or estate soever, whether ecclesiastical or civil." Ecclesiastical power was described as "care of God's church," including the right to call and dissolve councils.[50] This was nothing new. However, for any person to set up "any independent coactive power, either papal or popular," was declared to be "treasonable against God as well as against the king."[51] This was aimed both at papists and Presbyterians; the establishment of Presbyterian churches was treason. Damnation would be

---

47. Ibid., 2:305.
48. J. Morrill, "The Religious Context of the English Civil War," *TrRHS* 34 (1984): 155–78.
49. Bray, *Anglican Canons*, 553–78.
50. Ibid., 558.
51. Ibid., 559.

the fate of any who resisted the royal power, according to St. Paul. The canons insisted that there was no conflict between the powers of the king and the private property of his subjects, but in doing so they grounded the royal right to levy taxes in "the law of God, nature, and nations" (*ius divinum, ius naturale, ius gentium*). This aroused much antagonism. Moreover, as Bray points out, Convocation was intruding into a sphere recognized as belonging to Parliament.[52] In similar vein, the canons inaugurated a special day, 27 March, in which "all manner of persons within the Church of England" shall celebrate the inauguration of King Charles, again usurping the right of Parliament to institute new holy days of observance.[53]

However, the chief bone of contention in these canons was the notorious "et cetera oath." This required all clergy to take the following oath before 2 November, under penalty of law, resulting in deprivation of all ecclesiastical promotions and functions in the Church of England:

> I, A.B. do swear that I do approve the doctrine and discipline or government established in the Church of England as containing all things necessary to salvation, and that I will not endeavour by myself or any other, directly or indirectly, to bring in any popish doctrine contrary to that which is so established, nor will I give consent to alter the government of this church by archbishops, bishops, deans and archdeacons, *et cetera*, as it stands now established and as by right it ought to stand, nor yet ever to subject it to the usurpations and superstitions of the see of Rome. And all these things I do plainly acknowledge and swear according to the plain and common sense and understanding of the same words, without any equivocation or mental evasion, or secret reservation whatsoever. And this I do heartily, willingly and truly upon the faith of a Christian. So help me God in Jesus Christ.[54]

The use of "et cetera" implied that to swear the oath would be to swear to uphold the system of courts that had provoked such dissension. True, there were concessions to Puritan concerns: kneeling at

52. Ibid.
53. Ibid., 560.
54. Ibid., 568–69 (italics added).

25

the communion rail was no longer mandatory, as it had been in the Elizabethan Settlement and the Canons of 1604. In addition, against the insistence of Bishop Wren of Norwich that a communion rail be placed across the entire church, it was left open as to where the rail might be, allowing for it to be situated around the communion table. This was to prevent irreverent conduct by parishioners, who often lounged around or under the table during divine worship.[55] Yet these caveats could not hide the main thrust of the canons.

Warfield describes the issue at stake as "a secular one, the issue of representative government over against royal absolutism."[56] This is misleading, an anachronistic reading back into history of principles recognized only later. The English are—and always have been—a pragmatic nation. Political ideology has never been a governing factor, let alone anything ending in -ism. Nor is Warfield correct that the Civil War was a secular matter. Not only were the political and the religious so inextricably intertwined that "secular" was a meaningless category, but the religious issues alone had the strength to generate the passion needed for armed uprising against the king. Warfield is, however, on sounder ground in recognizing that between king and Parliament there was agreement that the church should be subject to the civil authority. The only question was whether this should be to the king or to Parliament.[57] The events of 1640 and beyond would catapult this question into view and drive the nation to war.

55. Ibid., 570–71.
56. Warfield, *Westminster Assembly*, 5.
57. Ibid.

2

The Westminster Assembly and the Breakdown of Order

Events Leading to the Creation of the Westminster Assembly (1640–43)

In 1640, trouble was brewing. By 1642, England was plunged into civil war. The following year, the legal and ecclesiastical structure of the Church of England was torn down and an Assembly of Divines was called. What aroused such passions? How did the crisis arise?

John Morrill has argued cogently that the primary factors precipitating the first Civil War were religious. Local issues never had the momentum for armed conflict; most people in the provinces wanted peace and remained, as far as possible, neutral. Parliamentary records show the legal and constitutional grievances were pursued hesitantly and lethargically. Neither were they matters of controversy. Members of Parliament right across the political spectrum saw them as problems needing solution. They surrounded one man, the king, not the system as such. It was the religious issue that ignited passionate feeling, provoked the formation of armed militias, and lit the fuse that exploded into civil strife. It is, says Morrill, "almost impossible to over-estimate the damage done by the Laudians." Charles, it was maintained, had abdicated his responsibilities to preserve the true Reformed religion. The specter was not so much the danger of persecution as the fear of popery.[1] Charles was being manipulated by unscrupulous papists at home and abroad, who were plotting to overthrow the Reformation. An apocalyptic battle with the forces of Antichrist loomed.[2]

The first positive achievement of the Long Parliament, besides denying Charles the taxes he needed to finance his military expedition and for which he had summoned it, was the annulment of the Canons of 1640,[3] with their notorious et cetera oath. Then, throughout the months following the promulgation of the canons, a rash of petitions came before Parliament, calling for the end of Episcopacy. The Commons, in November, appointed a Grand Committee of Religion, consisting of all its members, to consider these matters. Most notable among the petitions was one from London, called in popular parlance the "Root and Branch Petition." The description arose from its desire that "the government of archbishops and lord bishops, deans, and archdeacons, *etc.*, with all its dependencies, roots and branches, may be abolished, and all laws in their behalf made void, and the government according to God's word may be rightly placed among us." The petition mimicked the et cetera oath by its pointed insertion of the offending abbreviation. Elsewhere, the Grand Committee disclosed widespread corruption, leading to the review and overturning of a number of past convictions and sentences, together with the awarding of damages. It investigated and tried ten times as many clerics as civil officials. By the end of the first session of the Long Parliament, many MPs who originally looked for ecclesiastical pruning now saw that Episcopacy had to be destroyed and the established Church reconstituted.[4] After considerable thought, the Commons legislated the abolition of Episcopacy—but not until 26 January 1643 did it become law. At that point, there was no legal foundation for the Church of England.

However, by this time events had taken a dramatic turn. A rebellion in Ireland led to the deaths of many Protestants; some unsubstantiated estimates were as high as two hundred thousand,

1. There were fewer deprivations and suspensions under Laud in the 1630s than in most decades since the Reformation. See Morrill, "Religious Context," 163.
2. See ibid., esp. 155–64.
3. Ibid., 164.
4. Ibid., 166–68.

although these were impossibly exaggerated for propaganda purposes. These atrocities raised the political temperature to fever pitch; it seemed that a full-blooded papist attack was imminent. Meanwhile, in an attempt to bring the recalcitrant Commons to heel, on 4 January 1642 Charles entered the chamber (an unconstitutional act) to arrest the five leading members opposed to his autocratic rule—John Hampden, John Pym, Denzil Holles, Sir Arthur Hazelrigg, and William Strode—so as to impeach them for treason. They left before he arrived. The speaker, William Lenthall, faced with Charles's personal demand to reveal their whereabouts, uttered his classic defiance of tyranny: "May it please your Majesty, I have neither eyes to see nor tongue to speak in this place but as the House is pleased to direct me, whose servant I am." Yet "even the most important constitutional developments were swamped by literature on religious ones; in January 1642 four times as many pamphlets were devoted to the impeachment of the bishops as to the Attempt on the Five Members."[5] The main issue was not the king's past tyranny; it was his present moral and political incapacity.[6] Morrill concludes: "The civil war broke out because small minorities thrust themselves forward, volunteered, took to arms. Neither the militia nor the array were the instruments of war. It was individual captains and colonels, recruiting their own companies and regiments who created the armies that went to war." On 10 September 1642, the Houses of Parliament told the Scottish General Assembly that "'their chiefest aim' was 'the Truth and Purity of the Reformed Religion, not only against Popery but against all other superstitious sects and innovations whatsoever.'" Morrill asks,

> Have we been so confused into seeking parallels between the British Crisis of the 1640s and the wave of rebellions on the continent (brought on by war and the centralising imperatives of war), or between the English Revolution and the events of 1789 and 1917, that we have missed an obvious point? The English civil war was not the first European revolution: it was the last of the Wars of Religion.[7]

5. Ibid., 170.
6. Ibid., 174.
7. Ibid., 177–78.

When, on 22 August, Charles raised his standard at Nottingham, civil war had arrived.

The Establishment of the Assembly

One of the main tasks facing the House of Commons in this national emergency was to establish an Assembly of Divines to provide a legal and theological basis for the Church, now that the regular order had been abolished. The Grand Remonstrance of December 1641 had expressed this need. It had requested "a general Synod of the most grave, pious, learned, and judicious divines of this island, assisted by some from foreign parts professing the same religion with us, to consider all things necessary for the peace and good government of the church."[8] This was in keeping with the wishes of Cranmer, several generations before. A bill passed both Houses by June, but the king refused to give the royal assent. Two other bills met the same result later in the year. So Parliament had no alternative but to issue an ordinance under its own authority, introduced in the Commons on 13 May 1643, and receiving the approval of the Lords on 12 June. The Assembly's mandate was largely doctrinal: the "settling of the government and liturgy of the Church of England, and for vindicating and clearing of the doctrine of the said Church from all false calumnies and aspersions." Its first mandate was therefore doctrinal and did not include radical reform of church government. Parliament simply requested advice on ecclesiastical affairs. Only when Parliament was forced to negotiate with the Scots for assistance in the war against the king did the new allies, as a price for their help, request that the brief be extended to include church government as a priority.

The ordinance declared that the government of the Church "by archbishops, bishops, their chancellors, commissaries, deans, deans and chapters, archdeacons, and other ecclesiastical officers depending upon the hierarchy, is evil, and justly offensive and burdensome to the kingdom, a great impediment to reformation and growth of religion, and very prejudicial to the state and government of this kingdom," and signaled its imminent removal. In its place was to come a govern-

8. Mitchell, *Westminster Assembly*, 108–9.

ment in the Church "most agreeable to God's holy word, and most apt to procure and preserve the peace of the Church at home, and nearer agreement with the Church of Scotland, and other Reformed Churches abroad; and, for the better effecting hereof and for the vindicating and clearing of the doctrine of the Church of England from all false calumnies and aspersions." Its task was "to confer and treat among themselves of such matters and things, touching and concerning the Liturgy, Discipline, and Government of the Church of England, or the vindicating and clearing of the doctrine of the same from all false aspersions and misconstructions, as shall be proposed unto them by both or either of the said Houses of Parliament, and no other."[9] As Van Dixhoorn points out, its theological task was to show how the Church of England was in agreement with the Church of Scotland and Reformed churches abroad. It was not to revise the Church's doctrine.[10] In fact, before the Solemn League and Covenant was signed with the Scots, the divines could have eliminated one of the Thirty-Nine Articles only at peril to themselves, since the penalty for deviating from canon law was excommunication, according to canon 5 of the Canons of 1604.[11]

The Assembly met for the first time on 1 July 1643, although its real business did not begin for another week. It convened in the Chapel of Henry VIII, but when the weather turned cold in early October the divines decamped to more comfortable quarters in the Jerusalem Chamber in the Deanery next door. The Assembly continued to function throughout the civil wars and beyond the execution of Charles I in January 1649. Thereafter it soldiered on, examining pastoral candidates until it was disbanded on 25 March 1652, following Cromwell's dramatic ending of the Long Parliament.

The Composition of the Assembly

After much debate, on 12 February 1642 Parliament determined that members of the Assembly should not be chosen by the clergy,

9. Ibid., xiv.
10. Van Dixhoorn, 1:39.
11. Ibid., 1:44.

but by Parliament itself, on recommendation of the knights and burgesses of each county. Those selected did not necessarily come from the county they were to represent, and in many cases they were from elsewhere. According to Van Dixhoorn, there was no overriding basis for nomination, although proximity to London was an advantage and, as is almost invariably so, personal contacts and patronage were very important.[12] Most of those selected were Presbyterian, but there were a wide variety of views on the war.[13]

When the members were finally chosen, the Assembly—composed almost exclusively of English subjects[14]—consisted of 119 divines. Two came from each county in England, two from the Channel Islands, one from each county in Wales, two each from Oxford and Cambridge universities, and four from London. In addition to these, there were ten representatives from the House of Lords and twenty from the Commons. The majority were Presbyterian, but most not dogmatically so. There were a number of Episcopalians, a few Independents, and a few more Erastians. While only a handful of its members held to Erastian views, the body as such was Erastian in the sense that it was entirely under the jurisdiction of Parliament, and thus all members tacitly acquiesced to civil control.[15] Three of its members were from the French Reformed Church, with pastoral positions in England. The average attendance was in the low sixties.[16]

Opinions about the caliber of the Assembly differ widely. Many have disparaged it; Jonathan Edwards wrote of some who, from their

12. See C. Van Dixhoorn, "Westminster Assembly (act. 1643–52)," in *Oxford Dictionary of National Biography*, online edition (http://www.oxforddnb.com/view/theme/92780, accessed 22 April 2008).

13. That there was much ferment in England about the legitimacy of taking up arms is evident from the section of Lightfoot's journal transcribed by Van Dixhoorn. Writing of S21 TU 8.8.43, Lightfoot reports "a tumultuous company of women this day to the Parliament houses & cried for Peace." Tragically, the next day reporting S22 W 9.8.43, he says, "This day the tumult of women grew outragious & many men, and they Papists, were mingled amongst, so that the Parliaments guards was forced to violate resistance, & they slew 2 men & 1 woman." Van Dixhoorn, 2:24. Evidently, there is nothing new under the sun.

14. Phillipé Delmé was probably not English.

15. This is not to be confused with what became known as "the establishment principle." In the case of the Assembly, its whole operation was at the behest of Parliament. There was agreement on the role of the civil authority; the question at the time was whether king or Parliament was the legitimate ruler. Only Independents and sects argued for complete freedom from state authority.

16. Van Dixhoorn, 1:18–34; Warfield, *Westminster Assembly*, 17.

Enlightenment perspective, considered the divines to be lacking in a proper understanding of Paul.[17] At the other end of the scale is the famous comment of Richard Baxter, reported by Mitchell: "The Christian world since the days of the apostles had never a Synod of more excellent divines."[18] There is little doubt that the Assembly had biblical, patristic, and scholastic learning to spare. The prolocutor, William Twisse, was widely recognized in Reformed circles on the continent: he had edited Thomas Bradwardine's *De causa Dei contra Pelagium*. John Lightfoot, Thomas Coleman, and John Selden were all distinguished Oriental scholars. Thomas Gataker was a man of great learning, a distinguished Hebrew and Greek scholar, one of the first to point to the difference between Koine and classical Greek. John Arrowsmith and Anthony Tuckney became professors of divinity at Cambridge; Joshua Hoyle took the same post at Oxford. John Wallis, a scribe for the Assembly and one of the authors of the Shorter Catechism, became a mathematician and a friend of Sir Robert Boyle and Sir Isaac Newton. Even Lazarus Seaman, a fairly representative member, if such could be said to exist, carried in his pocket an unpointed Hebrew text of the Old Testament for daily reading.[19] There was also an array of distinguished preachers: William Gouge, Thomas Goodwin, Stephen Marshall, Edmund Calamy, Herbert Palmer, Jeremiah Burroughs, and William Green-hill.[20] While Baxter's endorsement may be exaggerated—one has only to think of the first Council of Constantinople, where Jerome, Gregory of Nyssa, and Gregory of Nazianzus, among others, were present for a pre-council reading of the first two books of Nyssa's *Contra Eunomium*—it deserves to stand with the Synod of Dort as at least the "first among Protestant councils."[21] What is often missed by later scholars is the diversity of views in the Assembly, which was far wider than one finds in many conservative Presbyterian denominations in North America. Moreover, the divines were free

17. Jonathan Edwards, *Works*, 1:233, available at www.ccel.org.

18. Mitchell, *Westminster Assembly*, 122.

19. W. S. Barker, *Puritan Profiles: 54 Influential Puritans at the Time When the Westminster Confession of Faith Was Written* (Fearn: Mentor, 1996), 232.

20. Mitchell, *Westminster Assembly*, 122–28.

21. Schaff, *Creeds*, 1:728.

to express their views and were not proscribed for doing so. We shall see evidence of this later.[22]

The Powers of the Assembly

The first thing to note is that the Assembly was *not* a court of the Church. At the time the Assembly was set up, no legal, governmental structure existed for the Church of England. The entire constitutional fabric of the Church had been abolished, and nothing had been put in its place. That was to be one of the tasks of the Assembly. To that end, much of its time was spent examining, licensing, and ordaining ministers, for there was no other body officially authorized to do so. The Assembly was basically an advisory body of the Houses of Parliament—nothing more, nothing less.

The Assembly was further limited by having to deliver its opinions and advice to the Houses of Parliament "in such manner and sort as by both or either of the said Houses, from time to time, shall be required," and its dissolution was to be "in such a manner as by both Houses of Parliament shall be directed."[23] Van Dixhoorn sums up the relationship clearly: "At every point in the ordinance, Parliament asserted its governing and determining role on this synod." It set the date and location of the Assembly's meeting. It set the quorum at forty, chose the prolocutor, and retained the power to choose his successor. The Assembly was to be dissolved at Parliament's pleasure. Its debates were to be such as Parliament proposed, and its opinions were to be given to Parliament alone. No information was to be divulged to any outside person without the consent of at least one House of Parliament. If disagreements arose, they were to be submitted to Parliament for further direction. This was to be Parliament's Assembly.[24]

22. See Barker, *Puritan Profiles*, for detailed biographical sketches of members of the Assembly and others, and S. Carruthers, *The Everyday Work of the Westminster Assembly* (ed. J. Ligon Duncan III; Greenville, SC: Reformed Academic Press, 1994), for detailed information about the work of the Assembly. Van Dixhoorn provides detailed information on the members and their work in his *Oxford Dictionary of National Biography* article, cited in n12.

23. Mitchell, *Westminster Assembly*, xiv.

24. Van Dixhoorn, 1:39–40.

We must be clear on this. The Assembly was a commission of Parliament, with no jurisdiction or authority of its own. It was called by Parliament, its members were chosen by Parliament, Parliament defined its rights and privileges, and Parliament determined its area of debate. Parliament delimited its authority and appointed its prolocutor. Parliament even imprisoned one of its members, Daniel Featley, in the Tower of London![25] It was to deal with matters presented to it by Parliament. It was emphatically *not* a church court; after all, no constitutional structure existed for the church. It had "a purely advisory function."[26] The empowering ordinance was emphatic; nothing in it was to be construed as giving to the Assembly "any jurisdiction, power, or authority ecclesiastical whatsoever, or any other power than is hereby particularly expressed."[27] The Westminster Assembly was an Erastian body, even though only a handful of its members had Erastian convictions. However, this did not mean that the Assembly was constrained in its freedom of debate. Indeed, at times it came into some conflict with the prevailing sentiment of the Commons, particularly over discipline at the Lord's Supper and the freedom of the church to exercise discipline over its members.[28]

Here the difference from Scotland is noteworthy. In England, Parliament was alive and well, fighting the king, while the structure of the church had been disbanded, whereas in Scotland the church was alive and well, but there were no viable central political institutions. While England was a highly centralized country for its time, Scotland had a history of localized power (rival clans, families, and lairds), with little to tie everything together at the center. Thus, while the English church was strong locally, but in a muddle nationally, the Scottish church was strong centrally, but had made one compromise after another at the local level, under pressure from dominant local lairds.[29] This puts Warfield's pejorative comments about the English

25. Featley had been found to have disclosed details of the Assembly's business to royalists.
26. Warfield, *Westminster Assembly*, 14.
27. Mitchell, *Westminster Assembly*, xvi.
28. Warfield, *Westminster Assembly*, 16.
29. See M. Graham, "The Civil Sword and the Scottish Kirk, 1560–1600," in *Later Calvinism: International Perspectives* (ed. W. F. Graham; Kirksville, MO: Sixteenth Century Journal Publishers, 1994), 237–48.

church and his laudatory remarks about the Scots in proper perspective. The Scottish church was not the paragon of Reformed rectitude to which the benighted English church somehow needed to aspire.[30] Moreover, there was a significant body of theological and ecclesiastical opinion in Scotland that was opposed to the National Covenant of 1638, in favor of Episcopacy, and intent on maintaining the catholicity of the Reformed church. Led by John Forbes (1593–1648), this movement was centered in Aberdeen, and its leaders were known as the "Aberdeen doctors." That many of the English were skeptical about the Presbyterianism of the Church of Scotland is evident in the recently discovered section of Lightfoot's journal, which reports on the debate on the first article in the Solemn League and Covenant in S36–37, both on M 28.8.43. The article states, "I will endeavour the preservation of the true Reformed Protestant religion in the church of Scotland, in doctrine, discipline, worship & government, according to the word of God." It was debated whether the last phrase was limiting, insofar as the practices of the Scottish church were in accord with the Word of God, or whether it was approbatory, indicating an acceptance that the Scottish discipline *was* undoubtedly in accord with the Word of God. It was eventually decided to accept it as meaning "as far as in my conscience I shall conceive it to be according to the word of God."[31] While this was more of a problem for the Independents, there was at least a high degree of uncertainty or skepticism in the minds of many of the divines as to whether some features of the Church of Scotland were in accord with Scripture.

The king was not amused. In a proclamation made from Oxford on 22 June, referring to "that pretended Ordinance," he prohibited the Assembly's meeting. It was "illegal" since it lacked royal authorization. He threatened to act severely against any who participated in it. As Mitchell recognizes, the divines knew that by taking part in the Assembly they were putting their liberties and livelihoods at risk, and possibly their lives also. "Under the terrible threat of *praemunire* they resolved to obey the Ordinance of the two Houses." On 1 July, sixty-nine of them were present.[32]

30. Warfield, *Westminster Assembly*, 18–20.
31. Van Dixhoorn, 2:40.
32. Mitchell, *Westminster Assembly*, 133–35.

The Assembly's First Task

The divines began their work by drafting an expansion and development of the Thirty-Nine Articles.[33] This was not a replacement; the Articles were a robustly Reformed document from 1563, but they had been given a misleading spin by high-church divines and those of Arminian persuasion.[34] Warfield thinks this was a trifling matter. He writes of the Assembly "marking time," only getting down to real work when instructed, as demanded by the Scots, to start on the worship and discipline of the church. The revision of the Articles was given to the Assembly "as an expedient to occupy them innocuously until its real work" could be begun—busywork to keep them out of mischief![35] The falsity of Warfield's comment is shown by the fact that these revisions (as far as they went) were used by Parliament in negotiations with Charles I while he was in custody in Carisbrook Castle on the Isle of Wight, with a view to securing a settlement that would keep him on the throne while establishing Presbyterianism. Moreover, as the first task that Parliament gave the Assembly, it was at the top of its list of priorities prior to the negotiations with the Scots and the signing of the Solemn League and Covenant, events that could not immediately be foreseen. This was not idle busywork, as Warfield thought. As Norris points out, not only was the initial mandate from the House of Commons a doctrinal one, but the Assembly was saved much time later on by these earlier debates.[36] This was also the assessment of Alexander Mitchell (which was available to Warfield), who wrote that the debates on the revision of the Thirty-Nine Articles were "probably as important in a doctrinal point of view as any that occurred at a later stage."[37] Indeed, three years later, in S754 TH 10.12.46, an order from the House of Commons required the Assembly to send up what was finished of the Articles of the Church of England and the Scriptures for it. The Assembly ordered Dr. Temple, Mr. Seaman, Mr. Bond, and Dr. Stanton to be

33. See Norris, "Thirty-Nine Articles."
34. Mitchell, *Westminster Assembly*, 146.
35. Warfield, *Westminster Assembly*, 34–35.
36. Norris, "Thirty-Nine Articles," xviii–lx.
37. Mitchell, *Westminster Assembly*, 121.

a committee to work on updating the Articles of Religion, and that they meet that afternoon. Five days later, in S757 TU 15.12.46, it was ordered that the Committee for the Articles of Religion "doe meete this afternoone." Some time passed before the Assembly again ordered, in S763 M 28.12.46, that the committee "doe meete this afternoone and made report on Wensday come seven night next, and Mr. Gower and Mr. Profitt be added to the committee." In short, the committee took significant care in updating the Articles, enough to spend at least six weeks on the task.[38]

These debates were no sideshow or preliminary bout. Mitchell agrees, suggesting that

> the keen and lengthened debates which occurred in the discussions on these Articles could not fail to prepare the way for a more summary mode of procedure in connection with the Confession of Faith. The proceedings then were more summary, or at least more summarily recorded, just because the previous discussions on the more important doctrines of the Protestant system, and especially that of Justification by Faith, had been thorough and exhaustive, and pretty fully recorded.[39]

Most of the discussion on the Thirty-Nine Articles pertained to article 8 on the three creeds and article 11 on justification. On article 8, objections were raised to the titles of the creeds—Nicene, Athanasian, Apostles'—due to doubts as to whether they accurately reflected authorship. However, Daniel Featley replied that the contents of these creeds were compatible with the theologies of Nicaea, Athanasius, and the apostles, regardless of who wrote them. The Assembly altered the wording of the article to make it clear that they did not regard the creeds as the work of those to whom they had been attributed, but rather as commonly so called. Further objections pertained to some of the contents of the creeds: the allegedly peremptory way in which the Athanasian Creed affirms the damnation of those who do not believe its contents; the statement in the Nicene Creed that Christ is God of God, to which Featley replied that this does not suggest

38. Van Dixhoorn, 6:386–94.
39. Mitchell, *Westminster Assembly*, 150–51.

that Christ derives his deity from the Father; and the phrase "he descended into hell" in the Apostles' Creed, which is capable of many orthodox interpretations, with Christ descending locally, virtually, or metonymically.[40] We will consider this discussion in more detail in chapter 7 on Scripture.

Regarding the article on justification, Twisse, Gataker, and Richard Vines—like Robert Rollock (1555–99) and Johannes Piscator (1546–1625) before them—argued strongly that only the passive obedience of Christ is imputed for justification. Others opposed them, led by Featley. The vote went in favor of Christ's "whole obedience," with "3 <or 4> only dissenting."[41] James I's request that the controversy between Molinaeus and Tilenus on the imputation of the active obedience of Christ not be discussed in his realm was read to the Assembly, although there is some doubt as to whether the whole of it was read or only part. James cautioned against making this an issue on the grounds that it was a new matter, not decided by any council, nor handled by the Fathers or scholastics.[42] In the Confession of Faith, the word "whole" is left out. We will discuss this issue in detail in chapter 12 on the order of salvation.

Therefore, the initial work of the Assembly concerned the Church of England alone. There is no indication that formal uniformity in religion between England and Scotland was envisaged. Warfield is correct here.[43] The reader should note that England and Scotland were separate kingdoms at this time. Political union awaited the Act of Union in 1707. Therefore, talk about Britain must be confined to geographical or generic senses.[44]

The Assembly formed three equal committees to do the preparatory work. The Articles were divided up among the committees, which then reported to the Assembly, which in turn debated the committee proposals and eventually voted. A small subcommittee was appointed

40. Ibid., 151–53. Metonymy is the substitution of the name of one thing for the name of a related thing: e.g., "the crown," referring to the king.

41. Van Dixhoorn, 3:77.

42. S49 F 8.9.46. See Lightfoot's journal, in Van Dixhoorn, 2:57.

43. Warfield, *Westminster Assembly*, 14.

44. But see J. E. A. Dawson, *The Politics of Religion in the Age of Mary, Queen of Scots: the Earl of Argyll and the Struggle for Britain and Ireland* (Cambridge Studies in Early Modern British History; Cambridge: Cambridge University Press, 2007).

to gather ancient copies of the Articles, so that the work could be based on the most authentic manuscripts.[45]

The Interposition of the Scots and the Solemn League and Covenant

Even before the Assembly began, Parliament recognized it needed help from the Scots in the war against the king, since the war had not been going well. A number of leading political, ecclesiastical, and theological figures from Scotland came to London, commissioned to negotiate with Parliament. When the Scottish commissioners appeared, Parliament—as part of the deal—subscribed to the Solemn League and Covenant. In this it agreed to bring the ecclesiastical government and belief in the three kingdoms of England, Scotland, and Ireland into conformity. This uniformity was to find expression in a confession of faith, a form of church government, a directory of worship, and a catechism. Due to this agreement, Parliament ordered the Assembly to suspend its revision of the Articles and to begin work on a directory of church government. By then, it had revised fifteen articles and had begun work on the sixteenth. Now Parliament requested the Assembly to produce a new confession and catechisms. Whereas the revision of the Articles was for the vindication of the doctrine of the Church of England, the new documents had in view the church in all three kingdoms. The political scene had changed dramatically and required an entirely new agenda. The Covenant was signed by both the English and the Scottish Parliaments on Monday, 25 September 1643. Its language was reminiscent of the original ordinance. At first, some Assembly members were reluctant to sign their approval. Certainly the document did not indicate what the future government or worship of the church would be like, nor did it specify whether an entirely new confession was needed or whether a revision of the Articles would do.[46]

45. For lists of committee members (as far as Mitchell was able to discover: see Dr. Williams's manuscripts), see Mitchell, *Westminster Assembly*, 149.
46. Van Dixhoorn, 1:45–50.

The agreement did not specifically require a presbyterian form of government. Indeed, the English insisted on the insertion of the qualifying clause "according to the Word of God." This underlined the point that while the Scots were dogmatic Presbyterians, insisting that God had laid down in Scripture such a system, the English were much more pragmatic, with varying degrees of commitment to Presbyterianism and usually on different grounds than the Scots. North of the border, Presbyterianism had been in effect for almost a century, since the Reformation under John Knox, and there was no question of any alteration. In view of this, it is obvious that conformity in church government entailed some form of presbyterian structure in England too.

The Solemn League and Covenant was an agreement between two nations, a treaty of sorts. In reality, it was a treaty between part of one nation and a Parliament of another—since half of the body politic in England was at war with Parliament, and civil union in Scotland was also under threat. The Scottish commissioners were sent south as representatives of the nation as much as of the church. Their task was not in relation to the Assembly but to Parliament; their brief was to safeguard the interests of Scotland. "They could treat with or act directly upon the Assembly of Divines only at the request of Parliament, to treat with which they were really commissioned; and only to the extent which Parliament might judge useful for the common end in view."[47] A committee of Parliament itself, called the Grand Committee, was appointed to meet and consult with them, to which was added a committee of divines. The points of uniformity were handled through this Grand Committee. Parliament also requested the Scots to sit in the Assembly as private individuals.

Therefore, it is wrong to call the Scottish commissioners members of the Westminster Assembly. They were not members at all. They were invited to attend and to participate in debates, but they had no vote. Their names are absent from all recorded votes. Nor were they commissioners to the Assembly as such; their commission was to deal with Parliament and the Assembly. The Assembly was an *English* body, even when it debated matters relating to the three kingdoms.

47. Warfield, *Westminster Assembly*, 32.

Chronology of the Assembly, Including the Subjects of Debate[48]

July 1643	Debates and revisions to the Thirty-Nine Articles
September 1643	Signing of the Solemn League and Covenant
October 1643	Directory of Church Government
January 1644	Directory for Ordaining Ministers pro tempore
February 1644	Directory of Church Government
end May 1644	Directory of Worship
July 1644	Cromwell wins the Battle of Marston Moor
October 1644	Directory of Church Government, Directory of Worship
January 1645	Directory of Church Government
June 1645	Admission to the Lord's Supper. Cromwell wins the decisive Battle of Naseby
July 1645	Directory of Church Government, Confession of Faith
August 1645	Admission to the Lord's Supper, examining of ministers
September 1645	Confession of Faith
April 1646	Directory of Church Government, debate on *jus divinum* of church government
June 1646	Directory of Church Government, *jus divinum*, Confession of Faith
July 1646	Directory of Church Government, *jus divinum*
August 1646	Confession of Faith
September 1646	Confession of Faith, Catechisms
October 1646	Confession of Faith
December 1646	Catechisms
January 1647	Confession of Faith
April 1647	Confession of Faith, Catechisms
May 1647	Catechisms, some days spent examining ministers
June 1648	Miscellaneous business, examination of ministers
July 1648	Examination of ministers
March 1652	Business ended

48. Reproduced by permission from Van Dixhoorn, 1:86.

Developments in the First Civil War and Beyond

Before long, the fortunes of war changed. Parliament, under Oliver Cromwell, won decisive victories over the Royalists at Marston Moor in July 1644 and at Naseby in June 1645. Cromwell's genius was such that, with no previous military experience whatever, he outclassed veteran generals tried and hardened by the grueling Thirty Years' War. He never lost a battle, going into combat at the place and time of his own choosing. By 1646, Parliament had won. However, power was passing inexorably to the army that had won the war. Cromwell and most of his army were Independents, not Presbyterians; the shift in power was irreversible. Moreover, the Presbyterians, who of various shades were a majority in the Assembly and in Parliament, were out-flanked politically by Cromwell. He knew what power was and how to use it. He was also ahead of his time in seeking religious freedom. The Presbyterians' unwillingness to grant such freedom to the Independents when the army was in the ascendancy was a monumental political error. They were intransigent and lacked the imagination to see the consequences of their actions. They also failed to grasp the realities of the political situation. If they had had the necessary gumption, Presbyterianism could have been achieved in the Church of England, supported by the army, if freedom of worship had been granted to the Independents. But the Scots were terrified of Independency, and that in all probability helped to tip the scales against accommodation and so eventually ruined the hopes that previously existed. Brian Levack argues similarly: "English Presbyterians were too Erastian for their Scottish co-religionists," and "the rise of the English Independents, who were feared and abhorred in Scotland, sealed the fate of presbyterianism in England, driving the Scottish presbyterians into a temporary alliance with the royalists and ending, for all practical purposes, the last real hope of religious union in the history of the nations."[49]

Eventually Charles was arrested, tried, and beheaded in January 1649. From 1649 to 1660 came the Commonwealth, with Cromwell as Lord Protector from December 1653 until his death in September

49. B. P. Levack, *The Formation of the British State: England, Scotland and the Union, 1603–1707* (Oxford: Clarendon Press, 1987), 129.

1658. In 1660, the monarchy was restored under Charles II, the son of Charles I. The Act of Uniformity (1662) forced 2,000 ministers out of their parishes and created English nonconformity—those Protestants unable to conform to this legislation. The Westminster Assembly failed to achieve in its own land the purpose for which it had been established.

PART 2

THE THEOLOGICAL CONTEXT

3

The English Context

It is a savage irony that, in terms of the purpose for which it was created, the work of the Westminster Assembly was a total failure. Set up by the House of Commons soon after the start of the First Civil War for the "vindicating and clearing of the doctrine of the Church of England from all false calumnies and aspersions," by the time it wound down power had irretrievably passed to the army, in which various shades of Independents predominated. Soon afterward, the restoration of the monarchy brought a savage backlash which forever dashed any prospects of its teaching receiving official sanction in England. Hence, the vast majority of its commentators have been from Scotland or North America. Some Scottish interpreters treat the English context as almost ancillary. We noted B. B. Warfield's dismissive comment on the Assembly's debates on the Thirty-Nine Articles, which were, he says, "marking time."[1] Overall, the English context has been neglected. Most commentaries usually provide a brief historical introduction to the Assembly, but thereafter ignore the historical context as a factor in interpretation. Robert Shaw is better than some, but still he views it from the Scottish perspective.[2]

This question of perspective is, of course, important in the interpretation of any text, ancient or modern. In northwest Scotland, there is a remarkable mountain, Suilven, an abrupt and bulbous protrusion

---

1. Warfield, *Westminster Assembly*, 34–35.
2. Shaw, *Exposition*.

when viewed from the southwest, an elongated ridge from the south, a jagged, nightmarish apparition out of Tolkien from the east. The contours are the same, but the appearance differs radically. The documents of the Westminster Assembly share with Suilven, and with any object in relation to which a human agent can be placed, a prospect shaped by the location of the observer.

It is proper hermeneutics to attempt to interpret a text in its original context. A striking example of carelessness, of failure to do basic homework, that renders a contextual reading improbable is this extract from the introduction to a recent popular treatment of the Westminster Confession:

> A distinguished body of Calvinistic scholars, churchmen, and theologians, representing the various religious constituencies from England and Scotland, met with representatives of Parliament, to forge the so-called Westminster Standards. . . . The goal of a greater Reformed unity throughout the British Empire was realized to some degree during the Cromwellian Interregnum, but it completely collapsed in England with a return to Anglicanism.[3]

This combination of anachronism and inaccuracy is by no means atypical. Not only did the Assembly not represent "the various religious constituencies from England and Scotland," but the British Empire lay in the future. While England had some colonies, Britain as a political entity did not exist until 1707 and so could not have had an empire.

Moreover, inordinate attention has been paid to the Scottish commissioners (Rutherford, Baillie, Gillespie—"Scotch what d'ye call," in Milton's memorable phrase[4]), who were simply advisers, commissioners to Parliament who had no voting rights in the Assembly.[5] The minutes published by Mitchell and Struthers in 1874 do not include the first two volumes, since they deal with English matters that would be of little interest to their Scottish readership. When the publishing

---

3. J. H. Gerstner, ed., *A Guide: The Westminster Confession of Faith: Commentary* (Signal Mountain, TN: Summertown Texts, 1992), vii.

4. D. Masson, *The Life of John Milton* (London: Macmillan, 1873), 3:468–71.

5. The Scottish commissioners are not listed as members of the Assembly in the minutes. See S87 TH 2.11.43, in Van Dixhoorn, 1:238–40.

project collapsed in 1904 due to insufficient funds, these records were still not transcribed.[6] Meanwhile, members of the Assembly such as AnthonyTuckney, who had a major influence on the Larger Catechism, have been virtually ignored.[7] As for more popular commentaries, these do not address the historical situation at all.[8] It is as if the Assembly were timeless, suspended above history.

Added to this, virtually everyone, of whatever persuasion, has accepted the spin given by Restoration historians, the eventual winners. According to this standard view, the Presbyterian Puritans who formed the bulk of the Westminster Assembly were extremists, not representative of the Church of England. John Henry Newman gave this notion added impetus by his claim that the Church of England was committed to a *via media* between Rome and Protestantism. In his famous *Tract 90* (1841), he argued that the Thirty-Nine Articles could be interpreted in harmony with the Council of Trent. After his move to Rome, in *An Essay on the Development of Christian Doctrine* (1845), he dismissed Protestantism in general as averse to history and the development of the church. Protestantism is not the Christianity of history, he maintained, for "to be deep in history is to cease to be a Protestant."[9] This thinking painted the Presbyterians as extremists, destabilizing both church and nation. This campaign was so effective that the conclusions of Restoration historians, until recently, have been

6. Van Dixhoorn, 2:xli; A. F. Mitchell and J. Struthers, eds., *Minutes of the Sessions of the Westminster Assembly of Divines While Engaged in Preparing the Directory for Church Government, Confession of Faith and Catechisms (November 1644 to March 1649): From Transcripts of the Originals Procured by a Committee of the General Assembly of the Church of Scotland* (Edinburgh: William Blackwood and Sons, 1874).

7. Contrary to those who portray the Assembly as designed to bring English practice into conformity with the Church of Scotland, general assemblies of the Church of Scotland at this time were overloaded with changes forced on them from England: the abandonment of the use of the Apostles' Creed and the Lord's Prayer in the liturgy, of reading Scripture without interpretation, of the minister's devotions before the sermon, of deacons reading Scripture (as in the French and Dutch Reformed churches of the time)—all standard liturgical practices in the Scottish church since Knox. See J. B. Torrance, "Covenant or Contract? A Study of the Background of Worship in Seventeenth-Century Scotland," *SJT* 23 (1970): 71–73, citing G. W. Sprott, *The Worship of the Church of Scotland During the Covenanting Period, 1638–1661* (Edinburgh: William Blackwood and Sons, 1882), 34–49.

8. E.g., Vos, *Larger Catechism*; G. I. Williamson, *The Westminster Confession of Faith for Study Classes* (Philadelphia: Presbyterian and Reformed, 1964).

9. J. H. Newman, *An Essay on the Development of Christian Doctrine* (Notre Dame, IN: University of Notre Dame Press, 1989), 7–11.

accepted virtually without question. Winston Churchill confidently predicted during the Second World War that history would paint him in a favorable light since he would be writing it himself.[10] So too the winners in 1660 wrote the received tradition. With the general acceptance of this paradigm came, particularly in Presbyterian minds, caricatures of Anglicanism as a halfway house to Rome, and this in turn affected perceptions of the relationship between the theology of the Assembly and what preceded it. In short, there is a pressing need for a more accurate placement of the Assembly and its theological documents in a wider context.

The Westminster Assembly in Its English Context

Any consideration of the Assembly must locate it in its *English* context, as an *ad hoc* advisory committee of Parliament, without any power or jurisdiction,[11] with its first task the revision of the Thirty-Nine Articles of Religion of the Church of England.[12] We noted in the previous chapter the falsity of Warfield's claim that in this the Assembly was merely "marking time." In this he was preceded by William Hetherington, who dismissively stated, "It is unnecessary to trace that part of the proceedings which led to no practical result, and which, terminating abruptly and unfinished, cannot properly be said to form any part of the Assembly's actual proceedings. Let us rather direct attention to the formation of the Solemn League and Covenant itself."[13] In 1843, in his remote study in Torphichen Manse, some way west of Edinburgh, Hetherington knew well his readers could ignore matters directly relevant to England. On the other hand, they were directly relevant *to the Assembly*. As Norris points out, not only was the initial mandate from the House of Commons a doctrinal one, but

10. See, e.g., R. Jenkins, *Churchill: A Biography* (New York: Farrar, Straus and Giroux, 2001), 819.

11. For the overall English context, see W. A. Shaw, *A History of the English Church During the Civil Wars and Under the Commonwealth, 1640–1660* (2 vols.; London: Longmans, Green, 1900), which is still valuable.

12. See Norris, "Thirty-Nine Articles."

13. Hetherington, *History*, 122. While there is some useful information and comment in this book, much of it is marred by overt anti-English prejudice and historical inaccuracy— including listing the Scottish commissioners as members of the Assembly.

the Assembly was saved much time later on by these earlier debates.[14] This was also the assessment of Alexander Mitchell (which was available to Warfield), who wrote that the debates on the revision of the Thirty-Nine Articles were "probably as important in a doctrinal point of view as any that occurred at a later stage."[15]

Again, Van Dixhoorn, in an earlier thesis, identifies Anglicans with those who did not want preaching, but thought the reading of Scripture was sufficient in divine worship.[16] This antipathy to preaching did emerge before the Civil War, under the direction of Laud, and was pursued with vigor in some dioceses, such as Norwich and Ely, by Matthew Wren, and Bath and Wells by William Piers, who maintained that preaching had run its course and that there was no more need for it. In particular, an attempt was made to eradicate preaching at evensong, normally held in the afternoon. Wren stamped it out in his diocese.[17] Yet such policies were contrary to the form for "The Ordering of Priests" in the Elizabethan Book of Common Prayer:

> When laying on hands, the receivers humbly kneeling, the bishop says ". . . be thou a faithful Dispenser of the Word of God, and of his holy Sacraments; in the Name of the Father, and of the Son, and of the Holy Ghost. Amen." Then the bishop shall deliver to every one of them kneeling, the Bible into his hand, saying, "Take thou authority to preach the Word of God, and to minister the holy Sacraments in the Congregation, where thou shalt be lawfully appointed thereunto."[18]

One can hardly call "Anglican" that which was diametrically opposed to what Anglican doctrine prescribed. Later, Van Dixhoorn helpfully connects the Assembly's comments concerning the keys of the kingdom with preaching, by referring to similar connections in the Heidelberg Catechism, yet the Book of Common Prayer has this also in the ordination service for priests.[19]

14. Norris, "Thirty-Nine Articles," xviii–lx.

15. Mitchell, *Westminster Assembly*, 121.

16. C. B. Van Dixhoorn, "Anglicans, Anarchists, and the Westminster Assembly: The Making of a Pulpit Theology" (Th.M. thesis, Westminster Theological Seminary, 2000), 70–71.

17. Davies, *Caroline Captivity*, 132–43.

18. *The Book of Common Prayer* (Oxford: Oxford University Press, n.d.), 602.

19. C. B. Van Dixhoorn, "Anglicans, Anarchists," 102.

Recent Reassessment of Pre-Restoration Anglican Theology

In recent years, there has been a significant reassessment of pre-Restoration Anglican theology. In turn, this requires a reevaluation of the relationship between the Assembly and the reassessed theology. In his magisterial and widely acclaimed critical biography of the great English reformer, Thomas Cranmer, Diarmaid MacCulloch demonstrates that Cranmer, throughout his career, was much in contact with continental Reformed churches and theologians. It is of course well known that, on a trip to Europe to arrange Henry VIII's famous divorce from Catherine of Aragon, he remarried in Nuremberg (his first wife had died in childbirth[20]), a daring move for an Anglican priest before the break with Rome. His wife was the niece of the wife of the reformer Osiander.[21] Thereafter, his career was a tortuous but persistent attempt to bring the Church of England into line with the Reformed churches on the continent, a trajectory that accelerated with the accession of Edward VI in 1547, but was abruptly reversed under Mary, claiming Cranmer's own life in the process. After Elizabeth came to the throne in 1558, Mary's depredations were removed, but Cranmer's trajectory was frozen short of its apogee. In MacCulloch's words, "The thread running through [his career] . . . is his fierce determination to promote the evangelical reform of the Church."[22] Cranmer's "middle way" was not a midpoint between the Reformation and Rome, but "between Wittenberg and Zürich," the path trod by Bucer and Calvin. He was "a Reformed Catholic" who sought to rebuild the Catholic Church on the basis of the Bible, the creeds, and the great councils of the early church.[23] This contrasts strongly with Mitchell's earlier negative assessment of Cranmer, one which lacked the benefit of the vast material that has accrued in intervening years.[24]

Similarly being reassessed has been Richard Hooker, widely regarded as the linchpin of historic Anglicanism.[25] Spinks, in his evaluation of Perkins and Hooker, finds that both "stand firmly

20. MacCulloch, *Thomas Cranmer*, 21–22.
21. Ibid., 69–72.
22. Ibid., 630.
23. Ibid., 617.
24. Mitchell, *Westminster Assembly*, 21–23.
25. Kirby, *Royal Supremacy*; Spinks, *Two Faces*; Atkinson, *Richard Hooker*.

within a broad-based Reformed theology." Hooker "never departs from a Reformed position." Both Hooker and Perkins are legitimate interpreters of the Thirty-Nine Articles, while "Hooker finds his theology expressed in the 1559 Book of Common Prayer; Perkins gave no hint that his theology was contradicted by it."[26] There are, Spinks holds, differences of emphasis between the two, and in 1630 Perkins was more typical of Church of England opinion than Hooker.[27] However, Hooker had ably defended the Prayer Book, something Perkins had not done, and so he was a more serviceable source for post-Restoration Anglicanism—especially after he was carefully sanitized by Izaak Walton's *Life of Hooker*, in which the last three books of the *Lawes of Ecclesiastical Polity* were discredited.[28] A different view had previously been propounded by Peter Lake, who argued that Hooker is notable mainly for a new style of sacrament-centered piety that came to full fruition during the Laudian ascendancy. Hooker was followed in this, so Lake maintains, by Lancelot Andrewes and John Buckeridge.[29]

The English Reformers and the Thirty-Nine Articles leaned toward the theology of Augustine and the Reformed, rather than toward the Lutheran churches.[30] The Lambeth Articles (1595) are an unequivocally Calvinist document, approved and superintended by Archbishop Whitgift, although never formally adopted as official Anglican dogma. Whitgift himself played an instrumental role in rejecting the views of William Barrett and Peter Baro, who had argued that the elect could totally and finally fall from grace. At the same time, he moderated the draft of William Whitaker, the chief opponent of Barrett and Baro. The Articles state that the nonelect are damned on account of their sins (*propter peccata sua*), which was to find an echo in WCF 3.7, where the rest of mankind other than the elect are said to be "ordained to

---

26. Spinks, *Two Faces*, 160–62.

27. We should note that there were clear differences on the principles governing the worship of the church. We shall examine this question in chapter 13.

28. Spinks, *Two Faces*, 168–71.

29. P. Lake, *Anglicans and Puritans? Predestinarianism and English Conformist Thought from Whitgift to Hooker* (London: HarperCollins, 1988), chap. 4: also Lake, "Lancelot Andrewes, John Buckeridge and Avant-Garde Conformity at the Court of James I," in *The Mental World of the Jacobean Court* (ed. L. L. Peck; Cambridge: Cambridge University Press, 1991), 113–33.

30. Mitchell, *Westminster Assembly*, 346; see P. E. Hughes, *The Theology of the English Reformers* (Grand Rapids: Eerdmans, 1965), *in passim*.

dishonour and wrath *for their sin.*"[31] The Irish Convocation in 1615 was permitted to incorporate the Lambeth Articles. In 1618, the British delegation to Dort sent by James I, with the approval of Archbishop George Abbot, took the Lambeth Articles with them as evidence of the faith professed in England.[32]

Calvinism continued to be the backbone of the Church of England for several generations after Hooker. R. Scott Clark points to the predominance of Calvinists at Oxford right up to the time of the Assembly. Calvinism was *de rigeur*, as doctoral theses routinely defended Calvinist positions until the 1630s. Indeed, one-third of the active divines at the Westminster Assembly had studied at Oxford.[33] The archbishop of Canterbury from 1611 to 1633, George Abbot, was a Calvinist. The British delegation to the Synod of Dort (1618–19), the greatest international Reformed synod, was also Anglican: George Carleton (bishop of Llandaff), John Davenant (Lady Margaret Professor of Divinity, University of Cambridge), Samuel Ward (master of Sidney Sussex College, University of Cambridge), Walter Balcanqual (fellow, Pembroke Hall, University of Cambridge, representing the Church of Scotland), Thomas Goad (chaplain to the archbishop of Canterbury), and Joseph Hall (dean of Worcester Cathedral), who was unable to attend due to illness.[34] Andrew Pettegree, in his extensive research into continental and English publishers' booklists, books bequeathed in Cambridge wills, and theological works published in English, confirms "the preeminent position of Calvin as the dominant theological influence in Elizabethan England." He easily outstripped all competitors, from whatever source, including England itself. Moreover, "England, on this evidence, was far and away the biggest market for

31. Porter, *Reformation and Reaction*, 368–69; Schaff, *Creeds*, 3:523; R. W. A. Letham, "Saving Faith and Assurance in Reformed Theology: Zwingli to the Synod of Dort" (2 vols.; Ph.D. thesis, University of Aberdeen, 1979), 1:286–89.

32. Mitchell, *Westminster Assembly*, 350.

33. R. S. Clark and J. R. Beeke, "Ursinus, Oxford, and the Westminster Divines," in *Westminster Confession into the 21st Century* (ed. Duncan), 2:5–7.

34. J. Platt, "Eirenical Anglicans at the Synod of Dort," in *Reform and Reformation: England and the Continent c1500–c1750* (ed. D. Baker; Oxford: Blackwell, 1979), 221–43; R. Letham, *Assurance in Theological Context: Reformed Dogmatics 1523–1619* (Rutherford Studies in Historical Theology; Edinburgh: Rutherford House, forthcoming); W. R. Godfrey, "Tensions Within International Calvinism: The Debate on the Atonement at the Synod of Dort" (Ph.D. dissertation, Stanford University, 1974).

Calvin's works in translation." The "Calvinist consensus" of the English church was intact. Indeed, when Calvinism seemed to be under threat on the continent, it was from England that help was requested, with confidence that it would be forthcoming.[35]

Anthony Milton has produced massive documentary evidence of the work of the British delegation at Dort. The extensive correspondence that Milton reproduces includes 116 letters between members of the delegation, James I, and others, and theological letters between the delegates and others. Additionally, he includes the delegation's judgment on various aspects of the Synod, and letters to and from a range of figures, including the moderator, Johannes Bogerman. He even includes references to the Synod made by the delegates after their return home. The delegation was sent by James I and Archbishop Abbott to represent the Church of England. Anglicans under the influence of Restoration and post-Restoration theology have tried their best to forget it happened, or to disown it, whenever the subject is raised. Milton points out that the presence of English divines at this, the most important international Reformed synod, has provoked "agonized debate among Anglican scholars and church historians ever since."[36] Indeed, "the general tendency . . . was to deny that the Synod of Dort had anything to do with the Church of England."[37]

That the delegation was not merely representing James's political interests in securing Dutch support against France and Spain is clear from their self-identification as spokesmen for their church. They reacted strongly against Gomarus's charge that they were not accurately representing the doctrinal formularies of the Church of England.[38] While there may have been other English theologians of different persuasions who could have been selected to go to Dort—Lancelot Andrewes was one obvious candidate—and whereas there was no question of any church but the Dutch being bound to the Canons, there was no significant attempt to distance the Church of England from Dort

35. A. Pettegree, "The Reception of Calvinism in Britain," in *Calvinus Sincerioris Religionis Vindex = Calvin as Protector of the Purer Religion*, ed. W. H. Neuser (Kirksville, MO: Sixteenth Century Journal Publishers, 1997), 267–89, esp. 280–82, 289.

36. Milton, *British Delegation*, xviii.

37. Ibid., xx.

38. Ibid., xxvii.

for at least a generation, until the dying days of the Commonwealth.[39] James himself was well pleased with the result, and all the delegates were rapidly promoted.[40] Nor were the members of the delegation merely observers. Bishop George Carleton arranged private meetings where differences among various delegations were discussed and agreements were reached; this was particularly the case when the Dutch were at odds with the Bremen delegation, and Mathias Martinius in particular.[41] In 1626, Bishop Carleton reproved Bishop Montagu for reviving the proto-Arminian doctrines of William Barret and Peter Baro and for calling those who supported the Lambeth Articles Puritans; he was supported in this reproof by Ussher, Downame, Davenant, and Hall.[42] This, as Spinks argues, is a "past which the Restoration ideology wished to deny, and the Oxford Movement pretended did not happen."[43]

In an earlier era, Mitchell also stressed the continuity of the theology at Westminster with the English movement for the reformation of the church a century earlier.[44] Bishop Carleton, of the Dort delegation, acknowledged, "Albeit the Puritans disquieted our Church about their conceived discipline, yet they never moved any quarrel against the doctrine of our Church. . . . It was then the open confession, both of the Bishops and of the Puritans, that both parties embraced a mutual consent in doctrine."[45] Mitchell argues that "the movement which culminated in the Westminster Assembly was designed . . . if possible to restore Augustinianism and the theology of the English reformation."[46] There were strong indigenous antecedents: Anselm, Bradwardine, Tyndale, Frith, and Barnes, as well as the powerful impact of Bucer and Peter Martyr. Mitchell points to the close connection between the Latin Article of 1553 and the views on election of Bucer and Martyr, adding for good measure the affinity between Calvin's 1543 edition of the

39. Ibid., xviii, xlix–l.
40. Ibid., lii.
41. Ibid., 193–95.
42. Mitchell, *Westminster Assembly*, 351.
43. Spinks, *Two Faces*, 173–74.
44. Mitchell, *Westminster Assembly*, 1–97.
45. Cited by Mitchell, *Westminster Assembly*, 335.
46. Mitchell, *Westminster Assembly*, 336.

Institutes and article 17 of the Thirty-Nine Articles of 1563.[47] That there was close and regular contact with the writings of Calvin, Bullinger, and Martyr in sixteenth-century England is well known. That there was a thorough theological commonality is seen in the Lambeth Articles, the Hampton Court Conference of 1604, the approval of the Irish Articles (1615), and the delegation sent to Dort in 1618. Non-Puritans agreed that Augustinianism was the doctrine of the Church of England. It was only in the reign of Charles I that the fashion arose to call those who held to this doctrine "Puritans." "Down to the time of Archbishop Laud there had been almost a continuous succession of Augustinian Professors of Divinity in the Universities. . . . Besides these there was a whole host of men who preached the same theology from the pulpits or expounded it through the press."[48]

So much is clear from the writings of Church of England leaders who defended the Elizabethan settlement against those pressing for further reform of discipline and ceremonies. Thomas Rogers, who was to be chaplain to Bancroft, archbishop of Canterbury after Whitgift and before Abbott, wrote in 1585 and 1587 that the doctrine of the Church of England expressed in the Thirty-Nine Articles was in conformity with the confessions of the Reformed churches on the continent, and that there was no contention over it in England itself. Although he was no Puritan—he strenuously opposed attempts to introduce presbyteries and rejected arguments that the church had no right to allow ceremonies or feast days not prescribed in Scripture— he was a consistent and thoroughgoing Calvinist, defending double predestination, justification by faith alone, and all the doctrines of the Articles.[49] His main opponents were papists and the Roman Church: "We, al of us, either simplie subscribe unto the forme of pub. praier prescribed, or humblie (which libertie the lawe giveth) desire resolution in some fewe things; we, al of us, iointlie both embrace the Articles of the English Creed, and renounce al haeretical opinions contrarie there-unto."[50]

47. Ibid., 336–46.
48. Ibid., 352–53.
49. Rogers, *English creede*. See, e.g., 59–67 on article 17.
50. Ibid., preface [3].

Yet there was another strain of indigenous English Reformed theology within the Church of England, one which was to surface at the Assembly and has sometimes been misunderstood. Jonathan Moore terms this "English hypothetical universalism." By this, he means to distinguish it from Amyraldianism, which emerged between Dort and Westminster. Usually these two movements are seen as identical. However, the English hypothetical universalists antedated the move of John Cameron (1579–1625) to Saumur and the publication of Moyse Amyraut's (1586–1664) major work, *A Brief Treatise on Predestination*, in 1634. Moreover, while Amyraut changed the Reformed order of decrees, placing the decree of election after the decree to send Christ, the English retained the original order, whether in an infralapsarian or supralapsarian guise.[51] Amyraut held that God intended Christ's death to be for all, but, foreseeing that not all would believe, he elected some. There was a rift between election and the atonement. The English argued that Christ died for all, obtaining a conditional salvation if they believe. This, Moore insists, was not a retreat from the scholasticism of high Calvinism, for all used scholastic methods, and in fact the hypothetical universalists relied on scholastic logic more than most.[52] This is a further nail in the coffin of the erstwhile idea that the pure biblical theology of Calvin and the Reformation was defaced by the renewed application of Aristotelian philosophy, a view popularized by such scholars as Hans Emil Weber and Brian Armstrong,[53] but fatally undermined by, among others, Richard A.

51. The debate between infralapsarians and supralapsarians concerned the order of decrees in the mind of God. Since there is no way we can know the order of decrees in God's mind unless he chooses to reveal it, the issue is inherently speculative, yet it was nonetheless a real one with significant ramifications for how theology as a whole was approached. For infralapsarianism, the decree of election is beneath (*infra*), or after, the decree to permit the fall. Hence, the elect are contemplated in God's mind as already fallen. This line of thought attempts to follow the historical outworking of salvation. On the other hand, supralapsarianism regards the decree of election as preceding the decree to permit the fall. In this view, the first thing in God's purpose is his election of a people for himself. The elect are contemplated as potentially capable of falling. Supralapsarianism follows the logical order in the decrees: what is last in activation is first in intention. As a consequence, supralapsarianism has a tendency to regard a range of theological issues as principally determined by the decree of election.

52. Moore, *English Hypothetical Universalism*, 217–22.

53. B. G. Armstrong, *Calvinism and the Amyraut Heresy: Protestant Scholasticism and Humanism in Seventeenth-Century France* (Madison: University of Wisconsin Press, 1969); H. E. Weber, *Reformation, Orthodoxie und Rationalismus* (2 vols. in 3; Gütersloh: C. Bertlesmann, 1937–51).

Muller and a variety of contributors to the volume on scholasticism co-edited by R. Scott Clark and Carl Trueman.[54]

What facilitated the emergence of this strain of theology was the changed historical context. The era of the Reformation was past; it was established and needed consolidation. Challenges had emerged from Arminianism. As Moore states,

> "Once the fact is reckoned with that England and Scotland were the only kingdoms in the sixteenth century in which the Reformed faith was established as the national religion, simple comparisons became impossible between seventeenth-century parish preachers in the English state church and sixteenth-century continental Reformers in their gathered congregations surrounded by the false church of Antichrist. Along with Scotland, England was an island [*sic!*][55] in covenant with God. Citizenship and church membership were but two sides of one coin, and choice and persecution were involved in neither."[56]

Moore continues by explaining that the whole parish was coextensive with the congregation, but not all were godly. England was an ungodly godly nation. Consequently, the Lord's Supper, not baptism, had effectively become the sacrament of initiation and the focal point of the free offer of the gospel, so facilitating the covenantal and soteriological structures of hypothetical universalism.[57] English Calvinism was a heterogeneous creature. A hasty application of the label "Calvinist" should be avoided, Moore advises, for underneath lay a spectrum of

54. C. R. Trueman and R. Scott Clark, eds., *Protestant Scholasticism: Essays in Reassessment* (Carlisle: Paternoster, 1999); R. A. Muller, "Scholasticism in Calvin: A Question of Relation and Disjunction," in *Calvinus Sincerioris Religionis Vindex* (ed. Neuser), 247–65; R. A. Muller, *The Unaccommodated Calvin: Studies in the Foundation of a Theological Tradition* (New York: Oxford University Press, 2000); R. A. Muller, *After Calvin: Studies in the Development of a Theological Tradition* (Oxford: Oxford University Press, 2003); R. A. Muller, *Christ and the Decree: Christology and Predestination in Reformed Theology from Calvin to Perkins* (Grand Rapids: Baker, 1986).

55. England is part of a larger island called Great Britain, and also includes a number of smaller islands, such as the Isle of Wight and the Scilly Isles. Scotland consists of another large section of Great Britain, plus a large number of smaller islands. Together with Wales, they form an archipelago, not an island.

56. Moore, *English Hypothetical Universalism*, 223. Moore is not strictly correct in claiming that the Reformers of the sixteenth century had gathered congregations. For the vast majority, in places such as Strasbourg, Geneva, Zurich, and Heidelberg, their congregations were territorial.

57. Ibid.

predestinarian beliefs.[58] This would become evident at the Westminster Assembly when debate focused on the decrees of God and many were spotted with copies of Amyraut in their hands. Moore writes of "a general softening of Reformed distinctives on other fronts as well, especially that of the extent of Christ's satisfaction and the nature of the gospel call to the reprobate." While anti-Calvinism may have helped to precipitate the Civil War, "it was not before the 'Calvinistic consensus' itself had undergone significant internal modification." This modification, Moore argues, took place over time and covered a spectrum of beliefs.[59]

It seems to me that the various alternative proposals on the order of decrees—those of Arminius, the English hypothetical universalists, and Amyraut—arose in a particular context. The Reformed had debated the order of decrees in the mind of God at some length toward the end of the sixteenth century. The infralapsarians had proposed this order: creation, fall, election, grace. Supralapsarians—William Perkins was the most prominent English representative, although William Twisse, the prolocutor at Westminster, was also to be a staunch advocate—held to election, creation, fall, grace. Franciscus Junius in Holland had suggested a compromise: creation, election, fall, grace. All of these had in common the belief that, in the mind of God, election was prior to grace. Out of this debate sprang the Arminian-Remonstrant controversy, with Arminius urging this order: creation, fall, grace, election.[60] The crucial point was that Arminius placed election after grace, making it conditional on God's foreknowledge of future human actions. Following in its wake came the two brands of hypothetical universalism that Moore identifies.[61]

---

58. Ibid., 225. See L. C. Boughton, "Supralapsarianism and the Role of Metaphysics in Sixteenth-Century Reformed Theology," *WTJ* 48 (1986): 63–96; Tyacke, "Anglican Attitudes."

59. Moore, *English Hypothetical Universalism*, 226.

60. See Letham, "Saving Faith and Assurance," 1:313; Franciscus Junius, *Opera theologica* (Geneva, 1607), 1:1279, 1618, 1621; 2:328; Junius, "Theses on Predestination," in *The Works of James Arminius* (trans. J. Nichols; London: 1825–28), 3:242, where the 1593 debate between Junius and Arminius is reported. See also R. A. Muller, *God, Creation, and Providence in the Thought of Jacob Arminius: Sources and Directions of Scholastic Protestantism in the Era of Early Orthodoxy* (Grand Rapids: Baker, 1991).

61. In support of Moore's argument, we can mention the comments of George Gillespie in the debate on the decree of God, in S522 W 22.10.45, where he cites Cameron and Amyraut,

When the Assembly was convened, the scene was marked by a number of major groupings. The non-Laudians, of which the Westminster divines are prime examples, demonstrated an ongoing commitment to the theology of the English Reformers and its underlying Augustinianism. This was developed and strengthened, as Muller has demonstrated, by prolonged reflection on the biblical text, for scriptural exegesis lay at the heart of their work. It was also informed by a wide-ranging familiarity with the history of exegesis from the Fathers onward.

Theologically, they faced a number of recent challenges. Arminianism was still a force with which to reckon. The Laudian attempt to wrest power in the interests of strict conformity to the Prayer Book and the canons of the Church was fresh in the recent past. Hypothetical universalism had attempted to make the Reformed faith more palatable to its cultured despisers. Lastly, but increasingly important once Episcopacy was ended, was the rise of antinomianism and a proliferation of sects that seemed to endanger everything—church, theology, society, the whole fabric upon which the Reformed faith in England was based. The antinomians held that Christ had so fulfilled the law of God on behalf of the elect that it no longer had any relevance for sanctification or daily life. Some went so far as to apply these ideas to the legitimacy of such things as private property. Despite the popular fears of popish plots, it was to this that most concern would be directed.

---

making a distinction between them: "Camero[n] saith for all upon condition of beleiving, but Amerauld, he hath drawn it further." Van Dixhoorn, 6:204.

4

Sources of the Assembly's Theology

The Westminster Assembly in Relation to the
Thirty-Nine Articles

Central to any contextual consideration of the theology of the
Westminster Assembly must be its relationship to the Thirty-Nine
Articles of Religion of the Church of England. The defense of these
Articles, the Assembly's first task, was suddenly aborted on Thurs-
day, 11 October 1643, by Parliament's demand that the Assembly
devote itself to matters of church government. This was provoked by
the Scottish commissioners who, as the price for Scottish support of
Parliament against the king, insisted on the signing of the Solemn
League and Covenant, with its call for uniformity of church polity
and discipline. The Thirty-Nine Articles are strongly—robustly—
Calvinist in nature. It is noteworthy that the proposed revisions of
which we have record (articles 11–16) indicate that very little was
altered.[1] Mitchell comments: "The keen and lengthened debates
which occurred in the discussions on these Articles could not fail
to prepare the way for a more summary mode of procedure in connection with the Confession of Faith . . . just because the previous
discussions on the more important doctrines of the Protestant system,
and especially on that of Justification by Faith, had been thorough

1. Norris, "Thirty-Nine Articles," 386–88.

and exhaustive, and pretty fully recorded."[2] We will refer to some of these debates in the following chapters.

The Influence of James Ussher and the Irish Articles (1615)

It is widely recognized that James Ussher had a strong influence on the Westminster Assembly, especially through the Irish Articles of Religion (1615).[3] At the time these Articles were composed, Ussher was professor of divinity at Trinity College, Dublin. Later he became bishop of Meath and Clonmacnoise and then, in 1625, archbishop of Armagh. In 1641, he moved to England as bishop of Carlisle. Warfield comments: "From these Articles [the divines] derived the general arrangement of their Confession, the consecution of topics through at least its first half, and a large part of the detailed treatment of such capital Articles as those on the Holy Scripture, God's Eternal Decree, Christ the Mediator, the Covenant of Grace, and the Lord's Supper. These chapters might almost be spoken of as only greatly enriched revisions of the corresponding sections of the Irish Articles."[4] He recognizes, however, that the Assembly did not take anything from these Articles without much revision and expansion.[5]

In his Articles, Ussher uses a range of sources from the confessional documents of the Church of England, some of which he expands, although mostly he leaves his sources unchanged. He also adds contributions of his own. The most recent document he uses is the Lambeth Articles (1595) on assurance, justification, and perseverance. These Articles were compiled following the predestination controversy at Cambridge. Otherwise, his main sources are the Thirty-Nine Articles (1563), the Anglican Catechism (1549), and the Homily on Fasting. Unless stated otherwise, references below to the Thirty-Nine Articles are to Ussher's verbatim or effectively verbatim quotations.

2. Mitchell, *Westminster Assembly*, 150.
3. Schaff, *Creeds*, 3:526–44.
4. Warfield, *Westminster Assembly*, 59.
5. See Mitchell, *Westminster Assembly*, 391ff., for a detailed comparison of the Irish Articles and the Westminster Confession of Faith on election and predestination.

Ussher's Contribution to the Irish Articles

The following articles and sections of the Irish Articles are from Ussher:

Article 1: sections 1, 4 (on the need for translation of the Bible), and 5 (on the perspicuity and difficulty of Scripture).

Article 2 on the Holy Trinity: section 9 on the generation of the Son by the Father.

Article 3: section 14, second sentence. According to Warfield, 27 percent of article 3 is from Usher.[6]

Article 5 on the fall of man and original sin: sections 27–28.

Article 6, of Christ, the mediator of the second covenant: bits of section 30.

Article 7, of communicating the grace of Christ: section 33.

Article 8, of justification and faith: sections 34–37.

Article 9, of sanctification and good works: sections 39–40, 43.

Article 10, of the service of God: sections 47–49, 51–54, 56.

Article 11, of the civil magistrate: section 60. Part of section 59 is an expansion by Ussher.

Article 12, of our duty toward our neighbors: section 64; the first sentences of sections 66–67.

Article 13, of the church and the outward ministry of the gospel: sections 68–69, 74.

Article 14, of the authority of the church, general councils, and the bishop of Rome: section 75, where Ussher's first sentence is added; sections 79–80.

Article 15, of the state of the Old and New Testaments: section 81, parts of section 82, section 83.

Article 17, of baptism: part of section 91.

Article 18, of the Lord's Supper: part of section 99, section 100.

Article 19 on eschatology: sections 101–4 in their entirety.

Barth comments that "the dominant role played by Calvinistic thought in this confession reveals the intellectual force that strictly

---

6. Warfield, *Westminster Assembly*, 148.

Reformed thought had accumulated before the Revolution in the island kingdom."[7]

The Influence of the Irish Articles on the Westminster Confession

Parts of article 1, section 5, of the Irish Articles form the basis for WCF 1.6, 8.

The WCF used article 3 (of God's eternal decree and predestination), section 11, almost verbatim. Moreover, the order of the Irish Articles—Scripture, God, God's eternal decree—was followed in the Westminster Confession of Faith.

The Influence of the Thirty-Nine Articles on the Irish Articles

Ussher builds largely on the Thirty-Nine Articles. Warfield found that 58 percent of the article on election and predestination is taken from the Thirty-Nine Articles, a figure with which I agree.[8] Overall, the Irish Articles show clear dependence on the Thirty-Nine Articles in the following ways:

Article 1 of the Irish Articles follows article 6 of the Thirty-Nine Articles in sections 2 (on the canon), 3 (on the Apocrypha), and 6 (on the necessity of Scripture). Section 7 follows article 8 of the Thirty-Nine (on the three creeds) almost verbatim.

Article 2, of faith in the Holy Trinity: section 8 is the same as article 1 of the Thirty-Nine, while section 10 is identical to article 5 on the Holy Spirit.

In Article 3, 58 percent of the text is taken from the Thirty-Nine, as noted above. As for particulars, section 13, a definition of predestination to life, is taken from article 17 of the Thirty-Nine. Section 15 is mostly from the same article. Section 16, on godly consideration of predestination and election, is taken straight from article 17, as is section 17 on receiving God's promises.

7. K. Barth, *The Theology of the Reformed Confessions* (1923; trans. D. L. Guder; Louisville: Westminster John Knox Press, 2002), 135.
8. Warfield, *Westminster Assembly*, 148.

Article 5, of the fall of man, original sin, and the state of man before justification, depends on article 9 of the Thirty-Nine in sections 22–24, while section 25 is taken from article 10, and section 26 from article 13.

Article 6, of Christ, the mediator of the second covenant, depends on article 2 of the Thirty-Nine in section 29, while section 30 comes from articles 15, 2, 3, and 4, with bits of Ussher tacked on.

Article 7, of the communicating of the grace of Christ, in section 31 depends on article 18 of the Thirty-Nine.

Article 8, of justification and faith, in section 34, is taken from article 11 of the Thirty-Nine, with some additions from Ussher. Sections 35–37 are largely composed by Ussher, with the last part of section 37 taken from the Lambeth Articles, section 6.

Article 9, of sanctification and good works, is taken from article 12 of the Thirty-Nine in section 41. Section 42 comes from articles 13–14, although not precisely verbatim. Section 44 is from article 16, while the following section comes from article 14.

Article 10, of the service of God, depends in section 55 on the final article of the Thirty-Nine.

Article 11, of the civil magistrate, is almost entirely dependent—section by section—on article 37 of the Thirty-Nine, with some expansion in section 3.

Article 12, of our duty toward our neighbors, after the first sentence in section 64, is taken from article 32 in section 64 and article 38 in section 65.

Article 13, of the church and the outward ministry of the gospel, shows obvious dependence on article 26 in section 70, on article 23 in section 71, on article 24 in section 72, and on article 33 in section 73.

Article 14, of the authority of the church, general councils, and bishop of Rome, after the first sentence of section 75, follows article 20, while section 76 follows article 21, section 77 follows article 34, part three, and section 78 follows article 19, part two.

Article 15, of the state of the Old and New Testaments, in section 82 follows the first part of article 7, with some additions, while section 84 follows the second part of article 7.

Article 16, of the sacraments of the New Testament, follows article 25, section by section.

Article 17, of baptism, follows article 27.

Article 18, of the Lord's Supper, in sections 92–95 follows article 28, with an expansion of the third part, while section 96 follows article 29. Section 97 is taken from the Eleven Articles, section 10. Section 98 then reverts to part 4 of article 28 of the Thirty-Nine. Section 99 is largely new, but also incorporates elements of article 31. Section 100 is entirely new.

Article 19, of the state of the souls of men after they depart from this life, together with the general resurrection and the last judgment, is new throughout sections 101–4, dependent on Ussher.

The Influence of the Lambeth Articles on the Irish Articles

Fifteen percent of article 3 of the Irish Articles, consisting of sections 11–17, is from the Lambeth Articles.

Section 12, on election and reprobation, refers to there being a definite number of both the elect and the reprobate. This echoes the Lambeth Articles, 1 and 3, which was a tightening of the Thirty-Nine Articles, which in article 17 explicitly teaches single predestination.

Section 14, sentence 1, referring to a cause in God of predestination, is taken from the Lambeth Articles, 2, while the next sentence is from Ussher.

Section 15, apart from the first part, which seems to come from the Thirty-Nine Articles, is from the Lambeth Articles, 4.

Section 32 is from the Lambeth Articles, 7–9.

The last section of section 37 is from the Lambeth Articles, 6.

Section 38 is from the Lambeth Articles, 5.

The Influence of the Catechism of 1549 on the Irish Articles

Article 10, of the service of God, section 46, and article 12, of our duty toward our neighbors, section 63, both show dependence on the Catechism of 1549.[9]

9. Schaff, *Creeds*, 3:519.

The Influence of the Homily on Fasting on the Irish Articles

Article 10, section 50 of the Irish Articles is dependent on the Homily on Fasting.

The Influence of the Eleven Articles on the Irish Articles

Part of section 91, on baptism, and section 97, on the Lord's Supper, may possibly derive from the Eleven Articles.

Ussher's Influence on the Westminster Confession of Faith

Evidently Ussher had a major influence on the structure of the Westminster Confession of Faith.

Ussher departs from the order of the Thirty-Nine Articles, which start with God the Trinity, then move on consecutively to Christ, Scripture, and the Holy Spirit. Ussher instead puts Scripture first, God second, and then the decrees of God, from which flow creation and providence; this would be the precise order of the Westminster Confession of Faith. What follows in the Irish Articles is also the order adopted by the Assembly for the Confession: sin, Christ the mediator, free will, justification and sanctification, the civil magistrate, the church and sacraments, and the last things. This is a more logical order than that of the Thirty-Nine Articles, which were more of an evangelical statement in opposition to the teaching of Rome, focusing on the issues most prominent at that time, rather than formally relating each element to the next. This latter task is one better undertaken when the original pressures have lifted and the church is in a more settled state, as it was in the first decades of the seventeenth century.

Some of Ussher's phraseology was to be taken over into the Confession, especially in the first article (on Scripture) and the third article (on predestination). The structure of the Confession was largely drawn from Ussher.[10] However, this does not mean that his impact was pervasive. The Larger Catechism, which if anything is even more

10. Warfield, *Westminster Assembly*, 1–148, esp. 59ff.

important theologically than the Confession, follows a quite different order, one based more on the traditional catechetical structure of creed, commandments, and Lord's prayer.

Moreover, Ussher's Irish Articles are a pastiche of the previous confessional literature in post-Reformation Anglicanism, topped up with his own expansions and additions in particular places. He is content to adopt large swathes of previous confessional material without alteration. In affirming that Ussher influenced the structure of the Confession, though not the Catechisms, and that other echoes of his work are to be found, we are simply pointing to the common heritage of confessional Augustinian Anglicanism, of which both he and the Westminster divines were heirs.

For instance, Ussher incorporated the Lambeth Articles where they were relevant—on predestination, justification, and perseverance. As a staunch Calvinist, Ussher agreed with these Articles. Yet the most prominent confessional influence on Ussher was the Thirty-Nine Articles. This should hardly be surprisingly, since he was both an Anglican archbishop and a Calvinist. There had been a succession of strongly Reformed confessions from the time of Cranmer onward. Ussher saw himself as a successor to Cranmer, Whitgift, and, by extension, Whitaker.

To say that Ussher had a strong influence on the Westminster Assembly is to affirm that the Assembly stood foursquare in the trajectory of English Calvinistic Anglicanism as it moved into the middle of the seventeenth century.

The Influence of the Thirty-Nine Articles

How much are the Thirty-Nine Articles to be found in the Confession of Faith and the Larger Catechism finally produced by the Westminster Assembly? Warfield comments that there are "minute" traces.[11] Here again, Warfield understates the case. Why was this? Is it possible to detect in this a lingering anti-English prejudice in American Presbyterianism, inherited from the Revolutionary War, once considered to be a Presbyterian revolt against the Anglican establishment?

11. Ibid., 59.

There are, of course, notable differences in the Westminster documents from the classic formularies of the Church of England. Some topics treated in the Thirty-Nine Articles are ignored by the Assembly (purgatory, the three creeds, works of supererogation, sin after baptism, ministering in the congregation, speaking in the congregation in such a tongue as the people understand, the marriage of priests, the avoiding of excommunicated persons, the traditions of the church, homilies, the consecration of bishops, and Christian men's goods that are not common). Other topics were treated by the Assembly that are not present in the Articles (God's covenant, adoption, perseverance, assurance, Christian liberty, the Sabbath, marriage and divorce, the communion of the saints, and the resurrection of the dead and the last judgment). Some of the articles are dedicated to themes mentioned in the Westminster documents, but not given distinct chapters of their own (Christ's descent into hell, his resurrection, the Holy Ghost, the sufficiency of Scripture, original sin, works before justification, the authority of general councils, the unworthiness of ministers which hinders not the effect of the sacraments, the wicked which eat not the body of Christ, and partaking of both kinds in the Supper).

These differences are, in great measure, to be explained by the differing historical contexts. The Thirty-Nine Articles, composed five years after the drastic Marian interlude and at the end of the Council of Trent, were aimed at establishing Protestant doctrine against Rome. Some questions were not at issue until later. For example, the extent of the atonement did not surface as a significant theological factor until 1586.[12] The Articles are more to be compared with the Scots Confession (1560) or the Heidelberg Catechism (1563), both composed at around the same time. It is anachronistic to judge the Thirty-Nine Articles by the Westminster Confession of Faith, written almost a century later. The Articles make no attempt to be systematic. They are an evangelical statement, distinguishing the Church of England from Rome. At Westminster, the need was vastly different, for the world itself had

12. Cf. article 31, "Of the one Oblation of Christ finished upon the Cross," with Heidelberg Catechism, 37.

changed. Now that Episcopacy had been abolished, the church had to be placed on a legal foundation. There was a need to say what the church *was*, rather than what it was not.

The Westminster Assembly also introduced important substantive differences: the absence of diocesan bishops in the Form of Presbyterial Church-Government, the altered spheres of responsibilities between church and state, the Sabbath (an issue when Protestantism was more established, rather than when the immediate battle was against Rome), and covenant theology (which was in its early stages in 1562, with as yet only one covenant proposed).

Often the Articles provided the base, and the Assembly added large chunks of explanatory material. Excursus 1 provides an example, comparing the Thirty-Nine Articles, 1, with WCF 2.1, 2.3, 4.1, and 5.1 and LC 6–11. The Assembly often takes over the language of the Articles, sometimes verbatim, and on more occasions the substance. In all cases, it adds a great amount of explanation and expansion. The Westminster Confession has an obvious antecedent in the Irish Articles (1615), but these were written by Archbishop James Ussher, himself an Anglican drawing on the Thirty-Nine Articles.

A Comparison of the Thirty-Nine Articles with the Westminster Assembly Documents

Article 1. Of fayth in the holy Trinitie.
See Excursus 1 at the end of the chapter. Note how phrases from the first article of the Thirty-Nine Articles are distributed among various chapters of the Westminster Confession of Faith and surface also in the Larger Catechism. The major point to note is structural; following Ussher, the Assembly relegated this subject to chapter 2 of the Confession. We will consider this critically later.

Article 2. Of the worde or sonne of God which was made very man.
WCF 8.2 is substantially the same as article 2 and adopts either identical or very similar phraseology. The description in the article of Christ's sufferings, death, and burial, with the consequent reconciliation, is taken up in WCF 8.4.

71

Article 3. Of the goyng downe of Christe into hell.

There is no corresponding chapter in the Westminster Confession. However, the theme was neither rejected nor ignored by the Assembly. The divines interpreted the phrase in the Apostles' Creed to refer to the time between Christ's death and his resurrection, during which Christ was "under the power of death." Hence, WCF 8.4 says that he "remained under the power of death, yet saw no corruption." According to LC 46, Christ's humiliation continued "after his death, until his resurrection." LC 50 equates Christ's humiliation after his death with the phrase in the Creed "he descended into hell." It refers to his burial, in which he continued "in the state of the dead, and under the power of death, till the third day, which hath been otherwise expressed in these words, *He descended into hell.*"

Article 4. Of the Resurrection of Christe.

Again, there is no chapter in the Confession devoted to this topic as such. However, the documents do refer to Christ's resurrection (how could they avoid it?). WCF 8.4 speaks of Christ rising from the dead "with the same body in which He suffered, with which also He ascended into heaven, and there sitteth at the right hand of His Father . . . and shall return . . . at the end of the world." The Larger Catechism develops these themes in LC 50–56.

Article 5. Of the holy ghost.

The Assembly has been criticized for having no chapter on the Holy Spirit. But does it lack a doctrine of the Holy Spirit? Each phrase in article 5 on the Holy Ghost is present in WCF 2.3. This is also the case in LC 9–10. We will consider how far the Assembly related the Holy Spirit to various theological loci in chapter 8.

Article 6. Of the sufficiencie of the Holy Scriptures for salvation.

The material of this article is adopted by WCF 1.6. The first clause of this section of the Confession conveys the entire substance of the first sentence of the article. See also WCF 20.2a, on Christian liberty, which reasserts the article's insistence that faith and practice are to be based on Scripture, not human teachings: "God alone is Lord of the conscience, and hath left it free from the doctrines and commandments of men which are in any thing contrary to his Word, or beside it in matters of faith or worship."

The rest of the article deals with the canon of Scripture. This is substantially adopted in WCF 1.2, which lists the canonical books, and 1.3, which excludes the Apocrypha from the canon. The article names the apocryphal books, whereas the Confession does not. This, again, may be due to the historical circumstances at the time the Articles were compiled, for it was necessary to distinguish the canon of the Church of England from the canon of the Roman Church, which included these books.

Article 7. Of the Olde Testament.

Here the first sentence of the article is mirrored in WCF 19.7. The Confession states that the uses of the law are not contrary to the grace of the gospel, "but do sweetly comply with it." This statement has a somewhat narrower focus than the article, which is concerned with the Old Testament as a whole. However, the article viewed in its totality puts it into perspective, for it thinks in the same terms. The law and the required obedience to it are entirely compatible with the eternal promises of the gospel. Cf. WCF 19.5–6; LC 97.

Article 8. Of the three Credes.

There is no counterpart to this article in the Assembly documents, except by implication where Scripture is compared with the teaching of the church, which can err. However, the framers of the Articles also held Scripture to be of supreme authority. The Creeds are "thoroughly to be received and believed," they argue, "for they may be proved by most certain warrants of holy Scripture." We will discuss this in detail in chapter 7.

Article 9. Of originall or birth sinne.

The substance of this article is clear in WCF 6.3–5. See also LC 25–28.

Article 10. Of free wyll.

Once again, the Confession accepts the entire substance of this article in WCF 9.3–4.

Article 11. Of the iustification of man.

All the salient elements in this short article are present in WCF 11.1–2 and LC 70.

Article 12. Of good workes.

The substance and even the phraseology of this article are present in WCF 16.2, 5–6.

Article 13. Of workes before iustification.

The substance of the article is present in WCF 16.7.

Article 14. Of workes of supererogation.

See WCF 16.1, 4, 5.

Article 15. Of Christe alone without sinne.

See WCF 8.2–3; LC 37–40.

Article 16. Of sinne after Baptisme.

There is no counterpart to this article in either the Confession or the Catechisms.

Article 17. Of predestination and election.

See WCF 3.3, 5a, 6, 8; LC 13. The article affirms single predestination. It says nothing about reprobation, but neither does it oppose it. Indeed, the warnings about "curious and carnal persons" and the dangers attendant on their consideration of the doctrine of election would hardly make sense apart from an implicit acknowledgment of reprobation. The Confession is, of course, much larger and more elaborate. Warfield's analysis of the contents of WCF 3 makes it appear that the contribution of the Thirty-Nine Articles is small. He suggests it comprises less than 10 percent of the chapter in the Confession.[13] However, since the Articles are themselves much shorter, it is inevitable that they would comprise a relatively small part of the larger document. It is more pertinent to ask how much of the article is incorporated into the Confession. Not surprisingly, this yields rather different results. Of the

13. Warfield, *Westminster Assembly*, 148.

first paragraph in article 17, 53 out of 130 words are used in the WCF, or 40.8 percent. Of the rest of the article, 11 words out of 166 are present in the Confession, or 6.6 percent. In total, 21.6 percent of the words of the article are carried over into the Confession. The differences between the two are largely explained by the absence of any mention of reprobation in the article and by the omission in the Confession of the pastoral advice at the end of the article, which is rather disappointing, for this connects election to assurance and the gospel in a way that the Confession fails to do.[14]

Article 18. Of obtaynyng eternall salvation, only by the name of Christe.

There is no counterpart to this article in the Confession, although LC 60 covers the same ground.

Article 19. Of the Church.

The first sentence of the article should be compared with WCF 25.2. The article considers the visible church to consist of "faithful men," while the Confession speaks of "all those . . . that profess the true religion, and . . . their children." The development of covenant theology in the years between 1563 and 1647 is largely to explain for this. LC 62 also includes the children of those who profess the true religion in the visible church. The latter part of this first sentence in the article is repeated, although not verbatim, in WCF 25.3. The substance of the second sentence of the article is expanded in WCF 25.4–6.

Article 20. Of the aucthoritie of the Church.

The authority of the church is not treated as a distinct topic in the Confession. However, WCF 32.4–5, 20.2, and 21.1 address the matter, asserting that Scripture is the rule of worship and that the church cannot ordain anything contrary to Scripture or beside it, which is exactly the teaching of this article.

Article 21. Of the aucthoritie of generall Counselles.

There is a significant difference between the first sentence of the article and the teaching of WCF 31.2. The article asserts that

14. See Letham, "Saving Faith and Assurance."

only princes may call general councils. This is the position of the Eastern church to this day. However, the WCF, while holding that the civil magistrate retains the right to call synods and councils, states that, if the magistrates are open enemies of the church, "the ministers of Christ . . . or they, with other fit persons, upon delegation from their churches, may meet together in such assemblies." In part, this is the consequence of a changed political environment. The Assembly met in the days when Parliament, its master, was at war with the king; the time of Good Queen Bess was quite different. However, the Confession has in common with the article that the responsibility in normal circumstances belongs to the civil ruler. Parliament had called the Assembly into being; Parliament determined its functions.

The second and third sentences of the article refer to the capacity of such councils to err. This entails the fact that if they declare certain things to be necessary for salvation, their declarations must be backed up by Scripture. The substance of this claim is adopted in WCF 31.4.

WCF 31.5 has no parallel in the Articles; this is not a contradiction of the earlier document, but rather a reflection of the unique times in which the Assembly met.

Article 22. Of Purgatorie.

This topic barely surfaces in any of the Assembly's documents. The change in context from the sixteenth century made comment on it superfluous. The framers of the Articles needed clearly to differentiate the Reformed English church from Rome. By the middle of the next century, this need had passed. The one occasion when mention is made of purgatory is in WCF 32.1, which has a dismissive comment. There is no mention of purgatory in LC 86.

Article 23. Of ministryng in the congregation.

WCF 27.4b forbids any but a lawfully ordained minister of the Word to administer the sacraments. LC 158 restricts the preaching of the Word of God to those duly approved and called to that office. These two statements accurately summarize the teaching of this article and are at one with it.

Article 24. Of speakyng in the congregation, in such a tongue as the people understandeth.

The one parallel to this in the Assembly documents is in WCF 21.3. There was no longer as much need to protest against the exclusive use of Latin in the liturgy.

Article 25. Of the Sacramentes.

The first paragraph of the article, defining and explaining what the sacraments are, is substantially echoed in WCF 27.1 and LC 162. The second paragraph simply lists the two sacraments, as do WCF 27.4a and LC 164. The third paragraph, which denies the other five ceremonies called sacraments by the Roman Church, is not repeated in the Westminster documents. Once again, the Articles distinguish the Reformed Church of England from Rome, which the Assembly had little need to do. Implicitly, the Confession agrees with the Articles in its assertion that "there be only two sacraments ordained by Christ our Lord in the Gospel" (WCF 27.4). The final paragraph of the article denies that the sacraments are to be gazed upon and affirms that they have "a wholesome effect" on those who worthily receive them. The latter claim is elaborated more extensively in WCF 27.2–3, which we will note in chapter 14.

Article 26. Of the unworthynesse of the ministers, which hinder not the effect of the Sacramentes.

This is substantially repeated, except for its last sentence, in WCF 27.3b.

Article 27. Of Baptisme.

This article is reflected in WCF 28.1 and LC 165, while the baptism of infants is considered in WCF 28.4 and LC 166. Both the Confession and the Larger Catechism provide a fuller theological explanation, more rooted in the covenant than the more individualist emphasis of the article, largely due to the development of covenant theology in the interim. This is especially evident in LC 166, where the covenant is expressly the rationale for the baptism of infants of a parent or parents who profess faith. The article refers only to "the baptism of young children." However, the baptismal liturgy in the Book of Common Prayer required the parents to make a profession of faith, so no distinct affirmation is required in the article. In practice, the same principles applied in 1563 as in the 1640s; the developed covenant theology of Westminster sharpens and crystallizes the underlying rationale for the baptism of infants.

Article 28. Of the Lordes Supper.

The first paragraph of the article, describing the nature of the Supper, is affirmed and developed by WCF 29.1, 5, 7 and LC 168. The second paragraph opposes the Roman Catholic dogma of transubstantiation, which WCF 29.2, 4, 6 also does, with a close correspondence in wording. The third paragraph is expanded and developed, but not substantially altered, by WCF 29.5, 7 and LC 170. The final paragraph is reaffirmed in WCF 29.4. The congruence of the article and the Westminster theology should be no surprise since Cranmer, Calvin, and the Assembly are here in concord.[15]

Article 29. Of the wicked which do not eate the body of Christe in the use of the Lordes Supper.

This was a distinctive of the Reformed faith. Whereas both Rome and Lutheranism believed that, since the body and blood of Christ are carnally present in the sacrament, all who receive the sign receive the reality also, the Reformed insisted that the reality—the body and blood of Christ—is received spiritually through faith, and so unbelievers receive the signs but not Christ. The teaching of this article is included in WCF 29.8, although there is no parallel in the Larger Catechism.

Article 30. Of both kindes.

The newer context, in which the teaching of Rome was no longer the main threat, relegates the affirmation that the laity are to receive both the bread and the wine to a single phrase in WCF 29.4.

15. R. Letham, *The Lord's Supper: Eternal Word in Broken Bread* (Phillipsburg, NJ: P&R, 2001), 31–47.

Article 31. Of the one oblation of Christe finished upon the Crosse.

WCF 29.2 says the same thing as this article, although not in exactly the same words.

Article 32. Of the mariage of Priestes.

There is no parallel to this in the Westminster documents. The need for such a statement had long since passed, as over a century had elapsed since clergy had left the jurisdiction of Rome.

Article 33. Of excommunicate persons, howe they are to be avoided.

WCF 30, which deals with church censures, makes no reference to the material in this article.

Article 34. Of the traditions of the Churche.

It is no shock to note that there is nothing at Westminster that corresponds to this article. This is one significant difference between the Assembly and the Articles, and it represents a change of outlook on the relationship between Scripture and the church. In particular, the article insists that anyone who "wyllyngly and purposely doth openly breake the traditions and ceremonies of the Church, which be not repugnaunt to the worde of God, and be ordayned and approved by common aucthoritie, ought to be rebuked openly . . . as he that offendeth agaynst the Common order of the Churche and hurteth the aucthoritie of the Magistrate, and woundeth the consciences of the weake brethren." Against this, WCF 20.2; 21.1 maintains that to submit for conscience' sake to the commands of the church, even if they are not opposed to the Scriptures but are beside them, is to betray true liberty of conscience. Additionally, WCF 31.4 points out that the decrees of the church are never to be made the rule of faith and practice.

Article 35. Of Homilies.

This article's commendation of the second book of Homilies as containing "a godly and wholesome doctrine," together with the first book of Homilies, produced during the reign of Edward VI, together with the request that they be read diligently in the churches, so as to be understood by the people, does not appear in the Westminster documents. The day had passed when these homilies were of direct and immediate interest in the church.

Article 36. Of consecration of Bishops and ministers.

This article lays down that archbishops, bishops, priests, and deacons be consecrated according to the form prescribed in the time of Edward VI and authorized by Parliament. Apart from the consideration that Parliament had recently abolished Episcopacy, the Assembly was charged with the task of producing a new form of church government. The licensing and ordination of new ministers was part of its brief and continued until its eventual dissolution in 1652.

Article 37. Of the ciuill Magistrates.

The counterpart of this article is WCF 23. The first sentence of the article is contrasted by WCF 23.1. The background to the article was the break of the English church from Rome. Hence, "the Queenes Maiestie . . . is not, nor ought to be subiect to any forraigne iurisdiction." The reference of the Confession is more general and establishes a hierarchy: God, the civil magistrate, and the people. Despite fears of a popish plot and the memories of the Spanish Armada and the Gunpowder Plot, indigenous authority in England was in no real danger in the 1640s, whereas in 1563 the Church had only fairly recently been released from the jurisdiction of a foreign power, the papacy.

The second sentence of the article and WCF 23.3 are in overall harmony, the difference being that the Confession goes into greater detail. The queen (or the civil magistrate) has no power to minister the word or sacraments, but only to suppress heresy, ensure the purity of the church, call synods, and be present at them to ensure that what is done is according to the Word of God.

The third sentence of the article denies the pope any jurisdiction "in this Realme of Englande," which WCF 23.4 also asserts.

The fourth sentence of the article affirms the right of the laws of the realm to punish Christian men with death "for heynous and greevous offences." Nothing like this is stated in either the Westminster Confession or the Larger Catechism.

The final sentence of the article is reaffirmed in greater detail in WCF 23.2.

Article 38. Of Christian mens goodes, which are not common.

This article expressly opposes the Anabaptists. By the time the Assembly met, a number of sects that were opposed to private property had arisen, including the Levellers. The same defense of the right of private property is affirmed in WCF 26.3b and LC 140–42.

Article 39. Of a Christian mans othe.

Arguments against the taking of an oath in a court of law were advanced in the 1640s, just as they were in the sixteenth century by the Anabaptists. The thrust of this article is reaffirmed in WCF 22.1–7.

The Thirty-Nine Articles were a major source for the Assembly, if not *the* major source. The Assembly is solidly in line with the English Reformed tradition. If the Assembly documents are like a sumptuous cheesecake, the solid, crunchy crust is Cranmer. If we were to suppose them to be a succulent piece of deep-fried plaice, the chips, salt, and vinegar come from the earlier English Reformed tradition. Or, to change the metaphor, if the work of the Assembly is a living being, the Articles provide the backbone and the nervous system.

Excursus 1: The Thirty-Nine Articles and the Westminster Confession on God

The following charts the adaptation of article 1 of the Thirty-Nine Articles in the Westminster Confession of Faith. The words in italics in the Confession are taken from the article.

THE THIRTY-NINE ARTICLES Article 1	THE WESTMINSTER CONFESSION 2.1
There is but one lyuyng and true God, euerlastyng,	*There is but one* only *living and true God,* who is infinite in being and perfection, a most pure spirit, invisible,
without body, partes, or passions;	*without body, parts, or passions;* immutable, immense, eternal, incomprehensible,
of infinite power, wysdome, and goodnesse;	*almighty, most wise,* most holy, most free, most absolute, working all things according to the counsel of His own immutable and most gracious will, for His own glory; most loving, gracious, merciful, long-suffering, *abundant in goodness* and truth, forgiving iniquity, transgression, and sin; the rewarder of them that diligently seek Him; and withal, most just, and terrible in His judgments, hating all sin, and who will by no means clear the guilty.

4.1

It pleased God the Father, Son, and
Holy Ghost, for the manifestation of
His eternal power,

the maker and preseruer of al
things
both visible and inuisible.

wisdom, and goodness, in the beginning,
to create, or *make* of nothing, *the world,
and all things therein whether visible or
invisible . . .*

5.1

God the great Creator of all things
doth uphold, direct, dispose, and
govern all creatures, actions, and
things from the greatest even to the
least . . .

2.3

And in vnitie of this Godhead
there be three persons, of one
substaunce, power, and eternitie,
the father, the sonne, and the holy
ghost.

*In the unity of the Godhead there be
three persons, of one substance, power,
and eternity:*
*God the Father, God the Son, and God
the Holy Ghost*: the Father is of none,
neither begotten, nor proceeding;
the Son is eternally begotten of the
Father; the Holy Ghost eternally
proceeding from the Father and the
Son. (cf. LC 9–11)

5

The Reformed and Catholic Contexts

On the basis of our discussion in the previous chapters, the Assembly should be placed in a Reformed context, in connection with the Reformed churches of the sixteenth and early seventeenth centuries. The Calvin-versus-the-Calvinists debate has now been largely exhausted, except in more popular thinking.[1] The consensus throughout much of the last century was that there was a deep division between Calvin and later Calvinists. The Westminster Assembly, according to this line of thought, was a leading representative of its *bête noire*, Reformed scholasticism, which forced theology into a straitjacket, constricted by Aristotelian philosophy. Holmes Rolston III exemplified this position.[2] However, this scholarship has been undermined by the recognition of the pluriformity and continuity of Reformed theology in the sixteenth and early seventeenth centuries.[3] Reformed theology was a relatively broad stream, and differences among those swimming in it were recognized and accepted.

1. See Muller, *After Calvin*, 64, where he lists the work of a number of scholars (Bray, Mc-Clelland, Donnelly, Godfrey, McPhee, Letham, van Asselt, Fatio, Muller, Trueman, Klauber, and Bierma) as bringing this about.

2. H. Rolston III, *John Calvin Versus the Westminster Confession* (Richmond: John Knox Press, 1972).

3. See, *inter alia*, Godfrey, "Tensions Within International Calvinism"; Letham, *Assurance in Theological Context* (originally Letham, "Saving Faith and Assurance"); Muller, *Unaccommodated Calvin*; Muller, *After Calvin*; Muller, *Christ and the Decree*; Trueman and Clark, eds., *Protestant Scholasticism*.

The criticisms of T. F. Torrance in his *Scottish Theology*[4] are pertinent at this point. We will address them more directly in chapter 6. Torrance has a programmatic, ideological opposition to federal theology. He regards the development of covenant theology in the seventeenth century as a distortion of the earlier, pristine theology of Calvin, Knox, and the Scots Confession. Torrance reserves his opprobrium for the Westminster Confession and says little about the Larger Catechism, which takes a rather different approach and obviates many of the alleged deficiencies he highlights. His comments about the Trinity in the Confession are well-taken. He deprecates its subordinate appearance. It is unfortunate, I agree, that the Trinity is not considered until WCF 2.3. However, Torrance does not mention that the Larger Catechism has a strongly Trinitarian doctrine of Scripture (LC 1–6). He does not even begin to consider the relationship of the Assembly to the Thirty-Nine Articles. As we have noted, the chapter in the Confession on God and the Holy Trinity is simply an expansion of the first article of the Thirty-Nine Articles (see Excursus 1), which dated from a time when Torrance claims that a dynamic Christocentric theology prevailed. Furthermore, he imposes on the Assembly the idea of a controlling central dogma—the dual framework of a covenant of works and a covenant of grace—whereas the idea of central dogmas only emerged in the nineteenth century, among German scholars, and was far from the minds of the Westminster divines.

On the other hand, many right-wing Presbyterians today interpret the Westminster Confession in detachment from the history of the Reformed church and its classic confessions. The militant adherents of the hypothesis that the days of creation were of twenty-fours duration are a prime example.[5] Neglect of this context is a barrier to understanding. The Assembly was frequently in touch with Reformed churches on the continent, giving and receiving greetings, ensuring that their pronouncements were in harmony. Arguments in debate were regularly backed up by reference to continental Reformed theologians. John Leith refers correctly to "a network of communication

4. T. F. Torrance, *Scottish Theology: From John Knox to John McLeod Campbell* (Edinburgh: T. & T. Clark, 1996), 125–56.
5. See R. Letham, "'In the Space of Six Days': The Days of Creation from Origen to the Westminster Assembly," *WTJ* 61 (1999): 149–74.

that had always existed between the Reformed communities of Britain and the continent,"[6] and so the divines "consciously sought the approval of the Reformed communities of the continent."[7] This had been helped down through the years by Latin being the *lingua franca* of the European intelligentsia, enabling easy communication between national elites. For their part, as Carruthers points out, "it must never be overlooked that the Assembly was a matter of great interest to the Reformed Churches on the Continent."[8]

The Interaction of English Reformed Theologians with the Continental Reformed

The Westminster divines drew on a heritage of interaction with continental Reformed theology. Way back during the Marian persecution, exiled English clerics had had much contact with Calvin and Bullinger. Later, John Whitgift made Bullinger's *Decades* required reading in 1577 when he was dean of Lincoln and in 1589 when archbishop of Canterbury. No fewer than ninety-six editions of Calvin were published in English by 1640, fifty of Beza, and thirty-eight of both Luther and Bullinger, but not one official of the Church of England had more than ten to his name. Calvin's *Institutes* was the recognized textbook for theology at both Oxford and Cambridge.[9] From another angle, the teachings of Moyse Amyraut posed a problem at the Assembly, although how much of a problem is disputed.[10]

As Muller shows, Reformed theology at this time had assumed truly international proportions. "The interrelationship of the English Reformed with the continental Reformed was such that neither development can be properly understood without the other: specifically, in the sixteenth and seventeenth centuries, British theology was receptive

6. J. H. Leith, *Assembly at Westminster: Reformed Theology in the Making* (Richmond: John Knox Press, 1973), 37.

7. Ibid., 38.

8. Carruthers, *Everyday Work*, 63.

9. Leith, *Assembly at Westminster*, 40.

10. A. C. Troxel, "Amyraut 'at' the Assembly: The Westminster Confession of Faith and the Extent of the Atonement," *Presbyterion* 22/1 (1996): 43–55; C. B. Van Dixhoorn, "Anglicans, Anarchists, and the Westminster Assembly: The Making of a Pulpit Theology" (Th.M. thesis, Westminster Theological Seminary, 2000), 114.

to continental thought, as citations of European thinkers in English works testify."[11] He refers to William Ames, whose *Medulla SS. Theologiae* (1623) was widely used both in England and in Europe—Voetius recommended that his students memorize it. Meanwhile, English reading of continental divines was "omnivorous." Major English thinkers were much appreciated throughout Reformed Europe. Furthermore, Muller indicates that Thomas Gataker's debate over whether Greek could be called an original language was with a German, while his debate over the tetragrammaton was with Louis Cappel of France. "A full picture of Reformed orthodoxy cannot afford to omit the English contribution to Protestant scholasticism—nor is it acceptable to attempt to interpret British theology in the sixteenth and seventeenth centuries without reference to continental developments."[12] Nicholas Tyacke agrees that "it is incontestable that much of the Elizabethan debate on subjects like predestination was conducted through the medium of foreign authors—either Latin republications or English translations."[13]

The Westminster Assembly and the Continental Reformed

We will now refer to some of the interaction that took place at the Assembly, and to occasions on which its members referred to Reformed authors and confessions to support their arguments. In this we will be somewhat selective. Partly, this is due to necessity, for not all the speeches made at the Assembly are recorded, there is more detail in the record on some occasions than others, and as time went on the minutes became increasingly cursory.[14]

Interaction with Continental Reformed Churches

On 27.7.43 the Assembly sent a letter to the classes of the Netherlands.[15] Nearly three months later, after the signing of the Solemn

11. Muller, *PRRD*, 1:66.
12. Ibid., 67.
13. Tyacke, "Anglican Attitudes," 143.
14. Of interest may be W. van 't Spijker, "A Comparison Between the Heidelberg Catechism and the Westminster Confession (I)," *Lux Mundi* 26/3 (September 2007): 56–61.
15. Carruthers, *Everyday Work*, 63.

League and Covenant, Dr. Burgess insisted in S78 TH 19.10.43 that the Assembly be governed by "what is most agreable to the best reformed churches." In a rough way, he urged, their method of procedure should be the same as "we doe find most of the churches of Christ to proceed in."[16] Later in the same session, Herbert Palmer pointed out that "we doe all agree that ministers ordained by the reformed churches ware lawfull ministers. 2. churches of that discipline in London: French & Dutch." John DelaMarch, addressing the question of whether those not yet ordained should be permitted to preach, referred to continental practice: "They in France are very cautious for the admitting of persons to preach without ordination; the church of Geneva did undertake to make ministers and send them in the parishes about them without advise of the French churches—the sinods in France, they did revoke that which was done & would not permit them to send their proposants to any citty about Geneva."[17]

Shortly afterwards, in S95 TU 14.11.43, the Assembly debated the question of whether the offices of pastor and doctor were identical. DelaMarch indicated that "by the practice of reformed churches we find them to be distinct officers & that one may doe what the other cannot." Afterward Dr. Joshua Hoyle cited the example of Calvin in Geneva: "Calvin desired the place of a doctor but being able for both he was admitted to both."[18]

The following day, in S96 W 15.11.43, Alexander Henderson, one of the Scottish commissioners, exhorted the Assembly in this way: "You are at this time as a citty set upon a mountaine; the eyes of E[ngland], S[cotland], I[reland] & of all reformed churches are upon you; a delight to this meeting [?]; a desire & fervent expectation. And the eyes of papists, Arminians, &c. are all upon you, & howsoever they may seeme to dispise the day of small things, yet they behould this Assembly with great feare and astonishment."[19]

One week later, in S101 W 22.11.43, a committee was formed to prepare letters to the churches of the Netherlands, stressing the Assembly's common commitment to the Reformed faith and pres-

16. Van Dixhoorn, 3:175.
17. Ibid., 3:192.
18. Ibid., 3:301.
19. Ibid., 3:311.

byterian church structure and its opposition to Independency.[20] As with most of the outgoing correspondence, the letter was not sent at once, but was dispatched in the new year. One of the constraining influences on the Assembly was the need for Parliament's authorization and approval; that took time. This was particularly evident when a letter was received on 8.12.43 from Hamburg. It referred to a case of conscience. The Assembly gave no reply, since the communication did not come through Parliament.[21] Carruthers refers to a range of correspondence during the next few months: on 4.3.43(44), a Latin letter from the church of Walcheren expressing distaste of the Independents; on 2.4.44, letters sent to the Protestant churches in Transylvania, Sweden, Poland, and elsewhere; a letter received on 22.12.43 from the French congregation in London, asking for help in dealing with an internal division; on 22.2.43(44), a request for help for a Greek minister suffering in Greece; on 29.4.44, a letter from churches in Zealand.[22] A letter arrived from the classis of Amsterdam, which was referred to the Committee for Letters from Churches Abroad in S248 M 1.7.44.[23]

Further letters were received as follows: on 19.7.44, from the church of Hanau; on 7.8.44, from the church of The Hague, from the synod of Holland, together with other letters from Switzerland and Germany; on 18.9.44, from the church of North Holland; on 19.9.44, from Guelderland; on 14.10.44, from Utrecht; on 6.6.44, from Switzerland; on 13.6.44, from Geneva; on 21.6.44, Bremen was added to a circular letter from the Assembly, on receipt of news that it had been offended by being left off. On 30.12.44, a letter was received from Zurich.[24]

On 4.12.44, a significant event occurred. Copies of a book by Guilielmus Apollonius were given to every member of the Assembly. The volume was written on behalf of the Walcheren classis and presented on its behalf by Mr. Calendrin and two elders. A unanimous vote was taken to write a letter of thanks for it. The next summer,

20. Carruthers, *Everyday Work*, 64.
21. Ibid., 65.
22. Ibid., 65–69.
23. Van Dixhoorn, 5:167.
24. Carruthers, *Everyday Work*, 70.

Apollonius was in England and was invited to come to the Assembly to receive thanks for the book. The following was ordered in S494 F 29.8.45: "Mr. Apollonius shall be desired at some time convenient <when the prolocutor shall be present> to come to the Assembly to receive publique thanks in the name of the Assembly by the prolocutor." Ten days later, in S498 M 8.9.45, this order was given: "Ordered Apollonius 'be entertained in the Assembly upon Wensday by Dr. Burges & notice be given unto him to come upon Wensday morning.'" The session to which he was invited would have been S500 W 10.9.45, although there is no record of this in the minutes.[25] We will refer to this book in chapter 14, for it has considerable significance for the Reformed doctrine of the covenant and baptism.[26]

On 3.1.44(45), the House of Commons ordered that a letter be written to the Dutch churches; on 6.11.46, the House of Lords stressed to the Assembly the necessity of Protestant churches abroad knowing that Parliament never intended to innovate on matters of faith. Further letters were received on 30.4.47 from Utrecht, and on 21.5.47 from Zurich.[27] A letter of thanks to the classis of Holland was read and ordered in S396 TH 13.3.44(45).[28]

In S250 W 3.7.44, in a debate on the Lord's Supper, Palmer referred to the practice of the French church of receiving communion at table—they did not sit, but all stood.[29] In discussing the lawfulness of dipping in baptism, in S263 TH 8.8.44, Charles Herle warned that "if you conclude against it [dipping], you condemne the reformed churches that practise it. Those that incline most to popery are all for sprinkling."[30] Later that month, in S269 TU 20.8.44, Samuel Rutherford reminded members that "the eyes of all Reformed churches is upon this Assembly."[31]

In S301 TH 10.10.44, in the course of a debate on whether the parents should make a profession of faith at the time of the baptism of their children, Stephen Marshall sounded a cautionary note to

---

25. Van Dixhoorn, 6:170, 173.
26. Carruthers, *Everyday Work*, 71.
27. Ibid., 71–72.
28. Van Dixhoorn, 6:85.
29. Ibid., 5:174.
30. Ibid., 5:219.
31. Ibid., 5:238.

the effect that "for the rest of the Reformed churches, our uniformity is not intended to reach so farre as that those things which they had nothing to plead for, but only seeing rules and prudence, that we should be tyed to that." Rutherford expressed surprise that no one as yet had produced an argument based on the only practice of Reformed churches or the sole practice of the Church of Scotland. Herle replied, saying that while he much prized conformity with Reformed churches, the Assembly should remember the former custom of a people and consider the possibility of adaptation to national circumstances.[32]

In S312 M 28.10.44, the Prince Elector was in attendance and addressed the Assembly.[33] In S310 24.10.44, he was given leave to come and go as he wished.[34]

The Citation of Continental Reformed Theologians

The Westminster divines frequently referred to leading Reformed theologians on the continent. In the debates on works of supererogation, undertaken while considering the Thirty-Nine Articles, in S45 M 4.9.43, Sidrach Simpson referred to John Cameron of Saumur, who commented on Matthew 5:48 against such works. George Walker added Chamier in further support, while Daniel Featley cited Calvin's *Institutes*, referencing Job 9:20–21 to the same effect. For good measure, Edmund Calamy added the Englishman, John Davenant.[35]

When the debates on justification got under way the next day, in S46 TU 5.9.43, Thomas Gataker, to buttress his distinctive views on remission of sins as subsequent to justification, quoted in support Caspar Olevian, Johannes Piscator, Sculbertus, and the French and Belgic Confessions. Walker, an inveterate opponent of Gataker, cited Luther against him.[36] The next day, in S47 W 6.9.43, Gataker fought back with references to Cameron and Daniel Tilenus.[37] His staunch opposition to the idea of the active obedience of Christ being imputed

32. Ibid., 5:391–92.
33. The minutes are silent as to the location of his Electorship.
34. Van Dixhoorn, 5:438.
35. Van Dixhoorn, 3:5–7.
36. Ibid., 3:16–18.
37. Ibid., 3:29.

to the believer in justification led him in S48 TH 7.9.43 to bring in Gomarus, Junius, and the French synod as witnesses on his behalf.[38] Herle, in opposition, quoted Piscator; Francis Taylor, Gomarus; Featley, "the judicious Calvin"; and William Twisse, Molinaeus and Tilenus.[39] In the next session (S49 F 8.9.43), Richard Vines, who lined up with Gataker, volunteered Peter Martyr.[40] Never one to be outdone, Gataker brought Calvin, Junius, and Gomarus to his aid in S50 M 11.9.43. William Gouge trumped this with the councils and synods, the Church of England homily, the Churches of Scotland and Ireland, the Synod of France, the Palatinate, as well as "beglise, Bohemia." Featley threw both Arminius and Socinus in Gataker's face.[41] Before the justification controversy was over, Twisse had himself cited Piscator in S52 TU 12.9.43.[42]

This gives a good picture of the divines' readiness to bring other Reformed authorities to their aid in debate. It shows their learning, and that their doctrine of Scripture in no way precluded appeal to the tradition of the church. Citations did not end there, although the scribe tired of recording speeches in such detail as time went on. For the record, here are some samples of further appeals to Reformed authorities:

In S54 W 13.9.43, Twisse cited Melanchthon, Chamier, and Calvin.[43] In S56 F 15.9.43, Hoyle cited Calvin.[44] In S57 M 18.9.43, Gataker referred to Cameron, while Lazarus Seaman sourced Beza.[45] In S66 M 2.10.43, John Philps cited Beza and Calvin on the question of whether we may know our faith by works.[46] In S71 TU 10.10.43, Simpson cited Beza.[47] In S72 W 11.10.43, Seaman cited Luther and Calvin, while Twisse cited Piscator.[48] In S82 TH 26.10.43, Herle cited Beza on different types of callings to the ministry—"immediate,

---

38. According to Lightfoot's journal, in Van Dixhoorn, 2:50.
39. Van Dixhoorn, 3:36.
40. Ibid., 3:46.
41. Ibid., 3:58–65.
42. Ibid., 3:72.
43. Ibid., 3:90.
44. Ibid., 3:94.
45. Ibid., 3:103, 107.
46. Ibid., 3:134.
47. Ibid., 3:155.
48. Ibid., 3:163–65.

mediate and mixt." Thomas Goodwin cited Whitaker and Piscator.[49] In S83 F 27.10.43, Herle cited Chamier.[50] In S96 W 15.11.43, William Bridge cited Beza.[51] In S261 M 22.7.44, Palmer cited Bucer in support of pouring, not dipping, in baptism.[52] In S262 W 7.8.44, an anonymous member referred to "powring water over the whole body as in Muscovy, & I have heard it used in Spaine."[53] In S301 TH 10.10.44, Henderson cited Calvin in a debate on the parents' confession at time of their children's baptism, as Calamy had done with Bucanus.[54] In S307 F 18.10.44, Bridge cited Cameron and Luther on excommunication.[55] In S522 W 22.10.45, in debating the decree of God, George Gillespie cited Cameron and Amyraut, making a distinction between them: "Camero[n] saith for all upon condition of beleiving, but Amerauld, he hath drawn it further."[56] In S603 F 13.3.45(46), Rutherford cited Calvin, Beza, Baynes, and Piscator on the issue of excommunication, while Gillespie referred to Erastus.[57]

Van Dixhoorn has properly noted the constant reference to continental divines in debate and the continued traffic of correspondence between the Assembly and the churches in Europe.[58] Morris comments on the affinity between the English Reformed and the continentals when he remarks that "in them as in a mirror we may almost see the entire doctrinal process of Protestantism making itself confessionally manifest." He observes: "It was this fact that led the Assembly, or at least some proportion of its members, to entertain the hope already adverted to, that the Confession they were framing might win its way to general favor and possibly to formal acceptance in the continental churches."[59]

49. Ibid., 3:202–4.
50. Ibid., 3:210.
51. Ibid., 3:306.
52. Ibid., 5:213.
53. Ibid., 5:214.
54. Ibid., 5:392, 394.
55. Ibid., 5:424.
56. Ibid., 6:204.
57. Ibid., 6:267–68.
58. Ibid., 1:371.
59. Morris, *Westminster Symbols*, 821.

The Westminster Assembly and the Western Catholic Tradition

The theology of the Assembly also needs to be placed in its Catholic context, its position in relation to the classic creeds and confessions of the church. An influential Reformed spokesman has questioned this recently. Robert L. Reymond has argued (though he no longer does) that Calvin rejected "Nicene trinitarianism" and that the Westminster divines may have followed him in this. In particular, Reymond has spoken of "Calvin's rejection of the ancient doctrine of the Father's eternal generation of the Son" and has asserted, among other things, that the doctrine of the eternal procession of the Holy Spirit goes beyond Scripture. Westminster Trinitarianism is Reformed, following Calvin, not Nicene, he has claimed.[60] In making this argument, Reymond fails to refer to primary sources from the fourth century, and his discussion of the patristic debates betrays a lack of firsthand familiarity. Moreover, his reading of Calvin is limited, being largely confined to the 1559 *Institutes*, and he does not refer to the Larger Catechism, which teaches the very things he opposes. In fact, the Larger Catechism more clearly follows the Niceno-Constantinopolitan teaching than the Thirty-Nine Articles do, although no one (including Reymond) would make a case that they were not faithful to the tradition.[61] I have reviewed Reymond's work elsewhere, and Paul Owen has written an excellent rebuttal, pointing out that Reymond's Trinitarianism is at best Anabaptist, and that his understanding of Calvin is distorted.[62] We will refer to this argument in detail in chapter 8.

That the Westminster divines saw themselves in continuity with the historic church needs little argument for those who have read their writings or considered the records of debate. William Twisse, prolocutor of the Assembly, had himself edited the works of Thomas Bradwardine. The divines' writings are full of citations of Augustine.[63] Their debates are replete with references to the Fathers and medievals,

---

60. R. L. Reymond, *A New Systematic Theology of the Christian Faith* (New York: Nelson, 1998), 317–41. These views were withdrawn in the second edition (preface dated 2001).

61. LC 10–11.

62. P. Owen, "Calvin and Catholic Trinitarianism: An Examination of Robert Reymond's Understanding of the Trinity and His Appeal to John Calvin," *CTJ* 35 (2000): 262–81.

63. Leith, *Assembly at Westminster*, 38–39.

far too many to list here. What we provide in the following paragraphs is again a sample, limited to a great extent by the varied detail of the reporting of Assembly discussion.

In the debate on works of supererogation, in S45 M4.9.43, Thomas Valentine referred to Cajetan and Cathoricus as using Mark 12:30–31 to prove the existence of such works. Thomas Carter, in discussing Job 9:20–21, spoke of "Gregory the Great, many excellent pasadges upon this place." Lazarus Seaman, in turn, referred to Duns Scotus and Savanorola.[64] During the debates on justification, in S47 W 6.9.43, Lightfoot recorded that Daniel Featley defined justification as an act of God, citing Justin Martyr, Jerome, Augustine, and Bernard to prove that that view was held before Luther.[65] In the same session, Joshua Hoyle drew attention to the fact that the article on justification was written "about the end of the councell of Trent, & against the papists."[66] The following day, in S48 TH 7.9.43, Lightfoot recorded Gataker citing Athanasius and Cyril in support of his distinctive position;[67] according to the minutes, he also added Tertullian.[68] In the same session, Featley cited Bernard.[69] Next Monday, in S50 M 11.9.43, Gataker cited Athanasius again, while Featley responded by referring to "St. Gregory" (no more specific description being provided in the minutes), Clement's epistle to the Corinthians, and Bernard again.[70]

Two days later, in S54 W 13.9.43, when the focus had shifted to justifying faith, Lightfoot recorded Twisse as arguing that reliance follows justification, citing the respected sixteenth-century Roman Catholic theologian Robert Bellarmine in support.[71] Hoyle cited Augustine.[72] In S56 F 15.9.43, classical authors had their turn, as Twisse cited Tacitus and Hoyle referred to Solon, Plato, and others.[73] Henry Wilkinson cited Augustine in S57 M 18.9.43.[74]

---

64. Van Dixhoorn, 3:4, 10.
65. Ibid., 2:47–48. See also 3:21 for another report of the same speech.
66. Ibid., 3:24.
67. Ibid., 2:50.
68. Ibid., 3:31.
69. Ibid., 3:42.
70. Ibid., 3:58, 64–65.
71. Ibid., 2:75; see also 3:90.
72. Ibid., 3:85.
73. Ibid., 3:94–95.
74. Ibid., 3:107.

In a discussion of procedure in debate, in S69 TH 5.10.43, Thomas Young referred to the Council of Nicaea (AD 325), noting how men such as Macarius were deputed to reason with the Arians.[75] Further references abound, most notably Herle citing Aquinas and Augustine in S70 M 9.10.43 and S83 F 27.10.43, respectively.[76] In S96 W 15.11.43, Young referred to "the antients," presumably the Fathers in general;[77] Herle could cite Stapleton—another strong Roman Catholic opponent of Protestantism—while Bridge cited Augustine, and Temple cited Beza, all in S84 M 30.10.43.[78] The next day, in S85 TU 31.10.43, Sidrach Simpson cited Augustine on the keys. The day after that, in S86 W 1.11.43, Young cited Chrysostom and the Greek fathers who say that the act of giving a person up to Satan denotes some temporal punishment, whereas the Latin fathers only understand it of excommunication, citing Tertullian.[79]

These details from debates that were more fully recorded indicate how often the Fathers were cited. As the record gets more sparse and cryptic, these details drop out. However, we do find people such as Arrowsmith citing Augustine on the three things required in a preacher—*ut doceat, ut delectat, ut flectat*—in S234 F 7.6.44.[80] In S238 TH 13.6.44, Gillespie referred to the ancient Jewish use of lectors in the synagogue,[81] and he later cited Augustine on the power of excommunication.[82]

This confirms the argument of Muller that all the Reformers, including Calvin, and the later Reformed orthodox operated in the context of their inheritance from the late Middle Ages. To understand them, it is necessary to have a grasp of the scholastic method, and of the history of medieval exegesis.[83] The Assembly's Reformed context establishes its Catholic credentials, for the Reformers were at odds, not with the Catholic tradition, but with its immediate representatives.

75. Ibid., 3:144.
76. Ibid., 3:148, 210.
77. Ibid., 3:307.
78. Ibid., 3:212–17.
79. Ibid., 3:223, 235.
80. Ibid., 5:145.
81. Ibid., 5:150.
82. Ibid., 5:419.
83. Muller, *Unaccommodated Calvin*; Muller, "Scholasticism in Calvin," 247–65.

Evidence abounds from Luther, Calvin, and their contemporaries.[84] This is abundantly demonstrated from the minutes, where the records we have show beyond the slightest doubt that every theological question was debated from a foundation of biblical exegesis, in dialogue with the history of exegesis reaching back to the early days of the church. So pervasive is the focus on biblical exegesis that it would be futile here to list the texts on which debate turned—the evidence is literally overwhelming.[85] However, it was not carried on in isolation; it took place self-consciously as part of the great tradition of the church.

Apart from the occasional reference to Chrysostom, Athanasius, Basil, and Cyril, was there any influence from the East? There is obviously a remote influence, just as a family divided generations earlier by emigration may show similar characteristics. The Assembly adopts as its own the ecumenical conciliar decisions (Nicaea I and Constantinople I on the Trinity, in WCF 2.3 and LC 9–11; Ephesus, Chalcedon, and Constantinople II on Christ the mediator, in WCF 8). Furthermore, recent interest in the Eastern teaching on deification and its presence in Augustine, Aquinas, Luther, and Calvin raises the question of the Larger Catechism's stress on union and communion with Christ in grace and glory, particularly in terms of glorification in LC 90.[86] Moreover, there is a possibility of a nearer influence—but one for which there is no documentary evidence, so far as I am aware. Only five years before the Assembly, Cyril Lucar, patriarch of Constantinople from 1623, was murdered by Turks. He was a Calvinist. He wrote a confession that included a clear statement on justification by faith. He had extensive contact with the Reformed in Poland and Hungary.[87] Was there any reciprocal impact, and if so,

84. On Calvin and the Fathers, see A. N. S. Lane, *John Calvin: Student of the Church Fathers* (Grand Rapids: Baker, 1999). On Calvin and the Trinity, see chapter 12 of my book *The Holy Trinity: In Scripture, History, Theology, and Worship* (Phillipsburg, NJ: P&R, 2004). On worship, see H. O. Old, *The Patristic Roots of Reformed Worship* (Zürich: Theologischer Verlag, 1975).

85. See the forthcoming multivolume critical edition of the minutes of the Westminster Assembly, edited by C. Van Dixhoorn, to be published by Oxford University Press, which will run to over 850,000 words.

86. I discuss this in chapter 20 of *The Holy Trinity*; it will also be considered here in chapters 12 and 15.

87. R. Letham, *Through Western Eyes: Eastern Orthodoxy: A Reformed Perspective* (Fearn: Mentor, 2007), 130; G. A. Hadjiantoniou, *Protestant Patriarch: The Life of Cyril Lucaris (1572–1638), Patriarch of Constantinople* (Richmond: John Knox Press, 1961).

what and how far?[88] This is a question for further research, taking us beyond the bounds of this book.

Arthur Cochrane notices that although there is a marked difference between the early creeds and the Reformed confessions, the latter were based upon the former, and sought to unfold and safeguard a proper understanding of them. He makes specific mention of the Westminster symbols in this context.[89] In general, the structure of the Westminster Confession of Faith is similar to that of the classic creeds—the Apostles' Creed and the Niceno-Constantinopolitan Creed. Both of these focus on God the Trinity, the life and work of Christ the Son, the church and sacraments, and the last things. I have drawn attention to the common ground between the Assembly and the Catholic tradition by including relevant sections from the Niceno-Constantinopolitan Creed at the head of the respective chapters that follow. While we will argue that the Confession is not shaped by any one central dogma, it does loosely follow this arrangement. God, his decree, the plan of salvation in Christ the mediator and its outworking, the church and sacraments, and the last things are all extremely prominent elements. That there are additional sections on law, gospel, and liberty, including church-state relations, is due to the historical context in which the Confession was written. As for the Larger Catechism, it follows the classic catechetical structure of creed, Ten Commandments, and Lord's Prayer. Together, these things demonstrate that the divines did not seek to innovate, but saw themselves as standing in the tradition of the Church of England. It was with the Enlightenment that a new and different focus was to emerge in the eighteenth century, as attention was directed to man and his salvation rather than God, church, and sacraments.[90]

---

88. Carl Trueman informs me that the sale catalogue of John Owen's library included volumes of Gregory Palamas, and that Owen refers to Cyril Lucar on occasion.

89. A. C. Cochrane, *Reformed Confessions of the 16th Century* (London: SCM, 1966), 8.

90. See R. Letham and D. Macleod, "Is Evangelicalism Christian?" *EQ* 67/1 (1995): 3–33.

PART 3

THE THEOLOGY OF THE ASSEMBLY

6

Perspectives on Westminster

The Westminster Assembly and Protestant Scholasticism

Through much of the last century, scholars of Reformed theology pitted Calvin against the Calvinists.[1] According to this view, Calvin's dynamic biblicism was lost by his successors. Aristotelian philosophical methodology, dominant in the late medieval period, was introduced into Reformed theology by Theodore Beza, who was Calvin's successor at Geneva, as well as by Zacharias Ursinus of Heidelberg and others. It produced a thoroughgoing rational theology in which logic and reason were paramount. Doctrines were deduced from masterful premises. Causal analysis was employed throughout. Reason was accorded a priority, and the biblical text was squeezed into a rigidly imposed grid. The tensions evident in Calvin, stemming from his determination to follow the Bible, rather than to form an internally consistent logical system, were ironed out by logic.

Prominent among the scholars taking this position were Hans Emil Weber, Karl Barth, Basil Hall, Walter Kickel, Brian Armstrong, R. T. Kendall, T. F. Torrance, J. B. Torrance, and latterly Alister McGrath.[2] In essence, they postulated a radical division between Calvin and those

---

1. The pithy phrase comes from B. Hall, "Calvin Against the Calvinists," in *John Calvin* (ed. G. Duffield; Appleford: Sutton Courtenay, 1966), 19–37.

2. Weber, *Reformation, Orthodoxie und Rationalismus*; Hall, "Calvin Against the Calvinists"; W. Kickel, *Vernunft und Offenbarung bei Theodor Beza: Zum Problem der Verhältnisses von Theologie, Philosophie und Staat* (Beiträge zur Geschichte und Lehre der Reformierten Kirche;

who followed in the Reformed tradition. The Westminster Assembly supposedly fits neatly into the Calvinist camp, as a prominent example of developed Reformed scholasticism, with its doctrine logically deduced from the premise of the eternal decree of God, and the history of salvation demarcated into two distinct covenants, the covenant of works before the fall and the covenant of grace after it.[3] This interpretation was notably advanced by Holmes Rolston III in *John Calvin Versus the Westminster Confession*.[4]

Among these critics, Barth sees the Scots Confession, together with Zwingli's *Short Christian Instruction*, Calvin's 1545 Catechism, the French Confession, and the Heidelberg Catechism as conveying "an accurate picture of what the early Reformed intended. All the rest are repetitions and variations, and when variations, often departures from the main tradition that then easily lead astray."[5] From this, the high noon of Reformed theology, the Westminster Assembly is a degeneration that Barth can only describe as "a tragedy . . . the death of Calvinism."[6] Barth, it seems to me, has set up an arbitrary canon within a canon, setting apart the early Reformed theology and confessions as definitive, and failing to take into consideration the peculiar historical circumstances of the time until 1563. Equally, he does not take account of changed conditions later. We noted Jonathan Moore's cogent counterargument above.

Earlier, Edward Morris was much more sympathetic and reliable.[7] The advantage of the Assembly over all other Protestant bodies, he said, was that "they had in their hands, not only all the antecedent creeds in Britain from the first Scots Confession down to the Articles of Ussher and the Irish Synod, but also most if not every one of the continental formularies which could be in any way helpful to them in shaping their

---

Neukirchen-Vluyn: Neukirchener Verlag des Erziehungsvereins, 1967); Armstrong, *Calvinism and the Amyraut Heresy*; R. T. Kendall, *Calvin and English Calvinism to 1649* (Oxford: Oxford University Press, 1979); J. B. Torrance, "Covenant or Contract?"; A. E. McGrath, *A Life of John Calvin: A Study in the Shaping of Western Culture* (Oxford: Basil Blackwell, 1990), 212.

3. See J. B. Torrance, "Covenant or Contract?" whose particular target was federal Calvinism, which he saw exemplified at Westminster.

4. Rolston, *John Calvin Versus the Westminster Confession*.

5. Barth, *Reformed Confessions*, 133.

6. Ibid., 135.

7. This is so, even though his book on the Assembly was published in 1900, just before the twentieth century began.

Symbols."[8] Indeed, they were inclined to adhere as closely as possible to the doctrine and language of those earlier creeds wherever practicable. Morris refers to their familiarity with the English Reformers and the continental divines, especially Calvin, whose *Institutes* had long been used in the universities. In fact, "at no date prior to the fifth decade of the seventeenth century could any body of men . . . have had such resources or such an opportunity to formulate a creed fitted to command interest and secure approval wherever Protestantism prevailed." This was "a conjunction which was nothing less than providential."[9] Morris draws attention to the Assembly's moderation, especially toward the Independents and those with tender consciences, and how it repeatedly avoided opinions that had aroused fierce debates in other quarters. He cites Gillespie's comment in a discourse to Parliament, in which he urged, "Let that day be darkness . . . in which it shall be said that the children of God in Britain are enemies and persecutors of each other."[10] Morris's own moderation was overtaken by the rise of the Calvin-against-the-Calvinists debate.

However, since the 1970s a growing movement has undermined the Barth-Weber-Hall argument. Richard Muller outlines the contours of its critique of the earlier model.[11] Early works by John Bray, Joseph McClelland, John Patrick Donnelly, W. Robert Godfrey, Jill Raitt, Ian McPhee, and Robert Letham pointed the way. Vast research by Muller has exploded the thesis, assisted by contributions from Lyle Bierma, Carl Trueman, Martin Klauber, Willem van Asselt, and others.[12] There is neither time nor space here to repeat these rebuttals. Certainly, it is not denied that there are definite discontinuities between the sixteenth-century Reformers and their successors a century later. Inevitably, there is historical development, involving new pastoral and theological contexts, with the need to defend the doctrine of the Reformation against new opposition, and to teach it in an orderly and systematic fashion to the church and its ministers. Equally inevitably, particular intellectual and philosophical tools were

8. Morris, *Westminster Symbols*, 795–96.
9. Ibid., 796–97.
10. Ibid., 802–4.
11. Muller, *After Calvin*, 3–102.
12. See the bibliographical references in Muller, *After Calvin*, 64, 207.

used for that purpose, as they are in any time or place. However, to label a theologian as a scholastic simply because he used Aristotelian causal analysis has little meaning, for everyone did so, Calvin included.[13] Carl Trueman's systematic demolition of the argument of Alan Clifford demonstrates the anachronistic and self-defeating nature of the accusation.[14] Moreover, the lines of continuity—downplayed or ignored by the previous scholarship—have been clearly brought to the surface.

Paul Helm has discussed in detail the Westminster Confession of Faith's chapter on providence in the light of the argument that the divines used the doctrine scholastically as a basis for logical deductions leading to their other formulations.[15] Helm argues that the place a doctrine occupies bears little or no relation to whether that person is a scholastic in method: "Each of the Chapters 2 through 5 presupposes the material of the immediately earlier chapter. But it does not follow from this that each chapter is *deduced from* the earlier material. The framers of the Confession sought to ground each of their assertions in the text of Scripture."[16] At no point do they offer a *theory* of divine providence, for they are "resolutely *a posteriori* in intent." Nor is there any trace of dependence on natural theology, nor an appeal to natural light or human experience—their Confession is thoroughly grounded on the assertions of Scripture. Their only concession in the chapter is the use of the idea of primary and secondary causality, a distinction used in the Middle Ages. But Calvin also used it.[17] There is no doubt that scholasticism is present in the sense of the technical development of theology by means of question and answer, careful distinctions, definition and argument, distinction of theological topics, and the like, but this is more "a presentational matter rather than theologically substantive."[18] Thus, Helm concludes, "there is no substance to the charge that,

13. See Muller, *Unaccommodated Calvin*, 39–61.
14. C. R. Trueman, *The Claims of Truth: John Owen's Trinitarian Theology* (Carlisle: Paternoster, 1998).
15. P. Helm, "Westminster and Protestant Scholasticism," in *Westminster Confession into the 21st Century* (ed. Duncan), 2:99–116.
16. Ibid., 103.
17. Ibid., 105–6.
18. Ibid., 107.

in this area at least, the Confession expresses a degenerate form of Reformed theology."[19]

Muller, as in his overall work in which he understands Reformed theology against its late medieval background, points to biblical exegesis as the Assembly's primary source of theology.[20] This is strikingly evident from the record of debates. The divines were constantly discussing the meaning of passages from the Old Testament and New Testament. Their theology was grounded, not on abstract logical speculation or a chain of causal deductivism, but on their grappling with the biblical text in its original languages in interaction with the history of interpretation, not only in the Reformed churches, but also in the medieval and patristic periods.[21]

The Ecclesiological Captivity of the Assembly

Van Dixhoorn reflects on the almost uniform preoccupation of scholarship on the Assembly with ecclesiology. Its membership has normally been defined purely in ecclesiological terms, as Presbyterian, Episcopalian, or Independent. One is given to believe that theology was of little concern, a matter on which general agreement existed, and that the real issues concerned church government. As Van Dixhoorn indicates, this approach was consistent until its crowning work, that of R. S. Paul.[22] In contrast, Van Dixhoorn's examination of the 1,333 plenary sessions from 1643 to 1652, the 209 ad hoc committees, and the 162 published manuscripts shows that the greatest part of the Assembly's energies were expended on theology, "a fact which cannot be gathered from any existing history of the Assembly."[23] Only

19. Ibid., 115.

20. R. A. Muller, "Either Expressly Set Down . . . or by Good and Necessary Consequence: Exegesis and Formulations in the Annotations and the Confession" (conference paper presented at Westminster Assembly 2004; Philadelphia: Westminster Theological Seminary, 2004); R. A. Muller, "Inspired by God . . . Kept Pure in All Ages: The Doctrine of Scripture in the Westminster Confession" (conference paper presented at Westminster Assembly 2004; Philadelphia: Westminster Theological Seminary, 2004).

21. Morris (*Westminster Symbols*, 807) notes that many have approached the documents anachronistically in terms of their language—focusing on expressions such as "mere love," "utterly, wholly," "pleasure," "estate," "guilt," and "good works," in particular.

22. Paul, *Assembly of the Lord*.

23. Van Dixhoorn, 1:5–10.

26 percent of the plenary sessions and 19 percent of the committees had church government as their main focus, whereas 36 percent of the plenary sessions were devoted to theological issues, as well as 31 percent of committees.[24] Occasionally this reigning paradigm has been questioned, but it has never been shaken from its dominance. Van Dixhoorn's work should help turn attention in a direction more compatible with the Assembly's main work. As he comments, ecclesiological classifications are essential to understand the Assembly on ecclesiastical and political matters, but they beg the question as to why the Assembly was bifurcated into Presbyterians and Independents. He suggests theological factors may even underlie the ecclesiological divisions: "These men were, after all, called divines for a reason."[25]

The Criticisms of T. F. Torrance

The sea change in recent Calvinism scholarship had little effect on Thomas F. Torrance. In his book *Scottish Theology*, he devotes a chapter to the Westminster Assembly and marshals against it a range of arguments familiar to those acquainted with his trenchant criticisms of the later development in Scottish Calvinism.

However, Torrance's arguments have some surprising holes and historical inaccuracies. His listing of James Ussher as a commissioner at the Assembly is technically correct, but Ussher refused to recognize the body, let alone attend it, due to his royalist sympathies. Torrance dates the Irish Articles as 1614, rather than 1615. Moreover, he says the purpose of the Assembly was to give rational cohesion to the participating churches in the Commonwealth, forgetting that the Assembly, as set up, was an English body and that the Commonwealth lay in the future.[26] He argues that the Confession did not follow the lead of Calvin and the 1560 Scots Confession in holding justification and union with Christ inseparably together. But while this may be true, Torrance ignores the Larger Catechism, where this connection is

24. Ibid., 1:212.
25. Ibid.
26. T. F. Torrance, *Scottish Theology*, 125–26.

clear.[27] This also evaporates his contention that the Confession's *ordo salutis* is medieval, with a series of steps leading to union with Christ, a reversal of Calvin's teaching on union with Christ as the source of his benefits.[28] The Confession, he insists, does not demonstrate the spiritual freshness and freedom of the Scots Confession. The earlier evangelical Calvinism was here replaced by a more legalistic variety of theology.[29] We can recognize here the approach typical of the scholarship undermined by Muller and others, in which the earlier vitality of Reformed theology was supposedly stifled by rigidly logical and legal thinking. Torrance gives little attention to the historical context, the purpose of the Assembly in the situation of ecclesiastical and political anarchy in 1640s England, or the quite different needs of the time. He does not pay attention to the whole theological output of the Assembly, but is fixated on the Confession. His comments on the "frigidly logical proof texts" ignores the occasion for their inclusion—the order of Parliament—and the divines' reluctance to provide them, their wider view of the sense of Scripture, and the way the proof texts were intended to function.[30] We will discuss this in more detail in chapter 7.

Overall, Torrance makes very clear that, for all its merits,[31] he dislikes the Assembly's work and does so from his distinctive theological position, which is very much his own, but owes much to Athanasius, his own reading of Calvin, McLeod Campbell, and Barth.[32] This is clear in his almost visceral opposition to limited atonement and the pre-fall covenant of works.[33] We should note

27. Ibid., 144.
28. Ibid., 128–29.
29. Ibid., 127.
30. Ibid., 128–29.
31. He states: "The powerful intellectual coherence in theological outlook achieved in the Westminster Confession has given an enduring unified character to Scottish theology and culture ever since." Ibid., 127.
32. I have written elsewhere that it is a mistake to label Torrance as a Barthian; he is too significant a thinker in his own right to be regarded in terms of someone else. However, it is clear that Barth had a significant impact on him, as he did on Barth. See Letham, *The Holy Trinity*, 356–73.
33. Torrance's caricature of limited atonement as requiring the Father to be "bought off" and "induced to reconcile us" (*Scottish Theology*, 137–39) would almost be laughable, were it not so tragically false. He rightly points to the Father's prevenient love as the root of Christ's atonement. However, this underlies WCF 3 and 8, in which the intent of the

that the theological connection between the covenant of works (or covenant of life) and the atonement is direct; Paul's exposition of the two Adams in Romans 5:12–21 makes that clear. In this case, Torrance believes that the overpowering impact of the doctrine of election reflects a defective view of God, in which justice and law have primacy over love. Thus, God's love is restricted to a certain number of people, fixed from eternity. Hence, following this, the sacraments do not display God as our Father, but are signs of the covenant, framed in a legal mold to which conditions are attached. This bred lack of assurance in later Scottish theology.[34] Apparently, the significant debates on the extent of saving grace passed Torrance by. We will refer to these below and in chapter 9. An indigenous brand of hypothetical universalism was present and active at Westminster and, although the divines did not adopt it, its exponents were able to voice their views and to continue to play an active role in the Assembly thereafter.

Torrance's criticisms are redolent of the movement begun in the nineteenth century that looked for large organizing principles or central dogmas that were held to govern thought across the theological spectrum. In particular, it has been claimed that election and predestination have shaped the Westminster Confession and thus the theology of the divines.[35] Again, Torrance and his brother James have pointed to the dual covenant framework—covenant of works and covenant of grace—as organizing and controlling the Assembly's approach to theology.[36] However, it is more than unlikely that a group of largely English theologians in the 1640s would shape their work in terms of an abstract principle devised two hundred years later in Germany. This is even more to the point when we remember the dominance of biblical exegesis in the Assembly debates. We have every right to ask whether it is, in fact, Torrance who has fallen prey to an abstract form of thought in which he criticizes a group of theologians in the seventeenth century for failing to anticipate Karl Barth of the twentieth

---

atonement is addressed—not to mention LC 32, which traces every aspect of the covenant of grace and Christ's mediation to the grace of God and his free offer of life and salvation in Christ.

34. T. F. Torrance, *Scottish Theology*, 125–50.

35. Ibid., 134–35.

36. Ibid., 136–37; J. B. Torrance, "Covenant or Contract?"

century, and for adopting a rationalistic *central dogma* when that whole idea was only to emerge in the nineteenth century.

Having said this, some of Torrance's observations carry weight. His criticism of the structure of chapter 2 of the Confession, with the Trinity relegated to the final section, is important. Even here, we have to add a rider that this is as much a criticism of the Western church and its consideration of the Trinity apart from the doctrine of God as it is of the Assembly as such. He is right to draw attention to the fatherhood of God belonging to God's eternal nature and not merely brought into effect in relation to the elect. This is correct, since the Father is the Father of the Son before he is ever our Father in heaven. However, the Confession explicitly acknowledges this in 2.3, where it speaks of the eternal relations of the Trinitarian persons. The Larger Catechism expounds this in more detail still. It undermines Torrance's claim that God is presented as Creator and Judge of all the earth, but as Father to his creatures only if they rigorously meet the requirements of his law. This assertion flies in the face of the Confession's expression of the sheer grace of God, both in election ("out of his mere grace and love") and covenant ("voluntary condescension," "freely offereth salvation").[37] We will address Torrance's criticism of the apparent lack of missionary vision at Westminster in passing in the next chapter, where we will note the Assembly's concern for the translation of the Bible "into the vulgar language of every nation . . . that they may worship Him in an acceptable manner; and, through patience and comfort of the Scriptures, may have hope."[38] Missionary activity, after all, has as its aim that people may know and worship the triune God.

Tim Trumper and Constructive Reassessment

More recently, Tim Trumper makes some apparently sympathetic criticisms of the Westminster Assembly in arguing for what he calls "constructive Calvinism."[39] Strongly influenced by the biblical theology

37. WCF 3.5; 7.3.
38. WCF 1.8.
39. T. J. R. Trumper, "Covenant Theology and Constructive Calvinism," *WTJ* 64 (2002): 387–404; Trumper, "A Fresh Exposition of Adoption: II. Some Implications," *SBET* 23 (2005): 194–215.

of Vos, Ridderbos, and Gaffin, he urges that redemptive history be given centrality in a Reformed confession in a way that it was not at Westminster. In particular, he laments the lack of attention given to adoption and the filial dimension of salvation. He bewails the juridical and legal focus. We need a new confession, he says, since the Westminster documents have lost their ecumenical force.

Trumper makes many good points. I have argued elsewhere for the balancing of the legal and judicial focus of Western soteriology by the Eastern doctrine of deification. Interestingly, this did not altogether escape the attention of the Westminster divines themselves![40] However, the Confession, uniquely among classic Reformed confessions—or any confession, for that matter—has a chapter on adoption. Furthermore, the strictly logical and sequential pattern of the Confession is balanced by a focus on union with Christ in the Larger Catechism. Overall, Trumper's proposal is more like "deconstructive Calvinism," as he peels apart one key doctrine of Reformed theology after another in support of a reconstruction. What Trumper misses is that biblical theology can *never* furnish the basis for a confession of faith, since the church is called to defend the gospel in words other than those of the Bible. Its task is not simply to repeat the nuances of the biblical authors, for it is all too often the meaning of the biblical language that is at stake. Its task is to bring out "the sense of Scripture," which includes not merely its express statements set in their redemptive-historical context—important though that may be for biblical exegesis—but also its entailments and implications. Trumper's line of argument would leave the church defenseless against heresy every bit as much as it would have done in the fourth century, when both orthodox and Arians could agree on biblical language, but gave to that language vastly differing meanings.[41] Certainly, the ongoing march of history has created new spheres of conflict for the church, and so the Westminster documents may not address all the issues that come to the surface. There may well be a need for a new confession in our own day. However, with the great ecumenical councils each affirmation merely restated the gospel in a new context, building upon

---

40. Letham, *The Holy Trinity*, 472–73.
41. See ibid., 108ff.

and *not replacing* what had gone before. Moreover, Trumper is simply over the top when he says, "While some readers may prefer the *status quo*, ongoing developments in biblical and historical theology suggest God may not."[42] We need to be careful about what we claim for our theology. This is doubly so when one can accurately be accused, as Trumper can, of substantial anachronisms and failure to be abreast of current scholarship on Calvin and Calvinism.[43]

Compromise and Flexibility

The Assembly documents need to be understood as *compromise documents*. Compromise is inevitable in a group of 150 people.[44] If we leave aside the Assembly's exclusion of what it considered false (the distinctive teachings of the antinomians, Arminians, Roman Catholics, Lutherans, and high church Episcopalians) and the well-known differences over ecclesiology between the Presbyterians and the Independents, as well as the issue of Amyraldianism, there were clear distinctions, nuances, and contours within what was considered acceptable doctrine.

The Ordo Salutis

First, there is a subtle but important distinction in the handling of the *ordo salutis*. The approach to the *ordo salutis* is strikingly different in the Larger Catechism than in the Confession. Instead of a purely logical order, the whole process of salvation is placed under the umbrella of union and communion with Christ in grace and glory (LC 65–90) and reaches its climax in a thoroughly Trinitarian view of glorification. We should note that, since these two perspectives exist side by side, the Assembly did not view them as incompatible. They are complementary, not competitive. For an adequate view of the process by which salvation is received and nurtured, both are required. We will discuss this at greater length in chapter 12.

42. Trumper, "A Fresh Exposition of Adoption," 215.
43. See the pertinent criticisms of T. L. Wenger, "The New Perspective on Calvin: Responding to Recent Calvin Interpretations," *JETS* 50 (2007): 311–28.
44. It is also necessary in your marriage.

The Covenant of Works (the Covenant of Life) and the Imputation of Sin

Second, since thought on the covenant was still developing, the Confession takes a different tack than the Larger Catechism. This is not merely a difference of nomenclature (covenant of life versus covenant of works), but concerns the imputation of sin. In the Confession, the sin of our first parents is imputed, they being the root of mankind. This is the sin of Adam together with, rather than in distinction from, that of Eve. Our connection with our first parents is organic here, rather than representative; they are together the root of mankind. This statement is placed in the chapter on sin (6:1–4), not the one on the covenant, where we might expect to find it, if it were viewed in connection with Adam as federal head. It echoes the earliest views in Reformed theology on the transmission of the first sin. Both Bucer and Calvin saw the connection between Adam and the human race in terms of natural generation, rather than legal representation. However, in the Larger Catechism, Adam is identified as "a publick person," who acted not for himself alone, but for his posterity (LC 22). The fall brought mankind into a state of sin (23). The guilt of Adam's first sin is conveyed to mankind, although the means of conveyance is unaddressed (25), while original sin is passed on by natural generation (26). There is no reference here to imputation, although it may be implied, for all the necessary building blocks are in place.[45] Thus, in the Confession the sin of our first parents is imputed to us, since they are the root of the human race, while in the Larger Catechism Adam's posterity incur the guilt of *his* first sin, he being a public person, but the manner of acquiring this guilt is left unsaid. This difference can be explained in a number of possible ways: flexibility, uncertainty in the face of ongoing development of the doctrine of the covenant, a preparedness to hold different positions in tension. This is a matter I will explore in more detail in chapter 10.

---

45. However, LC 22 appears to connect Adam to his posterity by natural generation. This is how the connection was understood in Reformed theology until at least 1600. Calvin, Bucer, and Vermigli all held this position. Although the idea of a pre-fall covenant of works emerged in 1585, the various ingredients of the doctrine were added, not at once, but over the course of time.

Justification and the Imputation of the Active Obedience of Christ

Even more vivid differences surfaced in the extensive debate on justification when revisions to the Thirty-Nine Articles were being considered. Many divines (roughly one-third of the recorded speakers) argued that it is improper to say that Christ's active obedience is imputed to us in justification. Richard Vines, for one, insisted that he had never taught it. The debate went on for seven sessions, although one of these was largely taken up with an answer to a request from the Scottish commissioners. Eventually the approved revision referred to Christ's "whole obedience and satisfaction being by God imputed unto us."[46] This statement satisfied the majority, who held to the imputation of Christ's active obedience. However, it was couched so as to avoid any idea that Christ's obedience is divided, an idea unacceptable to those who opposed the imputation of his active obedience. It also allowed Christ's obedience to be equated with his satisfaction of divine justice on the cross. It was a compromise enabling both sides to claim it as their own. During these debates, Thomas Gataker argued that these differences should not lead to the imposition of one position on everyone, so as to prevent some men from exercising their ministry, for only the Second Helvetic Confession had specified the exact nature of Christ's obedience; and while it was mentioned in the Irish Articles, there was no compulsion for people to subscribe to them.[47] Norris hits the nail on the head when he remarks, "It was a point on which difference was tolerated. It shows that the Calvinism of the Assembly, so long regarded as inflexibly rigid, and pilloried for being so, was capable of divergent opinions within it, and of tolerating and discussing these opinions without much of the acrimony that accompanied continental theological debates."[48] The Assembly clearly committed itself to regard the active obedience as imputed in justification, but the minority who disagreed were not run out of the Assembly. They continued to participate actively and productively.[49]

46. Norris, "Thirty-Nine Articles," 386.
47. Ibid., 54.
48. Ibid., lviii.
49. That the position of Gataker and Vines cannot be equated with the view of those in the early twenty-first century who deny the imputation of the active obedience of Christ in

This compromise on justification was carried over into both the Confession and the Larger Catechism. In fact, the word "whole" was omitted from both the Confession and the Larger Catechism. There is no mention of the active obedience of Christ anywhere in the Assembly documents. Later the Savoy Declaration (1658) of the Congregationalists referred to both the active and the passive obedience, as if it regarded Westminster as soft on the issue. Why precisely it was omitted remains uncertain—there is not enough historical evidence to make a firm judgment. We will discuss the matter in detail in chapter 12.

The Extent of Saving Grace

Significant debates were held in October 1645 on the universality of grace. Amyraut's theology was a hot topic at the time. Many members were spotted reading Amyraut during the proceedings.[50] At the same time, there was—and always had been—a strong strain of hypothetical universalism in English theology, distinct from Amyraut and less developed than his.[51] The debates thrust these significant differences into the foreground. Earlier they had been evident at the Synod of Dort, where the British delegation had mediated between the more universalist delegation from Bremen and the hard-line Dutch, brokering a final statement that gave full voice to the universal sufficiency of Christ's death before it added a statement about its intention being for the elect.[52] We will discuss this question in chapter 9.

Issues Concerning Baptism

Differences over the mode of baptism emerged during the course of debate, in S 261–63 22.7.44–8.8.44, eventually culminating in a vote as to whether, given that sprinkling was the correct mode, dipping was also acceptable. The initial vote supported dipping by 25–24, but then was reversed on a second vote by the same margin. The matter

justification is made clear by Jue, "Active Obedience of Christ," 99–130. All sides in the Assembly rejected any idea that the sinner contributes anything, including works of evangelical obedience, to his or her justification.

50. Troxel, "Amyraut 'at' the Assembly."
51. Moore, *English Hypothetical Universalism*.
52. Godfrey, "Tensions Within International Calvinism."

was debated further, another vote was taken, and the lawfulness of dipping was reaffirmed.[53] In this light, it is interesting to note that the *Annotations* commissioned by Parliament state that the meaning of *baptidzo* ("to baptize") is "to dip," in the course of which reference is made to the ancient practice of baptism as immersion.[54] Similar differences of opinion existed on the practical issues of whether baptism brings the one baptized into the covenant of grace or whether he is to be baptized because he is in the covenant already, and whether parents should make a profession of faith at the time their children are baptized. Furthermore, there was the question addressed to the Assembly by Apollonius on behalf of the church of Wallcheren—and the practice of the Reformed churches in general—as to the limitation of the covenant simply to believing parents rather than seeing it as extending back in time from one generation to the next.

General Considerations

All this is to leave to one side the well-known differences on church government that have been rehearsed many times before. The majority of divines were Presbyterian, although not for the same reasons or with the same degree of commitment. The Scots were, of course, Presbyterian, but they were at the Assembly only to give advice. There were a number of Episcopalians and a small but able and vociferous group of Independents. We have already seen that the body as a whole was Erastian, with all power in the hands of Parliament.

The distinctions between the Confession and the Larger Catechism, and the underlying differences between members of the Assembly, demonstrate, among other things, the Assembly's dynamism and flexibility, its ability and willingness to encompass a range of models for an understanding of salvation. A contextual approach

53. Van Dixhoorn, 5:210–20.
54. *Annotations* [Wing D2062]: annotations on Romans 6:1–2 re *baptidzo*, and also on Romans 6:5. Commenting on Romans 6.4 (where Paul states that believers have been buried with Christ by baptism), the *Annotations* read: "In this phrase the Apostle seemeth to allude to the ancient manner of Baptisme, which was, to dip the parties baptized, and as it were to bury them under the water for a while, and then to draw them out of it, and lift them up, to represent the buriall of our old man, and our resurrection to newnesse of life." The identical comments are found in the third edition of 1657 [Wing D2064].

to the Westminster Assembly provides the opportunity to locate its doctrinal documents in the context of Reformed theology as a whole and within the broad flow of doctrinal development in the Christian church—and in England in particular—as *Christian* teaching proper to the whole church.

A notable example of the Assembly's desire to reach as wide agreement as possible is provided by the Committee on Accommodation. In S536 M 17.11.45am, the Assembly received an order from both Houses for the Committee on Accommodation "to take into consideration the differences in opinion of the members of the Assembly in point of church government, and to endeavour a union if it be possible, and in case that cannot be done, to endeavour the finding out some way how tender consciences, who cannot in all things submit to the common rule which shall be established, may be borne with according to the Word, and as may stand with the public peace."[55]

Moreover, a few months later, the staunch Episcopalian Thomas Coleman, in S601 M 9.3.45(46)am, during the debate on whether church government is distinct from the civil government, voiced some concerns of conscience. Coleman disagreed with such a distinction and wanted to know whether, if he spoke his mind on this matter, it would be considered a breach of the Solemn League and Covenant to which he had given allegiance, and so open himself up to a charge of perjury. He clearly wished to be free to speak according to his conscience, even if that was contrary to the Covenant and to the overwhelming majority of the Assembly. The matter was debated "and the Assembly thought not fit to pass any resolution upon that, it being free to any member of the Assembly to speak his conscience in the Assembly; and so he was called into the argument."[56]

It is well known that the Independents were given leave to present their case to the Assembly and that this occupied a considerable amount of time in debate. In S639 TH 14.5.46am, it was resolved that "Goodwin, Ny, Burroughs, Bridge, Sampson, Greenhill, Carter junior, Phillips granted liberty to be a committee to bring to the Assembly

---

55. From the Journals of the House of Commons, 4:342, recorded in Mitchell and Struthers, eds., *Minutes of the Sessions*, 163–64.

56. Mitchell and Struthers, eds., *Minutes of the Sessions*, 204–5.

what they should think fit upon these questions [on the *jus divinum* of church government]."[57]

As Morris points out, "Traces of fraternal compromise, even on points which at first were matters of strenuous discussion, such as the order of decrees or the scope of the Gospel or the divine right of the Presbyterian polity, are frequently apparent." He finds "many indications . . . not only of a purpose to incorporate whatever was worthiest in the ancient creeds, but of a disposition to harmonize in belief, so far as possible, with other Protestant and especially with the Reformed communions."[58] Morris goes on to argue that the Westminster documents are less technical than the Canons of Dort, less strictly theological; yet, when compared with the Heidelberg Catechism, they reveal a more thorough doctrinal structure without the sacrifice of spiritual tone. In fact, "they exhibit much in both spirit and thought which the common Christianity for all time will continue to appreciate as the most consummate flower of historic Protestantism."[59] That these are not uncritical comments is evident from the fact that Morris points to the absence of such topics as the nature of the gospel and the person and work of the Holy Spirit, in suggesting that the Assembly may not have made the best grouping possible.

The Boundaries of Acceptable Doctrine

In short, the Assembly, within limits, was inclusive rather than exclusive. It sought to reach the widest measure of agreement possible, within acceptable limits of doctrine and practice. And what exactly was unacceptable doctrine and practice?

First, the Assembly obviously excluded the distinctive teachings of Rome. This is evident in its speaking of the pope as the Antichrist, its comments about churches degenerating into synagogues of Satan, its strong assertion of the supreme authority of Scripture, its rejection of transubstantiation and the Mass, and the limits placed on the power of synods and councils. However, this does not mean that the Assembly differed from Rome on everything; it expressed its adherence to the

57. Ibid., 231.
58. Morris, *Westminster Symbols*, 62.
59. Ibid., 63.

doctrines of the great ecumenical councils on the Trinity and Christology, its common opposition to Pelagianism, and so on. It disagreed with the teachings of Rome that had provoked the Reformation, and underlying these was, of course, the relative position of Scripture and the teaching authority of the church, which we will consider in the next chapter. This does not mean that the Assembly considered the Roman Church to be entirely a synagogue of Satan; clearly, it retained some of the marks of the church, including Trinitarian baptism. Indeed, much of the opposition to Rome was connected to fears of a popish plot emanating from France and Spain, aimed at overthrowing the Protestant establishment. Papists were not simply followers of the Roman Church, but threats to England.[60]

Second, and in a far less antagonistic light, the Assembly distanced itself here and there from some aspects of Lutheranism. This is particularly evident in the Confession's chapters on the sacraments. Its statements on the efficacy of baptism in part distinguish Reformed theology, with its insistence on the sovereignty of the Holy Spirit in effecting the reality to which the sacramental signs point, from the Lutheran objectivity. Moreover, the feeding on Christ in the Lord's Supper is not carnal but spiritual, but nonetheless real and true. Having said that, there is little in the documents directed explicitly against Lutheranism, and the differences, where they surface, are handled gently and discreetly. Luther and Melanchthon are cited with approval as authorities.

Third, the Assembly is stronger in its opposition to Anabaptism. This is especially notable in the sections on the church and the sacraments, but it also surfaces in connection with lawful oaths and vows—which many Anabaptists refused to recognize as legitimate—and on the right of private property. Overall, it could be said that the theology of the Assembly as a whole was largely opposed to the predominantly semi-Pelagian individualism and antisacramental direction of Anabaptism. At the same time, there was in England an emerging group of Particular Baptists, who differed from the Assembly mainly on matters of baptism and church government, but who were in general agreement with most of what the Assembly produced. These churches produced their own confession in 1644 and revised it in 1677, adopting large

60. See chapter 13.

swathes of the Assembly documents in doing so. In this, they had a certain commonality with the Congregationalists who composed the Savoy Declaration in 1658, which—guided by their leading light, John Owen—followed Westminster in all but church government.[61]

Fourth, and most vehemently of all, is the immense concern expressed in the Assembly against antinomianism, the belief that Christ had fulfilled the law in its entirety on behalf of his people, so that it no longer had any significance for them. This was the real perceived threat, not only to the church, but also to civil society. This was particularly urgent, given that the country was engulfed in civil war, its institutions in disarray. A standing committee on the antinomians was set up, and it was constantly reporting to the Assembly, questioning prominent antinomians, arranging for their books to be burned, and sending them to Parliament for penal sanctions to be enforced. These were the main opponents the Assembly had in mind throughout its work. A minor, but amusing, indication of the hostility the antinomians provoked was the habit of the scribe, Adoniram Byfield, to record the name of a leading antinomian, Paul Best, as "Paul Beast."

Fifth, the Assembly, following Dort, definitely excluded Arminianism. Its chapter on the decree of God and its various statements on the extent of the atonement and on the perseverance of the saints all oppose Arminius and his followers head on.

Sixth, Amyraldianism is implicitly ruled out by the strong teaching on the particularity of redemption, although hypothetical universalists such as Edmund Calamy were not excluded, but spoke up vigorously in debate and continued thereafter to play a prominent role in the Assembly's activities. Evidently, they were regarded differently than Arminians or, worse, antinomians. Yet Amyraldian doctrine was excluded—the first chapter was in part written against tendencies at Saumur.

Behind all this was a united commitment to the historic Christian creeds. Deviation from the orthodox formularies on the Trinity and Christology was entirely out of bounds. Adherence to these was an axiom that underlay all the rest of the Assembly's work. We shall refer to Robert L. Reymond's suggestion that Westminster rejected Nicene Trinitarianism in chapter 8. In connection with this, in chapter 7 we shall also consider the debate on the three creeds.

61. Schaff, *Creeds*, 3:707–29.

7

Holy Scripture

We believe in the Holy Spirit . . . who spoke by the prophets.

The first chapter of the Confession ranks as the most thorough statement of classic Reformed Protestantism on the subject of Scripture and possibly the finest to date from any source. Warfield points to its careful construction by the Assembly, together with the widespread agreement on its content. The minutes give no hint of significant discord.[1] The debates on the chapter lasted a good while, on and off from S463 M 7.7.45 to S472 F 18.7.45, but only two minor amendments were made to the committee report. A reference was inserted on the need for the inward illumination of the Holy Spirit, and the word "saving" was added to the expression "understanding of such things as are revealed in the Word," in recognition that people could understand Scripture without having saving faith.[2]

Warfield argues that the chapter represents "a consensus of the Reformed theology." The churches in the British Isles prized the support of other Reformed churches. They wanted to demonstrate their unity with them. Behind this lay a long history of interaction with continental churches and theologians, a commonality resulting from

---

1. There is one notable exception to this, stemming from the earlier debates on the Thirty-Nine Articles, to which I will draw attention later in this chapter.

2. Warfield, *Westminster Assembly*, 155–257.

an almost seamless web of consensual theology.[3] Warfield remarks:
"No reader of the Puritan literature of the seventeenth century will
fail to observe how hard it leans upon the great Reformed divines of
the Continent."[4] Behind the theology of this chapter lies not this or
that particular source, but Reformed theology in general. Warfield
provides extensive material from Heppe to show this agreement—
citing Heidegger, Wendelius, Crocius, Polanus, and Chamier, and
concluding that "no single assertion is made in the first chapter of
the Confession which is not the common faith of the whole Reformed
theology."[5] He also compares the chapter to the Irish Articles, the Belgic Confession, the French Confession, the Second Helvetic Confession, and, as examples of contemporary Puritan theology, John Ball's
Catechism and John Downame's *Body of Divinity*, which the author
published under the name of Archbishop James Ussher, much to the
latter's chagrin.[6] Wayne Spear also makes a strong case for continuity
with past Reformed thought on Scripture, especially Calvin and the
earlier Puritan, William Whitaker, whose 1588 treatise, *A Disputation
on Holy Scripture*, was a landmark work.[7]

Why did both the Confession and the Larger Catechism begin
with Scripture, rather than the more usual starting topic of God?
Three reasons are immediately evident. First, this was the order of
the Irish Articles, and we saw how influential James Ussher was. There
was a precedent. Second, starting with Scripture stresses the way we
know Christian doctrine. Epistemologically, it is the best starting
point, while a beginning with God would have given a more ontological focus. It was a matter of judgment. However, the third reason
is probably the most telling. It concerns the historical context. The
previous century had witnessed the development of textual criticism.
It stemmed from the humanist insistence on *ad fontes* (to the sources)
and led to a focus on the biblical text in the original languages. By the
1640s, debate centered on the vowel points of the Masoretic text of

3. See chapter 6.
4. Warfield, *Westminster Assembly*, 161.
5. Ibid., 162–69.
6. Ibid., 170–90.
7. W. R. Spear, "Word and Spirit in the Westminster Confession," in *Westminster Confession into the 21st Century*, 1:39–56; Spear, "William Whitaker and the Westminster Doctrine of
Scripture," *RTJ* 7 (1991): 38–48.

the Old Testament.[8] In 1538, Elias Levita had argued that the vowel points of the Hebrew consonantal text were added at a date later than the Talmud and the Midrash. They were not part of the original. These claims, confirmed by scholarship, shook the Protestant stress on the Bible as the supreme authority. Roman Catholic apologists such as Robert Bellarmine argued that these human additions showed the need for the authoritative interpretation of the Roman Church. While these polemics were answered by Reformed theologians such as Amandus Polanus and William Whitaker, and by textual critics such as the elder and younger Buxtorfs, the situation changed in 1624 with the publication by the Reformed scholar Louis Cappel of his *Arcanum punctuationis revelatum*. Cappel disputed claims that the vowel points were early. He suggested that the vocalization had been handed down by oral tradition from the time the Scriptures were written, and that the Masoretes had expressed this by the vowel points that they had added to the text. As Muller indicates, "Reaction to Cappel's arguments and subsequent movement to modify hermeneutics without losing irrevocably the formal doctrine of scriptural authority laid down by the early orthodox is most clearly and definitively seen among the English writers."[9] In this light, Torrance's criticisms of Westminster for starting with Scripture are shown to miss the vital point of understanding theological statements in terms of what they intend to say to the situation in which they are made. The reason why the doctrine of Scripture was addressed first was that it was an immediate and pressing issue.

The Necessity of Scripture (WCF 1.1; LC 2–3)

The Assembly stated that God reveals himself in the natural world. He does this through the light of nature, the works of creation, and the works of providence. The phrase "the works of creation" refers to the production of the universe, and "the works of providence" refers to its maintenance. "The light of nature" is a reference to the consciousness of God that he has imprinted on the human

8. For what follows, I am indebted to Muller, *After Calvin*, 146–55.
9. Ibid., 152.

mind. Calvin wrote of a *sensus divinitatis* common to the race as a whole.[10] There are things that can be known of God by human beings in general without regard to whether they are Christian believers—specifically, his goodness, wisdom, and power. In this, the Assembly reflects the comments of the apostle Paul that God's "eternal power and divine nature" are clearly perceived through the things he has made (Rom. 1:19–20). Enough is made known to leave people without excuse for rejecting him. However, creation, providence, and the *sensus divinitatis* are inadequate when it comes to salvation. There is a twofold inadequacy. First, due to sin, people resist this knowledge in creation and in their own constitution. Second, the revelation is itself not designed to deliver from sin. It discloses God's power, but makes known neither his law nor his grace.[11] However, it is reliable within its limitations[12] and in terms of God's intention, for it declares plainly that there is a God (LC 2). Additionally, since it is God who reveals himself through these means, his revelation is utterly without defect as far as it goes. However, after the fall it cannot lead one to salvation, no matter how diligently one may follow it (LC 60). The works of creation and providence, and the common human awareness that God exists, cannot between them teach us what God wants of us, nor can they lead us by themselves to know him savingly. As Barth puts it, the light of nature "refers to the inner light of the inborn image of God in the human. The light of nature appears as a source of knowledge, but immediately is placed beneath Scripture as ineffective and incapable of revealing to us the will of God."[13]

In this, the Assembly was moving within lines already charted by earlier Reformed theology. Calvin recognized the natural inability of fallen humans to acknowledge God through his revelation in creation. It was the springboard for his discussion of the necessity for the Bible

10. P. Helm, *John Calvin's Ideas* (Oxford: Oxford University Press, 2004), 209–45.

11. Even before the fall, Adam was given word-revelation in order for him to understand his place in the created order. His task and responsibilities were spelled out verbally (Gen. 2:16–17), while God's walking in the garden and calling out to Adam immediately after the fall imply that communion between God and man was part of the original created order and that this included personal communication.

12. Warfield, *Westminster Assembly*, 193.

13. Barth, *Reformed Confessions*, 48.

and, indeed, for his whole doctrine of Scripture.[14] Richard Muller traces this feature in Calvin, Zacharias Ursinus, Robert Rollock, and Amandus Polanus. He argues that Reformed theologians of the late sixteenth and early seventeenth centuries gave greater stress to the necessity of revelation by the Word than is found either in medieval thought or in the Reformers.[15]

Therefore, the Lord revealed himself and his will freely (note: "it pleased the Lord") *to his church*. At once, this particular form of his revelation is more limited or focused in its scope; it does not extend as far as creation itself, but is directed specifically to God's church. He did this in two distinct but inseparable ways, as the Assembly notes: he revealed himself and his will in acts of revelation, and afterward committed his revelation to writing in Holy Scripture. The point to note again is that this revelation, in both forms, was directed toward his church. *The Bible was given by God to his church.* This reflects the role of the Assembly. While it was not formally a church body, but rather a creation of Parliament, serving at Parliament's behest, its task was to establish biblical foundations for the church's doctrine, worship, and government. Moreover, while many members of the Assembly were in academic positions, especially at Cambridge, they saw the formulation of theology as essentially an ecclesiastical activity.[16]

This paragraph has as its principal theme *the necessity of Holy Scripture for the church's salvation.* Without Scripture, we are left inexcusable for our sin and bereft of God's grace. This is an extremely sophisticated and nuanced statement. "Therefore it pleased the Lord, at sundry times, and in divers manners, to reveal Himself, and to declare that His will unto His Church; and afterwards, for the better preserving and propagating of the truth, and for the more sure establishment and comfort of the Church against the corruption of the flesh, and the malice of Satan and of the world, to commit the same wholly unto writing: which maketh the Holy Scripture to be *most necessary*" (italics added). In the Larger Catechism, question 2 does

---

14. Calvin, *Institutes*, 1.6.1–2.
15. Muller, *PRRD*, 2:168–76.
16. Note the contrast with developments since the Assembly, where increasingly in the Western church, theology has become the special province of the academic realm, divorced from the life of the church, leaving a range of adverse consequences in its wake.

not explicitly tie the Word of God to Scripture, but LC 3 does draws the connection: the Holy Scriptures of the Old and New Testaments are the Word of God.

We note that (1) the Lord revealed *himself* to his church, and in doing so revealed *his will* to his church, and (2) afterward he committed the same to writing. The Assembly does a number of things here. First, it distinguishes between the Lord's revealing of himself and his revealing of his will. The two of course are inseparable, but the distinction is nonetheless important, for at all stages of redemptive history God progressively reveals who he is even as he acts in covenant, in law and gospel. Second, it makes a distinction between the Lord's revealing—of himself and of his will—and the committing of it to writing. However, there is also an identity between the revelation and the writing; that is, what was committed to writing was the same as what the Lord had revealed. A wedge cannot be driven between the revelation and the writing without altering the statement. Moreover, it is the Lord who revealed himself who also committed it to writing and preserved it. Between the acts of God in the history of salvation, and the written record and explanation of those acts, is a distinction but also an identity, a unity in diversity. It is important to distinguish between the Bible and God's actions in revealing himself and his will; it is equally vital to maintain their unity and identity. This statement provides a bulwark against the opposing dangers of bibliolatry, on the one hand—think of hymns addressed not to God but to the Bible, such as "Holy Bible, book divine"—and the Barthian separation of revelation and the Bible, on the other.[17]

This revelation, in both deed and written word, contains both personal and propositional elements. The Lord reveals *himself* and he also reveals *his will* relating to salvation. Here the Assembly reflects the biblical record that at each stage of redemptive revelation, God reveals his name—his character—alongside his action in covenant with his people. As Warfield comments, this revelation was in parts and by stages—it was progressive. Despite our earlier caveat about the inclusion of proof texts in the Confession, the Assembly's use of Hebrews 1:1 in support underlies that. Warfield also stresses the goodness of

17. See Warfield, *Westminster Assembly*, 194.

125

God, both in revealing himself and then in preserving this knowledge and propagating it, for it was due to his good pleasure that he had this committed to writing.[18]

God's committing of his revelation to writing is necessary for us to know him and his will for us. From one angle, it was not strictly necessary, for God could have chosen some other way to communicate his will for our salvation. The Assembly recognizes this when it says that Scripture exists "for the *better* preserving and propagating of the truth"; it does so better than any other method could have done.[19] It is preserved accurately. A written record stands permanently, whereas oral transmission can easily be corrupted. Thus, the inspiration of Holy Scripture enables an accurate "preserving and propagating of the truth." God always had a mind to the well-being of his church and its missionary task to spread the truth; the divines' recognition of this in the very first section of the Confession belies claims that they lacked missionary zeal.

The concluding reference to "those former ways of God's revealing His will unto His people being now ceased" must refer principally to the former ways of revelation by way of dreams, theophanies, and direct encounters; it can hardly mean that general revelation had come to an end, for the heavens continue to declare God's glory. Barth, with his rejection of natural theology and skepticism about the revelation of God in creation, refers to "the foolish second question" of the Larger Catechism, which states that the light of nature and the works of God "declare plainly that there is a God."[20] It is clearly foolish from the standpoint of Barth's theology, coming nearly three hundred years later, in all its multifaceted grandeur, which the divines could hardly have anticipated. Others may wonder whether the foolishness lies elsewhere.

Recently, Garnet Milne has argued that a number of the divines held to the continuation of dreams and visions as conveying God's will in a nonredemptive sense. In particular, he refers to William Bridge. The Scottish commissioner George Gillespie also refers to John Knox

18. Ibid.

19. Cf. a similar argument in Amandus Polanus, *Syntagma theologiae Christianae* (Basel: 1609), 69. Muller also cites this passage in *PRRD*, 2:173–74.

20. Barth, *Reformed Confessions*, 146.

as a prophet. However, Milne concludes, they confined this belief to the illumination of Scripture; that is, the Holy Spirit might providentially guide the mind to an understanding of this or that part of the Bible through various means. Even for Bridge, the determining factor was Scripture, while Gillespie wrote of Knox in terms of him mediating Scripture, not as the agent of immediate revelation.[21] In fact, there is no trace in the minutes of debate on the question; if there had been one, it would have certainly ignited interest, since any hint of continuing revelation would have undermined the Protestant and Reformed polemic against both Rome and the Quakers.

Warfield comments that the necessity of Scripture rests on two grounds: the insufficiency of general revelation, and the cessation of special revelation, the record of which Scripture is said to be. Thus the Scriptures are "the permanent embodiment and sole divinely safeguarded and, indeed, only trustworthy, extant form in which the revelation of God and of His will which is necessary to salvation exists." They are therefore more than the record of revelation—they are the revelation itself fixed in written form for its better preservation and propagation. And they are more than useful—they are necessary.[22]

The Canon of Scripture (WCF 1.2–3)

Having asserted that the Scriptures are necessary if we are to know the will of God for our salvation, the next question is, What exactly is Scripture? Where can we find that written record, where God reveals himself, and where he discloses his will for our salvation? The question of the canon of Scripture—or, more exactly, the canon of the New Testament—had come to focus in the early church, from the time Marcion rejected the Old Testament and much of the New Testament, and when various gnostic groups appealed to spurious "gospels." Formally, from Athanasius's *Festal Letters* and the Council of Carthage in 397, the New Testament canon had been clearly asserted,

21. G. H. Milne, *The Westminster Confession of Faith and the Cessation of Special Revelation: The Majority Puritan Viewpoint on Whether Extra-Biblical Prophecy Is Still Possible* (Carlisle: Paternoster, 2007).

22. Warfield, *Westminster Assembly*, 195–96.

although its recognition is evident from the writings of Fathers back to Clement and Irenaeus.

However, the canon of Scripture was a matter of debate again at the Reformation. With Luther's rejection of James, and his relegation of Hebrews, Jude, and Revelation (with James) to deuterocanonical status in the table of contents of his September Bible of 1522, and Zwingli's similar rejection of Revelation, this was a live issue. Many of the Reformed followed suit, albeit a minority, as witnessed by the Thirty-Nine Articles' list containing all twenty-seven New Testament books. Calvin considered that doctrinal content justified canonicity and, while he questioned the authorship of a number of New Testament books, he did not oppose their place in the canon. Moreover, Protestants rejected Rome's inclusion of the Apocrypha in the Old Testament canon, although they were not averse to citing or alluding to it in debate. Generally, the Reformed confessions of the sixteenth century find canonicity in the testimony of the Holy Spirit and not in the authority of the church. Here at Westminster, the canon was still a live issue. Barth points out that "the later writers, who did not share the doubts of the earlier ones, never formally disputed that questions may be raised concerning the constitution of the Canon as they had in fact been raised in the 16th century."[23] The very fact of the enumeration of the biblical books and the rejection of those not considered biblical demonstrates the reality of the question.

The list follows the accepted Protestant canon, leaving aside the caveats of Luther, Zwingli, and others. Barth indicates that the listing of canonical books is distinctive of Reformed confessionalism in contrast with Lutheranism, since the latter placed church councils on more or less a par with Scripture, and so for them the list of canonical books was a given: the Reformed, "with these lists, . . . wanted to document their fundamental right to reject what non-biblical history and even the church might prescribe as canonical, and to make such decisions themselves as the ancient church had done."[24]

The origin of the canonical books of Scripture is from God: "given by inspiration of God." The Assembly thus defined Scripture as those

23. Barth, *CD*, I/2, 476–78.
24. Barth, *Reformed Confessions*, 50.

writings that are inspired.[25] The phrase "immediately inspired" (1.8) denotes that the Father breathed Scripture out by the Holy Spirit without human means *in the origination* of the original manuscripts.[26] This refers to the *origin* of Scripture, rather than its full production, in which human means were obviously used by God to write it. The composition of Scripture was by human hands, and it flowed from human thought and sometimes historical research, but its ultimate origin was entirely from God. However, to my mind, inspiration of itself can hardly be Scripture's *defining* characteristic, since other utterances were inspired by God, and yet were not Scripture—for example, the letter of Paul to Laodicea, besides a whole range of prophetic utterances. There is no attempt to explain or define inspiration here since, as Warfield argues, the Assembly is defining Scripture itself. Inspiration pervades the whole sixty-six books. It involves their origin. It does not affect merely matters of faith and practice, as the Socinians alleged, but defines the *origination* of scriptural books. The purpose of Scripture is to be "the rule of faith and life," but it is so since it was originated by God.

Canonicity entails certain books being part of Scripture and equally other books being excluded. Here the Assembly denies, in contrast with Rome, the canonicity of the Apocrypha.[27] Further, John Lightfoot recorded in his journal how the Assembly presented its humble advice to Parliament that the Apocrypha should no more be read in the churches and should no longer be bound with Bibles. The Assembly wanted it to be very clear that this was no merely theoretical matter.[28] Since canonical books are inspired by God, the reason why the Apocrypha are not canonical is that those books are not inspired by God, but are purely human compositions. Consequently, they are of no authority in the church. This is in contrast not only with Rome, but also

25. So Warfield, *Westminster Assembly*, 202.
26. Inspiration would later be a battleground in the disputes between B. B. Warfield and Charles Augustus Briggs in the late nineteenth century—but this was 1643–47.
27. The Council of Trent had included among the books of the Old Testament Tobit, Judith, Ecclesiasticus, Baruch, Wisdom, and 1 and 2 Maccabees. Additionally, it stated that it received and venerated, with reverence equal to that afforded to the written books, the traditions dictated either by Christ's own word of mouth or by the Holy Spirit and preserved in the Catholic Church by a continuous succession. It anathematized any who did not receive all the books in their entirety.
28. S16 TU 1.8.43pm: Lightfoot's journal, in Van Dixhoorn, 2:20–21.

with Orthodoxy.[29] It rests on the consistent teaching of the Reformed churches and its representative theologians, who often point to the absence in the New Testament of direct citations from the Apocrypha, as well as the opinions of a range of Fathers and ancient councils.[30]

The connection in the Assembly's mind between inspiration and canonicity is obvious. There were other writings, some apostolic, extant in the first-century church—Paul refers to a letter he wrote to Laodicea—besides prophetic utterances, some of which are recorded in the New Testament, others of which are reported, and many more of which are unmentioned.[31] Hence the Assembly could hardly regard all inspired utterances as canonical. What is meant is that inspiration, while it may not of itself be sufficient, is a necessary condition of canonicity. The idea that the canon imposed itself on the church, while it may be correct, does not appear to be present, except implicitly, and in fact was a later development.

The Apocrypha are on a level with "other human writings." They are a human writings, not of divine inspiration, and therefore not canonical. This does not mean that the Apocrypha are of no use—this book you are reading is a human writing, not of divine inspiration, and so is not canonical, but I hope that it is of some use. There is therefore for the Assembly a clear distinction between Scripture, which is given by inspiration of God, and has God for its author (WCF 1.4, 8; LC 4), and human writings, such as the Apocrypha, which do not have God for their author and so are not part of the canon of Scripture.[32]

The Authority of Scripture (WCF 1.4)

In summary, the Assembly asserts that we believe Holy Scripture and obey it on the basis of its authority, its right to elicit faith. This is due to its own inherent qualities, preeminently because it comes from God. Here the origin of Scripture, its being inspired by God, is

29. See Letham, *Through Western Eyes*, 179–87.
30. Muller, *PRRD*, 2:390.
31. There are a range of references in the Old Testament to books which have subsequently been lost, although there is no evidence that these were composed under the inspiration of the Spirit.
32. Cf. Warfield, *Westminster Assembly*, 203.

the basis of the authority it exerts over the church. In this, it does not depend on human testimony, including that of the church. This is in obvious contradiction to Rome, which claims that the Bible can only be interpreted aright in the hands of the ecclesiastical authorities. The Assembly will have none of this. Scripture's authority depends wholly on God, its author. Both its own inherent authority to elicit faith and obedience, and our own response of faith, are together consequent on its origin from God. It carries the authority of God himself, who gave it in order to commit to writing his revelation of himself and his will for his church, thus preserving it and propagating it. Warfield describes this as "a paragraph of unsurpassed nobility of both thought and phrase."[33]

What this inspiration entails is well described by Morris: "It is nothing less than a movement of the Holy Spirit upon the minds and wills of the men inspired, by which they were led to produce a volume that is properly ascribed in its totality to God as its Author." Moreover, "to regard such inspiration as only a higher variety of mental power or of poetic or religious fervor, such as appears elsewhere in human experience, is to dissipate altogether its divine quality, and also to destroy its religious significance and worth."[34] There is no evidence that the Assembly made any attempt to describe or define exactly how this occurred; they produce no theory of inspiration, but only record the matter and attest their united belief that this is how the Scriptures came into existence.

That Scripture does not depend for its authority on the testimony of the church is evident by the Assembly's insistence that Scripture itself is the ultimate authority in the church. Synods and councils are to make decrees and determinations that are "consonant to the Word of God," and these decrees are to be received with reverence and submission, providing that they are in "agreement with the Word" (WCF 31.3). Moreover, all church councils may err, but since Scripture originates with God, it follows that it cannot err.[35] Therefore,

33. Ibid., 211.
34. Morris, *Westminster Symbols*, 78.
35. The later teaching of biblical inerrancy can find support in this contrast between the potentially errant church and the Bible, which originates from God. Inerrancy is an inference from the divine origin of Scripture.

church councils are never to be made the rule of faith or practice; they are simply a help, insofar as they conform to the Word of God in Scripture (WCF 31.4).

Therefore, the Word of God, committed to writing in Holy Scripture, is the source of our knowledge of God, together with the Holy Spirit's work in making effectual God's salvation. Scripture reveals what is pleasing to God. It is determinative for worship and Christian living. It provides the epistemological basis of the Christian faith. In it is made known the covenant of grace, the mediation of Christ, the way of salvation.

We must note that the Assembly gives no clear testimony to the human agents in the writing of Scripture. Nor does the Assembly explain how the inspiration of Scripture dovetails with the variety of personalities of the human authors. This might be thought something of a defect. However, criticism of the divines at this point is anachronistic; the role of the human author was not yet a real issue. As Warfield argues, "The time had not yet come when the true *concursus* of inspiration, by which we may see that every word of Scripture is truly divine and yet every word is as truly human, had become the common property of all."[36] Indeed, the tendency in the 1640s was not to limit divine inspiration in any way, but rather to conceive of it rather mechanically. John Owen was to adopt a particularly strong position on this point. This was true of the continental Reformed, as well as the English. Critical work on the Hebrew text of the Old Testament was to lead Francis Turretin to insist on the inspiration of the vowel points themselves, or at least the power of the points.[37] However, no less than John Lightfoot could, as Muller points out, "balance a strict view of inspiration with a strong sense of human activity in the writing of Scripture." Indeed, Muller adds that it would be mistaken "to

36. Warfield, *Westminster Assembly*, 276.
37. The Formula Consensus Helveticus, II (1675), of which Turretin was the prime author, states: "In particular, the Hebrew Original of the Old Testament . . . is, not only in its consonants, but in its vowels—either the vowel points themselves, or at least the power of the points—not only in its matter, but in its words, inspired of God." The text is given in A. A. Hodge, *Outlines of Theology* (repr., Grand Rapids: Eerdmans, 1972), 656. For a more extended discussion of the vowel points, see F. Turretin, *Institutes of Elenctic Theology* (ed. James T. Dennison; Phillipsburg, NJ: P&R, 1992), 1:114–16, where he concludes: "We have always thought the truer and safer way to keep the authenticity of the original text safe and sound . . . is that which holds the points to be of divine origin, whether they are referred to Moses or to Ezra."

view the seventeenth-century orthodox theory of inspiration as utterly opposed to the results of a more critical and textual exegesis or as incapable of accommodation to the various problems of authorship and composition raised by the critical approach."[38]

In Warfield's day, Charles Augustus Briggs argued that the Westminster divines were not committed to the idea of the verbal inspiration or inerrancy of the Bible and made a distinction between the word of God and the precise words of the Bible. For his part, Warfield expounds John Lightfoot's doctrine of Scripture—and Lightfoot, as a biblical scholar, might be expected to be less rigid than most—and finds that he maintained that inspiration reached not only to individual words, but also to the letters, even to the pointing of the Hebrew text by the Masoretes. Lightfoot concluded that Scripture is utterly trustworthy, free from the remotest falsehood, its words identical to the speech of the Holy Spirit.[39] Lightfoot is not the only Assembly member Warfield cites by any means.

Edward Morris agrees. There is no theory of how inspiration occurred, as far as we can discover in the minutes, he acknowledges, but "the Westminster teaching clearly rules out the opinion that inspiration relates merely to what are called the essentials, but not to the incidentals of Scripture," for the symbols "contain no suggestion of any recognizable distinction between the essential and the incidental, between the concept and the language; or of an inspiration which is but partial and variable." "They recognize that imperfect experiences are recorded in the Scriptures, but never suggest that these experiences are imperfectly recorded."[40] He correctly points out that the question of errors did not arise until the advent of English Deism in the eighteenth century. There are no traces of debate on the matter at the Assembly.[41] "In a word, the Bible must be something more, in form as well as in substance, than a transcript by fallible men in inaccurate language of a revelation once made on earth: it must itself be that Revelation."[42]

---

38. Muller, *PRRD*, 2:251.
39. Warfield, *Westminster Assembly*, 280–333.
40. Morris, *Westminster Symbols*, 80.
41. Ibid., 85.
42. Ibid., 82. Morris refers to LC 157, "with a firm persuasion that they are the very word of God."

In more recent times, Jack B. Rogers, in a study of the teaching of members of the Assembly, cites passages where they recognize human authorship and differences of style, which he considers to be evidence that they did not accept verbal inspiration. Like Briggs before him, Rogers pulls passages out of context, and sets up an unjustifiable polarity between the divine and the human. In the end, he is unable to establish that anyone at the Westminster Assembly believed Scripture contained errors.[43] In a later work, Rogers, together with Donald McKim, argues that the Westminster Confession holds a view of inspiration that does not entail inerrancy. The Word of God is simply the saving message of the Bible, rather than the Bible itself. The authors miss the point that the Assembly maintained that the Bible *is* the saving message, the written record by God of his own revelation, and that it—as a whole, in its sense and its details—is our only rule of faith and practice precisely because it comes from God in its entirety.[44]

Thus, the Scriptures, as the Word of God, are our "only rule of faith and obedience" (LC 3), teaching us how we may glorify God and enjoy him forever (SC 1). Since the Bible is God's revelation to his church concerning salvation, it also determines what we are to believe concerning him, and what we are to do in obeying him. Faith and obedience, justification and sanctification, are integrally related, although distinct.

We note the comment in SC 2 that the Word of God "is contained in the scriptures of the Old and New Testaments." To understand this clause in a neo-orthodox sense with the Word of God not equated with Scripture, somehow separating the word of God and revelation from the text of Scripture, would be anachronistic. The divines were not Barthians before Barth. In fact, the Assembly affirms *both* that Scripture is the Word of God *and* that it contains the Word of God. This stems from the fact that God speaks in Scripture; his words cannot be confined to a written text alone, for they have continued impact through

43. J. B. Rogers, *Scripture in the Westminster Confession* (Grand Rapids: Eerdmans, 1967), 298–302.

44. J. B. Rogers and D. K. McKim, *The Authority and Interpretation of the Bible: An Historical Approach* (San Francisco: Harper and Row, 1979), 461. It is disappointing that Andrew McGowan, in his recent book on Scripture, effectively ignores the Confession: A. T. B. McGowan, *The Divine Spiration of Scripture: Challenging Evangelical Perspectives* (Nottingham: Apollos, 2007).

the Holy Spirit. Moreover, the Word of God is living and active (Heb. 4:12–13). It goes beyond a printed page; it sits in judgment on us. It is precisely because Scripture *is* the Word of God that it can also be said to contain the Word of God.[45] This phrase merely indicates that the Assembly was able to distinguish between the text of Scripture as the Word of God, its continuing and ongoing efficacy, and the word of God eternal, essential, and unwritten. This was a commonplace among seventeenth-century Reformed theologians. As Muller states,

> The assumption of a radical discontinuity between the Reformation and the orthodox doctrine of the Word [Westminster falls into this latter group], thus, rests on a profound and dogmatic misunderstanding that falsifies both the teaching of the Reformers and the doctrine of their orthodox successors. Whereas it is incorrect to claim, on the one side, that the Reformers so stressed the concept of Christ as the living Word witnessed by Scripture that they either lost or diminished the doctrine of Scripture as Word of God written, it is equally incorrect to claim, on the other side, that the orthodox, by developing a formal doctrine of Scripture as Word, lost the Reformers' conception of Scripture as living Word. Theologically, such claims arise out of a mistaken either/or approach to the problem, where Word of God is taken to indicate either Christ or Scripture but not both. A multilevel understanding of Word is, however, quite typical of both the Reformers and the post-Reformation orthodox.[46]

How We Come to Believe That the Scriptures Are the Word of God (WCF 1.5; LC 4)

Given that Scripture is breathed out by God and is of final authority in his church, and so also for all aspects of faith and practice, how do we come to recognize it as such? The Assembly rehearses a number of ways by which Scripture displays its exalted nature, which carry persuasive power, but fall short of convincing us by themselves. They are unable to persuade because of the sinful state of the human heart, which can only be changed by the Holy Spirit.

45. Cf. also Irish Articles, 1.6; French Confession, 5; Belgic Confession, 7.
46. Muller, *PRRD*, 2:185–86.

135

The testimony of the church may induce us to a high view of Scripture. This may come through its decrees or its preaching, or a range of features in between. There are factors internal to the Bible—its heavenly matter, its speaking of realities that transcend our mundane perceptions; the efficacy of its doctrine; the majesty of its style, which even in translation was already shaping English language and culture, and would continue to do so for centuries; the consent, or agreement, of all its parts, though written at different times and by many different human authors, in their united focus on the glory of the God of Israel, the Creator of all things; the full discovery it makes of the only way of salvation, which the chapter will later claim to be clear to all; and many other incomparable excellencies, such as its entire perfection. All these things may lead the reader to a high view of the Bible. Together they have inspired some of the greatest creative work of human history, such as innumerable works of art and, later than the Assembly, Johann Sebastian Bach's *St. Matthew Passion*. Yet these do not convince us of its infallible truth and divine authority. That comes only from "the inward work of the Holy Spirit bearing witness by and with the Word in our hearts."

Why is this? First, there is the natural indisposition of the human heart to receive God's revelation due to sin. Sin's impact on our whole being renders us naturally incapable of obtaining the saving knowledge of God (WCF 6.4; LC 25). Moreover, the continued presence of sin makes us sluggish and slow to recognize the voice of the Holy Spirit and the truth of the revelation of salvation. Second, the Holy Spirit is the primary author of Scripture. The Bible is "immediately inspired by God," and it is the Spirit who carried its human authors along as they spoke from God (2 Peter 1:20–21). It follows that the Spirit is best able to convince us of the truth of what he has originated. This is exactly what Jesus said would be one of the principal features of the Spirit's ministry (John 16:12–15). Third, since the Bible has been given by God primarily to teach us about himself and his will, its many other wonderful features are conduits, as it were, to lead us to God—and that is something for which we are utterly reliant on the grace of the Holy Spirit. Here is that conjunction of the Holy Spirit, the primary author of Scripture who accompanies its reading and proclamation, with the Word written (*cum verbo*), that is distinctive of

Reformed theology. In this, the Spirit "does not give new revelation, or a purely mystical experience, but opens a person's spiritual vision to appreciate the marks of truth which were objectively present in Scripture all along."[47]

Neo-orthodox interpreters understand the authority of Scripture to rest upon this witness of the Holy Spirit in our hearts. But the Confession speaks of this witness simply as that by which we come to believe that Scripture is the Word of God. The question of Scripture's authority is not in view; rather, the human acceptance of Scripture as the Word of God is the subject. This is another instance of the anachronistic readings commonly made by the neo-orthodox, driven frequently by a preconceived theory of revelation.

Along similar lines, T. F. Torrance makes a dichotomy between divine revelation and the writing of Scripture. He criticizes the formal support for the Confession's teaching on Scripture and the inadequacy of the texts adduced. It is biblical nominalism! Doctrines logically derived from biblical statements are regarded as definite propositions and given a categorical character. Torrance displays a prime example of ahistorical eisegesis. The House of Commons required proof texts, against the Assembly's better judgment.[48] Its discussions carefully addressed the variety of linguistic, historical, and theological contexts that lay behind biblical passages. Furthermore, the Assembly's doctrine of Scripture—the same doctrine that Torrance criticizes—points to the sense of Scripture as Scripture. The proof texts were put there—reluctantly at the behest of Parliament—as indications of where to look in the writings and sermons of the Assembly members for support for what the Confession taught. Torrance has misconstrued the nature of the Confession, misread its doctrine of Scripture, and treated its historical context with scant regard.[49] In the same place, Torrance also

47. Spear, "Word and Spirit in the Westminster Confession," 50.
48. In S726 TU 13.10.46, there was a debate on "the annexing of Scriptures to the Confession of Faith as requested by the House of Commons." Van Dixhoorn, 5:369. Work on Scripture proofs began in S768 W 6.1.46(47). Committee work on the matter was completed by S804 F 5.3.46(47), when the Assembly voted to thank it for its work and established another committee to meet with it to review its work. The business was finally completed in S825 M 12.4.47. Van Dixhoorn, 6:397–434. See also, Warfield, *Westminster Assembly*, 102–3.
49. T. F. Torrance, *Scottish Theology*, 129.

criticizes the Assembly for giving undue prominence to Scripture over the fundamental doctrines of the gospel. But Scripture was a contentious subject at the time, due to the emergence of text-critical ideas at the school of Saumur. Moreover, Torrance has just accused the Assembly of minimizing Scripture in favor of logical deductions and dogmatic propositions. He wants to have his cake and eat it too.

The Sufficiency of Scripture (WCF 1.6)

Since Scripture is the Word of God, what does it contain? This section provides the answer: "the whole counsel of God concerning all things necessary for His own glory, man's salvation, faith and life." Note the order: first the glory of God (cf. SC 1), then our salvation, which in turn comprises first faith and then our life (cf. LC 5). Moreover, it is important to see what Scripture does *not* teach. The Assembly does not hold that the Bible contains all truth. If it were to have done so, it would have been inconsistent with its earlier teaching on the works of creation and providence and the light of nature. Those things are insufficient to teach us about salvation, but they do teach us something. They disclose the eternal power and deity of God and manifest his glory. There is such a thing as general revelation; although the term had not yet been coined, the reality was recognized. There are vast fields of knowledge that Scripture does not address. Scripture is complete and final only *for the purpose for which it was given*. The Confession does not deny the existence or value of other sources of truth. While the Bible talks about many things—"of ships and shoes and sealing wax, of cabbages and kings"—it does not talk about everything. Its message concentrates on God's glory and our salvation, faith, and life. The Assembly denies that Scripture needs to be supplemented to tell us what we are to believe about God and what duty he requires of us.[50]

Further, the question arises as to how we are to find this message of Scripture. The Assembly answers that it is to be sought in two ways. First, it is found "expressly set down in Scripture." There are clear and explicit statements in the Bible where the glory of God

50. See Warfield, *Westminster Assembly*, 224–25.

is unfolded as far as we are able to bear it, and where our salvation is explained both in terms of what we are to believe and how we are to respond. However, that is not all, for it is also true that the whole counsel of God "by good and necessary consequence may be deduced from Scripture."

This is a profoundly important statement. It points to the need for careful thought in reading, preaching, and thinking about the Bible. It mandates theology. In order to begin to grasp the whole counsel of God, we need to be able to make legitimate deductions from the Bible. Orderly thought is a *sine qua non* of the Christian faith. Attempts to disparage the mind, and dismiss intellectual reflection on Scripture as "cerebral" undermine the teaching of Scripture and begin to unravel the message of salvation. In short, this chapter mandates systematic theology. That, of course, is how the church has defended itself against heresy. In the early church, it was found that simply to repeat the words of the Bible left the church defenseless. The gospel itself was threatened by unthinking repetition of biblical words and phrases. A challenging intellectual response was required in order to defend "the sense of Scripture" against those who would use its words to overturn essential elements of the biblical gospel.[51]

This statement raises the question of the relationship between Scripture and tradition, and opens the door for a biblically based understanding of the development of dogma. It also preserves the role of human reason in reflecting upon Scripture, and guards against a literalistic fundamentalism. It is paradigmatic for all that follows; this cannot be overstated. Especially is it true when we reach the matter of the regulative principle of worship in the chapter on law and liberty (WCF 21.1). It rules out a fundamentalist requirement that proof texts be produced for everything.[52] It also undermines Torrance's criticisms, which we discussed above. In his own day, reflecting on this section, Warfield remarked: "The reëmergence in recent controversies of the plea that the authority of Scripture is to be confined to its express declarations, and that human logic is not to be trusted in divine things, is, therefore, a direct denial of a fundamental position of Reformed

51. See Letham, *The Holy Trinity*, especially 108–83.
52. It does not negate the legitimate use of proof texts to support doctrine where it is "expressly set down in Scripture."

139

theology, explicitly affirmed in the Confession, as well as an abnegation of fundamental reason, which would not only render thinking in a system impossible, but would discredit at a stroke many of the fundamentals of the faith, such e.g. as the doctrine of the Trinity, and would logically involve the denial of the authority of all doctrine whatsoever, since no single doctrine of whatever simplicity can be ascertained from Scripture except by the use of the process of the understanding." And he adds, "It is the Reformed contention, reflected here in the Confession, that the sense of Scripture is Scripture, and that men are bound by its whole sense in all its implications."[53]

To this, the sense of Scripture found both in its explicit statements and by deduction, nothing is to be added. Scripture is the complete and entirely adequate revelation of God for the salvation of his church. It is sufficient for these purposes. There were two potential sources for claiming additional revelation in 1640s England. First, there were the enthusiasts and antinomians, who were claiming "new revelations of the [Holy] Spirit," as have others down through church history. The Assembly rules these notions out of court, for if they were valid, they would make Scripture less than sufficient to disclose God's glory and to unfold our salvation, faith, and life. The Assembly rejects a mystical view of the Christian faith and asserts an evangelical view, defending a biblical but churchly Christianity in the face of an inherently individualistic one. Second, there was the threat from "traditions of men," which refers chiefly to the Church of Rome. The ideas opposed here are the dogmatic accretions accumulated by Rome, including, but not limited to, the sacramental notion of transubstantiation, together

---

53. Warfield, *Westminster Assembly*, 226–27. I am grateful to Sherman Isbell for pointing out the following works, which address the question of inferences from Scripture. Since they date from after the events that occupy this book, they are not guides to the Assembly so much as to later thought on the matter addressed by the Assembly here. See George Gillespie, *A treatise of miscellany questions* (Edinburgh: Gedeon Lithgow for George Swintoun, 1649) [Wing G371; Aldis, *Scotland*, 1367], 243. For the Westminster Assembly's use of necessary consequence, cf. J. R. de Witt, *Jus Divinum: The Westminster Assembly and the Divine Right of Church Government* (Kampen: J. H. Kok, 1969), 130. Important discussions of the role of necessary consequences in the interpretation of Scripture are found in J. Bannerman, *Inspiration: The Infallible Truth and Divine Authority of the Holy Scriptures* (Edinburgh: T. & T. Clark, 1865), 582–88, and Turretin, *Institutes of Elenctic Theology*, 1:37–43. See also John Owen, *The Works of John Owen* (ed. W. H. Goold; 24 vols.; London: Johnstone & Hunter, 1850–55), 2:379; 20:147; W. Cunningham, *Theological Lectures* (London: James Nisbet, 1878), 457–58; J. Bannerman, *The Church of Christ* (Edinburgh: T. & T. Clark, 1868), 2:409–13; Warfield, *Westminster Assembly*, 226–27.

with the recent imposition of the divine right of kings by the Anglican Canons of 1640. Instead, we are to look to Scripture as our only rule of faith and life.

That this commitment does not rule out the need for the Holy Spirit is clear by the immediately following recognition of "the inward illumination of the Spirit of God to be necessary for the saving understanding of such things as are revealed in the Word." The word "saving" was added by the Assembly to the committee report. The Assembly is opposed to fanatical claims of revelation by the Holy Spirit, but it also steers clear of rationalism. Just as the Spirit enables us to recognize that the Bible is the very Word of God (as we saw in the previous section), so we need the Spirit to enable us to interpret it correctly. These statements give a lie to the caricature that English Puritanism was devoid of a doctrine of the Holy Spirit.

Every bit as much as the Assembly steers clear of rationalism and relies on the Spirit for illumination—while rejecting the enthusiasts' claims to new revelation—so it rejects tradition as in any way supplementary to Scripture in disclosing the whole counsel of God, but does not reject tradition as such.[54] The light of nature and Christian prudence together can help us in certain "circumstances concerning the worship of God, and government of the Church, common to human actions and societies." There is a sphere where "the traditions of men" have a place; this corresponds to the fact that the Bible does not address everything, but those things necessary to disclose God's glory and our salvation, faith, and life. Scripture does not cover each and every particular concerning the worship of God or the government of the church—there is a sphere for Christian liberty, according to the light of nature and the rules of Christian prudence, while all such areas are still to be governed by the principles set down in the Word. Far from requiring proof texts for everything in everyday life, the Westminster divines left large swathes of human actions to the general rules of justice, faithfulness, and truth.

54. By "tradition" we mean the past teaching of the church, together with the cumulative thought of its leading theologians. Tradition can be false, as in the dogma of transubstantiation, or valid, as in the Trinitarian and Christological dogmas of the patristic period. The Assembly, we saw, referred constantly to past theologians and fathers. The point here is that Scripture has supremacy over all since it originates with God. Beyond this, "tradition" can also refer to circumstances common to human societies and activities.

141

The gist is that there is nothing in the way of truth required by God to be believed or duty required of us to attain salvation that is to be added from any source other than what is revealed in Scripture. The Bible, as Warfield puts it, is more than *a* rule of faith and practice; it is more than *the* rule of faith and practice; it is more than *a sufficient* rule of faith and practice; it is *the only* rule of faith and practice.[55] As we shall see, this is, in the mind of the divines, the charter guaranteeing Christian liberty and freedom from all forms of human tyranny. It is the basis for its far-reaching statements in WCF 16.1, 20.2, and 21.1.

The Clarity of Scripture (WCF 1.7)

A difficulty that arises in the discussion of Scripture is how far it is intelligible—and to whom? In the 1640s, Rome still maintained that Scripture should be interpreted only by the church authorities. Translations into vernacular languages were frowned upon, since they opened the door to aberrant theologies advanced by unskilled interpreters who would set at naught the sacred teaching of the church. In contrast, Protestants ever since Luther and Tyndale have insisted on translating the Bible into the common language of the people, since Scripture is the highest authority. In this the Assembly was at one with the Orthodox, for whom the translation of the Bible and the liturgy into the vernacular was of first importance in all missionary endeavor.

The Assembly in this chapter makes a number of crucial distinctions. There are varying degrees of clarity in the Bible. First, this is intrinsic to Scripture itself, since "all things in Scripture are not alike plain in themselves"; there are some places that are difficult to understand, as Peter comments on the letters of Paul, which he found difficult himself (2 Peter 3:16). Second, the relative clarity of Scripture is also dependent on the capacity of the reader; all things in Scripture are "not alike clear unto all." Some people are less able to understand than others, whether because of lack of knowledge or education, lack of Christian experience, or deficit of intelligence.

---

55. Warfield, *Westminster Assembly*, 225.

Second Peter 3:16, which features as a proof text, bears this out, too, for Peter mentions "the ignorant and unstable" who twist the meaning of Paul's letters to their own destruction. This clearly acknowledges the difficulty of interpreting some of the Bible. It recognizes that hard work is needed to explain it. It makes allowance for the role of the human interpreter, the knower, in the process of knowing.[56]

However, saving truth in Scripture is clear. "Those things which are necessary to be known, believed, and observed for salvation," the things on which the Assembly considered the Bible to focus, are clearly and openly propounded. However, this does not occur uniformly. The teaching of salvation can be found "in some place of Scripture or other," here or there. There has to be some effort expended; the places of Scripture have to be sought out. "Ordinary means" are to be used in this process; the ministry of the Word, the sacraments, and prayer come to mind, which the Assembly says are the principal means that God uses for the salvation of his elect (cf. SC 88; WCF 25–29). This task of encountering the message of salvation in "some place of Scripture or other," carried out through the use of "ordinary means," is open to anyone, whether learned or unlearned. The common person can come to a clear knowledge of the gospel through the Word of God propounded in the ordinary way by the ministry of the church.

These comments imply that everything taught in the Scriptures is not of equal weight or significance. Some things—those necessary to be known, believed, and observed for salvation—have a strategic significance and shed light on the rest. They are paradigmatic for the whole.

Moreover, saving truth is set forth "in some place of Scripture or other"; not in every single place is this or that aspect of saving truth set forth clearly. Additionally, these things are set forth so that a "sufficient" understanding may result—not an exhaustive understanding. Nor are they equally intelligible to all. In this light, the contention of Rogers and McKim that the Holy Spirit bears witness to the saving truth in Scripture, rather than to Scripture as a whole, evaporates.[57]

---

56. Note the crucial discussions of these issues in, e.g., M. Polanyi, *Personal Knowledge* (Chicago: University of Chicago Press, 1958); Polanyi, *The Tacit Dimension* (Chicago: University of Chicago Press, 1958).

57. Rogers and McKim, *Authority and Interpretation*, 126.

The divines were well aware that there is a diversity and a focus within Scripture, but its message is reliable because the whole comes from God. The whole of Scripture is the Word of God, not just some part of it that only an enlightened scholar can discern. In saving faith, we believe "whatsoever is revealed in the Word, for the authority of God Himself speaking therein" (WCF 14.2). That is, God speaks in the Scriptures, "whatsoever" the place or context may be.

Sometimes Scripture is obscure and difficult, while at other times it is clear as crystal, but it always points beyond itself to the God who gave it. Scripture is open to all through the use of ordinary means, so there is no need for an infallible teaching authority, such as the Roman magisterium, nor for special inner light, as with enthusiasts and the emerging Quakers. Yet the teaching of the church nevertheless has an integral place. The means of grace are there to lead us to the knowledge of those things that are necessary for salvation, with the indispensable illumination of the Holy Spirit. In short, the Bible has to be interpreted; it needs a human interpreter and the divine illuminator.

The Text of Scripture (WCF 1.8)

In what form do the Scriptures come? To what texts should we go for what kinds of knowledge? How do vernacular translations fit into the picture? How accurately has the biblical text been transmitted down through the centuries? These were important questions, not only because of the claims of Rome, but also because of the development of textual criticism since Erasmus and seen in the work of Levita and Cappel.

The Assembly presents a thoroughly nuanced discussion, with a number of distinct layers. First, the Hebrew text of the Old Testament and the Greek text of the New Testament were "immediately inspired by God." This is an appeal to the original *autographa*. The Scriptures as first penned were directly inspired by the Holy Spirit. We noted that the contribution of the human authors is not a matter for discussion; the assumption is that God is the author. It would be idle to argue that the divines discounted human authorship. However, it was not a major issue at the time, and so did not feature largely in their own writings, nor does it come into focus in the Assembly or its documents. That these originals are immediately inspired by God is the reason why, "in all controversies of religion, the Church is finally to appeal unto [the Old Testament in Hebrew and the New Testament in Greek]." This is in direct contrast with Rome, for which Jerome's Latin translation, the Vulgate, was the court of appeal, in tandem with its insistence that the common person could not have access to the text in his or her native tongue. In this, Rome denied access to the Bible to the common reader and based its authority on an ancient Latin translation. The Assembly, in common with the tradition of Protestant theology going back to Luther, appeals to the original sources, as the humanists had done—*ad fontes*.

It should be noted that the Assembly considers the Septuagint (the standard Greek translation of the Old Testament) a translation, and so not "immediately inspired by God," and consequently not to be the arbiter in religious controversy. The Assembly places it on a par with other translations. This was the version most frequently cited by Jesus and the apostles, and is the Old Testament text regarded as canonical by the Eastern church.

The Old Testament Hebrew text and the New Testament Greek text have been, "by [God's] singular care and providence, kept pure in all ages" and are therefore "authentical." This is the second category applied by the Assembly to the text. While the originals were immediately inspired by God, the text thereafter has been kept pure by the special providential care of God. This was written before the age when differing families of Greek manuscripts were discovered. However, the divines make no discrimination between manuscripts; the Greek text as a whole has been preserved. Some later argued that since what is now known as the "Byzantine text" was the standard in the 1640s, the statement refers to these manuscripts rather than others. There is little justification for such a claim. God's "singular care and providence" has hardly gone into remission. When large numbers of new manuscripts were found in later years, it was not as if he had gone to sleep; the same "singular care and providence" was evident in the discovery and analysis of these manuscripts. The principle stated here is of equal application to them.

Warfield argues that it is to the original manuscripts that inspiration applies, while to the copies of the originals, preservation by God's special providence is applicable. It is obvious that errors in transmission crept in through copying by hand; errors cannot apply to the originals. God's "singular care and providence" did not prevent errors from entering into individual manuscripts. Rather, it refers to the text as a whole. Thus, "our Tischendorfs and Tregelleses, and Westcotts and Horts . . . are all parts of God's singular care and providence in preserving His inspired Word pure."[58] The roots of Warfield's argument are evident in the Assembly. Such a belief mandates textual criticism, which at that time was in its relative infancy, but which now has yielded a text that gets us as close to the original as it may be possible to come, and one more complete than possessed by anyone in the first century.

The third layer identified by the Assembly is that of translations (including, we must suppose, the Septuagint). Translations are required so all can read and hear the Word of God in their own language, so that every nation may worship God in an acceptable manner—note again the missionary vision of the Assembly, extending to the ends of the earth. This is a far cry from Islam, for which the Koran is only the Koran in its Arabic original. In contrast, the universality of the gospel, together with the inability of most people to read the original languages, requires translations, and these translations—while distinct from the Bible in the original languages, and further distinct from the original manuscripts—are still the Word of God, conveying clearly that knowledge required for salvation. The earlier statements on the sense of Scripture underlie the fact that translations are still the Word of God. The result of Bible translation is that, "the Word of God dwelling plentifully in all" people, they may worship him in an acceptable manner and through patience and comfort of the Scriptures may have hope. In religious controversies, where precision is required, appeal must be made to the original languages, but translations are sufficient for all ordinary purposes.[59] Implicit is the missionary mandate: "into the vulgar language of every nation," as well as the need for individuals

58. Warfield, *Westminster Assembly*, 237–39.
59. See ibid., 240–41.

"to read and search" the Scriptures diligently and avail themselves of the ordinary means of grace.

Read in conjunction with the preceding section, there emerges a twofold layer to the Bible: (1) what is clear to all by the use of ordinary means, which is central to what the Scriptures as a whole teach concerning salvation, and (2) things inherently difficult to grasp, which many are unable to understand. Moreover, (1) translations are needed for the common person, and when made are the Word of God, with the above characteristics, while (2) the Hebrew and Greek texts are to be the basis for settling religious disputes. It is necessary to read WCF 1.7 and WCF 1.8 together. It is a complex and sophisticated statement. It follows in the line stretching back to Tyndale.[60] It also entails the fact that knowledge of the Hebrew of the Old Testament and the Greek of the New Testament is essential for the leaders of the church, especially the ministers of the Word. As one notable Puritan is said to have written in a presentation copy of the Bible given to a fellow minister upon his ordination, "Thou art a minister of the Word; know thy business."[61]

The Interpretation of Scripture (WCF 1.9)

Since not all of Scripture readily discloses its meaning, how are we to interpret it? Here the Assembly points to Scripture as self-interpreting. "The infallible rule of interpretation of Scripture is the Scripture itself." This follows from its being immediately inspired by God in the original *autographa*. If some principle other than Scripture were the key to its interpretation, then Scripture would not be the ultimate authority. Its divine origin also means that Scripture,

60. R. Letham, "Tyndale's Heirs? The Doctrine of Scripture at the Westminster Assembly" (paper presented to the Tyndale Society, Worcester Cathedral, 10 March 2007).

61. In a biting jibe at his Anabaptist opponents, the Westminster divine Daniel Featley proposes this syllogism: "First, by Authority, if you will dispute in Divinity, you must be able to produce the Scriptures in the Originall Languages; For no Translation is simply authenticall, or the undoubted word of God. In the undoubted word of God there can be no Error. But in Translations there may be, and are errors. The Bible Translated therefore is not the undoubted word of God but so farre onely as it agreeth with the Originall, which (as I am informed), none of you understand." Daniel Featley, *The dippers dipt, or the anabaptists duck'd and plung'd over head and eares, at a disputation in Southwark* (London: Nicholas Bourne and Richard Royston, 1646) [Wing F587], 2.

for all its diversity, is a unity. There is a common theme holding the various parts together, which in turn both justifies and requires its being interpreted as a whole. Thus, "the true and full sense of any Scripture" is one. This may also be a sideswipe against the interpretive model of Origen, propounded in his book *On First Principles*, in which he argued that the Bible is to be understood in a threefold manner akin to his trichotomist view of human nature. While the minutes say very little about the details of debate, they do recount that in S471 TH 17.7.45 the Assembly debated "the literal sense," implying that this may have been a factor behind the final draft.[62] Hence, questions about the meaning of any particular scripture are to be sought from the whole of Scripture. Difficult passages are to be understood from clearer ones.[63]

There is also the factor that the teaching of Scripture is not confined to the precise letter of the text, but also includes its sense, what may be deduced from the text (WCF 1.4). This requires interpretation. As long before as Athanasius and Basil, it was recognized that Christian doctrine was established, not by appeal to the letter of this or that text, but by understanding the sense of that to which Scripture referred, in its parts or as a whole. In this way, interpretation was a key issue before the Reformation, during it, and in the period that followed.[64]

62. The literal sense, as Aquinas understood it and so set the terms of debate thereafter, is the meaning intended by the author. At its most basic level, words signify things, which is the literal sense. However, the things signified by words can themselves signify other things, and so the Old Testament can signify the New Testament (the allegorical sense), things that signify Christ can signify what we ought to do (the moral sense), and can also refer to eternal glory (the anagogical sense). Thus a word can have multiple senses, but the key is that "all the senses are founded on one—the literal—from which alone can any argument be drawn." This literal sense can signify things that are proper or figurative. Thomas Aquinas, *Summa theologica*, Pt. 1, Q.1, Art. 10 (*St. Thomas Aquinas: Summa Theologica: Complete English Edition in Five Volumes* [Allen, TX: Christian Classics, 1948], 1:7. This understanding was shared by Reformation exegetes; see R. B. Strimple, "An Amillennial Response to Craig A. Blaising," in *Three Views on the Millennium and Beyond* (ed. D. L. Bock; Grand Rapids: Zondervan, 1999), 261–63.

63. In view of recent discussion in hermeneutics, the reader may ask where the interpreter fits into the picture. It is a matter of much debate as to how far meaning in a text is to be sought in the intention of the author, the text itself, or whether the reader either contributes to meaning or shapes the meaning in decisive fashion. To impose these discussions on our reading of the Assembly would be a classic case of anachronism, for these were not matters of debate at that time.

64. Muller, *PRRD*, 2:442–524.

The Supreme Authority of Scripture (WCF 1.10; 30.2; 31.3–4)

This final section in the Confession's first chapter reiterates the teaching of WCF 1.4. Scripture is the supreme authority because the Holy Spirit speaks there. The Spirit authored Scripture; he still speaks in Scripture today. As God has authority over humans, so the voice of God has determinative authority over the voices of his creatures, wherever they be located. Thus, all religious controversies are to be determined by the Holy Spirit speaking in Scripture, in the original languages of the Old Testament (Hebrew) and New Testament (Greek) (cf. 1.8). All decrees of church councils are to be examined in the light of Scripture. All the writings of the church fathers are to be considered in terms of how far they correspond to the voice of the Holy Spirit speaking in Scripture. All human teachings of whatever origin—the antinomians are primarily in view—are similarly to be examined. Moreover, we are to "rest" in the judgment of Scripture; that is, it is to be our authority, too. This is a comprehensive assertion of biblical authority. The Assembly obviously expected the papacy to submit to Scripture.[65]

Of particular note is the connection between the Holy Spirit and the Bible; there is no separation. The Spirit speaks in Scripture; Scripture is not viewed in isolation from the dynamic activity of God. As Warfield comments, it is not that the Holy Spirit speaks occasionally in Scripture, nor that he speaks through some passages rather than others. It is not—in twentieth-century terms—a matter to be reduced to the level of existential encounter. Rather, the Bible is both the rule that governs us and the judge that adjudicates.[66] Since the Holy Spirit speaks in Scripture so completely and continuously, the Word of God is living and dynamic and cannot be categorized as a dead letter.[67]

Later chapters in the Confession elaborate further on the authority of Scripture in the church. Church censures are to be carried out, when necessary, by the Word (WCF 30.2). Synods and councils may be called to govern the church, in which the voice of

65. At the present time, this expectation could equally be applied to biblical scholarship and theology.

66. Warfield, *Westminster Assembly*, 254–55.

67. See Spear, "Word and Spirit in the Westminster Confession."

the Holy Spirit speaking in the Hebrew text of the Old Testament and the Greek of the New Testament is to be heeded and rested in as the supreme judge. Such decrees, if agreeable to Scripture, "are to be received with reverence and submission," not only because they conform to Scripture, but because the power of such synods as an ordinance of God stems from Scripture (WCF 31.3). Indeed, since synods may be in error, all their judgments and determinations are to be examined in the light of Scripture, for that alone is our rule of faith and practice (WCF 31.4).

The Scope of Scripture (LC 5; cf. WCF 1.7)

What do the Scriptures principally teach? Thus asks the Larger Catechism. Its answer is that it teaches what we are to believe about God, and what duty God requires of us. Faith and obedience—that is the principle on which the structure of the Larger Catechism is based. Questions 6–90 are devoted to what people ought to believe about God, while the theme of questions 91–196 is what the Scriptures require as the duty of man.

What We Ought to Believe Concerning God (LC 6–90)

In summary, we are to believe in God, the Trinity (LC 6–11), and the decrees of God (LC 12–14), which encompass the rest of the section: creation (LC 15–17), providence (LC 18–20), the fall and sin, actual and original (LC 21–29), and the covenant of grace (LC 30–36), which in turn entails all that follows, not only to LC 90, but to the end of the Catechism: the person and work of Christ, the mediator of the covenant of grace (LC 36–59), whose work includes his incarnation (LC 37–42), the three offices (LC 43–45), his humiliation and exaltation (LC 46–56), and the benefits he has procured by his mediation (LC 57–59); and the outflow of Christ's work as mediator in the visible and invisible church (LC 60–65), and union and communion with Christ in grace and glory (LC 66–90). In this last section, the *ordo salutis*, which is described in logical and more sequential terms in the Confession, is here addressed as an aspect of union and communion with Christ. This material corresponds to WCF 2–18, 32–33, with elements of WCF 24–26, 30–31.

What the Scriptures Require as the Duty of Man (LC 91–196)

Here the Assembly teaches that Scripture requires obedience to God's revealed will (LC 91), which is found in the moral law, revealed initially to Adam (LC 92–97), and is summarized in the Ten Commandments (LC 98–99). There follows an exposition of the Decalogue, both in its positive and negative dimensions (LC 100–152). The rest of the Catechism is devoted to the outward means of grace (LC 153–96), in the observance of which God's revealed will is also obeyed. These means are the Word—the reading of Scripture, but especially the preaching of it (LC 153–60); the sacraments (LC 161–77), consisting of baptism (LC 165–67) and the Lord's Supper (LC 168–77); and prayer (LC 178–96), focusing on the Lord's Prayer (LC 186–96). This second part of the Catechism follows the traditional catechetical form, in which the Ten Commandments and the Lord's Prayer are two of the three component parts. The third, the Apostles' Creed, is missing, for reasons we shall shortly discuss. This second major section corresponds roughly to WCF 19–23, 27–29.

This division is borne out by the content of the Confession. There Scripture is said to be the object of saving faith and the yardstick of good works, the criterion for both what we are to believe and what we are to do. In the first place, saving faith is directed to "whatsoever is revealed in the Word" (WCF 14.2). This is in tandem with, and subordinate to, "receiving, and resting upon Christ alone"—which we will discuss at length in chapter 12. Similarly, assurance of salvation is founded on the truth of the divine promises of salvation found in Holy Scripture (WCF 18.2).

Moreover, Scripture provides the basis for Christian living and for Christian liberty and worship. Good works are what are commanded by God's holy Word, rather than what humans may devise (WCF 16.1). This is far from restrictive—in fact, it is supremely liberating, for it frees Christians from any obligation to be bound by anything that is contrary to Scripture, whatever the tyranny might be (WCF 20.2).

Thus, only Scripture can prescribe how worship is to be conducted (WCF 21.1), freeing us from any obligation to overbearing ecclesiastical authorities such as Archbishop Laud. Prayer must be according to God's revealed will (WCF 21.3), while the reading of Scripture and the preaching and hearing of it are an integral and indispensable part of the ordinary worship of the church (WCF 21.5; LC 155, 159), in contrast with the attempts of several bishops to restrict it in the preceding years. The reading of the words of institution of the sacraments as recorded in the New Testament is an essential element of their observance (WCF 27.3; 28.3). Marriage cannot lawfully occur if it is within the degrees of consanguinity and affinity forbidden by the Scriptures (WCF 24.4). These commands, together with the divine promises of salvation, are to be found in Scripture (WCF 4.2; cf. LC 17; WCF 7.1–3).

These factors, taken together, indicate that the Assembly viewed the Bible, not in isolation, but as integrally bound up with the whole of God's revelation of himself for us and our salvation. Thus, when we come to consider the object of saving faith (WCF 14.2), which is presented as whatsoever God has revealed in his Word *and* Christ, whom we receive and rest on for salvation, it is not to be viewed in some dualistic sense, as if Christ and the Bible were competing for our attention. For the Assembly, Scripture is subordinate to Christ as the means by which God draws us to himself in Christ to be saved. In this, as Muller indicates, "there is a continuity between the Reformation and Protestant orthodox language of Word that does not look in the direction of the neoorthodox usage."[68] In fact, Muller concludes, "the orthodox tread a fine doctrinal balance in their distinction between the essential, the unwritten and written, the external and internal Word."[69]

The Word and the Spirit

The Word and the Holy Spirit are coordinate at every point in salvation: the Spirit who authored Scripture employs the Word to effect

68. Muller, *PRRD*, 2:182.
69. Ibid., 183.

his saving purposes. The Word and Spirit effectually reveal God (LC 2), this being effected by Christ according to his prophetic office (LC 43; SC 24). God effectually calls by his Word and Spirit (WCF 10.1, 4; cf. LC 2, 43), the ministry of the Word being effectual and saving faith being produced through the Holy Spirit (WCF 14.1; LC 67, 72, 155). In turn, Christ governs the hearts of his elect by his Word and Spirit (WCF 8.8). Sanctification is by the Holy Spirit through the Word (WCF 13.1). Good works are such as are commanded by the Word (WCF 16.1), and the ability to do them comes wholly from the Spirit of Christ (WCF 16.3).

The Word of God, committed to writing in Holy Scripture, is the source of our knowledge of God, together with the work of the Holy Spirit, who makes God's salvation effectual. Scripture reveals what is pleasing to God. It is determinative for worship and Christian living. It provides the epistemological basis of the Christian faith. In it is made known the covenant of grace, the mediation of Christ, and the way of salvation.

Scripture and the Creeds

On the relationship between Scripture and tradition, the Assembly gives clear primacy to Scripture as the Word of God (cf. 1.6 on the "traditions of men"). However, there was great confusion at the Assembly on this point. It was by no means its finest hour. The divines came close to deviating from the rest of the Reformed churches and placing themselves outside the historic Christian tradition.

The problem surfaced long before the Confession of Faith and the Catechisms were on the agenda. Shortly after the Assembly was convened, during the debates on the Thirty-Nine Articles, the question arose as to the place of the three ancient creeds—the Apostles' Creed, the Nicene Creed, and the Athanasian Creed—in the life of the Church of England. These creeds were the subject of article 8 of the Thirty-Nine Articles.

Before discussion on article 8 was reached, the issue came to a head in the debates on article 2, on the phrase "Christ suffered," and on article 3, on Christ's descent into hell. Debate focused on a number of points. First was the question of whether the revised Articles should contain proofs from Scripture or be left as they were. The committee thought scriptural proof was unnecessary, but the Assembly voted that they be included.[70] Second, there came extended debate on whether the article adequately expressed the extent of Christ's sufferings of soul.[71] The Assembly adopted the position that no sense could be made of the article without express support from Scripture—what might be termed "something approaching biblicism," according to Van Dixhoorn.[72] It was a stance that seems at loggerheads with the later focus on the sense of Scripture in WCF 1.4, which takes the position that express textual support is not necessary for the whole counsel of God for his glory, our salvation, faith, and life. Eventually, a proposed clause expressing the opinion that Christ's sufferings were not sufferings of soul was revoked "for feare of offence to foraine churches."[73] According to Lightfoot, debate on article 3 "grew very earnest" as to whether the article should be entirely expunged—an astonishing proposal, given the Assembly's task to *defend* the Articles. Those who favored expunging were "generally opposed." Some lobbied for an altered translation of the creed. After a deferral of the question on 28 July 1643, the matter was taken up again on 17 August. The divines considered whether the clause should be expunged, altered, or retained. Eventually, the following statement was approved: "As Christ died for us, & was buried, so also it is to be beleved that he continued in the state of the dead & under the power & dominion of death untill his resurrection: which otherwaies hath bin expressed, he descended into hell."[74]

As Van Dixhoorn comments, the relationship between Scripture and the creeds was not self-evident for some divines. The report from the Third Committee said that it couldn't provide scriptural support for article 8, which recommended the creeds,[75] even though Thomas

---

70. S3 W 12.7.43; Van Dixhoorn, 1:215–16.

71. S6 M 17.7.43 through S13 F 28.7.43; Van Dixhoorn, 1:216–33; Lightfoot's journal, in Van Dixhoorn, 2:8–17.

72. Van Dixhoorn, 1:229.

73. S12 TH 27.7.43 and S13 F 28.7.43; Lightfoot's journal, in Van Dixhoorn, 2:15–17; see also 1:231.

74. Lightfoot, manuscript journal, fo.19v. See Van Dixhoorn, 1:232.

75. Van Dixhoorn, 1:226.

Rogers had popularized such a set sixty-five years before. Van Dixhoorn points out that the longest-running debate in the Assembly
was on the place of the three creeds, yet this was reduced to a single
paragraph by Carruthers.[76] Article 8, "Of the Three Creeds," states,
"The Three Creeds, *Nicene* Creed, *Athanasius's* Creed, and that
which is commonly called the *Apostles'* Creed, ought thoroughly to
be received and believed; for they may be proved by most certain
warrants of holy Scripture."[77]

The debate on this article produced a week of tumultuous agitation
and disagreement, from S30 F 18.8.43 to S35 F 25.8.43. Lightfoot
records in his journal "a long agitation on translating the creeds anew
& about some gloss in preface," and on the concluding words of the
Athanasian Creed, "which seem to be something harsh," but it was
concluded in S29 TH 17.8.43 that the creeds should be printed at
the conclusion of the Thirty-Nine Articles.[78] A few days later, in S32
TU 22.8.43, exceptions were raised to the article, and those who
had exceptions were requested to bring in their doubts the following
day. When the excepters raised their doubts, the whole day (S33 W
23.8.43) was taken up with "long & vehement debates & yet nothing
determined." Also on the next day (S34 TH 24.8.43), the Assembly
was thrown "into agitation againe: & was canvassed exceeding much
and long."[79]

It was argued that the phrase "they ought thoroughly to be received"
set them on an equality with Scripture.[80] According to Lightfoot, objections were raised by some on the use of the Apostles' Creed at baptism,
at confirmation, and after the reading of the Gospels.[81] Toward the
end, in S35 F25.8.43, a conciliatory proposal was made, that "the

76. Carruthers, *Everyday Work*, 105–6.

77. What is popularly known as the Nicene Creed dates from the Council of Constantinople
in 381, although the first explicit record of its existence is from the Council of Chalcedon in
451. It had for long been received by both Eastern and Western churches. The Athanasian Creed
was not composed by Athanasius, but probably by a disciple of Augustine; while accepted in
the West, it has never secured the same status in the East. The Apostles' Creed is a Latin creed,
owing its uncertain origins to baptismal formulas probably developed in the early centuries of
the church at Rome.

78. Van Dixhoorn, 2:37.

79. Ibid., 2:38.

80. Ibid., 1:233.

81. The creeds were used extensively in the Church of England, but in Scotland only the
Apostles' Creed was featured (Van Dixhoorn, 1.233–36). However, there were no Scottish

matter of them" may be proved by "most certain" warrants of Holy Scripture, replacing the claim that the creeds themselves could be proved by Scripture. The proposal was opposed on the grounds that it separated the theology of the creeds from their statements. Many pressed for a new translation of the creeds.[82]

The Assembly then resolved to print the creeds at the end of the Thirty-Nine Articles. But there were votes, revocations, and yet more votes. Confusion reigned. Those whom Van Dixhoorn terms "the excepters," who were not personally identified by Lightfoot, opposed almost everything, including the anathemas in the Athanasian Creed, the theology of the creeds, and the names of the creeds. According to Lightfoot, the main issue was the mandatory use of creeds. The excepters opposed the imposition of any forms, in this coming close to sectarianism and Socinianism.[83] A vote that the creeds are "thoroughly to be received" was revoked; the excepters again wanted (unsuccessfully) reference to the "matter" of the creeds inserted, freeing them from the creeds themselves while retaining the substance of doctrine to which the creeds referred. In the end, the settlement of the question of article 8 was put off until the Assembly had finished the revisions of all thirty-nine articles. This never happened. So "the creeds were left in an ambiguous position, as were the Thirty-Nine Articles."[84]

Despite the pledge to Parliament that the Apostles' Creed would be included, neither the Larger Catechism nor the Shorter Catechism includes anything about creeds.[85] This is particularly notable since the classic catechetical form consisted of the Apostles' Creed, the Ten Commandments, and the Lord's Prayer. The Westminster Catechisms incorporate the latter two into their structure, but not the Apostles' Creed. This can hardly be anything other than studied indifference

---

members of the Assembly, and at this time there was no onus to unite the doctrine and worship of the two churches, since the Solemn League and Covenant lay in the future.

82. Van Dixhoorn, 1:238.

83. The sectarian danger was that of cutting adrift from the confession of the historic Christian church, expressed in its creeds. If it was not acceptable to confess the ancient creeds, how, it might be asked, could it coherently be claimed to share the faith that the creeds confessed? This was not a question confined to the use of creeds in worship, but involved their function in belief.

84. Van Dixhoorn, 1:251–52.

85. Nor was there any reference to the creeds in the Directory for the Publick Worship of God.

and deliberate exclusion. It indicates that a significant portion of the Assembly's members were verging on a separatist mentality and that a firm historical consciousness was in the process of being lost. This was by no means uniform; there were sufficient members with a thorough knowledge of, and appreciation for, the past teachings of the church, the Reformed churches, and the church fathers to prevent this from being a blanket judgment. However, it is unfortunate that they were unable to carry the Assembly with them, and it weakens the claim that it is a body thoroughly representative of the historic Christian church. It demonstrates that "the divines did not approach the Scriptures and theological method in a uniform manner." These differences pointed to division over the relationship between Scripture and tradition, and even impacted, via the sufferings of Christ, the atonement.[86]

Van Dixhoorn points out that in their published writings the Assembly men all use the creeds, cite them, and support them. They never call for their removal or revision. Yet "most notable about the Assembly's corporate writings, by way of contrast, is not their contribution to an ongoing conversation, but their attempt to end the conversation by removing the creeds from the life of the church."[87] It is probable that this was an instance of groupthink, where the dynamic of pressure from a minority of strong voices carries a larger body with it, with many suspending their critical faculties and disregarding the consequences of their words and actions. It seems to be self-contradictory, for the Assembly was to spend several years painstakingly composing a Confession of Faith and two Catechisms in order to provide a solid foundation for the Church of England, while at the same time cutting the ground from under its feet by undermining the principial basis for producing such documents in the first place.

These debates aroused great concern among continental Reformed churches. It seemed that separatism was rife and was dominating the Assembly's discussions. In view of this, "the Dutch churches wrote to the Assembly arguing for the legitimacy of theological and liturgical forms."[88] On 4 December 1644, a volume was sent on their behalf,

86. C. B. Van Dixhoorn, "New Taxonomies of the Westminster Assembly (1643–52): The Creedal Controversy as Case Study," *RRR* 6 (2004): 82–106, esp. 103–6.
87. Van Dixhoorn, 1:265–68.
88. Ibid., 1:268.

written by Guilielmus Apollonius.[89] Apollonius produced a raft of evidence that the Assembly was in imminent danger of diverging from the settled teaching of Reformed churches throughout Europe from the time of Calvin onward. In the case in point, he argued strongly that it was a legitimate exercise of church power, supported by Scripture and Reformed theology, to make confessions of faith that were ecclesiastically binding. At the same time, these creeds and confessions were not of ultimate or absolute authority, being subject to Scripture. But they represented the digest of Christian teaching, and to digress from them was to err from the path of true doctrine. If anyone entertained doubts about the validity of this or that, he should keep the matter to himself until such time as the church as a whole was able to meet and consider the matter. But as for the validity of the creeds as such, Apollonius was able to present evidence on such a scale as to undermine the ideas of those who wanted to jettison them in the name of the Bible.

Within the parameters of the doctrine of Scripture propounded later in the Confession of Faith and the Larger Catechism, objection to the article on the creeds could theoretically have been raised if it had been considered that the contents of the creeds were not in conformity with the whole counsel of God found in Scripture. However, to object to the article as such made no sense, since the basis for its assessment of the creeds was that "they may be proved by most certain warrants of holy Scripture." The article conformed to the Confession's later position: if the creeds were in harmony with Scripture, then they ought to be received and believed. The Assembly betrayed confused thinking and appears to have veered in a direction out of harmony with its later considered judgment and in divergence from the other Reformed churches. Fortunately, when Apollonius came to London in August 1645, the Assembly invited him to attend its debates to receive public thanks.[90] The vote was unanimous—which was regarded by observers as unique. Evidently, on consideration the Assembly found his strictures to its taste.[91]

89. Guilielmus Apollonius, *A consideration of certaine controversies at this time Agitated in the Kingdome of England, concerning the government of the Church of God, written at the command and appointment of the Walachrian Classis. And sent from the Wallachrian Churches, to the Synod at London. Octob.16.1644* (London: G. M. for Tho. Underhill, 1645) [Wing (2nd ed., 1994) A3535], 130–51.

90. Van Dixhoorn, 6:170, 173.

91. Carruthers, *Everyday Work*, 71.

8

God the Trinity

*We believe in one God the Father Almighty . . . and in one
Lord Jesus Christ, the only-begotten Son of God, begotten by
his Father before all ages, Light from Light, true God from true
God, begotten not created, consubstantial with the Father . . .
and we believe in the Holy Spirit, the Lord and giver of life,
who proceeds from the Father, who with the Father and the Son
together is worshipped and glorified.*

The One Living and True God (WCF 2.1; LC 7; SC 4)

This majestic chapter starts out with a vigorous assertion of the
unity of the one God. This follows the tradition of the Western church
since Augustine.[1] Equally as prominent is the stress on God's infinitude
and uniqueness (LC 7; SC 4). WCF 3.1 presents a balance between
the infinitude of God ("immutable, immense, eternal, incomprehensible"), his sovereignty ("working all things according to the counsel
of his . . . will, for his own glory"), his holiness, his love and grace,
and his justice. He is full of grace, but he "will by no means clear the
guilty." Lurking in the background is the problem of sin, for human
corruption has provoked divine judgment, God's holy and settled
response to human sin.

1. See Letham, *The Holy Trinity*, 184ff.

One statement here has given rise to many questions. God is said to be "without body, parts, or passions." The meaning of "passions" is not entirely clear. The statement has suggested the idea of a God who is devoid of feeling, cold and detached like a judge, rather than a warm, loving Father. First, in the seventeenth century the word was used in a geometrical sense, referring, for example, to the passions of a parallelogram.[2] Similarly, the literature of the period frequently refers to the passions of the sun, moon, planets, and stars, in which their positions and movements are in view.[3] If used in this sense, the word would signify that God cannot be bounded; he has no spatial dimensions, since he transcends space and time. Since the phrase denies that God has a body or parts, this is a plausible meaning. A second possibility is that God cannot be the passive recipient of actions that impose themselves on him. He is not constrained by external forces, since he is sovereign over all that is other than himself. If the word is taken from the Latin, it could be a derivation from the perfect passive participle *passus, -a, -um* of the verb *patior*, which has a wide semantic field, but in all cases signifies some aspect of submission to outside forces, seen in such things as suffering. That Christ's sufferings were called his passion was commonplace at the time, but the word was also used for human suffering, as in the case of James, Marquess of Montrose, in George Wishart's memoir.[4] However, this reference might be a little odd in the immediate context, in conjunction with the denial that God has a body and parts. Third, it could be an anglicization of *passio, -onis*, meaning "natural effect," or "natural affections,"

2. See *The Oxford English Dictionary.*

3. Humphry Daniel, *An almanack for the year of mans redemption 1654: Various habitudes, passions and configurations of the coelestial bodyes, are artificially demonstrated* (London: T. W. for the Company of Stationers, 1654) [Wing A1582]; John Gadbury, *Prognostikon, or, An astrological prediction of the various changes likely to occur in most parts of Europe this present year 1658 from the manifold passions and positions of the coelestial movers, viz. the sun, moon and planets* (London: W. Godbid for the Company of Stationers, 1658) [Wing A1781]; Sir George Wharton, *Hemeroscopeion anni intercalaris 1652 containing the English calendar, and daily motions of the planets, &c in longitude, in latitude: their manifold passions and positions* (London: J. Grismond for the Company of Stationers, 1652[1651]) [Wing (2nd ed. 1994) A2667].

4. George Wishart, *Montrose redivivus, or The portraicture of James late Marquess of Montrose, Earl of Kincardin, &c. 1. In his actions, in the years 1644. 1645. and 1646. for Charles the First. 2. In his passions, in the years 1649. 1650. for Charles the Second K. of Scots.* (London: Printed for Jo. Ridley, at the Castle in Fleet-street, neer Ram-alley, 1652) [Wing (2nd ed., 1994) W3124].

relating to the mind or emotions, meaning that God is either incapable of the kind of emotions to which human beings are susceptible or, if capable, chooses not to have them. Since this is a cognate noun of *patior*, it may also have the connotation that God is not subject to the fluctuations and vagaries that accompany such experiences.[5] It may or may not be significant that Assembly member Edward Reynolds wrote a popular book on the passions and faculties of the soul in 1640.[6] Reynolds describes human passions as natural, involving an ebb and flow, and moral, for they can be either good or evil, but their proper place is in subordination to reason.[7] He regards its synonyms as "appetite" and "desire." Passions are the best servants, but the worst masters. However, as created, they are good: "naturall motion, ordained for the perfection or conservation of the Creature."[8] Two ideas here are prominent for Reynolds, that of motion (ebb and flow) and something distinctly creaturely, both of which are also present in the astronomical sense.

The proof text cited by the Assembly is Acts 14:11–15, where Paul and Barnabas rebuke the Lycaonians for attempting to offer sacrifice to them in the mistaken belief that they were gods. Paul stresses the uniqueness of God and the impropriety of the Lycaonians' actions. He says, "We also are men of like passions with you" (AV). In the Greek text to which the divines would have had access, the word is *homoiopatheis*, meaning "of the same kind of feelings or desires." Both in the biblical text and in the citation by the Assembly, the focus is on the difference between God and human beings. Human emotions may be an integral part of this, but the sense cannot be restricted to that.

5. It was commonly used for the passions of the mind or soul. See René Descartes, *The passions of the soule* (London: Printed for A. C. and are to be sold by J. Martin, and J. Ridley, at the Castle in Fleetstreet neer Ram-Alley, 1650) [Wing (2nd ed., 1994) D1134]; Thomas Hobbes, *Humane nature or, The fundamental elements of policie. Being a discoverie of the faculties, acts, and passions of the soul of man, from their original causes, according to such philosophical principles as are not commonly known or asserted* (London: T. Newcomb for Fra: Bowman of Oxon, 1650) [Wing (2nd ed.) H2242]; Thomas Jordan, *Pictures of passions, fancies, & affections Poetically deciphered in variety of characters* (London: Robert Wood, 1641) [Wing (2nd ed., 1994) J1052].

6. Edward Reynolds, *A treatise of the passions and faculties of the soule of man With the severall dignities and corruptions thereunto belonging* (London: R. H[earne and John Norton] for Robert Bostock, 1640) [STC (2nd ed.) 20938].

7. Ibid., 41–43.

8. Ibid., 45–47.

The meaning in the Confession seems to me to run along the following lines. God is not to be compared to the creature. He is spiritual and invisible. Immediately after our phrase, he is described as immutable, immense, eternal, incomprehensible, and almighty—all attributes that set him apart from his creation. In this way, he is without body and parts; he is not a composite being, he does not have the spatial and temporal limitations that are an unavoidable aspect of creaturely existence. He is therefore "without passions" in the sense that he is not, nor can he be, subject to the limits or external constraints to which the creation is restricted, to the changeable locations, or the ebb and flow, of human feelings or appetites.

However, a question must be posed as to whether the Assembly takes fully into account the astonishing fact of the incarnation. By becoming flesh, the Son has taken into permanent union our humanity, body and soul. God now has a *human* body and soul and experiences *human* thoughts and emotions. We are reminded of the heresy of Nestorianism, in which the deity and humanity of Christ were distinguished to such an extent that the unity of Christ's incarnate person was undermined. Is there a trace of Nestorianism here? This has been something of a tendency of Reformed Christology.[9]

It is good that the section states that God is "most loving," for the love of God is not mentioned in either the Larger Catechism[10] or the Shorter Catechism. This is an astonishing omission. It can only be described as culpable. John makes an absolute statement

9. A. B. Bruce lists among the leading peculiarities of Reformed Christology a stress on the distinctness of the two natures of Christ, which engendered the comment by the Lutherans that for the Reformed "the two natures were simply glued together like two boards, without any real communion." Bruce, *The Humiliation of Christ in Its Physical, Ethical, and Official Aspects* (Edinburgh: T. & T. Clark, 1905), 120. T. G. Weinandy, writing of Calvin, denies that he is a Nestorian, as he has been accused of being, but comments that "he was forced to give a 'Nestorian' flavor to his interpretation of the communication of idioms so as, like Nestorius, to protect the integrity of the natures." He agrees with E. D. Willis and J. Witte that "Calvin has no clear concept of the ontological foundation of the Incarnation." Weinandy, *Does God Suffer?* (Notre Dame, IN: University of Notre Dame Press, 2000), 188, where he cites E. D. Willis, *Calvin's Catholic Christology* (Leiden: E. J. Brill, 1966), 3–5, and J. Witte, "Die Christologie Calvins," in *Das Konzil von Chalkedon: Geschichte und Gegenwart* (ed. A. Grillmeier and H. Bacht; 3 vols.; Würzburg: Echter-Verlag, 1951–54), 3:458–59. See also my own observations on Calvin's comments on 1 Corinthians 15:28, in *The Holy Trinity*, 255–56.

10. Apart from tangential references in LC 13, 30.

about God in 1 John 4:8—"God is love." This is, of course, entirely consistent with his holiness, justice, and infinitude. He will not spare the guilty. His wrath against sin is real and terrifyingly awesome. Yet he *is* love. The Trinitarian persons are eternally in indivisible union and communion; their relations are pure love. The Father loves the Son, the Son loves the Father, the Son loves the Holy Spirit, the Father loves the Holy Spirit, the Holy Spirit loves the Son, the Holy Spirit loves the Father—all in indivisible union. God's wrath is the settled response of his holy nature to human sin, activated by human disobedience, but he is not wrathful in himself toward himself. God's holiness is his utter separation from his creation; he is holy precisely *in relation* to what he has made. However, he freely created. The universe had a beginning; God did not. In himself—in the eternal relations of the undivided Trinity—he is perfect love. And neither catechism mentions it! The Larger Catechism later refers to the decree of God in election as proceeding from his love (LC 13, 30), but any reference to love is missing from its description of God's character. The Shorter Catechism, the most widely read of all the Westminster documents, makes no mention of the love of God whatever, apart from a cursory and oblique statement in SC 36. True, God is "gracious, merciful, longsuffering, abundant in goodness [SC] and truth [LC]," forgives iniquity, and rewards those who diligently seek him, while the chief end of man is to enjoy him, but noticeably absent is mention of his love.

God's All-sufficient Sovereignty (WCF 2.2)

WCF 2.2 is a towering declaration of the supremacy of God over all his creation. He has all life, glory, goodness, and blessedness in and of himself. This entails his being the standard by which we are to make moral judgments. He is all-sufficient, the sole fountain of all being. He needs nothing outside himself, whereas we depend utterly on him. His sovereignty over all he has made will come to expression in WCF 3 onward, on the decrees of God and their outworking in creation, providence, and grace.

God's knowledge is infallible and independent of his creatures. In this, the Assembly rejects the Socinian denial of God's foreknowledge.[11] He is most holy, meaning that he is utterly distinct and separate from his creatures, and so he has the right to require from them whatever he pleases. This section is a litmus test of a theology. LC 7 covers the same ground. LC 8 focuses on the oneness of God. The doctrine of God's simplicity—teaching that God is not composite, for he cannot be divided into parts less than the whole of who he is—was held by both the Eastern and the Western churches, despite other differences between them, and apart from the particularly dominant form in which Aquinas propounded it.[12]

The Trinity (WCF 2.3; LC 8–12; SC 5–6)

WCF 2.3 seems almost perfunctory; yet the doctrine of the Trinity is distinctively the *Christian* doctrine of God, which sets it apart from Judaism and Islam. Two comments are in order. First, its brevity demonstrates the divines' acceptance of the Council of Constantinople's resolution of the fourth-century Trinitarian controversy. As the reference to the *filioque* indicates, this acceptance is firmly in the tradition of the Western church. Second, it is at least arguable whether this statement would have been better placed at 2.1. In its present location, the Trinity is introduced only after God has been described in terms that could equally be accepted by Muslims or orthodox Jews. The distinctively *Christian* doctrine of God is almost an afterthought.

In my judgment, Torrance is right that had the Confession begun with the Trinity it would have done more justice to God as a God of love.[13] Instead, it gives greatest prominence to God as omnipotent Creator and Judge, rather than as the Father.[14] Torrance comments that "the doctrine of the Trinity was tacked on to a doctrine of God," although he acknowledges its "awesome sense of the sheer majesty

11. The recent movement known as open theism, championed by Clark Pinnock, Gregory Boyd, John Sanders, and David Bassinger, is in reality a resurrection of the Socinian heresy of the sixteenth and seventeenth centuries.
12. See Letham, *The Holy Trinity*, 228–37.
13. T. F. Torrance, *Scottish Theology*, 131.
14. Ibid., 133.

of God."[15] This weakness means that in our own day the Confession lacks the focus to provide the tools to confront Islam effectively. On the other hand, it is balanced by the Larger Catechism, where the Trinity is more prominent. Unfortunately, however, few read the Larger Catechism, let alone allow its particular interests to impact their view of the Confession.

Part of the explanation of this question is the Assembly's place in the Western tradition. It was commonplace in the West to discuss the Trinity only after lengthy consideration of the existence and attributes of the one God. This tradition went back at least as far as Aquinas, who, in his *Summa contra gentiles*, considered God in the first of the four books, holding back discussion of the Trinity until Book Four. Then, in his *Summa theologiae*, while his treatment of the Trinity is an integral part of his doctrine of God, it still follows the discussion of his existence and attributes. Moreover, he is governed by such a powerful view of the divine simplicity that some critics question whether he is really able to hold a viable doctrine of the Trinity.[16] This pattern, by which the Trinity was in a semidetached relationship to the overall doctrine of God, became fairly standard in the Western church. Richard Muller examines the orthodox Reformed theologians of the seventeenth century and finds that it was typical of them to defer discussion of the Trinity. He points to the traditional basis in the Western church for this arrangement, and argues for its coherence as an appropriate order for knowledge, teaching, and discussion.[17] Criticism of the Confession at this point needs to be tempered in the light of the Larger Catechism and the ways in which Trinitarianism underlies the rest of the theological spectrum, as we will see shortly.

There is virtually nothing in the minutes on the debates on the committee reports on God and the Trinity in the Confession. These took place from S472 F 18.7.45am to S474 TH 24.7.45. In S480 TU 5.8.45am there was a debate about God in connection with the Catechism. It is here that the record is more interesting.[18]

15. Ibid., 131.
16. C. Hughes, *On a Complex Theory of a Simple God: An Investigation in Aquinas' Philosophical Theology* (Ithaca, NY: Cornell University Press, 1989).
17. Muller, *PRRD*, 4:143ff.
18. See Mitchell and Struthers, eds., *Minutes of the Sessions*, 114–18.

A number of years ago, in the first edition of *A New Systematic Theology of the Christian Faith*, Robert L. Reymond suggested that the Assembly may have rejected the doctrines of the eternal generation of the Son and the eternal procession of the Holy Spirit as espoused in the ecumenical councils. Instead, he proposed that it chose to follow Calvin, who, Reymond argued, considered the language of the Niceno-Constantinopolitan settlement at this point as speculative.[19] While Reymond withdrew these claims in the second edition of his systematics, they are sufficiently far-reaching to require investigation. Elsewhere, I have demonstrated that Calvin was in agreement with the Council of Constantinople (AD 381) on both of these doctrines.[20] In this respect, there is no dichotomy between Nicene Trinitarianism and Reformed Trinitarianism.

That Westminster did not depart from Nicene Trinitarianism is clear in the Larger Catechism. Question 10 asks, "What are the personal properties of the three persons in the Godhead?" Answer: "It is proper to the Father to beget the Son, and to the Son to be begotten of the Father, and to the Holy Spirit to proceed from the Father and the Son from all eternity."

The answer explicitly states that the Spirit proceeds eternally from the Father and the Son. In theory, it might be argued that while the Son is said to be begotten of the Father, this did not occur "from all eternity." Such a reading cannot be sustained for a number of reasons. First, it would be incongruous for the Spirit to proceed from eternity, but the Son's generation not to be from eternity. This is even more improbable since the key historically to the resolution of the Trinitarian crisis was the settlement of the deity and personal relations of the Son, after which the deity and personal relations of the Holy Spirit followed more readily. It would have been absurd for the Assembly to have supported the eternal generation of the Holy Spirit, but not the eternal generation of the Son. Second, Reymond's suggestion would require no comma before "from all eternity," thus restricting the reference of the phrase to the immediately preceding statement concerning the Holy Spirit. Although there is no comma

19. Reymond, *A New Systematic Theology*, 324–41.
20. Letham, *The Holy Trinity*, 252–68.

as the text is commonly printed today, Van Dixhoorn has discovered that the majority of early manuscripts include a comma before "from all eternity,"[21] thereby supporting the final phrase as covering the relations of the Son as well as the Holy Spirit. Reymond's suggestion might also require a semicolon after the second mention of "Father," separating the relations of the Son from the relations of the Spirit, but there is none at that point.

However, even if a comma did not precede "from all eternity," the draft questions for the Larger Catechism prove that the generation of the Son was understood as extending from all eternity. Presented in S708 TU 15.9.46pm, they read:

> Ordered: "9 Q: Is the sonne equall with the Father in the Godhead? A: The sonne of God who is the only begotten of the Father from all eternity, is true God equall with the Father."
> Ordered: "10 Q: Is the Holy Ghost also God, equall with the Father and the sonne? A: The Holy Ghoste who from all eternity proceeds from the Father and the sonne is also true God, equall with the father and the sonne."[22]

These questions show that the Assembly's committee understood the Son to be begotten of the Father from eternity, and that this in no way diminishes his equality with the Father or his true deity. No evidence suggests that the body as a whole had a different view.

Reymond also argued that the absence of the phrase of the Creed of Nicaea referring to the Son as "God of God" supports his thesis. This phrase, he argued, implies an element of subordination for the Son; moreover, it was speculative and went beyond the bounds of Scripture. He missed the point that the phrase is also absent from the Thirty-Nine Articles, both from article 1, "Of Faith in the Holy Trinity," and article 2, "Of the Word or Son of God, which was made very Man." I have yet to hear anyone advance the notion that the Articles diverged from Nicene Trinitarianism, still less since they conspicuously support the

---

21. Van Dixhoorn, 1:259n186. The punctuation of Bod Nalson 22, fol.133v., has a comma, supporting the generation of the Son from eternity, but Bod Nalson 22, fo. 159v., does not. The earlier printed version of c. 22 Oct 1647 and the c. 14 April 1648 Parliamentary printing with proof texts support fo.133v.
22. Van Dixhoorn, 6:357.

Niceno-Constantinopolitan Creed in article 8 as provable "by most certain warrants of holy Scripture." Even more striking, the phrase is absent also from the Creed of the Council of Constantinople, popularly known as "the Nicene Creed." If Reymond's thesis were correct, the Nicene Creed would reject its own Trinitarianism! Moreover, the phrase was from the Creed of Nicaea (AD 325), propounded at the very start of the Trinitarian crisis, but jettisoned along the way. I have demonstrated elsewhere that Calvin defends this creed against the Italian anti-Trinitarians.[23]

That the eternal relations of the three Trinitarian persons were not a matter of controversy at the Assembly, and that the classic Trinitarian settlement was fully accepted by the divines, is evident from the absence of any record of discord on the matter. For instance, in the debate on article 2 of the Thirty-Nine Articles, in S7 TU 18.7.43, in which the Son is said to be "begotten from everlasting of the Father," while there was, according to Lightfoot, "a great debating," this surrounded the later reference to the sufferings of Christ and whether it should be stated that he suffered in his soul. There is no record of controversy—or even debate—over the reference to the eternal generation of the Son.[24] In Morris's words, the Assembly adopted "the Nicene or Chalcedonian description, reproduced almost literally in the Confession . . . as the only one which in any adequate sense embodies or unifies these various forms and aspects of the revelation."[25]

The Catechisms summarily state the unity of God (LC 8; SC 5) and that he is three persons (LC 9; SC 6), the three being the one true God (LC 9). As such, they are of one substance, power, and eternity, equal in power and glory, but distinguished by their respective personal properties. These properties, or relations, are discussed in LC 10. The Father begets the Son, the Son is begotten of the Father, and the Holy Spirit eternally proceeds from the Father and the Son. The three are coequal (LC 11). Implicitly, all further references to "God" refer either to the Father or to the whole Trinity, depending on the context.

23. Letham, *The Holy Trinity*, 264–67.
24. Lightfoot's journal, in Van Dixhoorn, 2:9–10.
25. Morris, *Westminster Symbols*, 166.

The Confession and the Larger Catechism together are replete with Trinitarianism. It is far from true that the Assembly played down the Trinity. The following are examples of how the doctrine of the Trinity underlies the assembled divines' theology. God reveals himself for the salvation of human beings by his Word and Spirit (LC 2), which leads into questions 3–5 about the Scriptures. God's decree was made in Christ, for he chose his elect in Christ (WCF 3.5), to be redeemed by Christ, and called to faith in Christ by the Holy Spirit (WCF 3.6). This Trinitarian basis for election is not developed elsewhere. Creation, on the other hand, is fully Trinitarian (WCF 4.1): "It pleased God the Father, Son, and Holy Ghost . . . to create," whereas providence is not presented explicitly in such terms (WCF 5). All three persons of the Trinity are engaged in the covenant of grace (WCF 7.3; LC 32), for God offers life and salvation to sinners by Jesus Christ, and promises to give his Holy Spirit to make them willing and able to believe, to grant all saving graces, and to enable them to live in obedience to him. In the time of the law, its ordinances signified Christ who was to come and were sufficient for that time through the working of the Holy Spirit (WCF 7.5). In time, Christ the mediator was chosen and ordained by God—the reference appears to be to the Father, since the Lord Jesus is said to be his only Son—according to his eternal purpose (WCF 8.1). The Son—of one substance and equal with the Father—took human nature, being conceived by the power of the Holy Ghost (WCF 8.2; LC 37). The Lord Jesus was sanctified and anointed with the Holy Spirit, and as such it pleased the Father that in him all fullness should dwell (WCF 8.3; LC 42–43), and thus he exercises the office of a prophet in all ages by the Holy Spirit (LC 43). Furthermore, his atoning work is a Trinitarian event; allusion is made to Hebrews 9:14, where through the eternal Spirit he is said to have offered himself to the Father (WCF 8.5). Christ continues to govern the hearts of the elect by the Holy Spirit (WCF 8.8).

The order of salvation is also considered to be a work of the undivided Trinity. Effectual calling is seen in Trinitarian terms. God, the Father, calls his elect by his Word and Spirit to salvation by Jesus Christ (WCF 10.1; LC 67), while elect persons unable to hear the message of the gospel are regenerated and saved by Christ through the Spirit (WCF 10.3). Those whom God the Father calls he also justifies by virtue of the death and resurrection of Christ (WCF 11), while the Holy Spirit applies Christ to them (LC 72). In adoption, God, in his Son, adopts and gives the Spirit of his Son (WCF 12; LC 74). Sanctification is a work of God the Father's grace, by which those whom he has chosen before the foundation of the world are renewed by the powerful work of the Holy Spirit, applying to them the death and resurrection of Christ (WCF 13.1; LC 75). In union with Christ, they die to sin and are raised to new life.

Saving faith is the result of the work of the Holy Spirit in the human heart, accompanying the Word of God, and by such faith we believe whatever God says in Scripture and especially receive and rest on Christ alone for salvation (WCF 14.1; LC 72). Repentance is brought about by the Holy Spirit concurrently with faith (LC 76; WCF 15). Good works are done in accordance with what God has commanded in his Word, by the Holy Spirit, and are acceptable to God in and through Christ his Son (WCF 16). Perseverance is based on the unchangeable love of the Father, our union with Christ, and the indwelling presence of the Holy Spirit (LC 79; WCF 17.1–2). Assurance of salvation is effected by the Holy Spirit bearing witness with our spirits that we are the children of God, and by the promises of God, centering on Christ, which we believe in faith, and so enjoy "the first-fruits of glory with Christ" (LC 80, 83). Hence, the whole of salvation is seen by the Assembly in Trinitarian terms. Underlying each and every stage is the indivisible work of all three persons of the Trinity effecting, maintaining, and cultivating union with Christ.

Not surprisingly, the same theme comes into play in worship. Religious worship is offered to God the Father, Son, and Holy Spirit (WCF 21.2), and to him alone. Christian worship is, by definition, Trinitarian—or it is nothing. In support are cited Matthew 4:10, John 5:23, and the apostolic benediction in 2 Corinthians 13:14. Thus prayer, an integral part of worship, is "made in the name of the Son, by the help of His Spirit, according to His will" (WCF 21.3; LC 178). In this, the saints, united to Christ by his Spirit, have fellowship with Christ (WCF 26.1). The sacraments are also integral to the worship of the church (LC 161). Baptism is into the name of the Father, the Son, and the Holy Spirit (WCF 28.2; see LC 165, 167); this Trinitarian theme runs throughout the chapter. Similarly, in the Lord's

Supper, worthy partakers receive and feed upon Christ, not carnally but spiritually, by the Holy Spirit (WCF 29.7).

Oddly, the Larger Catechism makes no mention of the Spirit in connection with Christ's resurrection (LC 52), although this is a prominent theme of Paul's in Romans 8:1–11 and also features in his discussion of the nature of the resurrection body in 1 Corinthians 15:35ff. However, this lack is offset by its consideration of the way we come to share the benefits of redemption procured by Christ (LC 58); here it clearly affirms that it is "by the application of them unto us, which is the work especially of God the Holy Ghost." The theme is continued in LC 59. Furthermore, the resurrection of the just is by the power and Spirit of Christ (LC 87). Thereafter they will enjoy "the immediate vision and fruition of God the Father, of our Lord Jesus Christ, and of the Holy Spirit, to all eternity" (LC 90).

Having said this, in the section on the exaltation of Christ in the Larger Catechism, there is nothing at all on the Holy Spirit (LC 51–56). Torrance points to the absence from the Confession of a chapter on the Spirit or on God's infinite love as a "grave omission." He also points to the absence of any reference to the missionary outreach of the church, and in line with this, to a stress on God restricting his love to a fixed number of the elect, for, says Torrance, a God who restricts his love cannot be love.[26] Are not these serious problems, it may be asked?

First, we should bear in mind the context. The Assembly was called to establish a constitutional basis for the church in England, which no longer existed in legal terms. Then, upon the signing of the Solemn League and Covenant, it was charged with the task of unifying the church, its doctrine and government, in the three kingdoms. These pressing problems called for action. The Assembly did not intend to say everything that could be said. Second, the divines were not unaware of the missionary calling of the church and, as we saw, it is expressed in the first chapter of the Confession. Torrance, who was born in China to missionary parents and saw himself as an evangelist to Scottish culture, was clearly committed to this vital task, but, we suggest, he did not look closely enough at the Assembly's

26. T. F. Torrance, *Scottish Theology*, 141.

material. Third, there is more than a touch of anachronism in criticizing a seventeenth-century body for failing to anticipate interests and developments that were to arise several hundred years later. The massive interest in the work of the Holy Spirit, the encounter with non-Christian religions, and world mission all emerged in force in far more recent times. Fourth, the Confession and Larger Catechism in fact have what Robertson calls "a very full doctrine of the person and work of the Holy Spirit."[27] We saw the importance of the internal witness of the Holy Spirit that Scripture is the Word of God (WCF 1.4–5; LC 4), together with the necessity for the illumination of the Spirit for a saving understanding of the things revealed in the Word (WCF 1.6). Moreover, the Holy Spirit speaking in Scripture is the supreme judge in all religious controversies (WCF 1.10). In WCF 2, his full deity is proclaimed, for he is one in substance with the Father and the Son (LC 9, 11), sustaining relations to the Father and the Son in the unity of the indivisible Trinity (LC 10). Later, the Confession affirms that the Lord promises his Spirit to his elect to make them willing and able to believe (WCF 7.3), while it is the Holy Spirit who built up the faith of the elect in the Old Testament period (WCF 7.5). Creation is understood in a thoroughly Trinitarian way, with the Spirit integrally involved (WCF 4.1). He calls the elect effectually to faith in Christ (WCF 3.6). The Son of God became incarnate when he was conceived by the Holy Spirit (WCF 8.2; LC 37), and was sanctified and anointed with the Spirit above measure (WCF 8.3; LC 42). Jesus' obedience and sanctification were offered up to God the Father through the Holy Spirit (WCF 8.5). Christ effectually persuades the elect by his Spirit to believe and obey (WCF 8.8), governing their hearts by his Word and Spirit (LC 32, 58–59). Christ reveals the whole will of God to the church by his Spirit (LC 43). God effectually calls by his Word and Spirit (WCF 10.1; LC 67–68). The Holy Spirit applies Christ to the elect (WCF 11.4). He is the Spirit of adoption (WCF 12.1; LC 74). Sanctification is by the Word and Spirit (WCF 13.1–3; see 17.1; LC 75). Saving faith is a work of the Holy Spirit (WCF 14.1), by the ministry of the Word and sacraments (LC 72). Our ability to

27. O. P. Robertson, "The Holy Spirit in the Westminster Confession," in *Westminster Confession into the 21st Century* (ed. Duncan), 57–99.

do good works is wholly from the Holy Spirit (WCF 16.3); insofar as they are good, they proceed from the Holy Spirit (WCF 16.5). Perseverance in faith is due to the indwelling and abiding of the Holy Spirit (WCF 17.2; LC 79). The testimony of the Spirit of adoption gives assurance of salvation (WCF 18.2–3; LC 80–81). Meanwhile, the Spirit of Christ subdues the will of man to do what God requires (WCF 19.7). There are fuller communications of the Spirit of God under the gospel than under the law (WCF 20.1). Religious worship is directed to the Spirit, together with the Father and the Son (WCF 21.2). Thus we pray with the help of the Holy Spirit (WCF 21.3). The Holy Spirit makes the ministry of the church effectual, according to God's promise (WCF 25.3; LC 155, 159). The saints are united to Jesus Christ, and thus also to one another, by his Spirit through faith (WCF 26.1). The efficacy of the sacraments depends on the Holy Spirit and the word of institution (WCF 27.3; LC 161). Baptism is in the name of the Father, the Son, and the Holy Ghost (WCF 28.2; LC 165). The grace promised in baptism is conferred by the Holy Spirit to the elect in God's appointed time (WCF 28.6). In the Lord's Supper, worthy receivers feed on Christ spiritually, but truly and really, by the Spirit (WCF 29.7; LC 170). At the last day, the bodies of the just are raised by the Holy Spirit to honor and conformed to the glorious body of Christ (WCF 32.3; LC 83, 87, 90). For Torrance to complain that a chapter on the Holy Spirit is lacking from the Confession is to overlook the way the divines see the Spirit and his work pervading the whole of creation, active at every stage in grace, and undergirding the entire Christian life.

As for Torrance's criticism of the doctrine of election and its alleged restriction of the love of God, we will discuss that in the chapter on God's sovereign freedom, to which we now turn.

9

God's Sovereign Freedom

We believe in one God the Father Almighty, maker of heaven
and earth, and of all things visible and invisible . . . and in one
Lord Jesus Christ . . . through whom all things were made . . .
[who] sits at the right hand of the Father . . . and we believe in
the Holy Spirit, the Lord and giver of life.

God's Decree (WCF 3–5; LC 12–20)

Morris comments accurately that these chapters follow naturally
from what has gone before, particularly in view of the Arminian controversy that had brought the decrees of God into dispute.[1] God's plans
must have been formed from eternity, he agrees, and must include all
things and events; moreover, his supreme will carries them into effect.[2]
By placing the decree of God close to the beginning of the Confession,
the divines signaled that theology is to be a God-centered enterprise.
This is in keeping with the great ecumenical creeds, which focus on
God the Holy Trinity, the work of Christ, and the church and sacraments.[3] This placement was definitely not a principle from which the
rest of theology was logically deduced; we discussed the anachronistic
nature of this now-discredited argument in chapter 6. The Assembly's

1. Morris, *Westminster Symbols*, 179–82.
2. Ibid., 183–84.
3. See Letham and Macleod, "Is Evangelicalism Christian?"

stress on God's decree was greatly needed at a time of threatening instability, such as England was in during the 1640s. Nothing was certain. The institutions of state were in turmoil, the country was at war with itself, and no legal church existed. The foundations were shaken to their core. Yet in the midst of all this, God was working out his sovereign purposes to his glory and the good of his elect people. In the end, his kingdom would triumph, his church would be preserved, and his elect would be brought home to glory.

The Westminster Confession of Faith refers to the decree of God in the singular, while the Catechisms have the plural. Discussion occurred in the Assembly on this question. There was opposition to the Arminian division into separate decrees. Others raised the question of whether a commitment on such a matter should be put into a confession of faith. Morris thinks of the decrees—as the covenants—as many to our apprehension, while one in the sight of God.[4] The single nature of the decree, he suggests, fosters the idea that its execution is irresistible; it is balanced by chapter 5 on providence, where God is said to govern ordinarily in accordance with the nature of second causes, which takes account of the introduction and permission of sin.[5]

Debates on chapter 3, including the proof texts, occupied parts of twenty days and were "extremely searching and very comprehensive."[6] Robert Baillie referred to "long and tough debates."[7] The committee report followed the Irish Articles closely. Debate focused on two main issues. The first and relatively less important was the question of God's permitting the fall of man. It had to do with whether, as the committee reported, it happened by "the same decree" as that of election, and, if so, whether the phrase should be included in the Confession. Debate occupied two sessions (S520 M 20.10.45 and S521 TU 21.10.45).[8] Lazarus Seaman urged its inclusion; "great debate" would follow its omission, since the Arminians distinguish the decrees and from this arises all their "odious doctrine." Rutherford, on the other hand, urged caution. While all agree that God decrees both the

4. Morris, *Westminster Symbols*, 186–87.
5. Ibid., 190–92.
6. Warfield, *Westminster Assembly*, 122–24.
7. Robert Baillie, *The Letters and Journals of Robert Baillie: Principal of the University of Glasgow 1637–1652* (ed. D. Laing.; 3 vols.; Edinburgh: Robert Ogle, 1841), 2:325.
8. Van Dixhoorn, 6:200–202.

end and the means, and while it is probably one decree, it is doubtful whether such a statement should be included in a confession of faith, he urged. Certainly, if a proof was produced to establish the point, he believed the Assembly would be glad to hear it. Whitaker significantly (in view of the debate of the next few days) pointed out that "our conceptions are very various about the decrees," yet he did not know why the phrase should be left out, since it is the same decree in reference to time—since they are all "*simull & semel.*" Gillespie wanted the freedom of each man to "injoy his own sence." Reynolds argued strongly against inclusion: "Let us not put in disputes & scholasticall things into a confession of faith." Besides, he added, from our perspective they are different decrees. Seaman continued to be adamant for inclusion, again citing the Remonstrants for making two decrees concerning election. While Calamy supported Reynolds ("I desire that nothing be put"), Palmer to the contrary insisted that "it will be worse to leave it out." Meanwhile Gillespie pointed out that in the order of nature God's ordaining man to glory preceded his decree to permit the fall. In the end, the phrase was left out. However, the chapter avoids any idea that these decrees are separable by casting its title in the singular—"Of God's eternal decree"—and reaffirming the point in 3.3 by viewing both predestination to life and foreordination to death as aspects of this one "decree."[9] However, LC 12 speaks of God's decrees in the plural, as eternal acts of God's will. It could be argued that the plural signifies the variety of things decreed by God, while the singular refers to the unity of his purpose, but there is no evidence that this is how the Assembly saw it. Warfield wisely comments that the Assembly was after a generic Calvinism rather than any particular variety of it.[10]

The most significant differences emerged during the debate on the statement, "Neither are any other redeemed by Christ, effectually called, justified, adopted, sanctified, and saved, but the elect only" (WCF 3.6). The most vivid discussion occurred in S522 W 22.10.45 through S524 F 24.10.45,[11] although debates continued until S527 F 31.10.45.[12] The

9. Ibid.
10. Warfield, *Westminster Assembly*, 136.
11. Van Dixhoorn, 6:202–11.
12. Ibid., 6:212.

leading opponent of the clause was Calamy. His position, as Warfield accurately describes it, was hypothetical universalism. In S522 W 22.10.45, he insisted:

> I am farre from universall Redemption in the Arminian sence, but that that [sic] I hould is in the sence of our devines in the sinod of Dort; that Christ did pay a price for all, absolute for the elect, conditionall for the reprobate, in case they doe beleive; that all men should be *salvabiles, non obstante lapsu Adami*; that Jesus Christ did not only dy sufficiently for all, but God did intend in giving of Christ & Christ in giving himselfe did intend to put all men in a state of salvation in case they doe beleive.[13]

Reynolds was incredulous that Calamy was not differing from Arminius and the Remonstrants, since his proposal supposed that salvation was conditional on a response they could not perform and which God never intended to give them. However, Calamy proceeded to distinguish his position from Arminianism: Arminians say that Christ paid a price placing all in an equal state of salvation. "They say Christ did not purchase any impetration." Calamy insisted his views "doth neither intrude upon either [the] doctrine of speciall election or speciall grace." His point was that Arminianism asserted that Christ simply suffered; all people are in a potentially salvable situation, so that any who believe will be saved. In contrast, he himself believed that Christ's death saves his elect and grants a conditional possibility of salvation to the rest. Seaman, supporting Calamy, argued that the views of the Remonstrants were irrelevant; what mattered was the truth or falsity of the case. Calamy, he insisted, was talking not of a salvability in relation to man, but to God; he has so far reconciled himself to the world that he would have mercy on whom he would have mercy. Palmer probed closely, wanting to know whether Calamy understood this of all people. Calamy's rather limp reply was "*de adultis*" (of adults).

Gillespie intervened to stress that "ther is a concatenation of the death of Christ with the decrees." He outlined the differences between Cameron and Amyraut—according to Cameron, Christ died for all on condition that they believe, whereas Amyraut takes it further. The

---

13. Ibid., 6:202–3.

question for Gillespie was whether Calamy could hold to an absolute reprobation of all that shall not be saved.[14] Calamy affirmed: "I
am for speciall election & for reprobation I am for *massa corrupta.*
. . . By virtue of Christ's death ther is *ea administratio* of grace to the
reprobate, that they doe willfully damn themselves. I neither hould
sufficient grace nor speciall grace." In this Calamy clearly differed
from Arminius and did not go as far as Amyraut. He was in the line
of what Moore calls "English hypothetical universalism," a position
within the bounds of the Thirty-Nine Articles, which did not espouse
an explicit doctrine of reprobation.[15] As far as the Synod of Dort was
concerned, Reynolds's reply to Calamy has force: "The sinod intended
noe more than to declare the sufficiency of the death of Christ; it is
pretium in se of sufficient value for all, nay, ten thousand worlds . . . to
be salvable is a benefit and therfore belongs only to them that have
intrest in Christ."

If Calamy was the leading exponent of this hypothetical universalist position, Lazarus Seaman was a less-effective supporter. All in the
first Adam were made liable to damnation, so all are liable to salvation
in the second Adam, he proposed. Warfield correctly dismisses this
as inept; no Reformed confession would ever have admitted that the
result of the fall was that all people were potentially liable to damnation. What happened was that Adam plunged the race into ruin and
all are under the wrath of God in actuality. Equally, Christ does not
make salvation simply possible; he effectively saves.[16]

The biblical focus of the debate turned on the exegesis of "the
world" in John 3:16. Calamy argued that this referred to a love by God
for "the world of elect & reprobate & not of elect only."[17] It cannot

14. Ibid., 6:204.
15. Amyraut held that God, foreseeing the fall, sent his Son to atone for the sins of all
people. God also foreseeing that not all would accept the gospel, elected some to salvation.
Calamy and the English hypothetical universalists held to an atonement effective for the elect
and conditional for the nonelect, to a decree of election with the rest passed by. For these theological reasons, it is a mistake to describe these Assembly men as Amyraldians, as Fesko does;
it is also historically erroneous, since this strand of thought was present in England long before
Amyraut wrote on the subject. See J. Fesko, "The Westminster Confession and Lapsarianism:
Calvin and the Divines," in *Westminster Confession into the 21st Century* (ed. Duncan), 477–525;
Moore, *English Hypothetical Universalism.*
16. Warfield, *Westminster Assembly*, 141.
17. Van Dixhoorn, 6:204–5.

be meant of the elect, he argued, because of the phrase "whosoever beleiveth." Moreover, Mark 16:15 requires the gospel to be preached to all; "if the covenant of grace be to be preached to all, then Christ redeemed, in some sence, all—both elect & reprobate. But it is to be preached to all, [therefore] ther is a warrant for it." The alternative would be that there would be no truth in its preaching, yet we know that all of God's promulgations are serious and true. Rutherford countered by denying the connection; it proved too much, since it would equally apply to election and justification as to redemption. For his part, Calamy said he was not speaking of the application, but of the offer—it cannot be offered to Judas, except he be salvable. Rutherford summed up the ground of Calamy's position, which "is to make all salvable & soe justifyable." Seaman's comment was that "it comes only to this: looke as every man was *damnabilis*, soe is every man *salvabilis* & God, if he please, may choose him, justify him, sanctify him." Marshall, in support of Calamy's argument, maintained that it had not been answered properly, "that ther can noe *falsum subesse* to the offer of the gospell."

Wilkinson, opposing Calamy, argued that those against whom Christ takes special exception cannot be partakers of redemption. Yet Christ did not pray for the world. Gillespie answered Calamy's arguments from John 3:16. Calamy was taking for granted that the "world" means the whole world, but that point was much disputed. Their divines said that in some places it had to be taken in another sense. As for philanthropy, a universal love of God necessarily leads to a denial of absolute reprobation. Furthermore, from Mark 16:15 Calamy thought that the ground of the universal offer of the gospel was the institution of Christ in dying.[18] The mistake he made, Gillespie contended, was that "the *voluntas/voluntis decreti & mandati* are not distinguished." This is the distinction between God's decretive will—what he has determined shall happen—and his preceptive will—what he requires human beings to do. A man is bound to believe that he ought to believe and that by faith he shall be saved; it is a duty God requires of all humans. But God's command is not the same as his

18. At this time, the available manuscripts supported the integrity of the last twelve verses of the gospel of Mark.

intention; frequently God has decreed—with no subtraction from their personal responsibility—that people will not obey him. Marshall, however, asserted that there is more than a command in the gospel—that there is also a promise. Burgess pointed to the dualism inherent in Calamy's position: "You say the *novum foedus* doth intend; then there be either two covenants, one general to the elect and another special to the elect." Calamy was unabashed. The difference, he said, is not in the offer, but in the application. The decretive will of God is evident only in its application. The word "world" can indeed mean the whole world and it does so in John 3:16. There is also a double love of God—general and special.[19]

Gillespie continued to undermine Calamy's case. Calamy was taking for granted what he needed to prove. He had not reconciled a general love of God with absolute reprobation. The general offer of the gospel is not grounded on the secret decree. Lightfoot argued that the word "world" is in contrast with the nation of the Jews; God intends the salvation of the elect. Moreover, Price pointed out that even if mankind as a whole be meant, it did not follow that Christ intended "all" individual people. Nor does it follow that Christ died intentionally for the redemption of all. He challenged Calamy and his friends to prove that there is such a covenant with mankind—and if so, the signs of the covenant ought to be administered on a general basis. The reason for the promiscuous offer of the gospel is that we ourselves do not know who is elect and who is reprobate. On the other hand, Vines asked, is not the gospel a covenant, and is that not propounded to every creature? And on what is the gospel founded but the blood of Christ? By "world," he continued, he did not understand the Gentiles, but the word seemed to mean more than the elect: it denotes an intention in the gift and the love. We could not live if there were not a general love for mankind.[20]

The next day, in S 523 TH 23.10.45am, Thomas Goodwin intervened. It is true, he conceded, that the gospel must be preached to every creature, "but then the question is, what is the gospell there?" The answer is that God was in Christ, reconciling such a world to whom

19. Van Dixhoorn, 6:206.
20. Ibid., 6:207.

he does not impute their trespasses. The decrees of God concerning the world of his elect are expressed indefinitely, and so ministers are under a universal obligation to preach it to every person, so that every person may come to Christ.[21] Rutherford was equally emphatic. Referring to John 3:16, he said that "Christ speakes of a particular speciall love." There is not so much as one scripture in all the New Testament where it can be expounded for a general love. The love described in John 3:16 is restricted to the church. Rutherford also referred to Ephesians 5:21, Galatians 2:20, and Romans 5:8. All these passages speak of "an actuall saving love."[22]

In the following session, S 524 F 24.10.45, Vines insisted that the nonelect "have some fruits of the death of Christ & the benefits therof," but whether this makes them salvable we cannot say.[23] In opposition, Harris doubted whether there could be any such thing as a conditional decree. In John 3:16, he said, "the world" refers to the Gentiles, since it was spoken to Nicodemus, a Jew. The love there mentioned is the highest there can be, which cannot be meant of common love.[24] The debate ground on for another week. In S 528 M 3.11.45, there was discussion about leaving out the words "foreordained to everlasting death," but its opponents failed to persuade the Assembly to do so. In S 529 TH 6.11.45, the paragraph on reprobation was referred to the committee for a report on the morning of the following day.[25] However, there is no mention of it in S 530 F 7.11.45;[26] it waited until S 532 TU 11.11.45, where there are no comments on the debate.[27] In each case, the hypothetical universalists failed to gain the approval of the Assembly, which remained steadfast. This was despite roughly one-third of the recorded speeches favoring Calamy's position.[28] They could claim backing from the Thirty-Nine Articles and legitimately disavow any connection with Arminianism. It is also inaccurate to

21. Ibid., 6:208.
22. Ibid., 6:209.
23. Ibid., 6:210.
24. Ibid., 6:211.
25. Ibid., 6:212.
26. Ibid., 6:213.
27. Ibid., 6:214.
28. Calamy, Seaman, Marshall, and Vines are recorded as supporting the hypothetical universalist reading. They were opposed by Reynolds, Gillespie, Burgess, Rutherford, Wilkinson, Lightfoot, Price, Goodwin, and Harris.

describe them as Amyraldian; hypothetical universalism in England antedated Amyraut and did not go as far as he did in decretal dualism.[29] Warfield is correct in claiming that the clause was intended to exclude hypothetical universalism by ensuring that each element in the *ordo salutis* (order of salvation) was recognized as *intended* only for the elect, and was not merely a description of the fact that only the elect receive the benefits.[30] The inclusion of reprobation in WCF 3.7 was deliberate. This was "no hasty draft, rushed through the body at breakneck speed . . . on the credit of the Committee that had drafted it. . . . [It was] distinctly the work of the Assembly itself . . . [the] well-pondered and thoroughly adjusted expression of the living belief of that whole body."[31] In all this, Calamy and his supporters continued to play their part in the Assembly—Calamy a prominent one—and were not blackballed for their views. The Assembly was not a partisan body within the boundaries of its generic Calvinism, but allowed differing views to coexist.

According to LC 12, the decrees refer to acts of God's will, which is wise, holy, eternal, and free. The phrase "the counsel of his will" implies that in all God's plans all three persons of the Trinity are integrally and indivisibly involved. Moreover, God's decrees are "for his own glory"; viewed in a Trinitarian light, these are not the designs of a celestial megalomaniac insistent on imposing himself, but are the wise and holy plans of the God who is indivisible in communion and love. Thus, he has unchangeably foreordained whatever comes to pass in time, especially where angels and humans are concerned.

This special relation to angels and human beings is seen in election and rejection. God has elected some angels to glory. This he has done out of sheer love and grace. God has also elected some humans to eternal life. In this case there is a difference, for he has done this *in Christ*: "and in Christ hath chosen some men to eternal life, and the means thereof" (LC 13). Election is placed squarely in the context of the love and grace of God, and, in the case of humans, is in

29. *Contra* Warfield, *Westminster Assembly*, 142, who cites Robert Baillie in support. Mitchell and Struthers, eds., *Minutes of the Sessions*, lvff., correctly point to indigenous sources.

30. Warfield, *Westminster Assembly*, 142–44.

31. Ibid., 144–46.

Christ.[32] The difference between humans and the angels is that the elect angels had no need of salvation; God, in his decree, preserved them from sinning.

On the other hand, he has passed the rest by and ordained them to dishonor and wrath. There are two factors involved here. God's decree itself is in accordance with his sovereign power—he is free to do as he pleases with his creatures—and the unsearchable counsel of his will, into which we are unable to probe. However, this is not to be seen as a discordant imposition on "the rest," for it is inflicted "for their sin" and is in full conformity with his glorious justice. It is an entirely just determination. "The rest" have themselves opted to be separate from the grace of God; God's decree justly confirms it. From the other side, their choices in life, for which they are fully responsible and which they have freely made, are the result of God's own just decree.

We should note the disparity between election and reprobation. Election is by grace and is rooted in Christ; reprobation, or preterition (passing by) is in connection with sin and God's justice. There is asymmetry, not a parallel. Ultimately, both depend on the unchangeable, wise, holy, eternal will of God, but in themselves they differ considerably.

As to the dispute between infralapsarians and supralapsarians, the scales are tilted to the infralapsarian side, as is the case in all classic Reformed confessions.[33] There was a strong supralapsarian

---

32. As Isaac Watts (1674–1748) was to put it, "'Twas his own purpose that begun, to rescue rebels doomed to die; he gave us grace in Christ his Son before he spread the starry sky."

33. Differences regarding the order of decrees in the mind of God had existed for decades and had come to the surface in the Arminian controversy from 1603. Supralapsarians held that God first chose his elect and passed by the reprobate. Then he determined to create them. Third, he decreed that the fall should take place. Finally, he chose to send Christ to save the elect and to grant the Holy Spirit to enable them to believe and persevere. The order was election, creation, fall, and grace. The decree to elect preceded the decree to permit the fall. In election, the elect are regarded as creatable, or at least not fallen. Infralapsarians held to this order: creation, fall, election, grace. For them, when God chose his elect, he contemplated them as fallen. The decree to permit the fall preceded his decree to elect. The elect, in this case, are contemplated in the decree of election as fallen. This order found favor with the Reformed churches to a greater extent and was expressed in the confessions. It was an attempt to do justice to the historical order found in the Bible. Arminius proposed the order: creation, fall, grace, election. This placed election last, God choosing for salvation those whom he foresaw would believe the gospel. This has been called postdestination; in effect, God simply rubber-stamps the human decision. See the extended discussion of the matter in Fesko, "Lapsarianism," 495ff.,

representation at Westminster—Twisse and Rutherford were the leading exponents of the position in their day, and among the most notable in history. However, they did not get their interpretation inserted into the documents. WCF 6.1 says that "God was pleased, according to His wise and holy counsel, to permit [the fall]." Moreover, WCF 3.6 refers to those "who are elected, being fallen in Adam."

WCF 3.1. God has sovereignly, unchangeably, and wisely ordained all that happens. At the same time, he is not the author of sin. Fesko points out that, in contrast with the Irish Articles, the Assembly added the phrase "neither is God the author of sin" to undercut a possible criticism, and retained Ussher's scholastic distinction between primary and secondary causes so as to offset the charge of fatalism, thereby affirming the integrity of the created order, including human free agency.[34] God's decree does not override the liberty of his creatures or the contingency of secondary causes. In short, if something happens, it happens because God ordained that it happen. In the case of free agents, the thing that happens is of their own choosing. In the case of events in the natural world, the thing that happens is in accordance with the laws of nature. If it rains, God ordained it so. Yet it rains due to the atmospheric circumstances prevailing. In other words, God has so created the universe as to maintain its own contingent freedom within the scope of his unchangeable purpose. God and man are not competitors.

WCF 3.2. God's foreknowledge is utterly comprehensive, contrary to the Socinian heresy that had reared its head at the time. However, his decree is not based upon his foreknowledge, as Arminius had held. Warfield engages in undue speculation on this section, basing his comments on what he describes as "conjecture" and "general supposition."[35] Both Helm and Fesko correctly identify Molinism as the target of the final clause. Following Luis de Molina (1535–1600),

---

and in the published version of his doctoral thesis to which he refers: J. V. Fesko, *Diversity Within the Reformed Tradition: Supra- and Infralapsarianism in Calvin, Dort, and Westminster* (Greenville, SC: Reformed Academic Press, 2003), 257–96.

34. Fesko, "Lapsarianism," 487–88.
35. Warfield, *Westminster Assembly*, 129–30.

this was the proposition that God's decrees were based on his knowledge of all possible future actions.[36]

WCF 3.3–4. God's decree encompasses the everlasting destiny of both angels and human beings. Some he has predestined to everlasting life, others to everlasting death. The number in both categories is unchangeable; God's decree is irrevocable. All this is for his glory. Taken by itself, this statement might appear harsh and brutal. It should be read in the context of what precedes and what follows. Warfield writes that the Assembly was "unusually decided in its determination to have the doctrine of reprobation clearly asserted in this its appropriate place," and that it was "a matter which the Assembly deemed of the highest importance."[37] Fesko argues cogently for a distinction between "predestine," which he says is purely soteriological and refers exclusively to election, and "foreordain," which is used for the passing by of the nonelect with reference to providence. In this sense, he claims, God has foreordained providentially the means of salvation for the elect as well as the end (WCF 3.6). However, according to the divines, the means of the elect's salvation are soteriological, not merely providential, and consist of the ministry of the Word, the sacraments, and prayer (LC 154; SC 88). In WCF 3.6 itself, the means to glory are the various elements of the *ordo salutis*—one can hardly get more soteriological than effectual calling, justification, and the like. Again, the language is not quite as consistent as Fesko suggests; in WCF 3.6 the divines speak of God *appointing* the elect, rather than predestining them. Fesko goes on to argue that "the non-elect are not the specific subject of a decree of reprobation; they are instead the subject of God's providence," in support of which he points to the absence of the term "reprobation."[38] This argument is not spelled out in the minutes. The careful language is most likely in order to accommodate Calamy and his supporters. On the other hand, there is much to be said for the suggestion that the Assembly wished to keep as close as possible to the Thirty-Nine Articles, given its charge

36. Fesko, "Lapsarianism," 489.
37. Warfield, *Westminster Assembly*, 132–33.
38. Fesko, "Lapsarianism," 490–92.

to produce documents for the constitution of the Church, and for that reason chose to side with them instead of Ussher.

WCF 3.5. Human beings predestinated to life have been chosen *in Christ*. This is due to the sheer grace and love of God.[39] It is not based on God's foreknowledge of their faith or good works, contrary to the teaching of Arminius and the Remonstrants, which had been rejected at the Synod of Dort. There is nothing in the creature that in any way constrained God to this decision; it proceeded entirely from his own sovereign will, to the praise of his grace.

WCF 3.6. God has also foreordained the means by which the elect will be brought to glory. Those elected—regarded as fallen in Adam—are redeemed by Christ, effectually called to faith in Christ by the Holy Spirit, justified, adopted, sanctified, and preserved by his power through faith. Only the elect are saved; no others experience the saving grace of God.

WCF 3.7. The rest of the human race God has passed by. He has determined not to grant them grace for salvation. He has ordained them to wrath and dishonor. This is the doctrine of reprobation. There are two aspects to it. Negatively, God has determined to withhold grace from the nonelect. Positively, he has ordained them to wrath and dishonor. This goes beyond simply passing them by. The proof texts cited include Matthew 11:25–26 and Romans 9:17–18, 21–22, both of which speak of an action by God in concealing the truth from the wise and understanding, or in hardening the heart of whomever he pleases. These situations go beyond the providential to a judicial determination. Similarly, Jude 4 and 1 Peter 2:8 refer to an appointment to disobedience and stumbling at the Word, and an ordination to condemnation. It is an unsearchable determination of God's unchangeable will. He extends grace to whomever he chooses and withholds

39. This belies the critical attacks on Reformed theology for its alleged neglect of the biblical teaching that election is in Christ. See Barth, *CD*, II/2, 3–506; J. K. S. Reid, "The Office of Christ in Predestination," *SJT* 1 (1948): 1–12. On this see G. C. Berkouwer, *Divine Election* (Grand Rapids: Eerdmans, 1960), 154–62; Muller, *Christ and the Decree*, passim; Letham, *Assurance in Theological Context*, passim.

it from whomever he chooses. He is utterly free to do so, and all his ways are just. However, this is not blind fatalism. Those passed by are ordained to wrath *for their sin*. In short, all who endure everlasting death do so justly, in keeping with their sin. Their own choice freely echoes God's decree. No one will endure this destiny against his will; rather, it confirms his own free choices. As such, all will be to the praise of God's glorious justice. The Assembly saw this as important, not only because it was believed to be biblical, but also because it places all human events whatsoever under the sovereign direction of God. As such, it engenders assurance that his eternal purposes will be worked out in the course of human history, and that his elect will certainly be brought to salvation, whatever the current situation might be. When we remember the Civil War raging, the instability of political, social, and economic life, families divided down the middle by the conflict swirling around them, this apparently harsh teaching was in reality a source of great comfort and strength, rightly handled.

The divines also indicate a marked disparity between election and preterition (passing by). The latter is directly connected with the sin of the nonelect and is in perfect accord with God's justice. Election, on the other hand, is entirely a matter of free grace and love. The elect are chosen *in Christ*; the nonelect are left to *their own* sins. Election is "all to the praise of His glorious grace," while preterition is "to the praise of His glorious justice."[40] In the latter, the nonelect receive what is due to them for their own sin. In the former, the elect receive what is due to Christ, in whom they are chosen. Both are in accord with justice; in election, the justice is gracious because it is freely given in and through the mediator.

WCF 3.8. The Assembly appreciated the need for a careful approach to this "hard saying." This mystery is to be handled with great care. The aim of ministers of the gospel should be to proclaim it so as to encourage assurance of salvation in the elect, so as to bring praise to God and humility to those who obey the gospel. This

---

40. Morris comments: "Surely this peculiar emphasizing of the glory of God as the end of all things may be regarded as one of the distinguishing qualities, if not one of the chief excellencies also, of the Symbolism of Westminster." He remarks that the Assembly saw no conflict between the glory of God and the happiness of the creature. Morris, *Westminster Symbols*, 211–12.

section mirrors the comments in the second and third paragraphs of the Thirty-Nine Articles, 17.

Creation (WCF 4; LC 15–17)

The chapter on God's decree leads naturally into the various elements of the decree: creation (WCF 4; LC 15–17; SC 9–10), providence (WCF 5; LC 18–20; SC 11–12), the fall of man (WCF 6; LC 21–29; SC 13–19), the covenant of grace (WCF 7; LC 30–35; SC 20), the person and work of Christ (WCF 8; LC 36–56; SC 21–28), and the order of salvation (WCF 9–18; LC 57–90; SC 29–38). The old scholarship regarded this as a scholastic corruption that replaced the centrality of Christ with a logical straitjacket. The order is certainly a logical one, in the sense that it is orderly and rational. It is also historical; the progression from the decree to creation, providence, the fall, and the grace of God in salvation follows the line of the biblical narrative. Indeed, as we observed, much of the Assembly's time was taken up with the exegesis of biblical texts. Far from a cold set of logical deductions, the divines—most of whom were pastors—grappled with real questions germane to the gospel and its proclamation. This order is an outflow of chapter 3, in a way that preserves and honors the historical order and outworking.

There is little in the minutes on the details of debate on creation. The report of the First Committee was received by the Assembly in S536 M 17.11.45 and discussed in the following session the next day. In S538 W 19.11.45, debate took place on the creation of man, while in S540 TH 20.11.45 the report of creation and providence was considered.[41] Beyond this, nothing is recorded. This might be considered disappointing. What it shows is that creation was not a matter of controversy; it certainly did not interest the scribe.

WCF 4.1 presents a thoroughly Trinitarian view of creation, more so than LC 15. "God the Father, Son, and Holy Ghost" created the world. This was done for "His" glory. Note the singular, with its stress on the indivisibility of the Holy Trinity and the inseparability of God's

41. Mitchell and Struthers, eds., *Minutes of the Sessions*, 164–65; Van Dixhoorn, 6:217–19.

works, following Augustine. Creation is a free and sovereign action of the whole Trinity. In keeping with the historic Christian tradition, creation is described as *ex nihilo*; matter is not coeternal with God, for he brought into existence all things other than himself by his free decision. The world is not an emanation from God's being, but a product of his will. This includes both material and spiritual dimensions, "all things therein whether visible or invisible," echoing the Niceno-Constantinopolitan Creed. As Morris states, this refers to the absolute origination of all things by God at a time when no creature had any being.[42] The triune God has sole proprietary rights over the whole universe.

The Confession adds that this took place "in the space of six days." There are at least three possibilities for the meaning of this phrase. First, it appears to be a rejection of the most common historical interpretation, dating to Augustine, that creation was instantaneous.[43] This view had majority support from the time Augustine presented it in *De Genesi ad litteram* in the early fifth century up until at least the days of Anselm, when he wrote *Cur Deus Homo?* in 1098. Indeed, it was still a major interpretation in the thirteenth century, when Robert Grosseteste wrote his *Hexaemeron* (1230–35) and Thomas Aquinas his *Summa theologiae*. Second, it could also be understood as an affirmation of six literal, solar days of twenty-four hours each. All the Assembly divines who wrote on the topic held to this view, so much so that some were even able to pinpoint exactly when creation took place. Morris thinks this is the meaning in the Confession.[44] That this is compatible with the first possibility is obvious, although the first does not entail the second. Third, the divines could simply be repeating the words of Scripture, which in Genesis 1 speak of six days without necessarily defining the time. In this case, aware of the range of different interpretations in the history of the church, the Assembly would not be committing itself to any one in particular. This possibility is favored by Mitchell,[45] who cites Philo as saying that it was "rustic simplicity" to imagine that the

42. Morris, *Westminster Symbols*, 201. Morris argues that the statement gives theoretical ground for some form of theistic evolution, but rules out naturalistic evolution.
43. See Letham, "The Days of Creation."
44. Morris, *Westminster Symbols*, 202.
45. Mitchell, *Westminster Assembly*, 405–7.

world was created in six days, and by A. A. Hodge, who argues that the record in Genesis "was not designed to prevent or take the place of a scientific interpretation of all existing phenomena," and that the Confession simply uses the precise words of Scripture.[46]

Elsewhere I have written that this question was not a matter of controversy or even interest at the time, despite the variety of views in exegetical history and the scientific and philosophical ferment aroused by the work of Copernicus and its aftermath.[47] It had not featured in any Reformed creed or confession. As Rogland comments, "There is nothing in the Three Forms of Unity which could be even remotely considered as requiring a particular interpretation of the Hexaemeron."[48] Moreover, only two members of the Assembly wrote a treatise on creation or a commentary on the early chapters of Genesis. It is clear that John Lightfoot considered most of the days of Genesis 1 to be solar days, although he claimed that the first day lasted for thirty-six hours rather than twenty-four.[49] In *The history of the creation*, George Walker explored a variety of aspects of the theology of creation. He combined elements of the interpretations of Augustine, Grossteste, and Aquinas, and the literal theory. He distinguished between immediate creation, which was instantaneous, and which is mentioned in Genesis 1:1, and mediate creation, in which God formed the world in the space of six days. The instantaneous creation was in line with Augustine's idea. He combined this with a literal view of the six days, but wrote of these as mediate creation. At the same time, he recognized that the first three days are parallel to the second group of three. In this he showed a certain kinship with Grossteste and Aquinas in their formula of creation, formation, and adornment, where creation is reserved strictly for Genesis 1:1, formation refers to the first three days, in which God formed various spheres, and adornment describes

46. A. A. Hodge, *The Confession of Faith: A Handbook of Christian Doctrine Expounding the Westminster Confession* (London: Banner of Truth, 1961), 82ff.

47. Letham, "The Days of Creation."

48. M. Rogland, "*Ad Litteram*: Some Dutch Reformed Theologians on the Creation Days," *WTJ* 63 (2001): 233. See also W. S. Barker, "The Westminster Assembly on the Days of Creation: A Reply to David W. Hall," *WTJ* 62 (2000): 113–20.

49. John Lightfoot, *A Few, and New Observations, upon the Booke of Genesis. The most of them certaine, the rest probable, all harmlesse, strange, and rarely heard off before* (London: T. Badger, 1642) [Wing (2nd. ed., 1994) L20540].

the last three days in which God made various agents to populate these spheres. Walker was inclined to think that creation took place on the morning of 21 March, 3927 BC, 3960 years before Christ's death. Since the six days were each of twenty-four hours, the first day entailed equality between light and darkness throughout the world, and so occurred on an equinox. Spring was more appropriate than autumn, since it allowed for the growth of the vegetation described on the third day. This argument implies that Walker may not have been aware that the earth was spherical, and that the spring equinox for him is the autumnal equinox in the southern hemisphere.[50]

However, a number of books by the divines, in which it might be expected for creation to figure, hardly mention it at all.[51] Two books— one by a divine, the other by a scribe at the Assembly—make cursory mention of creation being in six days.[52] One book, which was published *after* the Assembly had disbanded, by John Richardson, not an Assembly man (but perused by Thomas Gataker, who of course was), refers to the days being of twenty-four hours duration.[53] Richardson was convinced that the first day began in the evening. It is clear from their comments on Genesis 1:5 that the compilers of the *Annotations* understood creation as six days of twenty-four hours each. They implicitly date the creation in comments on Genesis 2:3 to roughly the date suggested by Ussher. However, this was not an official document of the Assembly; indeed, it aroused some controversy.[54]

50. George Walker, *The history of the creation* (London: John Bartlet, 1641) [Wing W359].

51. Henry Wilkinson, *A Catechisme* (London: T. S. for Roger Pott, 1624) [STC (2nd ed.) 25644]; Herbert Palmer, *An endeavour of making the principles of Christian Religion plaine and easie* (London: G. M. for Tho. Underhill, 1642) [Wing P232]; Obadiah Sedgwick, *A short catechisme* (London: Stephen Bewtell, 1647) [Wing 1158:03].

52. William Gouge, *A short Catechisme* (London: John Beale, 1635) [STC (2nd ed.) 12130]; John Wallis, *A briefe and easie explanation of the Shorter Catechism* (London: Thomas Underhill, 1657) [Wing (2nd ed., 1994) W560C]. Wallis was a scribe of the Westminster Assembly.

53. John Richardson, *Choice observations and explanations upon the Old Testament* (London: John Stafford, 1655) [Wing (2nd. ed., 1994) R1385A].

54. The minutes of S504 TU 16.9.45 record a motion about the *Annotations*, noting "some things in them against the covenant & the votes of the Assembly." Debate was continued in the next session (S505 W 17.9.45) without scribal comment. In S506 M 22.9.45, Palmer presented a report on the *Annotations* (presumably a committee had been established for this purpose): "The stationers desired that some animadversions may be made suddenly, and they promised to sell noe more till tomorrow." In S507 TH 25.9.45, "Mr. Ley gave account of the Antidote prepared against the particulars complained of in the Annotations of the Bible." No

This paucity of literature, together with the absence of comment on the matter in the minutes, supports the view that there was little interest in creation or Genesis among the divines, despite the tumultuous developments following Copernicus. While there is no evidence that any divine at Westminster held to anything other than a literal view of the first chapter of Genesis, there were few who bothered to comment on the matter. Evidently, it was not seen as an important matter. The Assembly was well aware of the history of interpretation, as it was on other topics. It knew it was diverging from a major position in the history of exegesis, associated with Augustine in particular. Yet it did not make an issue of it, nor commit itself to a particular interpretation of the text of Genesis. This suggests that the third line of approach, supported by Mitchell and A. A. Hodge, has merit, regardless of the personal opinions of any particular divines. However, the most sobering thought is that the Copernican revolution, the biggest intellectual issue of the time, largely passed the Assembly by. Neglect of these revolutionary developments in thought would open the door to the Enlightenment and its aftermath. As Leith comments, "The kind of truth that interested the members of the Assembly was metaphysical and theological. They asked 'Why?' rather than 'How?' Though they knew about Copernicus, they lived and theologized in the old geocentric world in which theology could easily be imagined in spacial terms."[55] He argues that by the time of Westminster, theology was increasingly being conducted in isolation from the intellectual currents of the day.[56] This, as Leith agrees, is not to blame the divines—they had their hands full—but to point to a sad disconnection with the drift of current thought. The subtitle of Lightfoot's work on Genesis—referring to things "harmlesse, strange, and rarely heard off before"—illustrates the obscurity of the matters in the minds of at least some of the Assembly at this juncture.

One final but important point in this first section of WCF 4 is the comment, again reflecting the language of Genesis, that God saw that the creation was "very good." Such an affirmation

---

details are supplied of what the difficulties were, other than the comments on S504. See Van Dixhoorn, 6:178–80.

55. Leith, *Assembly at Westminster*, 31.
56. Ibid., 33.

undergirds the Assembly's conviction that the whole of life was to be lived to God.

In LC 16, the creation of the angels is considered, a topic absent both from the Confession and the Shorter Catechism, although the sins of angels are mentioned in WCF 5.4. These beings are spirits, created immortal and holy, with outstanding knowledge and power. They were made to execute God's commandments (Psalm 103:20–21 being cited in support). They were made to worship God, their Creator. However, they were not made in a state from which they were secure from the possibility of deviation. However mighty or knowledgeable, they are still creatures.

WCF 4.2, together with LC 17, focuses on the creation of man. The phrase "after God had made all other creatures" includes angels, affirming the prior existence of the angelic beings. God created man male and female, with rational and immortal souls. This was not an acceptance of the Platonic idea of the immortality of the soul, since the Confession affirms, in keeping with the Christian tradition, that human souls have a beginning, whereas for Plato the soul is eternal. In contrast with the angels and the rest of creation, man—both male and female—was created after God's own image, which is understood to consist in knowledge, righteousness, and holiness. Here the Assembly seems either to be unaware of, or to discount, the classic Greek patristic teaching that Christ is the image of God and that humanity was created in Christ. Instead, the divines take the language of Paul in Ephesians 4:24 and Colossians 3:10 and consider it to be the complete description of what being in the image of God entails. Its corollaries are that the law of God was written in human hearts and that people had, as created, power to obey it. They also received a specific command not to eat of the tree of the knowledge of good and evil. As they kept it, they remained in communion with God and ruled the rest of creation. However, as God created them, there was a possibility that they might break God's law. They had free will, but their wills were liable to change. Nevertheless, the state of man in creation has already been described as "very good" (4.1). In this, the Confession follows the overall pattern of Genesis 1 and 2. The Larger Catechism, on the other hand, in the first part of its answer, sticks to the description of man's creation in Genesis 2. The last section is the same as the ending of WCF 4.2, connecting the Pauline statements with the historical narrative.[57]

Providence (WCF 5; LC 18–20)

Paul Helm, in his examination of this chapter in the Confession, discusses the argument that the Assembly was unduly influenced by scholastic thought.[58] Recognizing that there is a logical order between the chapters on creation and providence, Helm argues that this does not mean that the one is deduced from the other. Rather, the discussion of providence preserves the centrality of God and, besides, makes practical applications from the doctrine as it proceeds. He argues, correctly in view of the records of debate, that the divines tried to be faithful to Scripture. They did not argue from logic, but from the Bible. Their use of the distinction between primary and secondary causes in WCF 5.2 could be said to be scholastic, in the sense that it was a category from Aristotelian philosophy, but if that was so, then virtually everyone in the sixteenth and seventeenth centuries, including Calvin, could be labeled scholastic. Barth, in keeping with his charge that the Westminster Confession was a degradation of Reformed theology, insists that God is the Creator, not the First Cause.[59] However, the Assembly was thinking here of God in relation to the order of the world and nature. It used these concepts to maintain the integrity of the created order, not to impose an alien philosophical framework upon pristine biblical thought. Moreover, it had emphatically declared in WCF 4 that God was the Creator, not an impersonal cause. In short, the arguments pressed by the consensus of scholarship in the middle of the last century are not helpful in understanding or interpreting classic Reformed theology.

57. That this powerful statement is in harmony with the historic Christian tradition and its affirmations on creation is pointed out well by Morris, who compares it to the declaration of Vatican I (1870) and similar commitments of the Greek Church. Morris, *Westminster Symbols*, 207.

58. P. Helm, "Westminster and Protestant Scholasticism," in *Westminster Confession into the 21st Century* (ed. Duncan), 2:99–116.

59. Barth, *Reformed Confessions*, 137.

Providence, according to the Assembly (WCF 5.1), is more than God's preservation of the universe, although it includes that; it is his upholding, directing, disposing, and governing of all things. God is actively engaged in ruling his creation. "All things" excludes nothing. The greatest to the least aspects of the cosmos are under his direction. His government is in accordance with his character; it is wise, good, and holy. His foreknowledge is infallible, his will unchangeable; everything redounds to the praise of his character. Providence is integrally connected with creation, not only because both are aspects of God's decree, but since providence is God's governing and maintaining of that which he has brought into existence. Morris remarks: "No definition of providence so exact and so comprehensive as this can be found elsewhere in Protestant symbolism."[60] The Lutheran creeds, for example, hardly mention the subject.

In WCF 5.2, the divines make use of the language of first and second causality. God is the first cause; he created and he governs. The various elements of creation are the second causes. Thus, God determined that it would rain yesterday in Bridgend, Wales. However, his government takes fully into account the atmospheric conditions that produce rain: the air pressure, wind speed and direction, air temperature, and so on. Thus, it rains according to regular meteorological conditions. Hence, while God decreed infallibly and immutably that it would rain yesterday in Bridgend, it happened in harmony with the principles that produce rain; he decreed the end and the means. The nature of this concatenation changes when we consider free agents such as human beings. Here the freedom of human agency is also preserved. "By the same providence, He ordereth them to fall out, according to the nature of second causes, either necessarily, freely, or contingently." This distinction is spelled out more clearly in LC 19, which refers to God's providence toward the angels in their creation, in his permission for some to fall beyond recovery, and his establishment of the rest in holiness, and LC 20, which considers God's providence toward man as he was created.

WCF 5.3 narrows the focus still more as it considers the different ways in which God governs creation. It mentions his ordinary

---

60. Morris, *Westminster Symbols*, 216.

providence and, while the term is not used, it also implies an extraordinary providence as well. In the ordinary course of his government of the cosmos, God uses means—the second causes mentioned in 5.2. However, God is not bound by his creation. He is free and sovereign. He brought the universe into existence freely, of his own will. Hence, he is equally free to deploy it in whatever manner he determines. He can govern it through the use of means, as he normally does. However, he is free to dispense with means if he so wishes. He is free to work above means. He can work against them too. Into categories such as these come events such as miracles. The greatest of such events, like the resurrection, are contrary to the normal process of second causes. When a person dies, his body decomposes in the grave or is burned to a cinder in a crematorium. Yet God, being almighty, sovereign, and free, is able to reconstitute the body as and how he pleases. On a lesser level, a person may contract a terminal illness beyond the power of medicine to cure. According to all the knowledge of bodily processes that human science possesses, there is no hope of recovery. Yet God is able to heal the person without the intervention of medical professionals, just as he heals through means such as surgery, therapeutic chemicals, or a cup of tea and an aspirin. This section rules out two contrasting positions. First, it contradicts the Enlightenment view that the world operates purely from immanent causes, from which the miraculous is in principle excluded. Morris classifies this argument against miracles as an argument against God.[61] In keeping with this, it also opposes the idea that God either does not or will not act apart from means, sometimes held in Christian circles. Second, it equally counters the idea that we are to look for or expect the miraculous or unusual, since in his ordinary providence God makes use of means.

WCF 5.4 states that the falls of man and the angels into sin are within the bounds of God's providence. This he not only permitted, but ordered and governed with "a most wise and powerful bounding." God was not a passive spectator watching helplessly as men and angels rebelled. Their sin was part of his greater purpose "to his own holy ends." He kept it within the limits he had ordained, which will ultimately be seen to be for his own glory and the creature's greater

61. Ibid., 219.

196

good. In this way, accountability for sin rests squarely with fallen angels and humans, while God himself cannot be held responsible. This raises big questions, but it is the agreed conclusion of the Christian tradition, with which the Assembly concurred and on which it did not spend inordinate time.

WCF 5.5 alters the direction of discussion to focus on God's providential dealings with his children. It speaks of spiritual desertion, a theme with which Puritan pastors were very familiar, as we shall remark in chapter 12 in relation to assurance of salvation. God leaves his children sometimes on a temporary basis and exposes them to temptations, their own corruption, and various chastisements. This is to lead them to rely more on his grace and to make them more watchful against sin. These experiences are often difficult to understand. In order to use them productively, they are to be seen in the context of God's supreme and all-encompassing government of his world. Nothing that happens to the elect is outside his control. All he sends is for our good. It is not by accident that great trials befall us. Not even death itself is beyond the Creator's care and disposal. Again, the uncertainties and sufferings of the 1640s cannot have been far from the Assembly's mind.

On the other hand, a very different picture is painted concerning the wicked in WCF 5.6. In their case, God withholds his grace. Sometimes he withholds his gifts and gives them over to their sins and to the power of Satan, so that they harden themselves in their impenitence. Romans 1:24–28 and 11:7–8 are among the proof texts used here in support.

Thus, while God's providence extends to the whole of creation, he takes special care of his church (WCF 5.7). This modifies Morris's suggestion that the divines emphasized too much the disciplinary aspect of providence at the expense of its comforting side.[62]

---

62. Ibid., 226.

10

Humanity and Sin

*We believe in one Lord Jesus Christ . . . who for us
and for our salvation came down from heaven.*

Man and Sin (WCF 6; LC 20–29)

Chapter 6 is crucial in the Confession, and the corresponding
section in the Larger Catechism is equally important. As in medicine,
where an accurate diagnosis of a patient's condition is needed before
effective treatment can be given, so in theology, the diagnosis of man's
condition in the sight of God will largely determine the remedy. In
this chapter, we will summarize the contents of the two documents
on the subject of sin, and then we will ask some important questions
as to what exactly they mean.

WCF 6.1 recounts the record of the fall in Genesis 3 and puts it
in the context of God's providential permission, for his own glory. Our
first parents are the subjects of the section and what follows (see LC
21). In the light of later developments of doctrine in the Reformed
tradition, it is important to note that neither the Confession nor the
Catechisms speak of our first parents being placed on probation, being
given a commandment as a moral test, nor of a promise of everlasting
life on their successful completion of such a probationary period. This
may be implied in the alternative title that the Assembly gives for the
covenant of works—the covenant of life—but it is not present in this

chapter of the Confession. A. A. Hodge, nonetheless, goes to great lengths to expound the idea in his comments at this very point.[1]

WCF 6.2 addresses the result of this first sin: our first parents fell from their state of original righteousness and communion with God, and so became dead in sin and wholly defiled in all parts and faculties. This is the doctrine of total depravity, by which is meant, not that people are as bad as they possibly can be, which is self-evidently false, but that they all are defiled by sin in every aspect of their being, with debilitating effects in relation to God (see also LC 21).

In WCF 6.3, the relationship between the sin of Adam and Eve and the rest of the human race is considered. Our first parents were the root of all mankind, and so the guilt of this first sin was imputed to their entire posterity. The sin imputed here is the sin of *our first parents* and the basis for it is a *natural* one: they were "the root of all mankind." Focusing on the Princeton doctrine of the imputation of *Adam's* sin on the ground of a *federal* relationship, A. A. Hodge ignores the text of the Confession at this point and instead expounds his own theology as if these words in this section did not exist.[2] Moreover, the death in sin and the corrupted nature which our first parents immediately incurred was also conveyed to all their posterity by natural generation. This is the doctrine of original sin, which refers to the transmission of a corrupt nature, which all people inherit from the moment of conception.

Taking a different line, LC 22 states that all mankind fell in that first transgression, since the covenant was made "with Adam as a publick person," that is, for him and all his posterity descending by ordinary generation. Jesus Christ is excluded by implication here, since he was not generated by ordinary means. Because of this connection between Adam and the race, all his posterity sinned in him and fell with him since they were in him. In comparison with the Confession, there is a significant shift, from our first parents to Adam. Additionally, God made a covenant with Adam as a public person, whereby he acted not only for himself but for everyone descended from him by natural

1. Hodge, *The Confession of Faith*, 105–6. This is not to say that this doctrine cannot be defended from the Assembly's documents; we shall shortly see that this can be done. Rather, the question is the meaning of this section of the Confession.
    2. Ibid., 109–15.

generation. The connection between Adam and the human race is established by a covenant, but runs along natural lines, formed by ordinary generation. While Adam was a public person, the relationship is not *explicitly* described as legal, but genetic. In view of the widespread, but not universal, acceptance at the Assembly of the immediate imputation of Adam's sin, this forensic relationship is clearly in view, but it is couched in language that allows for the idea that the contraction of sin by Adam's posterity is grounded in a realistic manner based on natural descent. This is underlined in LC 26, where the Assembly states that original sin is conveyed by natural generation.

The reasons for the apparent disparity between WCF 6.3 and LC 22 are not entirely clear, and there is currently insufficient evidence to explain it. Robert Strimple reports an interesting suggestion on this made by John Murray, in a class Murray taught on the Westminster Confession. Murray proposed that between the framing of the Confession and the later completion of the Catechisms, a controversy on the continent (1644–45) came to a head over Placeus (a Saumur theologian) and his doctrine of mediate imputation. Hence, the Larger Catechism is careful to indicate that the covenant with Adam was the basis for the imputation of sin, which the Confession did not deny.[3] This is worthy of further consideration. Another factor to bear in mind is that there were some at the Assembly, including Thomas Gataker and Richard Vines,[4] who did not hold to the covenant of works/life. Some thought that the idea of such a covenant encouraged antinomianism; others feared that it minimized the importance of Christ's sufferings or that it was simply bad exegesis. That these were a minority is evident in that this covenant takes its place in the Assembly's documents. However, these were the same people who objected to the view that the active obedience of Christ is imputed in justification. As

3. In a personal e-mail, dated 18 July 2008, cited with permission. In notes taken by Strimple in the class, Murray stated: "It is quite probable that in the brief interval between the framing of the Confession and the final framing of the Catechisms, the information respecting the controversy on the Continent had become better known to the divines. Placeus's doctrine of mediate imputation had been condemned (1644–45). Consequently, the divines were more careful in the Catechisms to enunciate what they had known all along; i.e., that it was the covenant that was the ground of the imputation of Adam's first sin."

4. Van Dixhoorn, 1:315. See the discussion in chapter 12 on the imputation of the active obedience of Christ in justification.

we shall see in chapter 12, there are good reasons to conclude that the Assembly's declarations on justification went some way to placating this group. It may be, following from this, that the discussion in WCF 6.3 was similarly intended to enable the whole Assembly to agree. This does not preclude Murray's suggestion as to why the statement in the Larger Catechism referred more specifically to Adam.

WCF 6.4 explains the connection between original corruption and actual sins, which proceed from it. LC 24 explains that sin is any breach of, or lack of conformity to, the law of God.

According to WCF 6.5, this inherited corruption remains throughout this life, even in the regenerate. Through Christ, it is pardoned (justification), and mortified (sanctification), yet it remains and is still sin.

WCF 6.6 states that all sin is a transgression of the law of God and so brings guilt upon the sinner, leading to the wrath of God, the curse of the law, death, and all spiritual, temporal, and eternal miseries for mankind in general.[5]

The Imputation of Sin

The most surprising point in WCF 6, particularly when it is read in conjunction with the following chapter, is how the sin of our first parents (not merely Adam) comes to the human race because they were the root of mankind. We might expect to find discussion on the transmission of sin in the chapter on the covenant (chapter 7), but instead it is in the chapter on sin (chapter 6). Indeed, the treatment of the covenant of works in WCF 7 is quite cursory, although more detail is provided in LC 20, 22, and 30 (in passing). This placement undermines claims that the Assembly's theology was governed by the dual covenants, the covenants of works and grace. Clearly, this is an important strand in the Westminster documents. It was something

---

5. T. F. Torrance argues that the Confession presents a moralistic notion of sin; it is not seen in the light of the gospel or in the death of Christ, in which our whole being, good as well as evil, comes under judgment. The moralistic doctrine of sin blunts its radicalness. Torrance is right in that there is no doubt that the gospel highlights sin's heinous nature. However, those who do not share Torrance's antipathy to what he elsewhere terms "the Latin heresy" may demur and point to the Pauline comment that "through the law comes the knowledge of sin" (Rom. 3:20), as well as the historical order of both the Confession and the Catechism. See Torrance, *Scottish Theology*, 142.

new, an addition to the Reformed confessional corpus. However, it is another case of anachronistic reading to suppose that the whole of the Assembly's theology was controlled by one particular perspective. Moreover, it is doubly anachronistic to read back later, more developed covenantal views into documents where they are not to be found in such an advanced state. A greater case can be made for the decree of God occupying the commanding heights of the Confession than can be put forward for the covenants. Even there, however, we noted how readings of this nature suppose theories of central dogmas, and those theories were unknown in the seventeenth century. Besides, it was the consistent attempt of the divines to exegete biblical passages, rather than to form grand, overarching theories.

Most surprising, in the light of the later solidification of Reformed thought, is the variety of nuance at this point. What is imputed to the race appears to be the guilt, not of Adam's sin, but of "our first parents," Eve clearly included. Moreover, this is based on the premise that they are "the root of all mankind." Imputation is here grounded on genetic solidarity, rather than a judicial appointment of a covenantal nature. The placement in the chapter on sin, rather than in the following one on the covenant, emphasizes this contrast. The Larger Catechism mirrors this emphasis in LC 21, where it is said that our first parents transgressed the commandment of God and thereby fell.

The main reason why this is so is that covenant theology was still developing in the 1640s. There were many who were not prepared to consider it to the extent that others were. Thus, for a confessional statement, a full degree of agreement was lacking. An individual theologian can write what he wishes, within the bounds of what is accepted as orthodoxy; this does not mean that everything he writes, or all that may be true, is appropriate for a confession. There may not be sufficient consensus at the time on the matter; the agreement may come later. Not until 1602 was there a clear statement to the effect that the sin of Adam in particular is imputed to the human race. This idea had not gained sufficient ground forty years later to secure the approval of all.

However, in WCF 6.3 there is a semicolon after "imputed." The nature of the imputation is unspecified, but the lengthy series of proof texts includes Romans 5:12–19. This may indicate that the imputation in view is that of the sin of Adam, whereas the death in sin and corrupted nature, mentioned after the semicolon, is attributable to both parents and to the process of natural generation. This is unlikely, and at best ambiguous, since the preceding clause points to both parents and highlights their being the root of mankind.

What Light Do the Minutes Shed on This Question?

The minutes contain only a cursory report of debate on the draft chapter of the Confession and the relevant questions in the Catechism. These texts occupied only parts of four sessions, from S536 M 17.11.45am to S540 F 21.11.45am, evidently excluding S538 W 19.11.45.[6] The most noteworthy event, in S540 F 21.11.45, was an attempt by Edward Reynolds to have this explanatory addition inserted: "Death did not flow out of the condition of the created nature of man as the proper cause thereof, but was brought into the world only by sin. Eternall death is not the extinguishing, abolishing or anihiliating of Reprobate men and angells, but their being everlastingly separated from the glory of God and undergoing of those hellish torments which the wrath of God shall inflict upon them."[7] Note its attempt to provide distance from the view that the wicked are annihilated after the judgment. This was a theme taught by the Socinians, who were beginning to pose a threat in Western Europe, having begun in Poland. This proposal did not meet with the Assembly's approval. There is no record of why it failed to gain inclusion. It is highly unlikely that the divines disagreed with its content; it is more probable that it was not considered necessary for inclusion in a confessional document.

There is slightly more detail on the discussions during the earlier consideration of the Thirty-Nine Articles, and the debate lasted a good deal longer. John Lightfoot records in his journal something of the debates on article 9 on original sin. These reports show clearly that there was overwhelming support at the Assembly for the idea of the imputation of Adam's sin. In S17 W 2.8.43, when the report on the article was presented, there was what Lightfoot records as a

6. Van Dixhoorn, 6:217–20.
7. Ibid., 6:220.

"slow and long" debate. A significant change was made to the report: instead of "Man is very farr gone," it was agreed to insert "Man is wholly deprived of Originall righteousnesse."[8] The next session, S18 TH 3.8.43, saw another attempt to strengthen the language, with a proposal to add "onely"—giving the phrase "of his [man's] owne nature onely inclined to evill."[9] However, in S19 F 4.8.43 "an earnest & vehement agitation & debate" erupted, during which the Assembly revoked the previous day's vote. Scriptural proof was added to the rest of the article. The reporter of the committee stated something on the imputation of Adam's sin, but there was insufficient time to discuss it.[10] However, the debate on this matter did take place when the Assembly resumed on Monday, in S20 M 7.8.43. It lasted until noon, but nothing was resolved. This was, of course, a development from the article. In S21 TU 8.8.43, the Assembly discussed the scriptural evidence for the imputation of Adam's sin. "Mr. Gataker onely of all the assembly opposed the Doctrine, but when he had spoken what he could, & had bin answered to the full, but would not be satisfied, it was at last concluded upon Affirmatively & these places voted for its confirmation: Rom. 5:12–19; Gen. 2:17; 1 Cor. 15:22."[11] In the next session, S22 W 9.8.43, the divines concluded their treatment of article 9, with the addition of the italicized phrase in: "Originall sin standeth . . . but *together with Adam's sin imputed*, it is the fault . . . ."[12] In all, the Assembly spent six sessions on the topic, occupying over one week. It is clear that at this early stage the Assembly was committed to the doctrine that Adam's sin was imputed to the race, and that this was connected with, but distinguishable from, the transmission of original sin.

Why then, when it came to the Confession and Catechism, was there this reluctance to mention something for which there was overwhelming approval? It is not that this was denied—it was absent because it had not yet been developed to such an extent that it had become the accepted currency. But how far did these nuances repre-

8. Ibid., 2:21.
9. Ibid., 2:22.
10. Ibid., 2:23.
11. Ibid., 2:24.
12. Ibid., 2:25.

sent a stage in the development of the doctrine of the imputation of Adam's sin, rather than a settled and finalized verdict?

Morris again shows himself a superior interpreter of the divines than A. A. Hodge, who failed to recognize the tensions present within the documents. Morris comments on LC 25–26, describing original sin as not merely the guilt of the original offense but also the lack of righteousness and the corruption conveyed from our first parents by natural generation. He recognizes that the same view is present in SC 16 and WCF 6; in all these places it is a natural process, rather than a legal imputation. This, he remarks, raises questions about legal imputation, particularly in view of the argument that it is a necessary accompaniment of the covenant of works.[13] He points to both continental and British creeds, none of which mention imputation,[14] although his case is weakened by their having been written long before; a lot of development had occurred in the meantime. Corruption is itself sin, Morris continues, and belongs to all the descendants of Adam— and it is in corruption itself that our true guiltiness is to be found. The proper distinction between Adam and his descendants must be maintained.[15] Hence, Morris argues that mediate imputation has warrant in the Reformed tradition. In view of this background, and the nature of WCF 6.3, he asks "whether indeed this is not an instance in which the divines of Westminster consciously admitted a variety of statements somewhat incongruous, in deference to the various opinions existing among themselves." They were not Pelagians, "nor were they partially Augustinian, recognizing a liability and an infection, but limiting sinfulness or exposure to retributive results, to personal action only." They held to the unity and solidarity of the race under a divine constitution, rendering certain the transmission of depravity from birth. "They affirmed as a fact what is beyond question a fundamental fact, however explained or inexplicable."[16]

While Morris is aware of the problem, and considers the historical background in some detail, the confessions he cites were all written

13. Morris, *Westminster Symbols*, 272–73.
14. Augsburg Confession, 2; Formula of Concord, 1; First Helvetic Confession, 7–8; Second Helvetic Confession, 8; Heidelberg Catechism, 10; Belgic Confession, 15.
15. Morris, *Westminster Symbols*, 274.
16. Ibid., 275–76.

generations before Westminster and in very different contexts. The latest Reformed confession he lists, the Second Helvetic Confession, was published in 1566, nearly eighty years earlier. A lot of thought had gone into the matter in the meantime, and the idea that Adam's sin was imputed to the race had gained ground. That it had not yet received universal approval is evident in the differing nature of the Assembly's documents. However, as the following historical excursus indicates, the trajectory of thought was pointing clearly to the imputation of Adam's sin as an entailment from Paul's discussion in Romans 5. As Reformed theologians reflected on the connection between Adam's first sin and our own participation in it, and in particular as they grappled with the apostle Paul in Romans 5:12–21, the questions listed below began to formulate in their minds, although, in the nature of theological thought, the answers took longer to reach and still further to achieve widespread approval.

Excursus 2: The Development of the Doctrine of the Imputation of Adam's Sin from Calvin to Westminster

A discussion of the development of the doctrine of the imputation of Adam's sin is important in understanding where Reformed theology stood as the Westminster divines considered the matter in the 1640s. The key questions to be worked out during the development of the doctrine included the following:

1. Was the connection between the first sin and the rest of the race based on natural propagation and thus to be understood as inherited corruption (original sin)?
2. Was this connection also to be seen as due to a determination by God that Adam was the representative of the race, so that his sin was reckoned or imputed to his posterity?
3. If the answer to (2) is positive, what is the connection between (1) and (2)?
4. Was *Adam's* sin or the sin *of the first parents* imputed to the human race? The former points to a representative relationship, although it does not require it, while the latter is more clearly based on natural descent and so places the transmission of original sin in the primary position.

5. Related to (3), on what basis was the sin imputed? Was it by natural propagation? Was it on the grounds of a decree by God? Was it related to a covenant that God had made with Adam by which he was constituted the representative of the race?

6. How does the development of answers to these questions relate to the emergence of the idea of the covenant of works or covenant of life?

7. Was obedience before the fall meritorious or instead something God accepted through grace? The important book by John Ball, *A treatise of the covenant of grace* (1645), published posthumously while the Assembly sat, and which was received with much favor by the divines, denies that Adam's works were meritorious and insists on the grace of God as permeating his covenant.[17]

In order to address these questions, we shall examine the contributions of a range of significant representative theologians in the Reformed tradition from 1536 to the time leading up to the Assembly. We shall proceed, as far as possible, in chronological sequence, allowing for the fact that since Latin was the *lingua franca* of the educated classes of Europe it provided the means for the cross-fertilization of ideas on a continent-wide basis.

Martin Bucer (1491–1551)

Martin Bucer was the leader of the church at Strasbourg until the Augsburg Interim (1548) forced his departure. He was appointed Regius Professor of Divinity at Cambridge and remained there until his death. He had significant influence on Calvin, who spent three years at Strasbourg between his first and second periods in Geneva. In his lengthy commentary on Romans (1536), Bucer understands the relationship between Adam and the race organically and realistically. Commenting on Romans 5:12ff., there is not a hint that he considered Adam to be a representative in a legal sense. This is not surprising, since the covenant idea had only come to the surface in a significant way a decade or so before, in the writings of Zwingli, Bullinger, and Œcolampadius, and at this time was used solely of the covenant of grace. Hence, he writes that "such as Adam was, such were those born to him: hence they sinned in the loins of Adam and were lost." This, Bucer concludes, applies to infants

---

17. John Ball, *A treatise of the covenant of grace* (London: Simeon Ash, 1645) [Wing B579], 6–12.

as well.[18] In this passage, Paul is speaking of the transmission of sin, not its entrance. Adam was responsible for sin's propagation. His sin was conveyed by generation. In turn, we convey depravity to our children.[19] The first sin was that of our first parents.[20]

John Calvin (1509–64)

In his commentary on Romans (1539), Calvin states that Adam received for his posterity, as well as for himself, the gifts of divine grace, so by falling from the Lord he corrupted, vitiated, depraved, and ruined our nature. We have all sinned because we are all imbued with natural corruption, and for this reason are wicked and perverse.[21] There is definite evidence that Calvin recognized that Adam's sin was imputed, but this was not the principal point he wanted to make: "We are condemned by Adam's sin not by imputation alone (*non per solam imputationem*), as though we were being punished for another's sin; but we suffer his punishment because we too are guilty, since God holds our nature, which has been corrupted in Adam, guilty of iniquity."[22] In this he was in agreement with Bucer, although there is evidence here that Calvin recognized that imputation was part of the picture, even though not a dominant one.

Fesko argues that Calvin speaks of the guilt of Adam's fall in terms of imputation in the 1559 edition of the *Institutes*, 2.1.7.[23] However, Calvin speaks there of the contagion of sin originating neither in the flesh (which Aquinas held) nor the soul, but because it had been ordained of God. His theme is original sin and its transmission, not the guilt of sin and its imputation. Fesko thinks Calvin's view is in harmony with the Westminster teaching on imputed guilt. But Calvin's stress here is on guilt by propagation of a corrupt nature, although he also mentions God's ordination that

18. ". . . ut enim in omnes homines a primo parente peccatum invasit: illa ingenii nostri corruptio, ut vera bona nec cognoscere . . . in Adam omnes fuimus, in eo ergo & peccavimus, & mortui sumus . . . sic & lumbis Adae peccarunt & perditi sunt, quotquot homines sunt & erunt." Martin Bucer, *Metaphrasis et enarrationes in perpetuae epistolarum d. Pauli apostoli* (Strasbourg, 1536), 1:253–54.

19. Ibid., 1:257–58.

20. Ibid., 1:263.

21. "Peccavimus igitur omnes, quia naturali corruptione omnes imbuti sumus; ideoque iniqui ac perversi." Calvin, Comm. Rom. 5:12.

22. "Prior est, quod peccato Adae non per solam imputationem damnatur, acsi alieni peccati exigeretur a nobis poena; sed ideo poenam eius sustinemus, quia et culpae sumus rei, quatenus scilicet natura nostra in ipso vitiata, iniquitatis reatu obstringitur apud Deum." Calvin, Comm. Rom. 5:17.

23. Fesko, "Westminster Confession and Lapsarianism," 521.

Adam was the representative of the race. As such, this is a natural connection before it is a federal one.[24]

Heinrich Bullinger (1504–75)

In his *Decades* (1550–51), a series of five groups of ten sermons each, covering the whole field of Christian doctrine, Heinrich Bullinger, who succeeded Zwingli as leader of the church at Zurich, gives extensive consideration to sin as hereditary depravity. However, there is nothing on the guilt of Adam's first sin, still less any hint that Bullinger saw Adam's relationship to his posterity in terms of legal representation with his sin imputed. The *Decades* were quite influential in England. John Whitgift made them compulsory reading for clergy in the diocese of Lincoln when he was bishop, and later followed suit on his elevation to Canterbury.[25]

Wolfgang Musculus (1497–1563)

Wolfgang Musculus did most of his creative work at Berne, from 1549 onward, and was frequently in correspondence with Bullinger. In his commentary on Genesis 2:15–17, he states that God spoke to Adam, not to Eve, because Adam was the head of his wife.[26] However, a law (*lex*) was given to both of them. But there is nothing in this whole section about a covenant. Musculus restricts the terms *foedus* and *testamentum* to the Noachic and Abrahamic covenants.[27]

Musculus deals more extensively with the matter in his Romans commentary, published around the same time. The word *sin* in the context mainly refers to corruption (*principaliter de corruptione naturae humanae*). He counters Pelagian arguments that this corruption affects the rest of the race through imitation by referring to the deaths of infants, who obviously cannot actively sin. He asks by whom sin entered. Both Jerome and Ambrose held Eve to be responsible. On the other hand, Tertullian thought that while the beginning of sin was due to Eve, its propagation

24. ". . . ita corruptionis exordium in Adam fuit, ut perpetuo defluxu, a prioribus in posteros transfundatur. Neque enim in substantia carnis aut animae causam habet contagio: sed quia a Deo ita fuit ordinatum." Calvin, *Opera Selecta*, ed. Petrus Barth and Guilielmus Niesel (Berne: Chr. Kaiser, 1928), 3:236.

25. Henry Bullinger, *The Decades of Henry Bullinger* (ed. T. Harding; Parker Society; Cambridge: University Press, 1850), 2:358–432.

26. Wolfgang Musculus, *In Genesim Mosis commentarii plenissimi* (Basel: Sebastian Henricpetri, 1554?), 61.

27. Ibid., 60–65.

was dependent on Adam.[28] In what way did all sin in Adam? The phrase *in quo* (in whom) can be explained in various ways, he suggests. The simplest is that we were in the loins of Adam when he sinned (*in lumbis illius primi peccatoris, ex cuius massa nati sumus*). He cites Hebrews 7, where Levi is said to have been in the loins of Abraham when the latter paid tithes to Melchizedek. This explains why infants die, even though they have not committed any actual sins. Just as we are not virtually justified through the obedience of Christ, but actually justified, so we are not virtually sinners in Adam, but actually sinners (*ita non solum virtualiter peccatores sumus in Adam facti, sed & actualiter*). We are condemned, not only because we ourselves have done evil, but because of the sin of Adam (*sed ipsum eitam peccatum Adae, nos condemnat*). Echoing Paul, since death still occurred from Adam to Moses, while there was no law, no transgression, and so no actual mortal sins, it follows that another sin was involved (*nempe ex illius peccato, qui primus legem Dei transgressus, hoc venenum in fudit in omnes posteros*)—the sin of Adam.[29] Musculus is more expansive here, since he follows the more detailed text of Romans. However, his view is that Adam's posterity is implicated in his sin by natural descent.

That the question for Musculus is the propagation of original sin is also clear in his *Loci communes*. The transmission of sin from Adam occurred by propagation; thus, the origin of sin is attributed to Adam, not to Eve, although it appears she was the first to sin.[30] There is no mention of Adam's sin being imputed to the race. The real question for Musculus is the propagation of original sin.

Pietro Martire Vermigli (Peter Martyr) (1500–1562)

Pietro Martire Vermigli, an Italian colleague of Bucer at Strasbourg until 1548, was then appointed Regius Professor of Theology at Oxford at the same time as Bucer took the corresponding post at Cambridge. When Mary acceded to the throne, he fled to Zurich, where he remained. He discusses our question at length in his commentary on Romans (1558). There is both a similarity and difference between Adam and Christ. The differences are greater. Adam brought sin, death, and damnation; Christ brings righteousness, life, and grace. There is a difference also in propagation; Adam's evil is transmitted to people through

28. Wolfgang Musculus, *In Epistolam d. apostoli Pauli ad Romanos, commentarii* (Basel: Sebastian Henricpetri, 1555?), 92–93.

29. Ibid., 94.

30. Wolfgang Musculus, *Loci communes theologiae sacrae* (Basel: Sebastian Henricpetri, n.d.), 20.

fleshly generation, whereas Christ's benefits come through faith (*Adamus enim mala sua per carnis generationem in homines transfudit: Christus autem per fidem*). There is not a true *similitudo* but an *analogia*. The gift from Christ surpasses the curse from Adam in many ways. Adam by one sin ruined all our race. Christ removed (*aboleverit*) not only that one sin, but many others. More grace is given to man (*imputationem iustitiae per Christum*) than was extinguished by sin.[31] In saying that "judgment comes from one to condemnation," it is unclear whether Vermigli understands it to be from one man or from one sin. Sins after Adam are the fruit of the sin of our first parents and the original guilt that was passed on to us (*ex originale culpa in quemlibet nostrum transfusa, alia peccata esse nata*). However, not all guilt is necessarily connected with that original sin (original in the sense that it was the first sin), for adults who are damned are damned on account of their own sins (*adulti vero, qui damnant, non eo solo pereunt, sed & propter actualia peccata, quae adiecerunt*).[32]

In response to the obvious point that no one is responsible for an alien sin, one in which they had no hand (*Nam alieno vitio nemo dicitur peccator*), Vermigli asks why then does it say that many were constituted sinners? The reason lies with concupiscence and the great depravity of nature in the human race through Adam's transgression (*concupiscentia enim, & naturae magna de pravatio in nostrum genus per Adami transgressionem irrupit*).[33] It is in this way that the race sinned in Adam. Pelagians say that Adam's sin is propagated through imitation, but Christ's righteousness is not received through imitation, nor does the argument hold with infants who die. God does not impute to us the sin of another, but our own (*in culpa originis imputare nobis alienum peccatum, sed nostrum ipsorum iniquitatem, quae naturae adhaeret iam inde ab ipsa origine*). Here there is an implicit acknowledgement of imputation, but it rests on inherited corruption; the sin is ours by virtue of a shared nature with the fallen Adam.[34]

In his *Common Places* (London, 1583), a posthumous synthesis of his theology compiled by Robert Masson, and structured artificially according to Calvin's *Institutes*, Vermigli locates the transmission of original sin in the heat of lust that happens in procreation, citing and following Augustine, with whom Aquinas had agreed.[35] However, corruption is not the natural effect

31. Pietro Martire Vermigli, *In epistolam S. Pauli apostoli ad Romanos commentarii doctissimi* (Basel: Petrum Pernam, 1558), 158.
32. Ibid., 159.
33. Ibid., 162–63.
34. Ibid., 170.
35. Pietro Martire Vermigli, *The common places of the most famous and renowned divine Doctor Peter Martyr, divided into foure principall parts* (trans. A. Marten; London: Henrie Denham, Thomas Chard, William Broome, and Andrew Maunsell, 1583) [STC 24669], 219.

of sin. Rather, it proceeded from divine justice, by which the grace of the Spirit and the heavenly gifts were withdrawn when man sinned. Corruption comes from God's justice, the blame resting largely with the first man. We do not eat and drink immoderately in order to get gout, but when we do these things, the gout follows of its own accord. So Adam would not have had all these things happen, but when he sinned, they happened of themselves.[36] Vermigli cites Augustine again, writing that "God is exceedingly good, and doth not impute the sinnes of others unto us . . . but the iniquitie of our owne selves, which cleaveth to our owne nature, even from the first beginning of all." Death and "an infinite heape of calamities" show there is some sin to be punished in Adam's descendants. Here imputation surfaces again.[37] So, original sin is a corruption of the whole nature of man, derived by generation from the fall of our first parent.[38] The seed is the instrument whereby this sin is conveyed from parents to their children.[39] The punishment of the sin of the fathers to the third and fourth generation shows that "no other children shall beare the offenses of their forefathers, but such as shall be like unto them."[40] The phrase in Romans 5, "by one man," refers to Adam, "who was as a certaine common lumpe or masse, wherein was conteined all mankind: which lumpe being corrupted, we cannot be brought forth into the world, but corrupted and defiled." Original sin is ascribed to Adam, although Eve transgressed first. Vermigli thinks "one man" stands for the common name of man, as well Adam as Eve. Paul views the root of sin in the succession and procreation ascribed to man, because Adam is the root of sin.[41]

There are hints in Vermigli that he recognized that the sin of Adam is imputed. However, his overwhelming interest is in original sin, the corruption of nature transmitted from Adam by natural generation. While he was in England for only four years, escaping to the continent on the accession of Mary in 1553, he is nevertheless a significant source for the development of English Reformed theology.

Dudley Fenner (1558–87)

Moving ahead a generation, we come to Dudley Fenner, whose major work, *Sacra theologia* (1585), was the first Puritan systematic theology. Fenner

36. Ibid., 220.
37. Ibid., 221.
38. Ibid., 224.
39. Ibid., 231.
40. Ibid., 237.
41. Ibid., 242.

considers that all participated in the sin of Adam since they were in his loins and are descended from him by natural propagation. So all took part in the sin (all who are descended by the natural law of propagation of the seed).[42] He also writes of all who were in the person of Adam by that contract (*illo contractu*), although he doesn't mention the covenant of works (the first time the term had appeared) until a few pages later.[43] Fenner, who introduces the term *foedus operum*, if not the concept,[44] brings together both realistic and representative elements. Both natural propagation and a contract made by God place the human race in Adam and account for its involvement in his first sin. He does not develop these ideas at length.

William Perkins (1558–1602)

Arguably no theologian exercised greater influence on English theology in the early decades of the seventeenth century than William Perkins. He was a fellow of Christ's College, Cambridge, and then lecturer at St. Andrews, Cambridge, and a prolific author. In *The foundation of the Christian religion*, published in 1590,[45] he states that all were wholly corrupted with sin through Adam's fall and so are slaves of Satan and guilty of eternal damnation. He refers to Romans 5:12, but makes no attempt to explain how this happened.[46] The same year he published *A Golden Chaine*.[47] Here Perkins focuses on inherited corruption, but also writes of Adam as representing the whole human race, which thereby was implicated, not only in corruption, but also in guilt. Out of the corrupt state of the first parents arose the estate of sin, whereby God included all our sins. In this estate, we participate in both Adam's transgression and his guilt, according to Romans 5:12. The reason for this is that "Adam was not then a private man, but represented all mankind." Again, when Adam offended, "his posteritie was in his loynes, from whom they should by the course of nature, issue: and therefore take part

42. "Peccatum illud posteritatis, est unicum illud παράπτωμα quod omnes in lumbis Adami ex lege naturali de semine propogando cum ipso perpetrarunt. Rom. 5.12." Dudley Fenner, *Sacra theologia, sive veritas quae secundum pietatem* (Geneva, 1585), 78–79.

43. "Reatus illius peccati est reatus poenae de toto illo contractu in Adami persona ad posteritatem totam, lege praedicta propogando." Ibid., 78–79. For his reference to the *foedus operum*, see 86–87.

44. See R. Letham, "The Foedus Operum: Some Factors Accounting for Its Development," *SCJ* 14 (1983): 63–76.

45. First English edition [STC 19709].

46. William Perkins, *The Workes of that famous and worthie minister of Christ, in the Universitie of Cambridge, Mr. W. Perkins* ([Cambridge:] Iohn Legate, 1608) [STC 19649], 1:1.

47. Perkins, *Armilla aurea*, 1590 Latin edition [STC 19655]. The first English edition appeared in 1600 [STC 19646].

of the guiltinesse with him." Here participation in Adam's sin and guilt is through natural descent, although he is a representative of all mankind. Out of Adam's transgression arises original sin, which is corruption engendered in our first conception, with every faculty of body and soul being prone and disposed to evil.[48]

By 1595, Perkins had developed this theme further. In his *Exposition of the symbol or creed of the apostles*,[49] he argues that the greatness of this sin is that Adam was not a private man, "but as a root or head, bearing in it all mankind, or as a public person, representing all his posteritie, and therefore when he sinned, all his posteritie sinned with him; as in a Parliament whatever is done by the Burgesse of the shire, is done by every person in the shire."[50] In this explanation, clearly, Adam has a representative relationship with the human race, rather than a merely natural one, although it is by no means clear that Perkins sees the connection between the representative and the represented as involving imputation. However, the relationship does rest on an appointment by God,[51] by which Adam was made the root of his posterity. From the fall of Adam springs original sin. "God took this order in creation, that whatsoever evil Adam procured he should bring it not onely on himselfe, but upon all his posteritie: by virtue of which decree, the propogation of sinne is continued without any interruption, though parents themselves be borne anew by the spirit of God."[52] The representative headship of Adam—ordained by God—is for Perkins the root of the transmission of original corruption to posterity. This is a reversal of the earlier order in Calvin, Bucer, and the others. However, the appointment by God of Adam to represent the race entails the transmission of evil, rather than *explicitly* the imputation of guilt.

What is implicit becomes explicit in Perkins's *A commentarie upon the 11. chaptere of the Epistle to the Hebrewes*, a book first published as *A cloud of faithfull witnesses, leading to the heavenly Canaan*.[53] He puts the matter in very straightforward terms:

> Every man that came from Adam, sinned in the sinne of Adam: thou must therefore knowe, that his sinne . . . was thy sinne: and thou sinnedst therein, as well as he (though thou wast then unborne) and that thou art guilty of

48. Perkins, *Workes*, 1:19–20.
49. First English edition [STC 19703].
50. Perkins, *Workes*, 1:164.
51. Ibid., 1:165.
52. Ibid., 1:166.
53. William Perkins, *A cloud of faithfull witnesses, leading to the heavenly Canaan* (London: Humfrey Lownes for Leo. Greene, 1607) [STC (2nd ed.) 19677.5].

it before God, and must answer for it to Gods iustice, unlesse Christ doe it for thee. The reason hereof is, because we are his seede and posteritie, we were then in his loines, he was the father of us all: and was not a private man as we are now, but a publike person, the pledge of all mankind, and bare the person of us all at that time: therefore what he did then, he did it for himselfe, and for us: What covenant God made with him, was made for himselfe and us: what God promised him, and he to God, he promised for himselfe, and for us; what he received in his Creation, he received for himselfe, and for us: and what he gained or lost by his fall, he gained and lost for us, as for himselfe. He lost the favour of God, and originall puritie: therefore he lost it for all his posteritie: guiltinesse, and Gods anger, and corruption of nature which he gained, he lost for us all, as well as for himselfe. If we doubt of this point, it is prooved by the Apostle.[54]

Perkins asks why we should suffer for another's sin. The objection would stand if it were Adam's sin alone, "but it was his and thine also."[55] Perkins has developed a realistic and organic connection between Adam and the race. He has introduced the covenant into the picture. He has proposed that Adam is the representative of all people. There is no specific mention of imputation as such, but all the ingredients are there.

Imputation is finally spelled out precisely by Perkins in *A godly and learned exposition upon the whole epistle of Jude*, published posthumously in 1606.[56] Here he states that Adam "sinned actually, and we by relation and imputation." We are the cause of our own sin—"himselfe is a cause, although not in himselfe, yet in Adam before he was borne he procured that he should bee borne a naturall man." Why God allowed this is "a iust iudgement of God silently to be with reverence rested in, and not with curiositie to be searched out."[57] Perkins has taken the discussion on from our sharing in Adam's sin by our hereditary connection, and the inherited corruption that entails, to an appointment by God in which we share in Adam's guilt, a judgment in which we are to rest with reverent silence.

Robert Rollock (1555–99)

From 1583, Robert Rollock was sole regent of the newly founded College of James VI, later Edinburgh University. Additionally, from 1586, he took pastoral charge of a congregation. In his commentary on Romans (1596),

54. Perkins, *Workes*, 3:2:415. He cites Rom. 5:12–14.
55. Ibid.
56. First English edition, 1606 [STC 19724].
57. Perkins, *Workes*, 3:2:75b.

Rollock argues that Paul's comparison is not between Adam and Christ, but between the sin that exists through Adam and the righteousness that comes through Christ.[58] It is also a comparison between their effects, life and death. Sin is in view, not only as a contagion, but also in terms of all kinds of sin, original and actual (*non tam solus Adami, quam nostrum omnium in lumbis euis, & corrupteli eam insecuta, positum: quam actuale*). For Rollock, we were all in Adam's loins—there is no hint of a federal relationship.[59] All without exception sinned; all are without merit; without exception death entered. All sinned, so to speak, actually (*ait enim omnes peccase, ut ita loquor, actualiter*). Sin is not imputed where the law did not exist; from these words, it is evident that Paul is talking about actual sin.[60] The universality of sin is seen in the case of infants who die while not having committed actual sins. For this reason, this sin is the corrupt nature we receive by heredity. Adam is presented here as a type; it is a comparison, not always an equal one.[61] The Father imputed to us the merit and grace of Christ. It is the second part of the comparison: on the one hand, the necessary penalty is attached to the fault of Adam; on the other, there is the gift of righteousness.[62] Rollock regards sin in Romans 5:12ff. as actual sin, not original sin. Notwithstanding, he does recognize that original sin is included within the scope of Paul's definition. He agrees that Christ's righteousness is imputed to us in justification, but he does not introduce any idea of the imputation of Adam's sin.[63]

In his *Tractatus de vocatione efficaci*, published the following year[64] and translated as *A Treatise of God's effectual calling*, an important work in the development of covenant theology, Rollock viewed sin not as a substance, but an accident; as privative, or want of conformity to the law of God.[65] In this he followed Augustine. Original sin "is in us & with us from our first being, conception, and nativity: for it comes by propogation, and is derived from parents to children, as an hereditary disease, as a leprie, the stone, or any such malady of the body."[66] Its nature is threefold. First, it is that

58. Robert Rollock, *In epistolam S. Pauli apostoli ad Romanos* (Geneva: Franc. lePreux, 1596), 93.
59. Ibid., 94.
60. Ibid., 95.
61. Ibid., 96.
62. Ibid., 98.
63. Ibid., 99–102.
64. Robert Rollock, *Tractatus de vocatione efficaci* (Edinburgh: Robert Waldegrave, 1597) [STC 19956].
65. Robert Rollock, *A treatise of God's effectual calling* (trans. Henry Holland; London: Felix Kyngston, 1603) [STC (2nd ed.) 21286], 127.
66. Ibid., 133.

apostasy into which we all fell away from God in the loins of Adam: "This we receive from our mothers wombs for we are al born Apostates." This apostasy was not Adam's only, "but did appertaine to us al," for we were all in his loins, as parcels of the substance and nature of the first man and so we all fell in him.[67] This first apostasy is past, but the guilt remains, "for every man is borne guilty by nature of that first Apostasie." "Wherefore every man is guilty of that first defection and falling from God, untill this guilt be taken away by the bloud of a mediator."[68] Second, it consists in the lack of original justice. Third, it is an inclination contrary to that original justice and integrity, described as our natural corruption.[69] The propagation of original sin is by the bodies of parents to their children.[70] How does that first sin have the power to transmit sin to every one of Adam's progeny? Rollock answers that it is "by reason of that word and covenant which God made with Adam in his creation" (*efficaciam illius peccati ex verbo & foedere quodem Dei esse, quod in prima creatione pepigit cum Adamo . . . sin minus steterit sed lapsus fuerit, labetur sibi & suis: & quodcunque malum in ipso est, id omne transmittet in posteros suos*). This "ought to content all sober wits," he concludes.[71] Rollock has brought the matter into connection with the covenant made by God with Adam, a prominent theme in this book. However, it is the transmission of corruption rather than the imputation of guilt that is in the forefront of his mind. This is confirmed by his citation of opinions of the schoolmen, including that "this sin in Adam was reall and actually his; but it is ours only by imputation" (*Secunda, Hoc peccatum in Adamo fuit re ipsa, in posteris autem ipsius est per imputationem*), alongside which is a marginal comment: "Three grosse opinions of papists concerning originall sin."[72] For Rollock, it appears that there is guilt attached to our participation in the first sin of Adam, but this guilt is identical with the inheritance of corruption we receive through having been in his loins. He dismisses the idea of imputation of Adam's sin as a dangerous view of the schoolmen.

Johannes Piscator (1546–1625)

Piscator, a prolific biblical commentator and theologian, taught theology at Heidelberg, Neustadt, and, from 1584 until his death, at

---

67. Ibid., 134–35.
68. Ibid., 135.
69. Ibid., 136.
70. Ibid., 141–42.
71. Rollock, *Tractatus*, 193–94.
72. Ibid., 196; Rollock, *Treatise*, 143.

Herborn. In commenting on Romans 5, as part of a larger set of commentaries on the Pauline epistles published in 1590, Piscator writes of us
having sinned in Adam's loins (*in illius lumbis*).[73] This sin is imputed, but
it is on the basis of hereditary propagation (*nempe per imputationem, idque
iure haereditatio, propogatum scilicet per generationis naturalis successionem*).[74]
In *De iustificatione hominis coram Deo* (1609), Piscator states that the
principal part of original sin is that by the sin of our first parents we were
made sinners.[75] This, Piscator contends, is by imputation. By that first sin,
we were made guilty and incurred the penalty of death; both guilt and
penalty spread to all.[76] Piscator's Roman opponents deny it, but Scripture
confirms it. Two Pontifical dogmaticians—Pighius and Catharinus—agree
that the sin of Adam is ours by imputation (*qui peccatum Adami nostrum
solum esse quam sententiam etiam Iesuita impugnat imputatione afferunt*).
The Jesuits, on the other hand, argue that original sin consists in the fact
that we were in the loins of Adam when he sinned. To us, however, this
is not a bare imputation, nor something that rests only on the fact that
we were in Adam's loins, but the first sin is really and actually ours (*Ad
nos autem quod attinet, peccati Adami reos non esse, non nuda imputatione,
non quod potentia solum in Adami lumbis eramus, verum, vere, & realiter, &
aliquo modo actualiter contendimus. Hoc autem hac ratione demonstramus:
Eodem modo quo mors, peccati Adami poena, derivata est in posteros, eodem
modo & peccatum: verum mors ipsa in nos dominetur vere, & reipsa, non
imputatione aut potentia tantum*).[77] It is conveyed to posterity in the same
way as death. Infants are subject to death, and so to sin. This is the chief
part of original sin—guilt and obligation to punishment (*reatus culpae, &
obligatio ad poenam*). The other part of original sin is the general depravity of the whole human nature.[78] In short, contrary to Rome, for Piscator
original sin is not merely the privation of original righteousness, but also
something positive, a true and real depravity.[79]

73. Johannes Piscator, *Epistolarum Pauli ad Romanos, Corinthios, Ephesios, Philippenses, Colossenses, Thessalonicenses* (London: George Bishop, 1591) [STC (2nd ed.) 19956], 44–45, 48.
74. Ibid., 48–49.
75. Johannes Piscator, *De iustificatione hominis coram Deo* (Leiden: Andreas Clouquius,
1609), 78.
76. " . . . prima est, qua eo peccato & peccati, & inobedientiae primorum parentum
rei facti sumus, quae propagatione est nostra . . . [he cites Rom. 5:19] simulque cum
culpa poena est propogata, id est, mors in omnes pervasit . . . [here he cites Rom. 5:12]."
Ibid., 78.
77. Ibid., 78–79.
78. Ibid., 79.
79. Ibid., 80–81.

Guilielmus Bucanus (d. 1603)

In a long section dealing with the soul and the body, Bucanus argues for the transmission of original sin from Adam by propagation. This is the *modus* of transmission; the reality is the just judgment of God. Thus all were comprehended in the one man, as the root and head of the human race (*qui sicut omnes homines in uno, tanquam radice & capite humani generis, iustitia originali ornaverat: sic postquam peccavit Adam, in eodem omnes merito donis suis spoliavit*). All sinned in Adam because they were in his loins, and Adam's sin was imputed. In this, Bucanus places the imputation of the guilt of Adam's sin as the root of the inheritance of a corrupt nature.[80]

Bucanus considers that if Adam had continued in that original righteousness, Christ would still have had to be a mediator, not to reconcile us to God or to heal us from sin, but to keep us in the grace of God and preserve us from sin permanently. There is no hint that Adam would have been granted everlasting life as an inherent right as a result of continued obedience. If he had persisted in that original righteousness, it would have come down to his posterity, for three reasons: first, it was a righteousness of human nature, and so not a personal or private righteousness; second, original sin was handed down to Adam's posterity; third, like produces like in nature. However, the main reason was the ordination of God (*sed ex Dei ordinatione*).[81]

Derived from original sin is not only the loss of original righteousness and natural corruption, but also guilt, an obligation to eternal punishment by which Adam involved his posterity by his first act of disobedience, which was imputed to all of us, so that it was our act. This follows from the whole race being in Adam's loins.[82] Christ did not sin in Adam, since he was conceived

---

80. "Nam quamprimum omnia per se munda, unitur corpori in peccatis concepto, imputatur homini tanquam sua inobedientia illa prima parentis, unde Apostolus dicit, nos omnes in Adamo, tanquam in radice pecasse, 1.reos factus esse, in ipsius videlicet lumbis inclusos, Rom. 5.12. Quo modo etiam Levi dicitur, antequam esset in rerum natura, declinatus in Abrahamo, Heb. 7.9,10. Imputatam autem illam inobedientiam Adami, statim ex iusta Dei ordinatione, consequitur in anima etiam contagium, sive corruptio, & ad malum propensio, tanquam poena illius primi peccati, quae poena & ipsa peccatum est: sicut obedientia Christi nobis imputata proprie est nostra iustitia, qua iustificamur." Guilielmus Bucanus, *Institutiones theologiae seu locorum communium Christianae religionis* ([Geneva:] Ioannes & Isaias lePreux, 1604), 97.

81. Ibid., 106–7.

82. " . . . non solum ipsa iustitiae originalis privatio totiusque naturae corruptio: sed etiam reatus, id est obligatio ad poenam aeternam, qua se Adamus, & posteritatem suam involvit, id est ipsa prima Adae inobedientia quatenus nobis omnibus imputatur, ac proinde quae licet nos actu, reatu tamen & imputatione in omnes homines pertransit, sicuti Rom. 5.12. Omnes in Adamo tanquam in radice & massa generis humani pecasse pronuntiamur, quippe qui omnes in eius lumbis eramus." Ibid., 170.

by the Holy Spirit, not by the seed of man. From this, original sin is transmitted to all of Adam's descendants apart from Christ, infants in their mothers'
wombs not excepted.[83]

Bucanus clearly introduces the imputation of Adam's sin. However,
it is not connected with a covenant; *foedus* and related terms are absent.
For Bucanus, there is no covenant of works before the fall. He talks of
testamentum only with reference to the Old Testament and New Testament, of law and gospel.[84]

Amandus Polanus (1561–1610)

Amandus Polanus was a significant figure in the consolidation of
Reformed theology at the turn of the century. Concise and clear, he
produced a number of treatises, commentaries, and works of systematic
theology.[85] In his *Syntagma theologiae Christianae*, first published in 1609,
Polanus explicitly argues that Adam's sin was imputed to his posterity,
but that this was on the basis of natural propagation, rather than a bare
decree by God. The first person infected human nature, but afterward
the nature infected the person (*primum persona infecit naturam, sed post
natura infecit personam*). Here Polanus deals with *the sin of our first parents*.[86] Therefore, the fall brought with it corruption, obscuring the image
of God, and turning the mind away from the true and entire knowledge
of God. This corruption followed the first sin which Adam committed
and it was transmitted to his posterity.[87] Hence, original sin is derived by
all from Adam and through Adam (*ex Adamo et per Adamum*) by natural
generation. It is the origin of all other sins; it is called original because it
is derived from Adam by heredity (propagation). It is natural in us and
will only be removed by death.[88] Polanus, in true Ramist fashion, presents
original sin as having a twofold aspect. First, there is the responsibility or
blame for disobedience (*culpa inobedientiae seu defectionis a Deo in lumbis
Adami*), or falling short from God, in which we were implicated in the

83. Ibid., 172.
84. Ibid., locus 19 on law, 198–210; locus 20 on the gospel, 210–17; locus 21 on agreements and differences between the law and the gospel, 217–21; locus 22 on the differences
between the law and the gospel, 221–22.
85. See R. Letham, "Amandus Polanus: A Neglected Theologian?" *SCJ* 21 (1990):
463–76.
86. Amandus Polanus, *Syntagma theologiae Christianae* (Geneva: Petri Auberti, 1612),
6.3.10.
87. Ibid., 6.3.11.
88. Ibid., 6.3.12.

loins of Adam. Second, there is the resulting corruption that dominates the whole of human nature. The *culpa inobedientiae* is not only Adam's, but also ours. Not only Adam sinned, but we did too in Adam, since he was the root of the whole human race. Moreover, the sin of Adam was imputed to us by virtue of the contract.[89] Polanus, then, is prepared to write of the imputation of Adam's sin in a legal, contractual way, but on the foundation of his natural connection to his posterity.

The Irish Articles of Religion (1615)

Article 22 of the Irish Articles simply repeats the words of Romans 5:12 without comment. Article 23 explains that original sin consists, not in imitation of Adam, but in the corruption of the nature of everyone naturally engendered and propagated from Adam. Therefore, everyone born into the world deserves God's wrath and damnation, based on the inheritance of corruption. There is no mention of legal imputation, despite the reference in the previous section to the covenant of the law given by God to Adam. The Irish Articles do not regard Adam as representing the rest of the human race.[90]

The Canons of Dort (1618–19)

The Synod of Dort, in the Third and Fourth Heads of Doctrine, articles 2–3, addresses the topic of original sin. According to article 2, man after the fall begat children in his own likeness, and so a corrupt stock produced a corrupt offspring. Hence, all the posterity of Adam, Christ only excepted, have derived corruption from their original parent by the propagation of a vicious nature in consequence of a just judgment of God (*sed per vitiosae naturae propagationem, justo Dei iudicio, derivata*).[91] The judgment of God relates to the inheritance of a corrupt nature, rather than to the imputation of guilt. The latter was not the issue with the Remonstrants in the way that corruption was, since a depraved nature would affect the capacity of fallen man to respond to the gospel, which was central to the controversy.

89. "Ita culpa non tantum Adami est, sed etiam nostra: qua non tantum Adamus, sed etiam nos in Adamo tanquam radice totius humani generis peccavimus, & legem transgressi sumus, Rom. 5.12.19. Nam transgressio Adae nobis imputatur, alioqui reque iniquitate inde contracta, neque reatu ullo teneremur." Ibid., 6.3.12.
90. Schaff, *Creeds*, 3:530.
91. Ibid., 3:564, 588.

The Leiden Synopsis (1625)

The Leiden Synopsis was written by four professors at Leiden in defense of the theology of the Synod of Dort (1618–19). Anthonius Thysius was the author of the section on sin. While both Adam and Eve sinned, Thysius writes, the apostle assigns responsibility solely to Adam. This was because he was the head and beginning of the whole human race, from whom Eve was made. This is the natural connection with posterity. However, God had made a covenant with Adam, and so all people are reckoned or counted in the first parent.[92] At the same time, all people sinned in the sin of both parents and received a contaminated nature. Thysius makes a distinction between the responsibility for sin, which is in Adam,[93] and the inheritance of a corrupt nature, from both parents.[94]

Andreas Rivetus considered the question of original sin. His definition referred to the fall of the first parents, which, by the just judgment of God, contracted both guilt and a depraved nature, which were transmitted to all their posterity. This derives from propagation, since all were in the loins of the first parent.[95] Adam was a twofold person, acting for himself and for all his posterity. As in Hebrews 7, where Levi is said to have been in the loins of Abraham, so Adam carried his whole posterity with him (*tum totius posteritatus cuius sustinebat massam; etiam peccatum eius geminen habuit respectum*).[96] Thus, Adam's sin has been passed on, not by imitation but by propagation, even though most of his posterity has never heard of his sin. Both Adam and Eve were involved in the transmission, but curious questions accusing one or the other should be avoided.[97] For Rivetus, all sinned in Adam, both seminally and also by the just judgment of God, and thus the sin was imputed to them.[98] Of the fifty-two chapters in the Leiden

---

92. " . . . ad solum tamen Adamum ab Apostolo referetur, Rom. [5.]12 tanquam ad caput ac principium universale totius generis humani, ex quo ipsa quoque Eva fuerit conditu, 1. Cor. 11.8.4 in quo Deus omnes homines, tanquam in primario parente, pro rationis pacti cum ipso initi, censuerit." Johannes Polyander et al., *Synopsis purioris theologiae, disputationibus quinquaginta duabus comprehensa* (Leiden: Ex officina Elzeverianus, 1625), 152.

93. " . . . omnes iam inde ab initio in Adamo peccaverunt." Ibid., 161.

94. " . . . omnes homines in utroque parente originaliter peccarunt, ac per eiusdem naturae vitiatae propagationem communi lve [?] sunt contaminati, sic eiusdem criminis ac mortis rei sunt constitui. Rom. 5.12." Ibid., 157.

95. "Efficiens huius peccati causa est primorum parentam lapsus, quo justo Dei iudicio reatus & pravitas naturae attracta est, & in totam posteritatem transfusa"; all were "in prius primi parentis lumbis factam." Ibid., 161.

96. Ibid., 162.

97. Ibid., 164–65.

98. "Forma peccati originalis consistit in ἀνομία illa & inobedientia qua cum Adamo peccaverunt omnes qui in eo fuerunt secundum rationem, ut vocant, seminalem, quae inobedientia

Synopsis, not one is on the covenant(s), except for one on the relationship between the Old Testament and the New Testament. The subject of law and gospel occupies more space, and it precedes the discussion of Old Testament and New Testament. This standard work of seventeenth-century Reformed theology does not use the concept of covenant to any degree of prominence, not even to explain the guilt or transmission of sin.

Summary

Our survey indicates a development in thought. In the earlier period after the Reformation, the general consensus was that the human race participates in Adam's sin by virtue of the natural connection it has with him through generation. Calvin recognized in passing that this sin was imputed, but his emphasis did not lie there. As time progressed, and the doctrine of the imputation of Adam's sin rose to the surface, imputation was generally regarded as based upon this natural connection. Because of the corruption inherited from Adam or our first parents by natural propagation, the sin either of our first parents or of Adam was reckoned to us. Only as the covenant of works became recognized after 1585–90 did the focus begin to shift from our first parents as the root of sin to Adam in particular. In due course, not only was the corruption of sin seen to be reckoned to the race by a decree of God, but Adam was said to be a representative person, so that the guilt of his sin was imputed to all. It remained for all these matters to be fitted into a covenantal framework. This took time. While the Assembly was sitting, the influential book by John Ball, *A Treatise of the Covenant of Grace* (1645), was published, securing widespread interest and approval by the divines. In this work, Ball denies that Adam was on probation before the fall and that he would have received everlasting life as a reward for continued obedience. He denies that Adam's obedience would have been meritorious and asserts that the grace of God alone was the root of the covenant of creation. He says nothing about the imputation of Adam's sin.[99] Even in the 1640s, the doctrinal complex relating to the creation situation was in a state of evolution and development. It was that dynamic trajectory that the Assembly sought to represent.

& culpa cum reatu consequente, juste a Deo judice omnibus Adami filiis imputatur, quatenus omnes fuerunt & sunt unus cum eo." Ibid., 168.

  99. Ball, *Treatise*, 6–12.

11

Christ and Covenant

We believe . . . in one Lord Jesus Christ, the only-begotten Son of God, begotten by his Father before all ages, Light from Light, true God from true God, begotten not made, consubstantial with the Father, through whom all things were made: who for us and our salvation came down from heaven, and was incarnate by the Holy Spirit and the Virgin Mary, and became man; and was crucified for us under Pontius Pilate, and suffered and was buried, and rose again on the third day according to the Scriptures, and ascended into heaven, and sits on the right hand of the Father. And he shall come again with glory to judge the living and the dead. Whose kingdom shall have no end.

For the Larger Catechism, the whole *ordo salutis* is considered part of the person and work of Christ. Christ is the mediator of the covenant of grace, and salvation consists in union and communion with Christ in grace and glory (LC 65–90). Anthony Tuckney, who played a major role in the creation of the Larger Catechism, wrote that the redemption of the world by Christ alone "was the most happy product of the most divine counsels of all three persons in the blessed Trinity from all eternity," and he asked whether we could be wiser than God to say that he ought to have spared his counsels and Christ his death, seeing there is no way to come to life without him.[1]

God's Covenant with Man (WCF 7; LC 30–36)

In WCF 7.1, the divines outline general principles that underlie God's covenant. The focus is on the great distance between God and his creatures. His morally responsible creatures—angels and humans— owe him obedience. His bountiful goodness to us is entirely due to his own free decision. There can never be any blessedness or reward for us, except by God's "voluntary condescension," expressed in covenant. Right away, God's covenant is seen as an expression of his sovereign freedom, where he stoops low to grant humanity blessings for which they have no intrinsic claim. However, what exactly does the Assembly mean by "some voluntary condescension on God's part"? In particular, what in this context is "condescension"?

While there was a debate about "condescension" in S516 F 10.10.45am, the minutes do not record any details of it.[2] Further debate on the covenant took place in S559 TU 23.12.45am, without any comment in the minutes.[3] According to *The Oxford English Dictionary*, in the 1640s the word *condescension* had acquired the established meaning of "the action of descending or stooping to things unworthy" (Jeremy Taylor, 1642), "gracious, considerate, or submissive deference to another," "the action . . . of acceding" (Thomas Manton, 1648), while the cognate verb *to condescend* meant "to come down from one's rights or claims" (1485, 1513), "to stoop voluntarily or graciously to a course of action" (Hugh Latimer, 1549), "to depart from the privileges of superiority by a voluntary submission . . . to sink willingly to equal terms with inferiors" (Holy Bible, AV, 1611; Rom. 12:16), and "to accommodate oneself" (John Foxe, 1563–87). In Protestant scholasticism, long entrenched by the time of Westminster, *condescensio* was used for God's accommodation of himself to human ways of knowing

---

1. Anthony Tuckney, *None but Christ, or a Sermon on Acts 4.12 preached at St. Maries in Cambridge, on the Commencement Sabbath, July 4.1652* (London: John Rothwell and S. Gellibrand, 1654) [Wing (2nd ed., 1994) 3217], 19.
2. Mitchell and Struthers, eds., *Minutes of the Sessions*, 148; Van Dixhoorn, 6:196.
3. Van Dixhoorn, 6:231; Mitchell, *Westminster Assembly*, 172.

in order to reveal himself. This was closely related to *gratia Dei* (the grace of God), the goodness and undeserved favor of God toward man, and to *gratia communis* (common grace), his nonsaving, universal grace by which, in his goodness, he lavishes favor on all creation in the blessings of physical sustenance and moral influence for the good.[4] These are the clearest senses of the terms for the Assembly, for they saw grace as fully compatible with law, not offsetting or limiting it, as in the late medieval notions of congruent and condign grace.

The Covenant of Works/Life

WCF 7.2 introduces the covenant of works, made by God with man before the fall. This is the first major confessional document in which this covenant is expressly mentioned. In it, God promised life to Adam and in him to his posterity on condition of perfect obedience. Hence, in LC 20 the covenant is called *the covenant of life*, focusing on the promise held out to Adam. The term *covenant of works* draws attention instead to the means by which Adam was to attain the promise. The condition expressed in LC 20 is personal, perfect, and perpetual obedience. In short, the obedience was to be sustained for an unspecified period of time, upon the completion of which life would result in accordance with God's promise.[5] The other side of the coin was that there was a penalty of death for eating of the tree of the knowledge of good and evil, as expressed by God in Genesis 2:15–17. The promise is not mentioned in Genesis, but can be inferred by two considerations. First, wherever threats are made by God in the Bible, the opposite is entailed, and vice versa. The results of one course of action entail the opposing consequences for the opposite conduct. This is clear when we examine the promises and sanctions of the Mosaic covenant in

4. R. A. Muller, *Dictionary of Latin and Greek Theological Terms Drawn Principally from Protestant Scholastic Theology* (Grand Rapids: Baker, 1985), 19, 130.

5. The insertion of the word "perpetual" in the Larger Catechism, absent from WCF 7.2 and SC 12, might convey the idea that the covenant of works remains in force. If that were so, it might undermine the idea that the covenant was for a limited time of probation. There is insufficient evidence to establish why the adjective was added. According to Robert Strimple, in an e-mail dated 4 August 2008, John Murray, in the elective class Strimple took as a student, considered that "there seems to be a slip, for it makes the condition personal, perfect, and *perpetual* obedience, scarcely compatible with the consummate nature of the covenant." On the other hand, concrete evidence that the Assembly included the adjective unintentionally is lacking.

Deuteronomy 28 and 29; there is blessing for obedience and judgment for disobedience. Second, there is the connection between Adam and Christ, the first and second Adams, which is spelled out in the New Testament and which we will discuss in more detail shortly.

Development of the Doctrine of the Covenant of Works/Life

While covenant theology in the Reformed tradition emerged with Zwingli and Bullinger in the 1520s, the term *foedus operum* (covenant of works) was not used until 1585, by the Puritan Dudley Fenner.[6] Earlier, in 1562, in his *Summa theologiae*, the German Reformed theologian Zacharias Ursinus had written of a covenant of creation,[7] so the idea had already been proposed. In the five years after Fenner's work, a spate of theologians adopted the pre-fall covenant—including Caspar Olevian, Franciscus Junius, Lambert Danaeu, and Amandus Polanus.[8] By 1590, it was common. However, it was by no means universally taught at this time. Bucanus's *Institutiones theologiae* (1602) does not mention it. Some at the Assembly were hesitant about it and even opposed it.[9] No confessional document prior to the Assembly had adopted it.

Neither in his Genesis commentary nor in the *Institutes* does Calvin describe the condition of Adam before the fall as covenantal, still less as a covenant of works. Peter Lillback argues that all the ingredients for such a view are present in Calvin, and that he has an *inchoate* (just begun) covenant of works, but I prefer the word *incipient* (about to begin), since, while the elements for such a covenant are present, the formulation itself is not.[10] Lillback thinks not only that all the ingredients for the meal are in the kitchen, but also that Calvin has put them into the oven

---

6. Fenner, *Sacra theologia*.

7. A. Lang, ed., *Der Heidelberger Katechismus und vier verwandte Katechismen* (Leipzig: Deichert, 1967), 153, 156.

8. Caspar Olevian, *De substantia foederis gratuiti inter Deum et electos* (Geneva, 1585), 12–13, 48, 62–63, 90, 251–55, 270; Amandus Polanus, *Partitiones theologiae* (2nd ed.; Basel, 1590), 79–80; Polanus, *Partitiones theologiae* (Basel, 1607), 152–53; Junius, *Opera theologica*, 1:1659–62.

9. In chapter 12, we shall see that Thomas Gataker and Richard Vines indicated their opposition to it.

10. P. A. Lillback, *The Binding of God: Calvin's Role in the Development of Covenant Theology* (Grand Rapids: Baker Academic, 2001), 276–304.

and is about to take them out properly cooked. I agree that for Calvin the ingredients are present, but the evidence is that, while he may have heated the oven, he had not yet put anything in. Fesko is correct: "It is undisputed: Calvin does not speak of a covenant of works."[11] However, he agrees that the two main concepts in the covenant of works/life are found in Calvin: a probationary period for Adam, with a promise of life for obedience, and Adam as the federal head of humanity.[12] We have already argued that Fesko's point here has to be qualified. Fesko considers that Calvin speaks of imputed guilt from Adam, but in the passage he cites from the *Institutes* Calvin is not talking about the transmission of guilt, but of the contagion of a corrupt nature by the ordination of God. Fesko takes an unwarranted leap by saying that Calvin was writing about their (Adam and Eve's) sin being imputed to the rest of mankind.[13] Why was *Eve's* sin imputed? It makes sense to talk of Eve's sin being passed on through her descendants by the natural processes of human generation and birth, but it does not make sense to talk of her sin being imputed since Eve was not a federal head.

The *Annotations* make no reference to the covenant of works/life in the comments on Genesis 2:16–17. But in considering Hosea 6:7, it speaks of "Adam, the first sinner of all, who brake Gods first Covenant with mankinde. . . . Or as if it had been the Covenant of some meane man." The compilers were aware of the Hosea passage being cited in support of there being a covenant of works, but were prepared only to refer to it as one of a number of possible interpretations.[14] Moreover, the compiler of the notes on Genesis was not prepared to commit himself to the doctrine.

Arguments Against the Idea of a Covenant of Works/Life

The idea of a covenant of works has come under severe criticism. Among the most notable opponents of the Westminster Assembly's

11. Fesko, "Westminster Confession and Lapsarianism," 519.
12. Ibid.
13. Ibid., 2:521–22.
14. Hosea 6:7 is best translated "like Adam," rather than "at Adam," for there is no evidence of a covenant being made at such a place, or "like man," which is virtually meaningless. Following the Vulgate, virtually all patristic and medieval commentators understood it to mean "like Adam": see Muller, *PRRD*, 2:436–41.

construction is Holmes Rolston III.[15] He argues that it was a radical departure from Calvin and had the effect of placing law prior to grace, in contrast with what had gone before in Reformed thought. Along similar lines, James B. Torrance is deeply critical of the development of federal theology, particularly in Scotland. He understands the covenant of works in Scottish theology to be a purely legal covenant, and so opposes it. He argues that this legal understanding bases God's primary dealings with man on law, not grace. In turn, this colors the covenant of grace, casting it in a legal framework and so subserving the ends of law, with disastrous consequences for both theology and piety. He states of the idea, "God's prime purpose for man is legal, not filial, but this yields an impersonal view of man as the object of justice, rather than primarily the object of love." He claims it led to a legalistic cast to the Christian faith and eclipsed the grace of God. He asks whether it is appropriate to interpret creation in terms of natural law and to restrict grace to redemption.[16] He is prepared to see the pre-fall situation as covenantal, but not if it is construed in predominantly legal terms.

The Rationale for the Covenant of Works/Life

The main point to note in support of this development is that the pre-fall covenant is an inference from the work of Christ as the second Adam. This is a frequent theme in the letters of Paul. It is particularly relevant in Romans 5:12–21. There Paul talks of two ages and two solidaric groups, headed by Adam and Christ, respectively. The first Adam, by his one act of disobedience, plunged the entire race into sin and death, since he was the head of all his posterity. On the other hand, the second man, Christ, by his obedience has brought righteousness and life to all with whom he is in solidarity. His actions have reversed the effects of the fall, with plenty of room to spare. His life was one of testing and temptation, from which he emerged obedient. In turn, he endured the penalty of sin—death—on the cross. Following his

---

15. Rolston, *John Calvin Versus the Westminster Confession*.

16. J. B. Torrance, "The Concept of Federal Theology—Was Calvin a Federal Theologian?" in *Calvinus Sacrae Scripturae Professor: Die referate des Congrès International des Recherches Calviniennes* (ed. W. H. Neuser; Grand Rapids: Eerdmans, 1994), 15–40, esp. 35, 23; J. B. Torrance, "Covenant or Contract?" See also T. F. Torrance, *Scottish Theology*, 136, 214ff.

obedience to God's law and his enduring of its curse on our behalf, he was raised from the dead and given eternal life. His obedient righteousness and everlasting life are granted to all who belong to him by the grace of God through faith. The connection between the pre-fall condition of Adam and the atonement by Christ is clear. The former is an entailment of the latter. For their part, opponents of the pre-fall covenant of works have often opposed any form of penal substitutionary doctrine of the atonement.

However, not all those with reservations about the covenant of works have had similarly hostile thoughts on the atonement. John Murray disliked the term "covenant of works" because he did not find a covenant in Genesis 1–2 and since "the elements of grace entering into the administration are not properly provided for by the term 'works.'"[17] He understood all of God's covenants to be sovereign administrations of grace.[18] The simple solution to Murray's problem would have been to use the term "covenant of life," which the Assembly also approved. As for the absence of any mention of covenant in Genesis 2, the Pauline parallel between the first and second Adams and the indisputably covenantal setting of the second Adam argues that the creation administration was indeed a covenant—all the more so since all the ingredients of a covenant are present.

On the other hand, some defenses of the pre-fall covenant have erred in the opposite direction. Drawing on ancient Near Eastern parallels, Meredith Kline saw the biblical covenants as essentially law covenants. "A truly systematic formulation of the theology of the covenant will define covenant generically in terms of law administration." The satisfaction of divine law underscores every administration of covenant promise. Thus, the promises are, in effect, ancillary to law. For Kline, this reflects the character of God—"Merciful he may be according to his sovereign will but all his works are in righteousness and truth."[19] Evidently, the priority of law in God's covenants is an outflow of who he is. For Kline, Adam's obedience was to be merito-

---

17. J. Murray, "The Adamic Administration," in *Collected Writings of John Murray*, vol. 2: *Select Lectures in Systematic Theology* (Edinburgh: Banner of Truth, 1977), 49.

18. J. Murray, *The Covenant of Grace* (London: Tyndale Press, 1954).

19. M. G. Kline, *By Oath Consigned: A Reinterpretation of the Covenant Signs of Circumcision and Baptism* (Grand Rapids: Eerdmans, 1968), 33.

rious. He would have earned everlasting life as a just reward for his compliance with the terms of the covenant of works. In turn, Christ the second Adam, by his perfect obedience, earned salvation for us meritoriously. This is applied to us by grace on the basis of Christ's having merited it for us. For Kline, a position on the covenant of works has as its entailment a particular view of the atonement. For the pre-fall situation to be construed other than in terms of law and merit leads inexorably to the abandonment of the meritorious obedience of the second Adam and an undermining of the atonement and justification by faith.[20]

That a reading of the Assembly's doctrine of the covenant of works from Kline's perspective is mistaken is evident from a number of considerations. First, the Confession stresses condescension as underlying all God's covenants, including the pre-fall one. Whatever the place of law may be, it is in harmony with God's free and sovereign stooping down to do us a favor. Second, for the Assembly, law and grace were not polar opposites; it saw no incompatibility between them. Law is present in the covenant of grace, both in the time of the law (WCF 7.5) and also in the time of the gospel.[21] In the covenant of grace, grace and law are not competing ways of salvation. Instead, they fulfill different roles. Grace constitutes; law regulates. The covenant is pervasively gracious, yet we receive the promise through the obedience of Christ, and the law continues to regulate the life of the Christian (WCF 20.2, 5–7). Hence, the Assembly insists that the uses of the law are not contrary to the gospel, "but do sweetly comply with it" (20.7). As John Leith indicates, reflecting on the Assembly's portrayal of the pre-fall covenant: "This was not simply a covenant of merit, for the covenant itself was a gracious act of God, the great disparity between God and man prohibiting any possibility of man's works by their own merit earning salvation."[22] That Leith is correct here can be gauged from the important book by John Ball, *A treatise of the covenant of grace* (1645), published while the Assembly sat and received with much favor

20. See M. G. Kline, "Covenant Theology Under Attack," *New Horizons in the Orthodox Presbyterian Church* 15/2 (February 1994): 3–5, available at www.opc.org/new_horizons/ Kline_cov_theo.html as of 24 July 2008.

21. See the chapters on the mediatorial work of Christ (8.4–5), justification (11.3), and the law of God (19.1–7).

22. Leith, *Assembly at Westminster*, 92.

by the divines, which denied that Adam's works were meritorious and insisted on the grace of God permeating this covenant.[23]

Kline's concern that Reformed theology is debased if it adopts a different perspective on the covenant of works than his is wrong from both historical and theological angles. First, Lutheranism had no covenant of works, yet that of itself did not precipitate a headlong flight from a biblical view of the atonement. Moreover, since the doctrine of the covenant of works developed over time, if Kline were correct, significant swathes of earlier Reformed theology would have proved defective before his full covenantal position was developed; that would include Calvin. Kline is historically inaccurate and theologically too blunt. On the absence of grace, Kline is simply wrong. The Westminster documents clearly affirm that grace was present before the fall. This no more undermines the doctrine of the atonement than Kline does. The divines were able to hold on to an orthodox view of the work of Christ. If Kline were correct, this could not have happened.

The Covenant of Grace

Unfortunately, Adam fell into sin and so plunged the entire race into a condition of guilt before God and produced a corrupt nature transmitted to all his posterity. Moreover, all people were now living under the active displeasure of God and left to their own devices would face judgment, everlasting severance of relations with God, and permanent condemnation. Man was incapable of putting matters right, and so was destitute of life and hope. Against the background of this dire situation, WCF 7.3 moves to a consideration of a second covenant made by God, the covenant of grace.

In the covenant of grace, God freely promised life and salvation by Jesus Christ, requiring faith in Christ for salvation. He also promised to give his Holy Spirit to all whom he ordained to eternal life, so as to make them willing and able to believe (LC 32). This covenant was made by God out of his sheer love and mercy, delivering his elect from the estate of sin and misery and bringing them into an estate of salvation (LC 30).

23. Ball, *Treatise*, 6–12.

According to LC 31, the covenant of grace was made with Christ as the second Adam and the elect in him as his seed. It joins covenant and election together and provides a rationale for various elements of the work of salvation. It places the promises given to Christ in the context of the covenant of grace.[24]

According to WCF 7.4, this covenant is often described as a testament with reference to the death of Christ and the everlasting inheritance bequeathed as a consequence.[25] This, reflecting biblical language, points to two distinct ways in which the covenant of grace could be viewed. In the first instance, it is an arrangement made by God with his elect people in Christ, in which he promises to give them righteousness and everlasting life and grants them faith to believe in Christ. It contemplates two living parties, however one-sided the covenant is in practice. Second, as a testament it contemplates a bequest, an inheritance granted unilaterally on the basis of the death of Christ on the cross, an inheritance that comes into effect only upon that death. Both lines of thought are expressed in Scripture, both are taken into consideration here, and both together present different, although complementary, dimensions to the covenant of grace.

WCF 7.5 introduces us to the difference between the Old Testament and the New Testament. The covenant is administered differently under the law and under the gospel (cf. LC 33). Here there is a redemptive-historical distinction recognized between the Old Testament and the New Testament. However, it is a distinction that relates to the administration of the covenant, not to its substance or intrinsic nature. This point had been brought out clearly by Calvin.[26] The Assembly acknowledges the contrast between law and gospel, a central theme in Lutheranism. However, both the Confession and the Larger Catechism say that law and gospel are different means of administering the one covenant of grace. While there is a difference between law and gospel, there is a more basic compatibility. Moreover, in speaking of the covenant of grace in the singular, the Assembly

24. I am indebted to Robert B. Strimple for this point.
25. The proof texts for the Confession are Heb. 9:15–17, 22; Luke 22:20; 1 Cor. 11:25. However, all references to salvation as an inheritance, and to the saved as coheirs with Christ, should be taken into account.
26. Calvin, *Institutes*, 2.9.1 through 2.11.14.

distances itself from the Anabaptists. The Anabaptists claimed that there are simply a series of individual, disparate covenants, implying that the New Testament is something so new as to abrogate the Old Testament, undercutting any arguments for covenant continuity and its grounding of infant baptism.

The Covenant of Grace Under the Law

WCF 7.5 spells out clearly that the law was an administration of the covenant of grace.

Through "the promises, prophecies, sacrifices, circumcision, the paschal lamb, and other types and ordinances" given to the Jews, God signified Christ, who was to come in the future. The whole Old Testament was a preparation for Christ, an integral part of God's redemptive plan. In its own day, it was both sufficient and efficacious, by the power of the Holy Spirit, for its intended purpose to prepare the people for the coming of the Messiah. It was by the Messiah who was to come that remission of sins and eternal salvation were effected. Meanwhile, Abraham, David, and others were justified by faith as we are, as Paul argues in Romans 4; only this was by virtue of the future work of Christ (LC 34). The law was not an alternative way of salvation, but the means of administering the one and only way of salvation in Christ in the covenant of grace.

The Covenant of Grace Under the Gospel

Now, as WCF 7.6 and LC 35 state, Christ the substance of the covenant of grace has come. Hence, the administration of the covenant has changed in accordance with this all-determining reality. The ordinances of the covenant of grace under the gospel are the preaching of the Word and the sacraments of baptism and the Lord's Supper. These are simpler than the Old Testament ordinances, but they more fully and evidently display the gospel and do so with greater spiritual efficacy due to the work of the Holy Spirit. Moreover, the gospel is directed to all nations in the New Testament, not only to Israel. Here, incidentally, is another expression of the missionary awareness of the Assembly. The divines' understanding of the covenant of grace is that the Old

Testament and the New Testament are not two covenants, but one and the same covenant under different modes of administration.

The Covenant of Redemption?

The idea of the covenant of redemption was beginning to surface around the time of the Assembly. Two of its earliest exponents were the Dutch theologian Johannes Cocceius in 1648[27] and the Englishman John Owen, probably the greatest English-speaking theologian at the time of the Assembly, but a few years too young to have been considered for membership in it.[28] Some time earlier, Caspar Olevian had hinted at such an idea.[29]

This covenant concerning human salvation was said to be between the persons of the Trinity. In practice, it was transacted between the Father and the Son. The Father required the Son to become incarnate, suffer, and die on the cross as the head and representative of his people in order to make atonement for their sins. As a reward for his faithful discharge of these responsibilities, the Father promised the Son that he would be raised from the dead, be glorified, and receive for himself a people without number drawn from the entire world.

However, although various elements of that putative covenant are present in the Assembly's documents, there is no trace of this covenant as such. As Morris notes, the Confession speaks of two covenants only.[30] Yet while the covenant of redemption is not mentioned in the symbols, "the fact which the phrase is designed to describe, is clearly suggested in the confessional chapter on Christ the mediator, wherein it is said that the Son accepted the office to which he was called by the Father, was appointed and endowed for this office by the Father, and by discharging the duties involved in the office secured, as if by contract, salvation for sinful man and heavenly rewards for himself."[31] Morris recognizes that there is some warrant for such a covenant in Scripture (specifically Psalms 2 and 110 and Isaiah 53). However, he correctly warns that this construction tends toward tritheism, by

---

27. Johannes Cocceius, *Summa doctrina de foedere et testamento Dei* (Amsterdam, 1648).
28. Owen, *Works of John Owen*, 19:77–89.
29. Olevian, *De substantia foederis gratuiti* (1585).
30. Morris, *Westminster Symbols*, 358.
31. Ibid., 359.

representing the persons of the Trinity as entering into agreements with one another (he refers to the Sum of Saving Knowledge, head 2, which speaks of "a bargain") and by representing the Father and the Son as the only two parties involved, leaving the Holy Spirit out of the picture.[32] Certainly LC 31 talks of the covenant of grace as made with Christ as the second Adam and in him with all the elect as his seed, but the parties to the first covenant were God and man, and to the covenant of grace, God and the believer in Christ (WCF 7).[33]

The doctrine of the Trinity should have provided a barrier against the idea of the covenant of redemption. That salvation rests upon the pretemporal plan or counsel of God is evident from WCF 3. This counsel is Trinitarian, as is clear from that chapter and the preceding one on the Trinity. However, to describe the relations of the three persons in the Trinity as a covenant, or to affirm that there was a need for them to enter into covenantal—even contractual—arrangements is to open the door to heresy. The will of the Trinity is one; the works of the Trinity are indivisible. For all the good intentions of those who proposed it, the construal of the relations of the three persons of the Trinity in covenantal terms is a departure from classic Trinitarian orthodoxy. In two generations that was precisely what occurred in English Presbyterianism. Some other language should have been used. However, the Assembly wisely avoided these dangers.[34]

Christ the Mediator (WCF 8; LC 36–59)

The only mediator of the covenant of grace is the Lord Jesus Christ, who is the eternal Son of God become man, and who con-

---

32. Ibid., 360.
33. Ibid., 363.
34. See my brief criticisms of the idea in R. Letham, *The Work of Christ* (Leicester: Inter-Varsity Press, 1993), 52–53. For a fuller discussion of Trinitarian orthodoxy, including the indivisibility of the Trinity, see Letham, *The Holy Trinity*, 127–200. My point is that the covenant of redemption opened the door to Trinitarian heresy. Some went through the door, others did not. John Owen, perhaps the best exponent of the idea, recognized the dangers, acknowledging that the will of God is indivisible, and wrote of the will of God in its particular manifestation in the Father, in the Son, and in the Holy Spirit. See *Works of John Owen*, 19:87–90.

tinues to be God and man in two distinct natures and one person forever (cf. LC 36).

In WCF 8.1, the decree of God is related to the mediation of Christ, connecting the whole outworking of salvation with the eternal purposes of God. Salvation in Christ is a free and sovereign decision of the triune God. God chose and ordained his Son to be the mediator between God and man. This forms a necessary foundation for the covenant of redemption, although that formula is not present. At the same time, that covenant need not be the consequence of this statement. It is clear that salvation rests on the decree of God. It is equally clear that God is triune and that all three persons are engaged indivisibly in all his works and ways. It follows that salvation rests on the eternal counsel of the Holy Trinity. It does not follow that the relations of the three persons are covenantal, bringing them into quasi-judicial relations with one another, to strike "a bargain," as the Sum of Saving Knowledge puts it. Such a construction borders on tritheism. The Assembly cannot be accused of that.

However, the formula here in WCF 8.1 does undermine the claim of Barth and his followers that Reformed theology abandoned a Christocentric doctrine of election.[35] There are echoes of Thomas Goodwin's extended treatment of election in Christ in his commentary on Ephesians. Unfortunately, the minutes do not disclose how far Goodwin participated in the debates on this point.[36] Contrary to Barth, Christ is presented here not only as elected man but as electing God, since

35. See Barth, *CD* II/2,1–506; Reid, "Office of Christ in Predestination," 5–12 ("Christ is merely the exhibitor of a decision already made in an eternity in which he has himself been, even if existent, at least inoperative. On the other hand, his role is to give effect to a decree, in whose formation he has apparently had no hand"); Berkouwer, *Divine Election*, 132–71. See the discussion in Letham, *Work of Christ*, 53–56. Muller, *Christ and the Decree*, fatally undermines the Barth-Reid argument. Anthony Tuckney, a member of the Assembly, addressed this question when he wrote that in this saving covenant "Christ is not brought in *per accidens*, or in an inferior subordination, as a subservient means to us and our salvation as the end . . . but Christ's and God's glory in him is the prime design in it." Tuckney, *None but Christ*, 21.

36. See Thomas Goodwin, *An Exposition of Ephesians* (repr., n.p.: Sovereign Grace Book Club, 1958), 23–102. This is also found in *The Works of Thomas Goodwin* (ed. J. C. Miller and R. Halley; Edinburgh: James Nichol, 1861–66), 1:23–102. Before Goodwin, Jerome Zanchius (1516–90) had expounded this in great detail; see Hieronymous Zanchius, *Omnium operum theologicarum* (8 vols.; Geneva, 1619), 2:535–40; 6:1:11.

the God who chooses and ordains has already been declared to be triune (WCF 2.3), and his decrees are made by all three persons indivisibly (WCF 4.1).

Section 8.1 also brings together election, the threefold office of Christ as prophet, priest, and king, and the *ordo salutis*, together with the church and the world. It is a comprehensive statement of the unity and indivisibility of God's saving purposes, breathtaking in its scope.

WCF 8.2 focuses on the person of Christ. It follows very closely the Definition of Chalcedon (AD 451). This is its great strength; it places Westminster squarely within the tradition of the Western church. Christ is the Son of God from eternity, true God, of one being and equal with the Father. In this, the classic Trinitarian settlement is reaffirmed. In the incarnation, he took on himself the nature of man to the fullest extent possible, apart from sin. He was conceived by the Holy Spirit and born of the Virgin Mary—echoing the Apostles' Creed. He is true God and true man, yet one person. This is an abbreviated version of Chalcedon, without its four famous privative statements—without confusion, without change, without division, without separation. It is a denial of both Nestorianism and Eutychianism. However, in common with much Reformed Christology, it stops at Chalcedon and does not assimilate the refinements brought about by the second and third Councils of Constantinople (553 and 680–81). After Chalcedon, the supporters of Cyril of Alexandria claimed that too many concessions had been made to the Nestorians. The picture painted by Chalcedon was of two natures coming together into one person. This appeared to fragment the person of Christ by overly stressing the dual natures. Hence, in the fifth and sixth ecumenical councils it was affirmed that Jesus Christ *is* the eternal Son of God. In the incarnation, he has added human nature to his divine person. In answer to the question of *who* Christ is, the church replied that he is the eternal Son of God. In reply to the question of *what* Christ is, it answered that he, the Son of God, had assumed into union our humanity. Thus, it is not a case of two natures coming together to form one person, but, instead, it is one divine person assuming into union a human nature. This the Confession does not deny, but its failure to address the question weakens its statement on Christology.[37] However, there is enough here to indicate that Westminster was within the trajectory that culminated at the fifth and sixth ecumenical councils and approved of their declarations. It is "[God's] only begotten Son" who is the mediator (8.1), while the Son of God took upon himself man's nature (8.2). Again, in LC 36 the Lord Jesus Christ is said to be the eternal Son of God.

LC 37 follows the Apostles' Creed—Jesus was conceived by the Holy Ghost in the womb of the Virgin Mary. LC 38–39 underlines why the mediator had to be both God and man, while LC 40 points out why he had to be one person. Here again, the procedure is to start with the two natures. Neither document is in danger of Nestorianism, but both adopt essentially the same procedure as Nestorius, by focusing on the two natures rather than the trajectory taken by the Son. In short, the person of Christ is not an amalgam of two natures, but rather is the eternally divine person of the Son who has taken a human nature into personal union. This the Assembly misses, as does most of the Western church.[38]

WCF 8.3–5 relate the person of Christ to the work of mediation. WCF 8.3 sets his ministry in a Trinitarian context, called by the Father, sanctified by and anointed with the Holy Spirit. The Lord Jesus is said to be sinless. He was called by the Father, commanded by the Father, and equipped by the Father with all power and judgment in his incarnate state. In 8.4, he is said to undertake the work of mediation willingly and in obedience. He suffered grievously, was crucified, died, and was buried; he arose from the dead, ascended into heaven, and sits at the right hand of the Father, to return to judge men and angels. Here the words of the Apostles' Creed are again noticeably present in the voice of Westminster. We note in particular that the resurrection of the Lord Jesus is "with the same body in which He suffered." This is by no means intended to deny that a change had occurred to that body; it only affirms his body's continuity and identity. LC 46–50

37. Reformed Christology is often accused of having a Nestorian tendency; see Bruce, *Humiliation of Christ*, 116–32; similarly on Calvin, see Weinandy, *Does God Suffer?* 187–88.

38. Witness the books on Christology that end with Chalcedon and do not follow through to Constantinople II and Constantinople III. It would be absurd to accuse the divines of Nestorianism, for Chalcedon rebutted it emphatically. What is involved here is the approach to the person of Christ on the basis of the two natures, rather than the trajectory of union by the hypostasis of the Son.

traces the work of Christ in his humiliation, the state of lowliness he assumed from his birth to the grave.

In WCF 8.5, the work of Christ comes to the foreground. His perfect obedience and sacrifice were offered through the eternal Spirit to the Father. Echoing Hebrews 9:14, this is a clear Trinitarian statement about the cross. The language of "perfect obedience" takes on greater significance when we consider it in the light of the early debates on justification, which we will scrutinize in the next chapter. For now, we note that the Assembly avoided comment on whether this includes his active obedience to the law throughout the course of his life or whether it is restricted to his passive obedience in suffering the just demands of the law for the sinners he had come to save. The context, with its reference to the cross, would point in the latter direction. There is, we shall see, a third alternative, equally possible: that the phrase is deliberately ambiguous, so as to secure the widest possible agreement. The section also includes a clear commitment to particular redemption. The Lord Jesus purchased reconciliation and an everlasting inheritance for all those whom the Father had given him—neither for all people without exception, nor for all people provisionally, as the Arminians held.

LC 43–45 outline the work of Christ as prophet, priest, and king. LC 46–50 consider him in his humiliation, when he took the form of a servant. This proceeded via his incarnation (LC 47), his subjection to the law and his enduring of weakness and temptation (LC 48), his death (LC 49), and his burial (LC 50). This last point takes the position that the statement in the Apostles' Creed, "He descended into hell," refers to his "continuing in the state of the dead . . . till the third day," as had been proposed during the debates on the Thirty-Nine Articles. LC 51–56 trace the work of Christ in his exaltation, from his resurrection from the dead via his ascension to his heavenly session and intercession for his people.

In WCF 8.6, the work of Christ is said to be efficacious in all ages, including the period before his incarnation. Hence, although he had not yet achieved the reconciliation—here the significance of the historical process is recognized—the promises of God and the sacrificial system of the Old Testament signified the same realities and were effective for the elect who lived before his coming.

WCF 8.7 is devoted to the *communicatio idiomatum*, the communication of idioms. This classically recognized that since the Son had taken human nature into union, there were things said of him that might apply specifically to his humanity. In these cases, such human features—hunger, thirst, weariness and the like—are predicable of his person, just as are his divine characteristics.

Finally, WCF 8.8 is an emphatic affirmation of effective redemption. Christ's mediation achieves what God intends it to achieve. For all those for whom it is intended—the elect—Christ has purchased and will communicate redemption, by his Spirit bringing them to faith, governing them by his Word and Spirit, and overcoming all their enemies. Particular redemption is clearly close to the Assembly's heart. See also LC 57–59.

LC 60–61 discuss the case of those who have never heard the gospel. These persons, the divines insist, cannot be saved. Later, WCF 10.3 will allow that elect infants dying in infancy and other elect persons incapable of being called by the outward preaching of the Word will be saved. Clearly, these two Catechism questions do not have the elect in these categories in mind. At the same time, the Catechism denies that all who hear the Word preached will be saved. Evidently, some will not believe.[39]

---

39. Here, Anthony Tuckney is again of help. See Tuckney, *None but Christ*, 29, 34, 68.

12

The Order of Salvation

We believe in one Lord Jesus Christ . . . [who] was crucified for us under Pontius Pilate and suffered and was buried and rose again on the third day according to the Scriptures, and ascended into heaven, and sits at the right hand of the Father.

Blessed be the God and Father of our Lord Jesus Christ, who has blessed us in Christ with every spiritual blessing in the heavenly places. (Eph. 1:3)

WCF 9–18; LC 65–90

T. F. Torrance castigates the Assembly for what he considers to be a medieval conception of the *ordo salutis*, with various stages of grace leading to union with Christ.[1] Superficially, it might seem so, since there is no chapter on union with Christ in the Confession, nor is union with Christ significant in the discussion of the elements of salvation. However, Torrance's thesis is shattered by Larger Catechism 65–90, where all of God's grace is said to be found in union and communion with Christ. The two documents

1. T. F. Torrance, *Scottish Theology*, 128.

need to be taken together, for their lines of approach are different but complementary. Torrance refers to the alleged revival of the medieval *ordo salutis* by William Perkins (1558–1602), and claims the support of an article by his brother, James B. Torrance[2]—whose argument Richard Muller had destroyed in one of his early publications.[3] Torrance completely ignores Muller, rather like missing the proverbial elephant in the room.

Earlier, Karl Barth made trenchant and far-reaching criticisms of the Confession, including apparent compliments that were in reality thinly disguised condemnations. He acknowledges the elaborate care that went into its production, affirming that "no other Reformed confessional document was worked on as long and as carefully (three to four years, based on how one counts), with the possible exception of Bullinger's Second Helvetic Confession. Every phrase, every Biblical citation, is introduced consciously and with deliberation." Nonetheless, Barth snarls, "it is entirely justifiable for us to submit the final product to a thorough investigation. But this final product is a tragedy. It can only show how Calvinism's triumph was its death."[4] The problem for Barth seems to be that the focus has shifted from the works of grace by God to the marks of grace in the believing individual—to "a religious psychology arranged from the perspective of temporal-biographical sequence or phases of Christian experience."[5] In short, the focus on the *ordo salutis* indicates a turning to human experience at the expense of the grace of God. With brilliant and hilarious irony, he looks ahead to the nadir of nineteenth-century liberalism:

> The dark night of objectivism, in which the Reformers, under the weight of the medieval tradition, had still remarkably enough remained, now begins to *fade*, and gradually, from very far away, the pleasant morning of that day dawns on which Schleiermacher, that self-styled "Moravian of a higher order," will discover, as the actual finisher of the work begun by Luther, that the essence of

2. Ibid., n10.
3. R. A. Muller, "Perkins' A Golden Chaine: Predestinarian System or Schematized Ordo Salutis?" *SCJ* 9 (1978): 68–81.
4. Barth, *Reformed Confessions*, 135.
5. Ibid., 139.

theology is the analysis of the pious self-consciousness. This will be the day on which the Erlangen theologian Hofmann will compose the statement that defines at least two centuries of theology: "I, the Christian, am the most appropriate content of my science as a theologian."[6]

Barth may be correct in his strictures against Pietism, yet he commits the fallacy of looking for anticipations of later developments in authors who cannot be credited with an awareness of what lay in the distant future.[7] Moreover, he forgets that Calvin wrote at the start of his *Institutes* of a twofold knowledge, knowledge of God and knowledge of oneself, and that the two go together.[8] It is indubitably to the work of God that the Assembly attaches priority—indeed, its focus on the decrees of God has itself come in for attack by the same critics who here decry its attention to the human reception of grace. Not only Calvin, but the Bible itself, addresses these same questions, and the divines throughout their debates were preoccupied with biblical exegesis. Did Barth add to his anachronism by forgetting SC 1?

Moreover, Barth contradicts himself a few pages later, where he points to the distinctive feature of the characteristically Reformed confessions as

> the understanding of Christianity as the connection, grounded in God and effected in humans, of the invisible divine truth of life and the visible renewal of human life, of divine turning and human converting, of the knowledge of God and the self . . . of gift and task, of justification and rebirth, of covenant of grace and covenant of law, of faith and duty . . . or however else it may be phrased. This *connection* is the positive Reformed doctrine of Christianity.[9]

If this connection is both positive and central to Reformed theology, why is it a tragedy that the Confession draws that connection?

6. Ibid., 140.
7. See Skinner, "Meaning and Understanding."
8. Calvin, *Institutes*, 1.1.1.
9. Barth, *Reformed Confessions*, 147–48.

The *Ordo Salutis* and Its Critics

Some have argued that the concept of the *ordo salutis* (order of salvation) does not accurately reflect the progression of redemptive history found in the Bible. According to this argument, the best way to unfold salvation is in terms of biblical theology. This discipline regards redemptive history as the key to understanding the ways and works of God. It was at its height in the middle decades of the last century, but has lost favor since then. However, many conservative Reformed scholars—building on the work of Geerhardus Vos, Herman Ridderbos, and Richard B. Gaffin Jr.—still maintain this to be the most fruitful line of approach. It is said to capture the dynamism of the Bible and the centrality of Christ. The *historia salutis* (history of salvation) is a more pertinent theme, the argument goes.[10] There is little doubt that biblical theology is a useful discipline, especially for the exegesis of passages in the Old Testament. However, by itself it is incapable of defending the church against heresy, since most heresies make use of biblical language and thus cannot be refuted by recourse to that alone.[11] Moreover, it makes no sense to expect the Westminster divines to anticipate a movement three hundred years in the future and to criticize them for their failure to do so.

Others have argued that union with Christ must be given priority. There is something to be said for this position. I have mentioned elsewhere that Paul sees every aspect of our salvation as received *in Christ*, and that the rampant individualism of the Western world, especially since the eighteenth century, has robbed us of this vital teaching.[12] The point is recognized by Gaffin, who remarks, "Union with Christ by faith—that is the essence of Paul's *ordo salutis*."[13] Gaffin does not want to downplay the vital importance of justification by faith or of sanctification. His point is that union with Christ is for Paul the overarching factor within which the various elements of the order of salvation are to be considered. This argument is an important one.

10. See Trumper, "Covenant Theology and Constructive Calvinism"; Trumper, "A Fresh Exposition of Adoption."
11. See Letham, *The Holy Trinity*, 108–83.
12. Letham, *Work of Christ*, 75–87.
13. R. B. Gaffin Jr., *"By Faith, Not by Sight": Paul and the Order of Salvation* (Milton Keynes, England: Paternoster, 2006), 43.

It seems to me to be shared by the Assembly in its discussion of the matter in the Larger Catechism. On the other hand, neither they nor we are bound simply to repeat the theology of the apostle Paul. We are called to respond to the challenges of the day, building upon the Bible, by working out effective answers in the language and thought forms of our respective worlds.

As we consider the *ordo salutis* as both the Confession and the Larger Catechism describe it, an important point should be remembered. Elements of the order that occur at the outset of Christian experience (effectual calling, justification, adoption, saving faith, repentance) have a clear temporal priority over other elements that relate to its ongoing outworking (sanctification, good works, perseverance, and assurance of salvation). In turn, glorification occurs at the completion of salvation. Among the elements present at the start of the Christian life, the Assembly was not attempting to convey a temporal order, as if one necessarily followed the other in time. Moreover, we cannot discount the fact that those elements most associated with the start of faith continue to be in force later. Those who persevere are the justified, and they do so with saving faith and repentance as their ongoing experience, as adopted children of God. What the Larger Catechism brings to the fore is that all these are aspects of union and communion with Christ in grace and glory. At no point should they be isolated from union with Christ. The Assembly displayed, not two different views of the way of salvation, but one view seen from complementary vantage points.

Free Will (WCF 9)

Man is a free agent (WCF 9.1). His will is not forced by necessity of nature to do good or evil. It follows that the good and evil he does are by his own volition and so are his own responsibility. He cannot hide behind the sovereignty of God and argue that God is responsible for his predicament. Nor can Satan be blamed. In fact, all notions of blame stop here, since sin exposes human beings as fully accountable for their actions.

Before the fall, man was in a state of innocence (9.2). He had freedom and power to do what is right, good, and pleasing to God.

He was created in the image of God for fellowship with God, to rule the earth on his behalf. However, there was a possibility of deviating from this position.

In the state of sin after the fall, man has wholly lost the ability of will to do any spiritual good accompanying salvation (9.3). He is not incapable of doing good deeds, but he has no innate capacity to restore himself to the situation prevailing at creation, when he was in relationship with God and ruled the earth in its pristine state. Rather, he is averse to spiritual good and has a natural inclination to rebel against God. He is dead in sin, unable to effect any change; a dead man cannot restore himself to life. So pervasive is the effect of sin that he cannot even make himself receptive to spiritual good. He can only will what is spiritually evil.

In the state of grace, man has been converted by God (9.4). The change comes from outside, from the power and grace of God alone. God converts; he translates from the one state to the other. Moreover, God frees the person from his natural bondage under sin. God, by his grace, enables him freely to will and do what is spiritually good. However, "corruption" remains, and so he does not perfectly will or do spiritual good, but also wills and does what is evil. He is now free to do good, but still has a tendency to will also what is evil. This is the state of all believers in this life.

In the state of glory, after the resurrection, God enables the will of man to do good alone (9.5). He is unable to will or do evil. Moreover, there is a major difference from the state of innocence before the fall. Then, Adam had the possibility of falling into evil. In the state of glory, that possibility will not exist, for the condition will be immutable. This is no limitation on human freedom, for our true identity is to will and do what is spiritually good, and to will and do so unchangeably.

Effectual Calling (WCF 10; LC 67–68)

In effectual calling, God brings people out of the state of sin and death prevailing since the fall and into grace and salvation by Jesus Christ (WCF 10.1; LC 67). He does this to his elect, and only his elect. He does so at his own appointed time; it is not in their own power to effect this change. In LC 67, the Assembly stresses the love and grace of God in this action, for there is nothing in the elect themselves that would elicit grace. Here the focus is on God's inviting them to the state of salvation, drawing them by his Word and Spirit. The scene has subtly shifted from God's power to his gracious invitation.

In both the Confession and the Larger Catechism, calling is said to come about by God's enlightening the minds of the elect spiritually and savingly, so that they understand the things of God. Reflecting the words of Ezekiel, God takes away their heart of stone and replaces it with a heart of flesh. He renews their wills and by his almighty power makes them ready and willing to answer his call, to do so freely, and to accept and embrace his grace. Both Confession and Catechism here preserve the delicate balance between the almighty, sovereign power of God—seen in his gracious and loving invitation in the gospel—and the free agency of the ones called, for God's call results in the elect responding freely of their own will, God having granted them the capacity to understand, believe, and respond. This call is the point where union with Christ is effected. The Father calls, and the Holy Spirit grants faith and brings into union with the Son. The Son united himself to us in the incarnation, in one indivisible person, permanently, everlastingly. Now we are united to him, as the Father calls countless human persons.

This effectual call is by God's grace alone and hinges on nothing in man. Nor is it based on God's foreknowledge of future events (WCF 10.2). This rebuts the Arminian idea that God's decisions in salvation are based upon his foreknowledge of who will respond in faith to the gospel. This theology denies that faith and repentance depend on God's determination in election, insisting that God simply ratifies the choices humans make themselves. The divines posit two stages in the call. In the first, the called are passive, for God changes the heart. However, in the second phase, they become active. Having been quickened and renewed by the Holy Spirit, they answer the call, embracing the grace offered in the gospel.

How about those who are unable to hear the Word and so are incapable of being effectually called (WCF 10.3)? Is there no hope of salvation for them? The Assembly deals with two classes of person in this category. Elect infants who die in infancy are regenerated and saved by Christ, through the Holy Spirit. This does not apply to all infants, but to *elect* infants who die. It is clear that all the elect will be saved; consequently, any elect infants who die before they can hear the gospel themselves will be saved. This is, of course, grounded on the covenant of grace, in which the Lord promises "to give unto all those that are ordained unto eternal life His Holy Spirit" (WCF 7.3; cf. LC 32). This covenant was made "with Christ as the second Adam, and in him with all the elect as his seed" (LC 31). Moreover, "infants descending from parents, either both, or but one of them, professing faith in Christ, and obedience to him, are in that respect within the covenant" (LC 166). WCF 10.3 does not explicitly state that all infants within the covenant who die in infancy will be saved, but instead relates it to election. There is a delicate balance here between sovereignty, seen in election, and history, in terms of the covenant and the *ordo salutis*. As for the other category, "all other elect persons who are uncapable of being outwardly called by the ministry of the Word," the Assembly intended for us to understand mentally handicapped persons. These too will be saved. The rationale for these claims is twofold: God's settled purpose in election and the inscrutable work of the Holy Spirit, who works as and how he pleases. Both of these factors are entirely outside human control, and so leave room for some of God's elect to be beyond what we ourselves can readily observe.[14]

This touches the discussion today on whether those who have never heard the gospel may be saved. The statement here in WCF 10.3 must be seen in the light of the next section, which denies that

---

14. Anthony Tuckney comments on this question referring to infants and "distracted persons . . . which want the use of reason." As for infants: "How God worketh in, or dealeth with elect Infants, which dye in their infancy . . . the Scripture speaks not so much, or so evidently, as for me (or it may be for any) to make any clear or firm determination of it. But yet so much as that are have thence ground to believe, that they being in the covenant, they have the benefit of it, Acts 3.25, Gen 17.7. Whether God may not work and act faith in them then, (as he made John Baptist leap in the womb) which Beza, and others of our Divines deny, and others are not willing to grant, I dare not peremptorily determine. Yet this I may say, that he acteth in the souls of Believers *in articulo mortis*, when some of them are so little able to put forth an act of reason, as they were *in articulo nativitatis*." Moreover, Scripture "giveth us ground to believe, that they being in the covenant may be so wrapt up in it, as also to be wrapt up in the bundle of life, and did it give us but as good hopes of the Heathens (of whom it rather speaks badly) as it doth of such Infants, I should be as forward as any to perswade my self and others, that they were in a hopeful condition." Tuckney, *None but Christ*, 134–36.

anyone not professing the Christian religion can be saved (10.4). Moreover, LC 60 answers the precise question: "Can they who have never heard the gospel, and so know not Jesus Christ, nor believe in him, be saved by their living according to the light of nature?" The answer is a resounding no. No matter how diligently people live according to the light of nature or the laws of the religion they profess, they cannot be saved. This is because there is only one Savior, Jesus Christ. Here the proof text cited is relevant. It is Acts 4:12, where Peter asserts to the Sanhedrin that there is salvation in no one else, for there is no other name under heaven by which we must be saved. These considerations force the conclusion that the elect infants and elect persons incapable of being called by the outward preaching of the Word are persons within the covenant who for reasons outside their control either die before they can personally understand the gospel or are incapable of understanding it when they hear it. The section also undermines the case of those who assert that conscious faith in Jesus Christ is an indispensable necessity for salvation. This is so in normal circumstances, but, thanks be to God, his grace reaches to the unusual and tragic conditions of his elect who are deprived of these opportunities.

Excursus 3: The Early Debates on Justification

The debates on justification during the early phase of the Assembly, when the Thirty-Nine Articles were considered, are of immense interest. They lasted for a week of intense discussion and not a little division. The doctrine of justification by faith was at the heart of the Reformation and is enshrined in article 11 of the Thirty-Nine Articles. The Articles expressly counter the Roman doctrine of justification by faith working through love, with its conflation of justification and sanctification and its teaching that the Holy Spirit infuses the righteousness of Christ in the believer.

Chapter 9 of the decree on justification of the Council of Trent anathematized anyone who taught that "it is by faith alone that the wicked person is justified." In turn, chapter 11 added, "If anyone says that people are justified either by the imputation of Christ's righteousness alone or by the remission of sins alone, to the exclusion of grace and the love which is poured forth in their hearts by the Holy Spirit and inheres in them . . . let him be anathema." For good measure, chapter 12 asserted, "If anyone says that justifying faith is nothing other than trust in the divine mercy, which remits sins for Christ's sake; or that it is this trust alone by which we are justified: let him be anathema."[15] This to Protestants was an erosion of the gospel, because it based justification on something in the believer, albeit the result of the grace of God. Instead, Protestants taught that we are justified on the sole ground of the righteousness of Christ reckoned or imputed to us and received only by faith. Since Christ is the ground of justification, faith by virtue of its looking outside ourselves to Christ is the appropriate instrument through which we are made right with God in a legal or forensic sense.

However, the Assembly's main concern was no longer Rome, but the antinomians. As Van Dixhoorn points out, this was the preoccupation of the justification debates; the main enemy was located not in Madrid but in London.[16] In particular, it was a form of antinomianism that he describes as "soteriological," which so stressed the completion and finality of the work of Christ that there was nothing left for the believer to do.[17] However, it was not long before the Assembly was effectively hijacked by the concerns of Thomas Gataker, backed up by wide and deep learning and dogged persistence.

The original article 11 was as follows: "We are accompted righteous before God, only for the merite of our Lord and saviour Jesus Christe, by faith, and not for our owne workes or deservynges. Wherefore, that we are iustified by fayth onely, is a most wholesome doctrine, and very full of comfort; as more largely is expressed in the Homilie of iustification."[18]

The proposed revision was as follows:

> We are justified, that is, we are accounted righteous before God, and have remission of sins, not for nor by our own works or deservings, but freely by his grace, only for our Lord and Saviour Jesus Christ's sake, his whole

---

15. A. N. S. Lane, *Justification by Faith in Catholic-Protestant Dialogue: An Evangelical Assessment* (London: T. & T. Clark, 2002), 79–80.

16. Van Dixhoorn, 1:28, 276.

17. See T. D. Bozeman, *The Precisianist Strain: Disciplining Religion and Antinomian Backlash in Puritanism to 1638* (Chapel Hill: University of North Carolina Press, 2004); D. Como and P. Lake, "Puritans, Antinomians and Laudians in Caroline London: The Strange Case of Peter Shaw and its Contexts," *JEH* 50 (1999): 695 [684–715]. The idea probably arose due to an excessive stress in Puritanism on self-examination and precise directives for godly living, for "antinomians offered a relief from the perceived tyranny of puritan practical divinity." Jue, "Active Obedience of Christ," 110–11. The leading antinomian, John Eaton, in *The honey-combe of free justification by Christ alone* (London: Robert Lancaster, 1642) [Wing E115], taught that both the active and the passive obedience of Christ were imputed for justification. This led to a focus on justification both completed by Christ and in God's eternal decree.

18. Schaff, *Creeds*, 3:494.

obedience and satisfaction being by God imputed unto us, and Christ with his righteousness, being apprehended and rested on by faith only. The doctrine of justification by faith only, is an wholesome Doctrine, and very full of comfort: notwithstanding God doth not forgive them that are impenitent, and go on still in their trespasses.[19]

In S46 TU 5.9.43, the chairman of the First Committee reported on article 11, and its report was debated. It was proposed to add the words "in the sight of God," reflecting, as Hoyle explained, the language of Romans 3:20.[20] This proved problematic for many of the divines since it seemed to open the door to an antinomian interpretation, in which God is held to see no sin in his servants, for the antinomians "hold justification without faith, and faith to be only a manifestation."[21] The debate took most of the morning, and the matter was sent back to the committee.[22] Then Gataker maintained that remission of sins *followed* justification and so was separable from it. As he said, "I apprehend Re[mission] to be a thing distinct from Justification. I confesse that's in the mold of the article is most true: our sins are remitted for the merit of Christ, & it doth always accompany Justification, but it is noe part of Justification, but a thing distinct from it."[23] This line of argument was a departure from classic Reformed confessions such as the French and Belgic, which both equated justification with remission of sins. For Gataker, justification was a legal matter, and remission was an act of grace based on the changed legal status. As soon as Gataker finished his speeches, on this and other occasions, two men pounced on him to rebut his arguments: George Walker, a persistent opponent of Gataker, whose main interest was union with Christ, and Joshua Hoyle. On this occasion, a lengthy debate followed, with point-by-point rebuttals on both sides.

The next day, in S47 W 6.9.43, the chairman reported the committee's response, incorporating the alternative phrase "before God." The beginning of the article, it was proposed, should now read, "We are justified, that is, we are accounted righteous before God, & have remission of sins, not for, nor by our owne workes or deservings, but freely by his grace onely for our Lord and Saviour Jesus Christ's sake, his whole obedience and satisfaction being by God imputed to us." Following an unsuccessful attempt to insert a statement on certainty of salvation, the title and first clause of the article

19. Van Dixhoorn, 1:320.
20. Ibid., 3:12.
21. Ibid., 3:12–15.
22. Lightfoot's journal, in Van Dixhoorn, 2:46.
23. Van Dixhoorn, 3:16.

were approved.[24] Daniel Featley pressed unsuccessfully for a definition of justification as an act of God, citing Justin Martyr, Jerome, Augustine, and Bernard to prove this was held before Luther.

A proposal was then made that justification entails being accounted righteous as well as having our sins forgiven. To many, this seemed to confuse justification and sanctification since, Gataker objected, accounting righteous applies also to sanctification. A considerable debate followed. Herle disagreed that the phrase was ambiguous, while Walker argued that the choice was not simply between forensic and inherent righteousness, for there was another possibility: "justification by communion of the righteousnesse of Christ."[25] Lightfoot also objected to the committee proposal, but on different grounds, since he considered it was close to an antinomian interpretation of eternal justification. Instead, he favored the phrase "made and accounted righteous," apparently oblivious to the probability that this would be even closer to the Roman Catholic view. The Assembly was not prepared to go that far and defeated his suggestion.[26] Yet, as Van Dixhoorn comments, "concern over antinomianism had risen to such a pitch that a handful of divines, Lightfoot included, were willing to sacrifice soteriological clarity and anti-Catholic polemic on the altar of anti-antinomianism."[27]

However, the main controversy regarding justification had to do with whether the active obedience of Christ is imputed to the one justified by faith. The Assembly took from S47 W 6.9.43 to S52 TU 12.9.43 to settle this matter. The majority held that Christ's active obedience was indeed imputed. On the other hand, a significant minority were either unsure or opposed the idea. The leaders of this second group were Gataker and Richard Vines. Vines, in contrast with Gataker, maintained that justification consisted solely in the remission of sins. He argued that Scripture connected our justification to the sufferings and blood of Christ.[28] Hoyle, Walker, and Bathurst all replied that while justification relates more to the blood of Christ, Scripture also attributes it to his obedience, which on the basis of Romans 5 must include his active obedience to the law.[29] Gataker held that Christ's passive obedience was imputed and that remission of sins was something separate, following justification. Neither he nor Vines was

24. Ibid., 2:47.
25. Ibid., 3:23.
26. Ibid., 2:48.
27. Ibid., 1:289.
28. Ibid., 3:25.
29. Ibid., 2:48–49; 3:25.

ready to accept that the active obedience of Christ was imputed. In this they were supported, of those whose contribution to debates was recorded, by Woodcock[30] and Taylor.[31]

For Gataker, Christ, according to his human nature, owed obedience to God. He went so far as to claim that the human nature of Christ was a creature.[32] Hoyle immediately sprang to his feet to rebut him, for "the obligation is not betwixt God & a nature, but God & a person. The person in which this human nature lyes is not a creature."[33] Walker thought Gataker's statement sounded uncomfortably like Socinianism.[34] Gataker, however, saw no reason why this was heretical; "to say that Christ being as man inferior to God did in that regard owe duty to God, I see not why erroneous."[35] He referred to the special *pactum* between God and Christ, which became known as the covenant of redemption. Since Christ was under obligation to God, his fulfillment of that obligation is not meritorious and so is not imputed. Therefore, in justification we are simply restored to the pre-fall situation of Adam; it is adoption that fits us for heaven.[36]

On the following day, in S48 TH 7.9.43, long lists of authorities were trotted out in support of various arguments. Hoyle, as usual, strongly opposed Gataker "as trenching too neere upon heresy" and then, from Romans 5, established that Christ's active obedience must be joined to his passive obedience or the latter would not be obedience at all; his sufferings and death avail because of his life of obedience. The question was whether his passive obedience was sufficient of itself for justification.[37] Gataker apologized for having called Christ a creature the previous day. He affirmed that the dignity of Christ adds to the merit of his person, since it is the blood of God. Moreover, he produced a range of authorities in his support of the controverted expression: Athanasius (the minutes list Tertullian, but Van Dixhoorn suggests Athanasius resisted using "creature" of Christ, and that maybe Gataker was making an inference from *Ad Episcopos Aegyptii*, NPNF 2, 4:232, or *Orationes contra Arianos*, ibid., 418–19), Cyril (*Opus in evangelium Ioannis*, Paris, 1508, 2:92; *Opera*, Basel, 1566; Paris, 1572: PL 73:386–87), Gomarus (possibly referring to

30. Ibid., 2:49.
31. Ibid., 1:303–4.
32. Ibid., 3:26–27.
33. Ibid., 3:27.
34. Ibid., 3:28.
35. Ibid., 3:29.
36. Ibid.
37. Ibid., 2:49–50.

Disputatio XXVI de hominis coram Deo justificatione, in *Opera,* Amsterdam: John Jansson, 1644, vol. 3), Junius (*Opera,* Geneva: Peter and Jacob Chovet, 1613, vol. 2), the French synod (in Gap, 1603, *Epistola ad Piscatorem;* see Norris, 211).[38]

According to Gataker, Vines, and Woodcock, Christ needed to fulfill the law in order to be a perfect sacrifice. He had to do this for his own sake, because he was man in relation to God.[39] Vines doubted the imputation of the active obedience. "He confessed his [Christ's] active obedience did conduce to our justification, nor did he deny an active obedience in his suffering, but his passive obedience was that which is the matter of our righteousnesse" since the current of Scripture runs this way when it deals directly with justification in Romans 3:24; 5:9–10 and Galatians 3:13. Scripture talks of our being justified "by his blood." All things in the law were purged by blood, and "even sacraments speake death." In contrast, Christ's active obedience was not typified in the law, nor does Romans 5 lend support. In fact, Philippians 2:8 identifies Christ's obedience with the death of the cross.[40] Later, Herle answered him by stressing that Christ is the end of the law, the consummating end, achieved not by his passive obedience but by his active obedience; this we all owed to God, and only the antinomians would question it.[41]

In opposing Gataker, Walker referred to a range of biblical passages, such as Isaiah 54:14, Isaiah 61:10, Revelation 19:8, Jeremiah 23:6, Jeremiah 33:16, Psalm 24:5, Psalm 40:8, Psalm 69, and Philippians 3:9. Wilkinson made a more theological argument, finding an active righteousness in each of Christ's three offices. Gibson, for his part, based his argument on his exegesis of Romans 5:18–19. Thomas Goodwin entered the fray, insisting that Christ was not obliged to keep the law because he was a divine-human person. Daniel Featley agreed; Christ is not a human *person* and the law was given to persons, not natures, and therefore Christ fulfilled the law for his people, and had no need to do so for himself.[42] For Goodwin, the active obedience is intended by Paul in Romans 5:12–19 because of the contrast between Adam's sin and Christ's obedience; he pointed to Paul's terming it "a justification of life" and to his referring to the righteousness of the law being fulfilled. Moreover, the main object of this obedience is Christ's person, and so it is called "the blood of God";

38. Van Dixhoorn, 3:31, who tracked these sources down.
39. Ibid., 1:297.
40. Ibid., 2:50; 3:31–32.
41. Ibid., 3:36–37.
42. Ibid., 1:299; 2:51; 3:32–36.

it is the obedience of more than a creature, since the human nature was united personally to the son of God.[43]

Gataker saw this as a serious mistake. On the basis of the *communicatio idiomatum*, the human attributes are attributable to Christ's person, and so he was obliged to keep the law. Even George Walker sided with Gataker here.[44] Gataker cited Tilenus and Cameron; Walker referred to "St. Gregory" (which one is unclear).[45] Herbert Palmer countered Gataker with lexical and theological reasons: it was unclear from Scripture whether the sufferings of Christ's soul were part of the satisfaction; therefore, the argument that Scripture focuses on the passive obedience is undermined; moreover, the word *dikaioma* in Romans 5:18 never signifies passiveness, or sufferings, but rather agrees with the phrase in Galatians 4, "under the law," which means under obedience.[46] Bathurst joined Palmer with a redemptive-historical argument. Redemption must answer the fall. Adam broke the law; Christ must keep it. The two tables were put in the ark; the ark was a pregnant type of Christ; Christ could not break the law; therefore, he set himself to keep it.[47] Moreover, those who rejected the imputation of the active obedience overlooked a necessary distinction between the exclusion of guilt and positive acts.[48]

Vines painted a picture of the situation before he came to the Assembly. He never referred to the active obedience of Christ, since so many people disagreed about it, but instead focused on his sufferings. Since everything under the law was purged by the shedding of blood, what more was needed? Moreover, he added, the sacraments point to Christ's death, not his life. With Gataker, Vines agreed that adoption gives the right to heaven since the adopted are sanctified and so righteous themselves. Walker's riposte was that those who enter heaven are sanctified and *sinful*, so justification gives the right to heaven.[49] The Assembly was all over the place. There was agreement that the sufferings of Christ are at the heart of redemption; the question was not that, but whether his passive obedience solely justifies.

The specter of antinomianism appeared when Francis Taylor, supporting Gataker, argued that if Christ obeyed the law perfectly for us, there would be no need for us to obey it ourselves, and so the antinomians would be right after all; besides which, Christ did not obey the whole law, since he was nei-

---

43. Ibid., 3:34–36.
44. Ibid., 1:300.
45. Ibid., 1:301.
46. Ibid., 3:38–39.
47. Ibid., 2:52.
48. Ibid., 3:39.
49. Ibid., 1:303–4.

ther a magistrate nor a husband.[50] Lightfoot fought back by repeating that our redemption overcomes the fall, and so Christ must obey the law since we broke it.[51] Goodwin agreed. A double debt arose in the fall: not only a requirement of satisfaction, but one of obedience. Undergoing punishment is not the same as satisfying the law, or else those in hell would achieve it. The antinomian threat is not real, he said; the discussion concerns justification, not sanctification. Moreover, love is the fulfilling of the law, and since Christ was full of that he satisfied for all relations: the same love that made him obedient to his parents would have made him so to a master, had he been a servant, and to a husband, had he been a wife. There were many parts of the ceremonial law that he did not perform, such as the rites of a cleansed leper, and so he did not undergo many particular branches of the curse.[52] And so the discussion continued. Seaman referred to Christ's "whole obedience and satisfaction." Featley, citing Bernard and Calvin, agreed that the topic was a matter of disagreement: "ther are very accute divines of both opinions, as Molinaeus. Contrary Piscator & Tilenus." He added that Adam and Christ must be seen here as public persons representing others. Twisse reinforced Featley's observation about the controversy on the continent: "The Duke of Bolian acquainted King James with it & his motion was to lay that question aside because never united amongst the fathers." Vines's last words in the session were that the argument that Christ was to do for us all that we had failed to do was untenable. We were bound to repent; Christ was not.[53]

In S49 F8.9.43, Wilson insisted, referring to 2 Corinthians 5:21, that the active and passive obedience are divided only in *rationis* and not in *rei* (in our reasoning and not in themselves), arguing that Christ's active obedience was in view in Romans 5:19. Price warned that if the imputation of Christ's active obedience was denied, the imputation of Adam's sin would be denied as well; and the imputation of the passive obedience would be under threat too. Vines made clear that he recognized Christ's active obedience, but his point was that it related to sanctification, rather than justification, since "it properly is not opposed to guilt & condemnation." He reinforced his claim by reflecting on the phrase "the law of the Spirit of life" in Romans 8:2, where the habitual holiness of Christ relates to sanctification, not justification. The nub of the matter was whether Christ's active obedience "is a <proper> distinct foundation of title to heaven" and whether it is part of justification.[54] Vines

50. Ibid., 1:307; 2:53; 3:39–40.
51. Ibid., 3:40.
52. Ibid., 2:53; 3:40–41.
53. Ibid., 3:41–43.
54. Ibid., 2:56; 3:44–45.

explicitly did not deny the merit of Christ, but he questioned whether the phrase "justification of life" in Romans 5:18 denotes active obedience; he did not see how it followed.[55] Nor could he see how the holiness of Christ's nature could be imputed.[56]

Goodwin, in another lengthy speech, stated that "if the passive obedience of Christ only ware it that ware imputed, it would but set us in the state we ware in [which] Adam was in the moment of his creation." This would take care of past omissions, "yet I must have an eternall active righteousnesse soe Adam was to have—& wher shall we have this unlesse it be active?"[57] Lazarus Seaman declared that Christ not only submitted to death, but also obeyed the substance of the ceremonial, moral & judicial laws, so therefore his obedience is to be joined together in imputation. The whole Christ is imputed to us, therefore his whole obedience is involved. The justice of God could not be satisfied without all kinds of obedience. The active obedience was not necessary for Christ alone, since all he did was for our good and in our place. He acted not as a creature or a person, but as a mediator. Finally, Christ's sufferings only had value since he was a righteous person. Herle repeated his argument of the previous day, that whatever the law required us to do and we failed to do, Christ did for us. An opponent might reply that Christ did not repent, but according to Herle repentance is required not by the law but by the gospel.[58]

When the Assembly resumed in S50 M 11.9.43am, after a much-needed weekend's break, Woodcock reasserted his fear that joining the active obedience of Christ to justification would lead to antinomianism. If it were so, then a justified person would be looked on as having no sin. If merit belongs to Christ's righteousness, and it is imputed to me, then there is merit in me. God will then see no sin in me.[59] This was a prominent theme of the soteriological antinomians.[60] A flurry of rebuttals followed. Walker said the same argument could be used against the imputation of the passive obedience.

55. Ibid., 3:46.
56. Ibid., 3:47.
57. Ibid.
58. Ibid., 2:57; 3:49–50.
59. Ibid., 3:52.
60. According to the leading antinomian, John Eaton, the perfect obedience of Christ, both active and passive, is the formal basis of justification, with the result that God sees no sin in justified persons. They are also freed from the requirement to obey the law as evidence of their justification. Behind this was an excessive stress on the finality of the decree of God and the work of Christ to the exclusion of human participation. Justification had priority over faith and was grounded in the eternal decree of God. Eaton, *The honey-combe of free justification by Christ alone* [Wing E115], 182, 262–63.

Bathurst pointed out that imputative righteousness entails inherent sin in us. Gouge made clear that God looks on us as having fulfilled the law, not by ourselves, but by a surety. Case stressed that God sees no sin in us in terms of justification, but does see sin in us when it comes to sanctification. Vines himself countered Woodcock's fear by stressing that imputation does not imply that I have done what Christ did, but that what Christ did is mine.[61] Herle warned against speaking of the merit of Christ being imputed to us, since "the law did not require of me merit, but obedience, soe as that obedience is mine but the merit is Christs."[62]

Then Raynor joined the fray by questioning whether there was sufficient biblical warrant for the idea that the active obedience was imputed in justification. As far as he could see, righteousness is not ascribed in Scripture to Christ until his death. Moreover, the debt a man owes to God is obedience, "but this debt which is over & above that in remission of sins, that a Christian doth truly pay in sanctification." Moreover, as with Gataker, Raynor argued that adoption gives us the right to heaven.[63] Both Arrowsmith and Coleman answered him. Gataker returned to the debate with a massive speech, citing a barrage of authorities from Athanasius, Calvin, Junius, and Gomarus to Aristotle, dealing largely with his opponents' exegesis of biblical passages from both Testaments. His main sticking point was the word "whole" in "whole obedience." The question at stake, according to Gataker, was "if Christs habituall holynesse, his obedience to the law naturall & morall, be cast into that price that was payed for the dischardge of our guilt. It is a question named unto me by a professour at Bazill, whether any place in scripture wher Christ's active obedience is called the price or ransome by which we are redeemed." The theological point he emphasized was that whatever someone does in our stead, we are not bound to do ourselves; therefore if Christ obeyed the law in our stead, we are not bound to obey it. Hence, antinomianism would follow from an acceptance of the imputation of the active obedience of Christ in justification. Moreover, Gataker pointed out, only in the Second Helvetic Confession was there express mention of the imputation of Christ's active obedience.[64] He urged upon the Assembly a motion as to whether it was convenient to dissent from the majority position: "whether in an article to be generally allowed and soe many learned men differing from it, to pitch

61. Van Dixhoorn, 2:58.
62. Ibid., 3:54.
63. Ibid., 3:55–56.
64. Ibid., 3:57–62.

upon that that may exclude many that [dissent] & keepe them out from exercising of their ministry."[65]

Gouge argued that the doctrine of the imputation of Christ's righteousness is ancient, constant, and universal,[66] evidently received by the churches of England, Scotland, France, the Palatinate, the Netherlands, Switzerland, and Bohemia.[67] However, he made a telling statement that may help to understand the rather cryptic terminology of the Assembly. The ground of the controversy, he suggested, was not the phrase "whole obedience," since "it makes no distinction of active & passive."[68] If this was so, the phrase in the eventually revised article was probably intended to unite the Assembly in accommodating Gataker and his friends. Ley, urging that the matter be brought to a vote, remarked that "the passive delivereth onely from hell; it is the active that giveth us interest in heaven."[69] Featley, bringing a touch of humor to the occasion, announced: "I have been passive this 2 days in hearing soe much & soe acutly objected; I desire now to be a littel alive. As St. Gregory spake of Thomas, I am much indebted to that learned brother that first made doubt of this. Many texts for active aleadged." He went on to add others himself, besides citations from 1 Clement, Chrysostom, and Augustine.[70] Vines insisted that "we are for whole Christ for every use, but we are to distinguish upon respects. We are wholly for Christ's active obedience, but *quaerimus* upon what this obedience is terminated. We confesse we have all we have by Christ & shall have ten times more glory then Adam's righteousnesse was capable of, but *quaerimus* whether this be founded upon the active obedience." After a long discourse, he concluded that justification is opposed to condemnation, and so his *quaere* remains, that the active obedience is not properly called justification.[71]

After more discussion that afternoon, in S51 M 11.9.43pm, the matter was finally put to a vote the next day, in S52 TU 12.9.43. Not surprisingly, this only came after still more debate. Hoyle urged the Assembly against a

---

65. Ibid., 3:62.

66. Cf. the well-known criterion of Vincent of Lerins, *quod ubique, quod semper, quod ab omnibus creditus est* (what is believed everywhere, always, and by all people), displaying the characteristics of ecumenicity, antiquity, and consent.

67. Van Dixhoorn, 2:60–61. Van Dixhoorn suggests the following sources: the Third Homily of the Book of Homilies; Scots Confession (1560), 8–9; French Confession (1559), 18; Heidelberg Catechism (1563), 56 (?); Belgic Confession (1561), 22; Second Helvetic Confession (1566), 15; Confessio Bohemica, 8.

68. Van Dixhoorn, 3:62.

69. Ibid., 2:61–62.

70. Ibid., 3:64–65.

71. Ibid., 2:63; 3:67–68.

"fallacy of division" of the whole Christ.[72] Otherwise, the same arguments were presented as had been rehearsed before. The question was whether the words "his whole obedience & satisfaction" should pass. After much hot debate, it was resolved that the wording should be "his whole obedience and satisfaction being by God imputed to us."[73] Only three or four dissented.[74]

Biblical exegesis was central in these debates; much of the time was spent in discussion of, and arguments derived from, Romans 5:12–19, but underlying the exegesis were deeper theological questions.[75] As Van Dixhoorn suggests, there were some in the Assembly who accepted that Christ's obedience could be understood as having both active and passive dimensions. Some of these considered that both elements were imputed in justification; others, such as Gataker, restricted the imputation to the passive obedience. However, there were others in the Assembly who did not hold to there being biblical evidence to support a twofold classification of the obedience of Christ. Some thought that the whole undivided obedience was imputed, while still others, like Vines, maintained that this necessarily ruled out talk of imputation of an active obedience.[76] Clearly, English Reformed theology had not reached a settled position on the question by 1643. Van Dixhoorn points to there being "constantly shifting allegiances during each debate."[77] Still further muddying the waters were differences over covenant theology, and in particular the pre-fall covenant of works or life. Neither Gataker nor Vines held to a covenant of works. Some thought it encouraged antinomianism, others considered that it minimized the importance of Christ's sufferings or that it was simply bad exegesis.[78] These obviously were a minority, since this covenant took its place in the Assembly's documents—although we have seen that there were underlying tensions in how to understand it and where to place it.

Was the phrase "the whole obedience of Christ" intended to include both the active and the passive obedience? Or was it instead a compromise, a form of words, allowing for differing interpretations? Van Dixhoorn suggests that it was intended to include active as well as passive obedience.[79] As we indicated before, Gataker urged that men not be excluded from their ministries over the question. The phrases "active obedience" and "passive obedience"

72. Ibid., 3:74.
73. Ibid., 2:66.
74. Ibid., 3:77.
75. Ibid., 1:310–15.
76. Ibid., 1:315.
77. Ibid., 1:316.
78. Ibid., 1:317–18.
79. Ibid., 1:293.

do not appear in the documents at this or at any later time; the phrase in both the Confession and the Larger Catechism is "perfect obedience."[80] In Van Dixhoorn's words, it is unclear whether these refer to both the active and passive obedience or only to the passive. "That the Assembly decided not to use the language of the active obedience of Christ in the *Confession* or in either catechism appears to have been a deliberate decision." The phrases could be taken to include or exclude the active obedience, but "it appears that the Assembly chose not to make its statement as clear as was possible."[81] It seems to me that the care the Assembly took over the phraseology indicates a desire to include all its members in accepting the statement.[82] In support of this possibility is the Savoy Declaration of 1658, produced by the Congregationalists led by John Owen and Thomas Goodwin, and virtually a reproduction of the Westminster Confession with appropriate modifications on church government. It also amends the chapter on justification, specifically referring to the imputation of Christ's active and passive obedience, as if to correct the undue flexibility and ambiguity at Westminster.[83]

What is clear is that the Assembly outlawed three unacceptable views of justification. Whatever the differences between the Gataker-Vines group and the majority, they were at one in rejecting the Roman Church's doctrine of justification, as expressed at the Council of Trent in canons 9 and 11. There was no place for any element in the believer contributing even in an instrumental sense to his justification. All positions that included inherent righteousness in this sense were excluded. Hence, "faith, thus receiving and resting on Christ and His righteousness, is the alone instrument of justification" (WCF 11.2). As Jue observes, "Whatever theological disagreements emerged during the Assembly's debates on justification, no one wanted to return to Rome."[84] In the committee's words in its original report, "A papist that lookes upon this article might see their doctrine condemned."[85] Morris observes, in referring also to WCF 15.3 and 16.3, that "the Symbols are careful to guard against the impression that good

---

80. Ibid., 1:323.

81. Ibid., 1:326.

82. Carl Trueman tends to agree. See C. R. Trueman, *John Owen: Reformed Catholic, Renaissance Man* (Aldershot: Ashgate, 2007), 105–6.

83. Schaff, *Creeds*, 3:706–29, omits the article on justification. The salient section in 11.1 reads "by imputing Christ's active obedience to the whole law, and passive obedience in his death for their whole and sole righteousness." *A declaration of the faith and order owned and practiced in the Congregational Churches in England* (London: John Field, 1658) [Wing (CD-ROM, 1996) N1486], 11.1. See also Trueman, *John Owen*, 108.

84. Jue, "Active Obedience of Christ," 106, 114.

85. Van Dixhoorn, 3:11.

works, even the good works of justified men, are in any way the ground of such abundant pardon."[86] Joshua Hoyle summarized the point pithily when he asked, "Why is faith imputed but because it hath relation to the righteousnesse of Christ which it takes as a hand. It doth only as a hand, else we shall confound it with workes."[87]

Even more striking is the deep concern to avoid any hint of antinomianism, with its claim of eternal justification. Both Vines and Gataker were strongly anti-antinomian. They feared that the inclusion of the active obedience of Christ in justification would lead in that direction, since there would be no reason for believers to be obliged to follow the moral law.[88] Anthony Tuckney is a good example of an Assembly divine who was concerned to avoid both "the scylla of Rome and the charybdis of antinomianism," by his claim that redemption depends on the active obedience of Christ as well as the passive, but that God regards as just those who are truly just, due to the imputation of the perfect righteousness of Christ.[89]

Third, the Arminian doctrine was also proscribed. Jue refers to Joseph Mede, whose work was highly regarded by many at Westminster. Mede argued that since the righteousness of Christ is reckoned to the justified, their own works are thereby rendered acceptable and so contribute to their justification at the final judgment.[90] In contrast, Gataker stressed that there is no eschatological reward attached to justification as such, while both he and Vines insisted that justification is forensic and does not contemplate renewal.[91]

Later, in 1645, the word "whole" was omitted from the Confession. Later still, LC 70 refers to "the *perfect* obedience and full satisfaction of Christ, by God imputed to them [sinners], and received by faith alone." Here it could be argued that Christ's "perfect obedience" refers to his active obedience, since his "full satisfaction" is almost certainly intended to point to the cross and his sufferings. The debates on article 11 one week later on the phrase "his whole obedience and satisfaction" tend strongly to support this possibility—

86. Morris, *Westminster Symbols*, 441–42.

87. Van Dixhoorn, 3:101.

88. Jue, "Active Obedience of Christ," 119–20; Van Dixhoorn, 3:39–40, 61. See Thomas Gataker, *Antinomianism discovered and confuted: and free-grace as it is held forth in God's Word* (London: E. G. for F. Clifton, 1652) [Wing (2nd ed., 1994) G312].

89. A. Tuckney, *Praelectiones theologicae, nec non determinationes quaestionum variarum insignium in Scholis Academicis Cantabrigiensibus habitae; quibus accedunt exercitia pro gradibus capassendis* (Amsterdam: Ex officina Stephani Smart, impensis Jonathanis Robinsonii, & Georgii Wells, Bibliopolarum Londinensium, 1679), 134–42.

90. Jue, "Active Obedience of Christ," 108–9.

91. Ibid., 116, 121.

Gataker, Vines, and their friends of course excepted.[92] On the other hand, the word "active" is studiously avoided, and an element of ambiguity is retained. Again, some scholars suggest that this indicates accommodation on the part of the Assembly to Gataker and Vines.[93] However, as Jue comments, there is no clear historical evidence that the Assembly had changed its mind, and the minutes do not record the details of the later discussions. Any conclusions on this can only be speculative.[94] Most likely, as Van Dixhoorn suggests, there were a range of reasons behind it,[95] just as the minutes disclose there to be on other areas where they supply detail. The Assembly was quite a diverse body, and it would be a mistake to seek single reasons for its actions on this matter and many others. On occasion, there may not even have been clear-cut reasons of any kind.

Jue may be accurate in observing that "the two-Adam Christological structure in the Standards supports a doctrine of justification that includes, in substance, the active obedience of Christ."[96] However, while this structure was considered in debate, it would be pressing the point to conclude that the divines applied it with rigorous logic, as theologians did later. Jue's comment is more theological than historical. The danger of the fallacy of coherence is a real one at this point, and later interpreters would do well to avoid it. Jue's comment that Gataker and Vines were "demonstratively voted down" is correct, insofar as the overwhelming majority rejected their position. On the other hand, they were not excluded from the Assembly, but continued to play a prominent part, in keeping with Gataker's own request that this not be made a litmus test of a man's ministry.[97]

---

92. Van Dixhoorn, 3:101–14. Supporting the idea that this phraseology distinguishes between the two aspects of Christ's obedience is the "Report of the Committee to Study the Doctrine of Justification," presented to the Seventy-third General Assembly of the Orthodox Presbyterian Church, July 2006, 73–75, although the tenor of the report suggests that the committee had made its mind up already. Moreover, it is not a primary witness.

93. J. R. D. Kirk, "The Sufficiency of the Cross (1): The Crucifixion as Jesus' Act of Obedience," *SBET* 24 (2006): 36–64; Barker, *Puritan Profiles*, 176.

94. Jue, "Active Obedience of Christ," 126.

95. Van Dixhoorn, 1:328.

96. Jue, "Active Obedience of Christ," 128.

97. I agree with Jue that the rejection of the imputation of the active obedience of Christ by Gataker and Vines cannot be compared with similar rejection of the doctrine by proponents of the New Perspective on Paul or the Federal Vision theology. Norman Shepherd, in *The Call of Grace* (Phillipsburg, NJ: P&R, 2000), ignores biblical passages that address the question and might undermine his argument; see Jue, "Active Obedience of Christ," 129. Everyone at the Assembly was strongly opposed to any inclusion of the good works of believers in the doctrine of justification; the latter was, of course, the position of the Roman Church, expressed at the Council of Trent.

The Nature of Justifying Faith

The Assembly continued, in S53 TU 12.9.43pm, with discussion of the nature of justifying faith. Wilkinson asserted that *fiducia* is the key point, meaning "layed hold of and applyed."[98] Bayly distinguished among general assenting or believing to be true all things to which God testifies, special resting whereby we put our trust and confidence in Christ for the benefit of his mediation, and particular applying faith whereby we appropriate the promises of Christ and make them our own. A man is saved by the second and second only, not by general assenting nor by particular applying, since God's special mercy in pardoning sins is not the object of justification. Sins are not forgiven until they are forgiven, he concluded.[99] Gataker thought talk of applying was dangerous. In justifying faith, there are six elements, he argued. First is *notitia*, an apprehension of something to be believed. Second comes *creditio scientiae*, assent to its truth. Third is conditional application, believing that the gospel will be saving if one performs the condition required. Fourth is *fiducia*, or a special resting upon Christ. Fifth is an apprehension of my own faith. Sixth comes a special application or persuasion—that you may know that you have eternal life—two steps after justifying faith, and so it cannot be the justifying act of faith. He cited Augustine in support of his view.[100]

Carter introduced a new twist. He commented that the focus had been on the act of faith, whereas it could be placed on the habit of faith; in some persons, such as infants, the habit may predominate. There is only a gradual difference between the two, "& therfore he that hath the habit, when by an inevitable necessity he cannot act, he is a true beleiver." There was a need to include "some phrase that may be meant as well of the habit as the act, & exercise of faith as that of 'receiving', because it is the scripture phrase."[101] Vines opposed Carter. We are not justified by the habit of faith; if it were this way, the faith through which we are justified would tend to be seen as a quality. "There must be something to answer imputation & must be by an act . . . a reception ther is, but

---

98. Van Dixhoorn, 3:78.
99. Ibid., 3:79–80.
100. Ibid., 3:81–82.
101. Ibid., 3:82.

a passive reception I understand not." He also questioned whether infants could be said to have the habit of faith. Walker pointed out that the crux of justifying faith is "the beleiving that we shall have in Christ remission of sins, & be constituted righteous before God." It reaches to those things that comprise our justification. Justifying faith comes from the Spirit of God.[102]

In S54 W 13.9.43, Herbert Palmer wanted a definition that included repentance with faith. This was a constant theme of his, provoked by fear of antinomianism. Gouge replied that it would be dangerous to place repentance before faith.[103] Vines argued that justifying or saving faith must be distinguished from general faith (indefinite belief that the whole Word of God is true) and temporary faith—for "this hath for its object the gospell of Christ." It is not believing the truth of an action or proposition, but it is the applying of oneself to Christ and his righteousness, a going out to Christ, a receiving or laying hold of Christ. The seat of it is in the heart. General faith it is not; temporary faith it is not; neither is it that certitude which we call an evident knowledge that I am justified and some call a reflex act of faith. This follows justification, for I cannot believe or know that I am justified until I am justified.[104] Price stated that the object of justifying faith is Christ in the promise. It has the nature of fiducial assent. Its acts include assurance.[105] Temple summed up the general consensus that it is *fiducia*, and that it is more than general belief, but less than assurance of salvation. For Goodwin, its object is Christ invested with his righteousness, while its act is an act of the will toward Christ.[106] The prolocutor, Twisse, brought the debate to a conclusion: "I am against this opinion that our relying upon Christ doth goe before our justification; it rather followes after." His argument was that faith is a work of grace. Since it is a work of grace, God treats us as a friend in giving us faith. Hence, the status of being justified has precedence over the act of faith. After all, how can we call God our Father if we are not

102. Ibid., 3:83.
103. Ibid., 3:85–86.
104. Ibid., 3:87.
105. Ibid., 3:87–88.
106. Ibid., 3:88.

persuaded that he is our Father?[107] Here, Twisse's supralapsarian-ism is evident, which caused some to think that he had a certain sympathy with soteriological antinomianism.

Repentance

In S55 TH 14.9.43 through S56 F 15.9.43, pressure was exerted to mention repentance in the article on justification. The discussion has obvious bearing on the Assembly's later consideration of repentance in its own right, although at this point it was brought into the debate simply as an element of justification. Not surprisingly, Herbert Palmer raised the matter. In S55 TH 14.9.43, he wanted "the expressing of something concerning repentance against the damnable opinion of the Antinomians"—a typical Palmer statement. There is no doubt that the antinomian menace, particularly in London, was the dominant motivation, not only for Palmer, but for many others.[108] Bayly made a surprising attack on William Perkins (1558–1602), perhaps the single most influential figure in English Puritanism, for perverting the people! The precise terms of his argument are missing from the record of his speech in the minutes, although later discussion shows that Bayly considered Perkins ambiguous and contradictory on the relationship between saving faith and assurance.[109] The Assembly decided to set up a committee to report promptly. This was despite Gataker's plea that when diseases are desperate, there should be no delay in getting medical attention; and, since this issue was as desperate as any that had sprung up in recent days, it should be discussed at once by the full Assembly. The committee consisted of Calamy, Seaman, Goodwin, Channell, Gataker, Palmer, Herle, Featley, and Temple. Gouge soon spoke against Bayly's outburst. An aspersion had been laid against a very learned and worthy man (Perkins), charging that he had contradicted himself. He asked for these words to be considered by the Assembly. Bayly insisted that it was far from his intent to cast an aspersion on Perkins. His point was that in his Catechism

107. Ibid., 3:90.
108. Ibid.
109. Ibid., 3:91.

he defined faith as assurance, but three pages later retracted his definition.[110] Gataker commented enlighteningly that repentance and faith are comparable to thunder and lightning; although occurring together in time, we apprehend them separately.[111]

After the weekend break, the Assembly returned to the question in S58 TU 19.9.43. Palmer, pressing again for mention of the necessity of repentance, reminded the divines that the apostle makes it one of the two main things in his preaching—repentance for the remission of sins.[112] Temple thought it needed to be put in some of the articles. Herrick said that it was already handled in other articles; since it is a work of sanctification, it should not be put in the article on justification. Gataker agreed; the best place would be in the next article, for "it is true, repentance of itselfe simply hath noe influence into justification; I doe not find them any where joyned together."[113]

A committee was appointed to add something concerning the nature of faith and repentance and to see if there was anything to this effect in the Homilies. Goodwin argued that the danger would be minimized if remission of sins was in suspension until the act of repentance.[114] Palmer assured the assembly that he did not have the least intention of eroding the doctrine of justification, but "the scripture doth speake of a repentance antecedent to remission of sins." Hoyle on the other hand wondered exactly what repentance it is that goes before faith. The Old Testament warnings speak of legal terrors, but not a true grace. Vines disagreed with suspending justification until repentance and affirmed "an immediate justification upon beleiving."[115] Herrick was even stronger: "that repentance must goe before remission of sins is not only erroneous but dangerous."[116]

Once again, the Assembly was divided down the middle. There were those, motivated by fear of antinomianism, who wanted to stress the necessity and precedence of repentance in relation to remission of sins. They were prepared to go to great lengths to

110. Ibid., 3:91–92.
111. Ibid., 3:93.
112. Ibid., 3:108.
113. Ibid., 3:109.
114. Ibid., 3:110.
115. Ibid., 3:111.
116. Ibid., 3:112.

safeguard against antinomian aspersions, but in doing so they were coming perilously close to eroding the gospel. The first centuries of the church showed that the easiest way to dilute the gospel was to emphasize the law where it should not be intruded. Usually, it was due to a zeal for righteousness. On the other hand, there were others at Westminster who wanted to preserve the gospel message that repentance flowed from remission of sins, and they managed to keep cool heads and clear minds.

Justification

We will now consider the final statements on justification in both the Confession and the Larger Catechism. After the mass of detail recorded on justification when the Thirty-Nine Articles were debated, there is next to nothing on record from the time when these documents were considered. Indeed, the time taken to deal with the chapter and the relevant questions was comparatively brief. As Norris affirms, "There can be no doubt that, when the Confession of Faith came to be drafted, the clear and defined thinking that resulted from these first debates on the revision of the Thirty-Nine Articles reduced the time needed for discussion, and conduced to the clarity and conciseness that are the hallmarks of the Westminster Standards."[117]

T. F. Torrance accuses the Assembly of departing from Calvin's teaching and that of the Scottish Reformation, in which justification is held inseparably with union with Christ. But he fails to consider LC 65–90.[118] It is astonishing that such a careful and meticulous scholar should be so neglectful on a matter that is so close to home. The exposition that follows should make clear how the Assembly saw these things in harmony.

First, the Confession's chapter 11 begins by relating justification to effectual calling. Justification is the result of the work of God's grace to his elect by which he powerfully and graciously draws them to Christ by the Holy Spirit. As such, justification is freely given, a work of his grace. Here, in 11.1, is a refutation of

117. Norris, "Thirty-Nine Articles," lx.
118. T. F. Torrance, *Scottish Theology*, 144.

both the Roman Catholic and the Arminian doctrines. Justification does not involve the infusion of righteousness. Instead, it consists in the remission of sins and the accounting righteous of the persons justified. This is accomplished by imputing to them the obedience and satisfaction of Christ. Thus, justification is forensic, by the imputation or accounting of Christ's righteousness, not renovative by the impartation or infusion of grace, as Rome taught. On the other hand, contrary to Arminian teaching, faith itself is not imputed, neither is any other evangelical obedience involved. This would simply be another form of the Roman Catholic doctrine, for justification would then be related to something present in the one believing, albeit the consequence of grace. This the Confession strenuously opposes, since justification does not depend on "any thing wrought in them, or done by them." It is based on Christ alone. For their part, the justified simply receive and rest on Christ and his righteousness by faith. This faith itself is the gift of God. Faith is appropriate to justification, since it is described in WCF 14.2 as "accepting, receiving, and resting upon Christ alone for justification, sanctification, and eternal life, by virtue of the covenant of grace." Faith looks to Christ alone; it does not contemplate the works of grace or the self. It answers from the human side the exclusively gracious, objective, and forensic nature of justification in Christ and his righteousness alone.

The phrase "by imputing the obedience and satisfaction of Christ unto them" reflects the earlier debates and raises the kind of questions we considered. On the face of it, the Assembly would appear to refer both to the passive and to the active obedience of Christ; if satisfaction is taken as meaning his sufferings and death, then obedience would comprise his conformity to the law of God throughout his life. This is the most probable meaning, in the absence of countervailing evidence.[119] However, the omission of the terms "active" and "passive," used continuously in the debates, is equally impressive. It allows

119. In favor of this reading, as long before as 1559 Calvin understood the justified person to be one who "grasps the righteousness of Christ through faith, and clothed in it, appears in God's sight not as a sinner but as a righteous man. . . . And we say that it consists in the remission of sins and the imputation of Christ's righteousness." John Calvin, *Institutes of the Christian Religion* (trans. F. L. Battles; ed. J. T. McNeill; Philadelphia: Westminster Press, 1960), 3.11.2. See also *Institutes*, 3.11.12; comm. 1 Cor. 1:30.

those who aligned themselves with Gataker and Vines to accept the statement, interpreting "obedience" and "satisfaction" as synonymous terms, which would not have been possible if the words "active" and "passive" had been used.

In WCF 11.2, faith, understood as receiving and resting on Christ alone for salvation, is the only instrument of justification. This is in alignment with the insistence in 11.1 that justification is grounded only in Christ, not in anything present in the justified, not even if it be there by grace in evangelical obedience. Faith is the only instrument of justification because Christ is its only ground. As the later popular hymn puts it, "On Christ the solid rock I stand, all other ground is sinking sand."

In order to balance the equation, the section adds that saving faith is never alone in the one who is justified, but is always accompanied by other saving graces. It works through love. It is living faith, for without works faith is dead. In short, the believer is a repentant believer or he is no believer at all. The question then arises as to what effect these other graces have in relation to justification. If the faith through which we are justified is always accompanied by love, does not love justify? If the one with saving faith is also repentant, should not repentance have something to do with justification? The Confession has already answered that these things have nothing to do with justification. We must remember the menace of the antinomians and the concern that motivated much of the earlier debates on justification. This statement at the end of WCF 11.2 is directed against antinomianism, but it is not an acceptance of Romanism. We are not justified by faith working through love, as Rome held. We are justified only by faith, since only by Christ. The faith through which we are justified has reference exclusively to Christ. However, it happens to bear fruit at all times in love and evangelical obedience. But these latter things have to do with sanctification, the renewal brought about by the Spirit, not with our legal status before the bar of God's justice. They are inseparable from the faith that justifies, but they are disconnected from the justification received through faith. They define the person justified, not the justification of the person. They describe the

271

one who has faith, but do not constitute his standing before God received through faith.[120]

The divines emphasize the sheer grace of God in justification in 11.3. Christ made full and complete satisfaction to the Father's justice for all the justified. This secures their complete acquittal and the perfection of their righteousness, which is Christ's righteousness reckoned to them. This is entirely of God's free grace. The exact justice and rich grace of God meet together.

God eternally decreed to justify all the elect, and in human history Christ died for the sins of all the elect and rose from the dead for them (11.4). The insistent theme of the antinomians was that the crucial center of gravity of justification was the eternal decree and the historical accomplishment of Christ. To counter this position, which the divines saw would undermine the doctrine of sanctification, the section goes on to assert that the elect are not *actually* justified until the Holy Spirit applies Christ to them through faith. This means that our receiving Christ in our own life-history is the Archimedean point of justification, not the decree of God in eternity. However, the sovereign decree of God is asserted, and the application of salvation to the elect is maintained. The Confession will have nothing to do with antinomianism; neither will it make concessions to Arminianism.

God continues to forgive the sins of the justified (11.5). They may incur his fatherly displeasure until they humble themselves and confess their sins. In this the continued need for repentance is underlined, in keeping with Herbert Palmer's concerns in the debates on the Articles. Finally, in 11.6, justification is said to have been the same—that is, only by faith—under the Old Testament as it is in the New Testament.[121]

---

120. Latter-day exponents of this passage, who argue that evangelical graces should be considered in relation to justification, have wrenched the words from their immediate polemical context and thus distorted the Assembly's teaching, which in this case was accepted right across the board, Gataker and Vines included.

121. On imputation and the forensic nature of justification, Morris says that justification is an act of God, with its sole basis in the mediation, the righteousness, of Christ. It is a judicial procedure, and so must be appropriated by faith. He continues: "The conception of a forensic procedure which the term suggests, is Pauline only, and . . . in the Revised Version the less rigid term, reckon, evidently commercial or social rather than judicial, is used as a more exact translation of the original word. In the Confession (XI) and in the Larger Catechism (70) the cognate terms, *accounting, accounteth*, are used as nearly synonymous with the word, *impute*."

When we turn to the Larger Catechism, we see a different, but entirely congruous, picture. Whereas in the Confession justification is the first of the blessings of salvation, followed by adoption, sanctification, perseverance, and assurance, the Catechism treats them all as aspects of our union and communion with Christ in grace and glory (65–90). Obviously, the Assembly saw no discrepancy between these two perspectives. They understood them as complementary, not competitive. The divines were hardly schizophrenic in their theology.

Morris makes the point very clearly that union with Christ undergirds justification by faith. He points out that pardon itself is not enough for salvation—for there is still the sinner who remains corrupt. Hence, "nothing but his union with Christ through faith can render him worthy of such cordial acceptance before the throne of the Father." So God by his Spirit does not infuse righteousness into regenerate souls so as to make them instantly holy; he does not treat them as holy by imputing faith to them, or evangelical obedience in any form, but he accounts and treats them as holy by virtue of their union with Christ established through faith. In support of his understanding, he cites the Augsburg Confession, the Formula of Concord, the Second Helvetic Confession, the Scots Confession, the Thirty-Nine Articles, and the Irish Articles.[122]

The divines are treading here the path previously trodden by Calvin. We cited him as advocating the imputation of the righteousness of Christ in justification. In his *Institutes*, 3.11.10, he does so again in direct connection with union with Christ. In rebutting the extreme Lutheran, Osiander, he says:

> Therefore, that joining together of Head and members, that indwelling of Christ in our hearts—in short, that mystical union—are accorded by us the highest degree of importance, so that Christ, having been made ours, makes us sharers with him in the gifts with which he has been endowed. We do not, therefore, contemplate him outside ourselves from afar in order that his righteousness

He refers back to the character of God, who is willing to forgive, but is also ready to vindicate his justice. Morris, *Westminster Symbols*, 440.

122. Ibid., 442–43.

may be imputed to us but because we put on Christ and are engrafted into his body—in short, because he deigns to make us one with him. For this reason, we glory that we have fellowship of righteousness with him.[123]

From another angle, in his commentary on 1 Corinthians 1:30, Calvin remarks that justification and sanctification are distinguishable, but yet "those gifts of grace go together as if tied by an inseparable bond, so that if anyone tries to separate them, he is, in a sense, tearing Christ to pieces." Tony Lane has compared them to two legs of a pair of trousers.[124] Paul ascribes to Christ alone the fulfillment of all— righteousness, holiness, wisdom, and redemption.

LC 70, like the Confession, describes justification as an act of God's free grace for sinners. As such, it is an aspect of union with Christ in grace. In union with Christ, our sins are pardoned and our persons are accepted as righteous. This is only due to the perfect obedience and full satisfaction of Christ imputed to us, received by faith alone. The nuance the Catechism introduces is that justification is received in union with Christ. In the background is Christ as "a publick person" who represents his people. His perfect obedience was exercised on their behalf; his sufferings were undergone on behalf of the elect. It would be tempting to see here also some of the dynamic aspects of union with Christ that are mentioned in the New Testament, but as far as I can see there is no specific evidence that this was discussed by the Assembly. Indeed, the care with which the debates on the Articles sought to safeguard justification from the Roman Catholic position, together with the denial of any instrumental role for imparted grace, leads in the opposite direction.

So much is borne out by LC 71. Here justification is said to be of free grace, although Christ made full satisfaction to God's justice. This is so because God accepts the fulfillment of his law from a surety,

---

123. Calvin, *Institutes*, 3.11.10. For an extensive study of Calvin's teaching on union with Christ, see M. A. Garcia, "Life in Christ: the Function of Union with Christ in the Unio-Duplex Gratia Structure of Calvin's Soteriology with Special Reference to the Relationship of Justification and Sanctification in the Sixteenth-century Context" (Ph.D. thesis, University of Edinburgh, 2004). This has recently been published as *Life in Christ: Union with Christ and Twofold Grace in Calvin's Theology* (Eugene, OR: Wipf & Stock, 2008).

124. Lane, *Justification by Faith in Catholic-Protestant Dialogue*, 18.

which he himself provided, namely, his own Son. He requires nothing for justification but faith, which in turn is his gift. The Catechism brings together law and grace, and shows clearly how the full provisions of the law are fulfilled in a way in which God's grace is clearly dominant. Man had sinned, breaking God's law and incurring guilt and condemnation. Christ the Son, in mercy, stepped in, took the place of his elect, fulfilled the law, and bore its penalty on their behalf. Thus the claims of God's justice were completely discharged, and in this way his people are delivered from their dire condition and given a new status, invested with the righteousness of Christ. Moreover, all this is based on Christ being fully man, one with us through his incarnation, and thus our head and representative. Furthermore, not only did he do everything for us, but, because of our union with him, we are in him in all that he did. Union with Christ is no more incompatible with forensic justification than justification is incompatible with sanctification. This undermines Torrance's caricature of Westminster as conveying a harsh legal view of God and salvation, which, we argued, requires him to ignore the Larger Catechism.

LC 72 addresses justifying faith in much the same terms as the debates on the Articles had done, and as WCF 14 does:

> Justifying faith is a saving grace, wrought in the heart of a sinner by the Spirit and word of God, whereby he, being convinced of his sin and misery, and of the disability in himself and all other creatures to recover him out of his lost condition, not only assenteth to the truth of the promise of the gospel, but receiveth and resteth upon Christ and his righteousness, therein held forth, for pardon of sin, and for the accepting and accounting of his person righteous in the sight of God for salvation.

Finally, LC 73 asks how it is that faith justifies a sinner in the sight of God. The answer makes a number of denials. Faith does not justify because of the other graces that always accompany it. It is true—we saw the Confession state it—that justifying faith is never alone, but always has fruit, hope, and especially love. However, these graces have no part to play in justification. Justification is a legal action. It rests on the fulfillment of God's law by a surety, Jesus Christ. Christ is received only by faith, not by the outworking of faith. The key is not the faith that receives Christ, but the Christ who is received by faith. Nor does faith justify because of the good works that are its fruit. Both here and in the Confession, the divines reject the doctrines of Rome, Arminianism, and antinomianism.

Nor is faith itself imputed for justification, as Arminians have held. If that were true, faith would be a work and the gratuitous nature of justification would be jeopardized. Instead, faith is merely an instrument by which Christ and his righteousness are received. Faith is the appropriate means of reception since it simply receives and rests on Christ alone (14.1–2). Once again, we see how union with Christ fits perfectly with justification by faith alone. Precisely because the righteous status is achieved only by Christ and is reckoned or imputed by God to his elect, who have done nothing to merit it, it is only by faith—abandoning self and trusting only in Christ—that this becomes actual for the elect.

Saving Faith (WCF 14; LC 72–73)

In WCF 14.1, the divines affirm that saving faith is ordinarily produced by the Holy Spirit through the ministry of the Word. Thereafter, it is strengthened by the Word, together with the sacraments and prayer. These, as SC 88 maintains, are the normal means that God uses to bring his elect to salvation. They are the provisions he has made for their lifelong pilgrimage of faith. The Christian life is inseparable from the ministry of the church and the sacraments, a point often missed by post-eighteenth-century evangelicalism.[125]

Saving faith is directed to a twofold object. A Christian believes whatever is revealed in the Word of God, because God is the primary author. This faith takes various forms, in keeping with the literary genre and what in today's parlance is termed the speech-act. Thus, in faith we obey the commands of God's Word, embrace the promises, and tremble at its threatenings. In a narrower sense, saving faith involves "accepting, receiving, and resting upon Christ

125. See Letham and Macleod, "Is Evangelicalism Christian?" 3–33, and Letham, *Lord's Supper.*

alone for justification, sanctification, and eternal life, by virtue of the covenant of grace."

Does this represent a dualistic view of faith? Is the central personal element eroded by the wider and more general belief in whatever the Bible says? Elsewhere, I have argued that this is not the case. The same Christ who is the principal object of saving faith is the one who sent the Holy Spirit to guide his apostles into all truth and, among other things, to write the New Testament documents. Thus, the Holy Spirit is the ultimate author of whatever is written in Scripture, while the Spirit himself was sent by the Son, who is the one whom we receive and rest in for salvation.[126]

This faith may vary in strength. With some it may be very weak and may come under attack in different ways. Yet it will normally grow through the means God has given. In some it may reach full assurance (WCF 14.3). This last statement raises questions that we shall address shortly.

Adoption (WCF 12; LC 74)

Chapter 12 in the Westminster Confession, on adoption, is unique for a creed or confession. There is a corresponding question in the Larger Catechism. Tim Trumper, to name but one scholar, has claimed there are grounds for thinking that adoption has been greatly neglected in the Western church.[127]

Adoption is an act of the free grace of God, given to all who are justified; it is therefore simultaneous with justification. The Father adopts us in and for his Son Jesus Christ. Those who are adopted are made God's children. This entails the fact that all people are not children of God; adoption is a privilege given by God to his elect people. God the Father puts his name on them; on the surface, this probably refers to baptism, where the one name of the Father, the Son, and the Holy Spirit is pronounced on the person baptized. The

126. See Letham, *Work of Christ*, 91–102.
127. See, e.g., T. J. R. Trumper, "The Metaphorical Import of Adoption: A Plea for Re- alisation. I: The Adoption Metaphor in Biblical Usage," *SBET* 14 (1996): 129–45; Trumper, "The Metaphorical Import of Adoption: A Plea for Realisation. II: The Adoption Metaphor in Theological Usage," *SBET* 15 (1997): 98–115.

drift of WCF 14, together with SC 88, underlining the role of the church and sacraments, points to baptism. However, the proof texts (2 Cor. 6:18; Rev. 3:12) do not refer to baptism. Additionally, the chapter continues, the Spirit of the Father's Son is given to them, referring to Galatians 4:6. Thus, those who are justified and adopted are placed under the care of the Father, are given the status and privileges of sons of God, and are made heirs of all God's promises and fellow-heirs with Christ in glory. They have access to the throne of grace and call on God as Father.

These features speak of a status. Those who are adopted share the same relation the Son has with the Father. This is astonishing! By this, believers call on God as "our Father in heaven." There is a difference, of course, for the Son is Son eternally by nature, whereas the adopted are made God's sons by grace. However, since, according to the Larger Catechism, union with Christ is the overarching theme that connects the various elements of salvation, adoption most vividly displays what this union entails. It means that those upon whom God has set his love, and whom he has united to his Son, in grace are regarded as identical in status to Christ, the Son of God.

Sanctification (WCF 13; LC 77–78)

Sanctification occurs through the virtue of the death and resurrection of Christ (1 Cor. 6:11; Acts 20:32; Phil. 3:10; Rom. 6:5–6) and by the instrumentality of the Holy Spirit, who indwells the regenerate, accompanying the Word. Hence, sanctification is rooted in the means of grace and the ministry of the Holy Spirit located in the church. Sanctification does not occur in private, but in the community of God's people. It happens in union with Christ. Since Christ died once for all, in him believers died to sin. He rose from the dead, never again to die; so they too in union with him rise to new life.

What happens in sanctification is twofold. First, something takes place at once, decisively: "the dominion of the whole body of sin is destroyed" (WCF 13.1). The proof texts cited by the Assembly are Romans 6:6 and 6:14. They both refer to what has happened to all believers by union with Christ in his death and resurrection. An irreversible change has taken place. They have died with Christ and risen with him to newness of life. They are no longer under the dominion of the law, but are under grace. They have been set free from the rule of sin.

Second, there are continuous and lifelong aspects to sanctification. The lusts of sin are "more and more" weakened, and believers are accordingly "more and more" quickened and strengthened in all saving graces. This is ongoing and indispensable, for without holiness no one will see the Lord. This whole process is rooted in the eternal decree of God. It consists in the renewal of the whole person according to the image of God, the seeds of repentance being placed in their hearts, stirred up, and increased "as that they more and more die unto sin, and rise unto newness of life" (LC 75).

However, believers must continue to battle against the "remnants of sin abiding in every part of them." The conflict of the flesh against the spirit is perpetual. Temptations will often foil believers; they will fall into various sins from time to time, while even their best works will be defiled (LC 78; WCF 13.2). Nevertheless, it is a winning struggle, for "more and more"—a constantly recurring phrase, thank God—the saints will grow in grace (WCF 13.1, 3).

The picture painted here is thoroughly realistic, yet also triumphant in the best sense. It does not downplay the struggles that believers face, nor does it minimize the continued presence of corruption within. It does not hold out false or unrealistic prospects. Yet it displays the hope and promise of growth in grace, and it points back to a decisive change that occurred in union with Christ. In this it operates within biblical parameters, unlike the later development of holiness teaching—seen in the Keswick movement[128]—which trumpeted the false promise of a victorious Christian life by letting go, minimizing the battle with sin, downplaying the Christian's personal responsibility, and belittling the

---

128. See J. I. Packer, "'Keswick' and the Reformed Doctrine of Sanctification," *EQ* 27 (1955): 153–67.

decisive change for all believers brought about by Christ in his death and resurrection.[129]

Repentance (WCF 15; LC 76)

Chapter 15 in the Confession is more expansive on repentance than is the Catechism. It starts by affirming the necessity of the preaching of repentance by every minister of the gospel (WCF 15.1), for it is as essential as faith. This is a clear safeguard against antinomian tendencies. Repentance is an evangelical grace, given by God, but it is also a human responsibility—the minister must preach it, and the believer must practice it. What it entails is a hatred for one's sins, turning from them all to God, and a determination to live according to his commandments (15.2). The divines are careful to acknowledge that repentance is a consequence of a "sight and sense . . . of the filthiness [of sin] . . . , as contrary to the holy nature, and righteous law of God" and of "the apprehension of His mercy in Christ to such as are penitent." It is, after all, an evangelical grace and so stems from the knowledge of the gospel. It flows from the faith that rests in Christ for salvation. Clearly, the Assembly regards repentance in the light of both the law and the gospel. R. T. Kendall's idea that Westminster placed repentance before faith and so construed it in legalistic terms is without foundation.[130] As careful as the divines were to avoid antinomianism, they were also determined to guard the gospel itself.

So much is underlined in WCF 15.3, where it is denied that repentance can in any way secure our pardon. Yet it is necessary, and pardon cannot come without it. Underlying this is the inseparability of faith and repentance. We receive pardon for sins on the basis of the work of Christ on our behalf, received through faith. Repentance goes together with faith, and so where pardon exists, there repentance will be also—not as the cause, but as the consequence. As impossible as

---

129. Barth points to some infelicitous language, when the Confession talks about "the regenerate part" overcoming the remaining corruption. He asks, "Is regeneration a larger or smaller quantity?" See Barth, *Reformed Confessions*, 141. This is a valid criticism, for since depravity is total, affecting every human faculty, so also sanctification is total, though incomplete.

130. See Kendall, *Calvin and English Calvinism*, 184–208. Kendall's arguments have been so thoroughly refuted that it is unnecessary to refer in any detail to their rebuttals here.

it is for there to be an unbelieving penitent, so too there cannot be an impenitent believer.

The necessity of repentance is highlighted further in 15.4–6. Everyone must repent of all sins, great and small, since there is no sin so small that it cannot of itself damn us. We must all confess our sins to God and turn from them. Where our sins have caused others to stumble, we must confess them to the person or persons concerned. Such confession may be private or public, depending on those affected. At the same time, no sin is too great for the mercy of God; for those who truly repent, no sin can bring damnation.

Good Works (WCF 16)

In S27 TU 15.8.43, during the debates on the Thirty-Nine Articles, there was a move to eliminate the phrase "and good works" from article 10 on free will. This was forestalled on the grounds that Rome used these words, and it was best to counter the papists on their own terms.[131] Moreover, on the following day, in S28 W 16.8.43, an addition was supplied since the article did not seem to oppose Rome and the Arminians clearly enough. It stressed the work of the Holy Spirit in granting a good will and enabling it to be effective: "that we may have a good will *& working effectually in us as that it determineth our will into that which is good, and also working with us when we have that will unto good.*"[132] In considering article 12, on good works following justification, which the Assembly maintained to be truly good and pleasing to God in Christ, the divines were equally emphatic that in themselves good works cannot put away sins or endure the severity of God's judgment.[133] However, there was much concern that if good works were said to be "acceptable to God in Christ," too much ground would be ceded to the antinomians, for whom God sees no imperfection in our good works.

This chapter in the Confession is unusually long, due, one suspects, to concerns over antinomianism. Good works are defined only by what

131. Lightfoot's journal, in Van Dixhoorn, 2:32.
132. Van Dixhoorn, 2:33.
133. S66 M 2.10.43, in ibid., 2:98.

God commands in his Word (WCF 16.1), and are fruits and evidences of a true and living faith (16.2). Only the Spirit of Christ can enable believers to will and to do good works, yet they are responsible to do them and are to be diligent in cultivating the grace of God in them for that very purpose (16.3). On the other hand, works of supererogation, as taught by Rome, are out of court—to do more than God requires is impossible. On the contrary, we constantly fall short of what he wants (16.4). Moreover, good works are of no avail for obtaining salvation. We cannot merit pardon of sin or eternal life by our deeds. The goodness of good works stems from the Holy Spirit, but our own contribution is mixed with sin (16.5). Yet, our good works are acceptable to God! This is because we are accepted in Christ. Because of our union with Christ, the Father accepts our sincerity and overlooks our many imperfections (16.6). As for the unregenerate, even if they were to do what God commands, their works do not spring from faith, nor do they seek the glory of God. Consequently, they cannot please God, nor can they prepare themselves for grace by what they do (16.7).

The Larger Catechism lacks a question on good works. However, the lengthy section on the law (LC 91–152), in expounding the Decalogue—particularly the positive duties required by the commandments—describes the outward form of good works. These consist in loving God with all our heart, soul, strength, and mind (LC 102) and loving our neighbor as ourselves, and doing to others what we would want them to do to us (LC 122; cf. SC 42).

In a sophisticated discussion of the matter, Anthony Tuckney argues that good works are necessary for salvation.[134] They are qualities required in a person who is to be saved, not things required in order to be saved; they are the means of administering salvation, but do not effect salvation.[135]

Perseverance (WCF 17; LC 79)

The doctrine of the perseverance of the saints had been challenged in the 1590s and defended by the Lambeth Articles of 1595. Both the

---

134. Tuckney, *Praelectiones theologicae*, 228ff.
135. Ibid., 233.

Confession and the Larger Catechism restate this defense. In 17.1, the doctrine is stated: "They, whom God hath accepted . . . can neither totally nor finally fall away from the state of grace, but shall certainly persevere therein to the end, and be eternally saved." This does not depend on their own will, but upon God (17.2; LC 79). First, it follows from his decree, which is unchangeable and is an outflow of the free love of God the Father. He has also covenanted to give them eternal life. Moreover, Christ's merit and intercession are continuously effectual for their salvation. The union which true believers have with Christ is inviolable—they are inseparable from him, and he is in the Father's presence, continually interceding for them. In keeping with this, and as part of what union with Christ entails, the Holy Spirit has been given to them and remains within them.

The divines are nonetheless realistic about the tensions of the Christian life and the dangers that confront us (17.3). Believers may fall into grievous sins. They face the temptations of Satan and the corruption of their own flesh, and they may for a time neglect the means of grace. If they succumb in any of these ways, God may be displeased with them and they may incur a range of temporal chastisements. Sanctification is always imperfect, as long as this life lasts (LC 78). Believers are responsible to live by faith. But in all these trials and uncertainties, they are kept by the power of God—through faith (LC 79). God's sovereign care and our full responsibility are both at work. This doctrine is the necessary foundation for assurance of salvation, which is treated next in the Confession. Without the confidence that God's power will keep us in the faith to the very end of our present life, despite all drawbacks and obstacles, we would be cast into a deep well of uncertainty and Christian living would be undermined. Knowing that those who come to Christ will never be cast out, we can have the strength to face whatever life may throw at us. We know there is a higher, ultimate power that will preserve us to the end and bring us at last to Christ's everlasting kingdom.

Assurance (WCF 18; LC 80–81)

Barth argues that chapter 18 "requires so much verbiage because something about it is not quite right"; "making sure" has to be added

THE THEOLOGY OF THE ASSEMBLY

to "infallible certitude."[136] He fails to take into account the pastoral situations in which many of the divines worked. Many of their parishioners were having questions about assurance.

That theological questions underlay the matter is virtually axiomatic. Rome denied that it was possible to have certainty of ultimate salvation in this life, apart from special revelation or the pronouncement of the church. The Council of Trent anathematized anyone who taught its normal possibility. On the other hand, Calvin, in common with other reformers, considered it so integral to the Christian life that he defined saving faith *as* assurance.[137] For him, the sovereignty and faithfulness of God, seen especially in the promise of the gospel in Christ, undergirded it. Rome's semi-Pelagian doctrine of salvation, together with its penitential system, cast a perpetual cloud of uncertainty over the believer's status.[138] Later, Arminius and the Remonstrants questioned whether a true believer might fall from grace so as finally to perish. They did not positively affirm this, but merely posed a question over the Reformed doctrine of the perseverance of the saints. As a result, the Arminians could have no doctrine of assurance of ultimate salvation, since no one could be sure that he might not fall from grace. In reply, the Synod of Dort affirmed emphatically that such assurance was to be expected, despite the struggles that the Christian may undergo, since all God's elect will persevere in faith to the very end.[139]

Within the Reformed churches, there was discussion and disagreement as to whether this assurance was, as Calvin described it, a normal aspect of saving faith, or whether it came after justification. Some have argued that the doctrine of limited atonement undermined assurance,[140] but this does not seem likely. In the Arminian controversy, election and definite atonement supported assurance, while the weaker views of the Remonstrants undermined it. I have suggested that a conditional view of the covenant of grace may have encouraged

136. Barth, *Reformed Confessions*, 144.
137. Calvin, *Institutes*, 3.2.7.
138. R. W. A. Letham, "The Relationship Between Saving Faith and Assurance of Salvation" (Th.M. thesis, Westminster Theological Seminary, 1976), 5–12.
139. Schaff, *Creeds*, 3:550–97, esp. 554, 571–76, 583–44, 592–95.
140. Kendall, *Calvin and English Calvinism*; G. M. Thomas, *The Extent of the Atonement: A Dilemma for Reformed Theology from Calvin to the Consensus (1536–1675)* (Carlisle: Paternoster, 1997).

introspection. If God's promise were to depend on the presence of grace within us, then people would obviously ask whether they had love, patience, and the rest of the Spirit's fruit before they could ever attain assurance. This idea has not gained universal support.[141]

Among the Assembly members, Thomas Goodwin propounded distinctive views about assurance in his commentary on Ephesians. He argued that the seal of the Holy Spirit, mentioned in Ephesians 1:13, refers to a particular work of the Spirit by which he grants immediate assurance of salvation. He does not give this to all who believe in Christ; it is for advanced Christians and is something that must be sought with diligence. Goodwin urges his readers to "sue God" for it. He based this idea on the aorist participle, translating "*after you believed* you were sealed with the Holy Spirit of promise."[142] John Owen disputed this interpretation, establishing that the sealing is coincident with the believing, and so Paul does not refer to a particular work of the Holy Spirit sealing us, but to the Spirit himself as the seal. As a result, the Spirit is the seal of salvation for all who believe, not the giver of a special experience to elite Christians.[143] However, Owen was not a member of the Assembly, and there are hints in WCF 18.3, where Ephesians 1.13–14 is cited in the proof texts, that Goodwin's ideas were accommodated in the chapter. This would explain why assurance was treated as an elite experience and hence so difficult to get and so easy to lose.

It is clear that the Assembly downplayed the note of confident assurance found in the New Testament. For one thing, assurance and saving faith are discussed in separate, noncontiguous chapters, obscuring the connections between them that WCF 14.3 tries hard to draw. In contrast, the apostle John's first letter mentions "we know" no fewer than 55 times, clearly distinguishing those who live in the light from those in darkness. The divines may also have exaggerated the possibility of

141. See R. Letham, *Assurance in Theological Context*, a revision of R. W. A. Letham, "Saving Faith and Assurance." From a pastoral experience in 1975, in a congregation drawn from the Scottish Highlands and Islands, it seemed to me that assurance was a very pressing concern, exacerbated by this form of covenantal conditionalism.

142. Thomas Goodwin, *An Exposition of Ephesians* (n.p.: Sovereign Grace Book Club, 1958), 227–52.

143. John Owen, "The Holy Spirit as a Comforter," in *Works of John Owen*, 4:399–406. I am indebted to James I. Packer, who pointed this out to me in a personal letter dated 28 August 1974.

spiritual desertion; this was evidently an important concern in their own ministries, since English Puritanism bred a barrage of books on spiritual desertion.[144] The chapter in the Confession presents assurance of salvation as very difficult to attain and extremely easy to lose—but cheer up, you will be kept from utter despair! This is realistic in terms of the lifelong battle between the flesh and the Spirit, described by Paul in Galatians. It was no doubt forged in the midst of the struggles of many of the divines' parishioners. However, this viewpoint is far from the tenor of the bulk of the New Testament. Even the book of Revelation, written to churches about to undergo intense persecution, sounds the unmistakable note of triumph in the midst of adversity. The Confession's own doctrine of perseverance should have had greater sway at this point.

In 18.1, the Confession affirms that true believers who seek faithfully to follow Christ *may* be assured that they are in the state of grace and *may* rejoice in the hope of the glory of God. This is much the same as in LC 80. However, it is at odds with the apostle Paul; those who are justified by faith, while they suffer, *do* rejoice in the hope of the glory of God (Rom. 5:1–5). It is also at variance with the Niceno-Constantinopolitan Creed and its concluding affirmation that "we look for the resurrection of the dead and the life of the world to come."

The next section strongly dissents from Rome. Assurance is not a conjectural probability. It is an infallible assurance of faith. This is due to a number of factors. This assurance is founded upon (1) the divine truth of the promises of salvation, (2) the inward evidence of those graces to which these promises are made, and (3) the testimony of the Spirit of adoption, witnessing with our spirit that we are children of God. The Holy Spirit is the earnest (guarantee) of our inheritance. LC 80 repeats this almost verbatim.

This section has been subjected to trenchant criticism from R. T. Kendall, who has argued that the theology of Westminster was part of

---

144. E.g., William Bridge, *A lifting up for the downcast*, in *The Works of the Rev. William Bridge, M.A.* (5 vols.; London: Thomas Tegg, 1845), 2:3–279; Thomas Goodwin, *A childe of light walking in darknes: or A treatise shewing the causes, by which God leaves his children to distresse of conscience* (London: M[iles] F[lesher] for R. Dawlman and L. Fawne, 1638) [STC (2nd ed.) 12038]; Richard Capel, *Tentations: their nature, danger, cure* (London: R. B[adger], 1633) [STC (2nd ed.) 4595]; Joseph Symonds, *The case and cure of a deserted soule* (London: M. Flesher for Luke Fawne, 1639) [STC (2nd ed.) 23590]. Both Bridge and Goodwin were members of the Assembly.

a radical movement away from Calvin. Under the impact of scholastic methodology, he claims, Reformed theology turned in a voluntaristic direction in which faith became an act of the will. Limited atonement raised huge questions in people's minds as to whether Christ had died for them. Thus faith and assurance were separated, and assurance itself was based on introspection; hence, the promises of salvation are here said to be made *to the inward evidence of grace*.[145] This, Kendall argues, was in contrast with Calvin's identification of faith and assurance, with faith being a sure and certain knowledge of the Father's benevolence toward us. Elsewhere, in a number of places, I have pointed to the inadequacy of Kendall's research and argued that his claim is untenable.[146] Others have also joined the fray. By now, Kendall's thesis is dead in the water.[147]

In 18.3, the Confession asserts that assurance is not *so* of the essence of faith that a true believer may wait long for it. LC 81 goes a step further in asserting outright that assurance of grace and salvation is *not* of the essence of faith. This justifies the divines in dealing with assurance in a separate chapter, apart from saving faith. The true believer may attain to this assurance apart from special revelation, in the due use of ordinary means. This is contrary to Rome, which teaches that assurance can be received only by revelation or ecclesiastical pronouncement. LC 80 also stresses the use of ordinary means apart from extraordinary revelation, while LC 81 reinforces the WCF by saying that a true believer may have to wait long for it. Nevertheless, it is a Christian duty to seek it. It is associated with peace and joy in the Holy Spirit, thankfulness to God, and cheerful obedience. Contrary to those who might think it is a cloak for antinomian ideas, it does not lead to looseness.

This assurance can be shaken (18.4). Neglect of the means of grace, sin, and temptation can threaten it. God may withdraw the light of his countenance. Spiritual desertion was a familiar theme in Puritan

---

145. Kendall, *Calvin and English Calvinism*.

146. See Letham, "Saving Faith and Assurance"; R. Letham, "Theodore Beza: A Reassessment," *SJT* 40 (1987): 25–40; R. Letham, "Amandus Polanus: A Neglected Theologian?" *SCJ* 21 (1990): 463–76; R. Letham, "Faith and Assurance in Early Calvinism: A Model of Continuity and Diversity," in *Later Calvinism* (ed. Graham), 355–84; Letham, *Assurance in Theological Context*, a revision and relative updating of the 1979 thesis, "Saving Faith and Assurance."

147. After a range of books and articles, R. A. Muller dealt the coup de grâce in *After Calvin*. See also J. Beeke, *Assurance of Faith: Calvin, English Puritanism, and the Dutch Second Reformation* (New York: Peter Lang, 1991); Trueman and Clark, eds., *Protestant Scholasticism*; Moore, *English Hypothetical Universalism*.

literature. Ministerial careers were often built around it. Yet the true believer will never be utterly destitute. In due time, this assurance may be revived by the Holy Spirit, and meanwhile the believer will be kept from utter despair (see also LC 81). Instead of the affirmations of 1 John—we know we have passed from death to life—we are simply kept from utter despair. While the connection with real pastoral situations is to be commended, this was one of those occasions when the Assembly was not at its best.

Finally, we return to Barth. He attacked the whole idea that assurance of salvation was addressed by the Assembly. "This intention of *reassurance*, which is profoundly pietistic and egotistic, is the worm in the timberwork, not the doctrine itself!"[148] Indeed, "the intolerable approach of the English" is seen, not in the answer they give to the question of whether this or that person might be elect, but insofar as "the actual interest in this *question* was the first crack in the wall of the church itself."[149] This tirade overlooks the point that the Thirty-Nine Articles had exactly the same emphasis, only more so, for there was a repeated pastoral concern to encourage and protect weak consciences. It seems almost incredible that Barth should overlook this. Moreover, the vast majority of the members of the Assembly were pastors who had dealt with the concerns and questions of their parishioners. Barth had been a pastor, but of a different kind, interested at the time and until 1914 in Christian socialism. From a slightly different, although related, angle, T. F. Torrance opines that the effectual calling of only some people for salvation, together with the doctrine of limited atonement, bred a lack of assurance.[150] However, without a robust doctrine of the perseverance of the saints, no assurance is possible. Historically, Arminius undermined assurance; Dort maintained it.

Glorification

LC 86 addresses the nature of the communion in glory with Christ that the elect will enjoy immediately after death. Their souls will be

148. Barth, *Reformed Confessions*, 136.
149. Ibid., 216.
150. T. F. Torrance, *Scottish Theology*, 136–37.

made perfect in holiness, they will be received into the highest heavens, and they will behold the face of God in light and glory (2 Cor. 5:1, 6, 8; Phil. 1:23; cf. Acts 3:21; Eph. 4:10). They will see the face of God (1 John 3:2; 1 Cor. 13:12). On the other hand, their salvation will not yet be complete, for they will await the full redemption of their bodies (Rom. 8:23; Ps. 16:9). However, even in death their bodies remain united to Christ. Not even death and the grave can sever the union with Christ which we enjoy now and will come to fruition at his return.

At the resurrection, according to LC 87, true believers will be raised up by the power of Christ in the selfsame bodies they now have. Their bodies, united to their souls, will be raised in power. They will have spiritual and incorruptible bodies, made like the glorious body of Christ. Here again, salvation is in union with Christ: our resurrection is based upon and integrally connected to his. Then comes the final judgment (LC 88–90; WCF 33), after which the righteous, fully and forever freed from all sin and misery (Rev. 14:13), will be filled with inconceivable joys (Ps. 16:11), made perfectly holy and happy in body and soul (Heb. 12:22–23), especially in the immediate vision and fruition of God the Father, of our Lord Jesus Christ, and of the Holy Spirit to all eternity,[151] which is the perfect and full communion that members of the invisible church shall enjoy with Christ in glory. The Confession speaks of everlasting life, receiving that fullness of joy and refreshing, which shall come from the presence of the Lord (WCF 33.2). This is a theme which at present we can only anticipate, looking for the resurrection of the dead and the life of the world to come.

However, as the New Testament indicates, and as the divines also held, this should direct and shape our life here and now. In the Eastern church, deification is the focus of salvation, understood as transformation into the image of God by the Holy Spirit. As such, it encompasses what in Reformed theology is together regeneration, sanctification, and glorification, seeing it as one. This perspective has been lost in the West. It helps us to recognize—with the Assembly—that union with Christ here and now is of a piece with union with Christ in the future, that the difference is in degree rather than kind, that being united to

---

151. This Trinitarian view of glorification undermines many of Torrance's criticisms noted in chapters 6 and 8.

Christ in regeneration, justification, and sanctification is to come to its perfect expression in the complete fruition of our knowledge of God, when in undisturbed and fulfilled union we enjoy the Father, the Son, and the Holy Spirit, in indivisible union forever.

Excursus 4: Anthony Tuckney on 2 Peter 1:4: "The Highest Exaltation Imaginable"

One of the most influential Assembly members, Anthony Tuckney, who played a large part in the production of the Larger Catechism, preached at some length on the idea of being conformed to the divine nature. In a sermon on 2 Peter 1:4, he remarked that "only the Divine power can produce this Divine nature, and precious faith in Christ, which alone instates the Christian believer in this most precious promise, or promised mercy of being made partaker of it."[152] Tuckney asks, "What is meant by this Divine Nature and our communicating or being made . . . *partakers* of it?" He considers a number of different interpretations, which are reducible to three. The most corrupt interpreters argue that there is a real participation in the divine essence. Osiander and Servetus claim that the essential Godhead is transfused into the godly, as the soul is into the body by which it is animated. The ranting enthusiasts and gnostics of this and former ages have held to this view. It flies higher than Lucifer's pride; it is anti-Christian blasphemy. Some of the Fathers, especially the Greek—Athanasius and Gregory of Nazianzus— "indulge themselves a sufficient liberty . . . but it is not as though they ever meant any such abolition of our nature, and transformation of it into God's, or a participation of his essence." This shows good judgment by Tuckney, indicating his learning. It is common among conservative Protestants to tar the Eastern view of deification with this brush, but in doing so it is clear they have not made an attempt to understand it.[153]

Tuckney compares our sharing in the divine nature with the incarnation and notes that "if Christs hypostatical union did not confound the natures and their properties; much less will this mystical union of God and the soul work any commixtion, or transfusion of it into the Godhead." Tuckney then compares it with two other unions: (1) the three consubstantial persons of the Trinity, in common partaking of the divine nature essentially, and (2)

---

152. Anthony Tuckney, sermon XVII on 2 Peter 1:4, in *Forty sermons* (London: J. M. for Jonathan Robinson and Brabazon Aylmer, 1676) [Wing T315; Arber's Term Cat. I/225], 224.
153. Ibid., 225. See Letham, *Through Western Eyes*, 253–63.

Christ's human nature, *hypostatikos* and personally. He concludes, "It's our highest honour and happiness that we may be made partakers of it by a participation of Divine grace and image, which is wrought in us by him, and by which we are made conformable to him, so far as the image of his infinite holiness is expressible in a limited and restrained being, as the wax receives the impression of the Seal, not the essence," or as a picture is called a face *accidentaliter per donum gratiae sanctificantis.*[154] He cites the "sober and pious" words of Cyprian, that our conjunction is in terms neither of persons, nor essence, *sed affectus consociat & confoederat voluntates.*[155]

He acknowledges here that the Reformed theologian Cloppenburg thinks otherwise—the words, he suggested, point to God in his own nature and being—so that what Peter intends is not only a communion of grace "but also a true and blessed communion with God himself," referring to John 17:3. Tuckney recognizes that the words in 2 Peter 1:4 "seemeth to sound a more inward and inherent communication of something, and not only a bare communion and fellowship, as one friend hath with another, though that be included, and of it some good Interpreters expound it."[156]

Others, such as Ambrose and Oecumenius, Tuckney says, interpret the passage with reference to Christ in his incarnate state, in which his human nature partook of the divine because it was hypostatically united to it. But, Tuckney argues, Christ took our nature, rather than we the divine. This union was in force ever since his conception and birth, while ours is still to be accomplished. It would follow that all who have human nature are partakers of the divine, whereas the apostle restricts it to believers. Cyril, who follows this argument, refers it to the Eucharist, which the papists eagerly swallow down. Yet here the apostle speaks more generally than of the sacrament, and more spiritually than any grossly absurd and blasphemous commixture and concorporation of Christ's body with ours.[157]

Others more rightly interpret the passage of the Holy Ghost. Cornelius à Lapide argues not only for *accidentaliter* (by the Holy Ghost we are endued with divine qualities and graces, made conformable to him and like our heavenly father), but for *substantaliter:* the very person of the Holy Ghost is united to us. He agrees with Lombard, Lib. 1 dist. 14, that the Holy Ghost is given to and dwells in believers, but he knows nothing of the *novus modus* they talk about.[158] Moreover, the Holy Ghost is not hypostatically united to believers.

---

154. Tuckney, *Forty sermons*, 226.
155. Ibid., 227.
156. Ibid.
157. Ibid., 227–28.
158. Ibid., 228.

Tuckney's own view is that, by the grace of adoption and sonship, what Christ is by nature we are made by grace—sons of God. Christ's Father is our Father, his Spirit our Spirit. Consequently, the nature of all three is in this relative sense communicated to us. We are sons having our subsistence from the Son, who is one with the Father, and we in our manner and measure one with them both. He finds support in Athanasius: we are partakers of God by being partakers of the Son of God, in *Oratio 4 contra Arianos*. He also has a marginal reference to Forbes, *Justification*, ch. 8, 23–25; Bellarmine, *Justification*, 1 2,c5 Quomodo autem etc.[159]

From this it follows, Tuckney argues, that as we are sons of God on a double title (by adoption and regeneration), for whom he adopts as sons he begets as sons (John 1:12–13), so we are made partakers of the divine nature upon a double interest, as relative in adoption, so positive and inherent in regeneration, and carried on in sanctification. He cites in support Gregory of Nazianzus, *Oratio* 47: Cyprian, who wrote that we are made partakers of the divine nature by partaking of the Holy Spirit—as Athanasius, *de S. Trinit. Dialog.* 2.164, while by the Holy Spirit in heart and life we are made like God (Eph. 4:24, Col. 3:10). This is "not by any partnership of his Essence and substance, but of excellent graces," or "as the child to the father . . . or in the wax to the seal . . . or in the *glass, face to face, being changed from glory to glory as by the Spirit of the Lord* 2.Cor.3.18." This likeness to God "is as a transcript of what is in God originally and infinitely." He cites Jerome, Calvin, "*quantum modulus nostra feret, sumus unum cum Deo.*"[160]

The following words in 2 Peter 1, "having escaped the corruption," tell us what it is in and by which we are made partakers of the divine nature. It is not a partaking of God's divine essence, but rather a participation of his heavenly grace whereby we escape worldly pollutions. The words preceding indicate that we have it by promise, and so again do not have the essence or nature of God. There is not one promise in the whole book of God that we will have his essence or nature, except the devil's promise to Eve.[161] "On God's part it is the lowest condescension, and on our part the highest exaltation imaginable," for "man can be raised no higher, and the Angelical nature of it self cannot rise so high." The amazing thing is that "we so vile and filthy, by nature children of wrath . . . [are] to be made partakers of that Divine nature, which is so glorious and holy."[162]

159. Ibid., 229.
160. Ibid., 230.
161. Ibid., 231.
162. Ibid., 233.

13

Law and Liberty

The Law of God (WCF 19; LC 91–152)

WCF 19.1 refers to the law of God in creation and in the covenant of works. In this, God bound Adam and his entire posterity "to personal, entire, exact, and perpetual obedience," giving a promise of life on condition of obedience and a threat of death for breaking it, while giving Adam the power to fulfill it.

The rest of the chapter develops the threefold classification of the law that had become standard in Reformed theology. The previous confessional literature provided the basis for this distinction, although it was not always explicit. Behind it lies a particular understanding of Scripture. According to the New Testament, Christ has terminated the laws governing worship, sacrifices, and ritual. The letter to the Hebrews makes clear that the Old Testament sacrifices were brought to an end by the cross of Christ. In Galatians, Paul insists that circumcision is no longer of covenantal significance. On the other hand, the Ten Commandments are interpreted and intensified by Jesus (Matt. 5–7) and reinforced by Paul and James. In this sense, Paul insists that the gospel establishes the law (Rom. 3:31). At root, the Decalogue is a reinforcement of creation ordinances and so transcends the time-limited Sinai covenant.[1] The plethora of civil laws given by the Lord

1. The first four commandments govern human relations with God, while the next five commandments protect the creational institutions and entailments of the family, life, marriage, private property, and personal reputations. The tenth commandment applies to inward personal

to Israel was part of the covenant he made, which, Paul argues, was for the specific purpose of preparing Israel for the coming of Christ (Gal. 3:19).[2]

Of the classic Reformed confessions, the French Confession, 23, states that "the ordinances of the law came to an end at the advent of Jesus Christ; but, although the ceremonies are no more in use, yet their substance and truth remain in the person of him in whom they are fulfilled. And, moreover, we must seek aid from the law and the prophets for the ruling of our lives, as well as for our confirmation in the promises of the gospel." There is a distinction here between "the ordinances of the law," which include "the ceremonies" that are now obsolete, since they were fulfilled in Christ, and "the law and the prophets" that help us in "ruling our lives" and in turn confirm the promises of the gospel. The latter are of ongoing significance, whereas the former have ended.[3] It adds later, in article 39, that "God wishes to have the world governed by laws and magistrates, so that some restraint may be put upon its disordered appetites." He has established kingdoms and republics—all that belongs to a just government—"so he has put the sword into the hands of magistrates to suppress crimes against the first as well as the second table of the commandments of God."[4] Here the Decalogue is said to be the basis for civil law. There is no reference here to the civil legislation of Israel; we can only conclude that it has expired, since the Decalogue is to be the basis for civil authority.

The Scots Confession, 14, states that the works regarded as good by God are the works of the first and second tables of the Decalogue. Here the continuity of the moral law is clearly taught.[5]

The Belgic Confession, 25, speaks of the abolition of the ceremonial law. The ceremonies and figures of the law ceased at the coming of Christ, and all the shadows are accomplished—they are abolished among Christians—yet the truth and substance of them remain with

---

motivations—greed—and also reaches beyond the particular relationship between Yahweh and Israel established at Mount Sinai.

2. See the discussion of this question in Letham, *Work of Christ*, 39–49.

3. Schaff, *Creeds*, 3:372–73.

4. Ibid., 3:381–82.

5. Ibid., 3:454–56.

us in Jesus Christ, in whom they have their completion.[6] Article 36 teaches that God, being "willing that the world should be governed by certain laws and policies," has appointed kings, princes, and magistrates, although there is no indication of what is to be the basis for these "certain laws."[7] In Article 24, sanctification is seen as the practice of those works which God has commanded in his Word.[8] We might infer that these works are founded on the moral law, but the Confession does not state it in such terms.

The Heidelberg Catechism makes no distinction between the various aspects of the law. One of its main sections considers the application of the Decalogue in the Christian life, but there is no mention of the ceremonies or the sacrificial system.[9]

The classic confessions provide evidence of the threefold division of the law, but do not put it in precise terms. They recognize that the sacrifices, ceremonies, and circumcision ceased with the advent of Christ, although they are of use in understanding how he brought them to fulfillment. They all acknowledge that the Decalogue is of continuing validity and provides the basis for the Christian life. They are, as a rule, more reticent when the role of civil government is in view, preferring not to deal with the subject. When the matter is considered—by the French Confession—it is stated that civil rulers are responsible to implement the two tables of the law, that is, the Decalogue. There is no reference to the civil legislation of Israel—what the Westminster Confession calls "the judicial laws."

WCF 19.2 situates the law as a perfect rule of righteousness after the fall. It was delivered by God at Mount Sinai in ten commandments, the first four containing our duty to God, the other six relating to our duty to man. As 19.3 mentions in passing, this is the moral law, and for a while the chapter puts it to one side before returning to it in 19.5. We have often noted the perceived threat of the antinomians; this chapter is crucial in rebutting them, and this statement is at the heart of it.[10] The ceremonial law is the theme of 19.3. This law God

6. Ibid., 3:412–13.
7. Ibid., 3:432–33.
8. Ibid., 3:410–11.
9. Ibid., 3:307–55.
10. There was considerable discussion of the antinomians during the debates on the Thirty-Nine Articles. The Assembly petitioned the House of Commons, asking for antinomians

gave to Israel as the church in its minority. It consisted of a number of ordinances that were types prefiguring Christ. Some of these ordinances related to worship; evidently the sacrificial system is in view. Of the ordinances not specifically related to worship, circumcision is the most prominent. These typical ordinances foreshadowed Christ in his graces, actions, sufferings, and benefits. In part they demonstrated a range of moral duties.

The next section focuses on the judicial laws. These God gave to Israel "as a body politic." Once Israel as such ceased to be the particular vehicle for God's saving purposes, these laws expired. Therefore, the function they had in the Old Testament no longer exists. This does not mean that they have lost all relevance for today. They may place an obligation on the present insofar as "the general equity thereof may require." According to the Assembly, the judicial laws no longer have any obligatory function and their usefulness is indirect, insofar as they reflect general principles of natural justice relating to the natural law of creation.[11]

who specifically argued against the seventh article (on the Old Testament) to be stopped, citing works by Crisp and Eaton and a range of preachers in London (Van Dixhoorn, 2:26–28). In S24 TH 10.8.43pm, debate occurred on the proposition that the civil precepts of Moses ought not of necessity to be received in any Christian commonwealth. The proofs of this were Matt. 5:31–32; 19:7–8; cf. Deut. 24:1; Matt. 5:38–39. It was argued that Christ repeals two civil laws, on divorce and retaliation. In S25 F 11.8.43, debate continued on the ninth proposition of the seventh article. In S26 M 14.8.43, texts were produced in support of the perpetuity of the moral law. The committee on the antinomians (of which Lightfoot was a member) pointed to the antinomians' argument that those in Christ have no sin and so Christians have nothing to do with the moral law, that to repent and ask pardon for sin is to crucify Christ again and is blasphemy, while to look for grace in Moses is wrong. In S27 TU 15.8.43, it was asked whether the Mosaic law should be explained by anything more than the Ten Commandments. Palmer proposed, and it was accepted, that it refers to the Ten Commandments in their full extent (Van Dixhoorn, 2:28–32). Later, in S59 W 20.9.43, Thomas Temple reported on the antinomian ideas that the law is of no use to believers and no rule to walk by, that it was as possible for Christ to sin as for a child of God, that a child of God needs not, may not, and ought not to ask for pardon from sin—indeed, that it is blasphemy to do so—that God does not chastise any of his children for sin, and that there ought to be no fasting days under the gospel. They argued that when it seemed Abraham was lying, in reality all his thoughts were holy and righteous, free from all spot of sin in the sight of God, and that if anyone by the Spirit knows himself to be in a state of grace, then God sees no sin in him, whatever he does. Temple proposed reasons why the Assembly should urge the House of Commons to quell these heretics—including the stability of the kingdom, the reputation of faithful ministers, and the infection of the army (Van Dixhoorn, 2:89–93). Debate continued in S60 TH 21.9.43, S61 TH 21.9.43(pm?), and S62 F 22.9.43 (Van Dixhoorn, 2:94–95).

11. See A. C. Troxel and P. J. Wallace, "Men in Combat over the Civil Law: 'General Equity' in WCF 19.4," *WTJ* 64 (2002): 307–18. They consider the phrase "general equity" against the

Attention returns to a detailed consideration of the moral law in 19.5. The Decalogue binds all people to obedience, whether they are justified persons or not. This ultimately stems from the authority of God, who gave it. The Ten Commandments have in no way been abrogated by Christ. Indeed, the gospel strengthens the moral law, rather than weakens it. It applies not only to the church or Israel, but to all people. This is a direct repudiation of antinomianism.

The relation of the moral law to the justified is in view in 19.6. Believers are not under the covenant of works; it neither condemns them, since Christ by his obedience has satisfied its demands for them, nor does it justify them. However, "it is of great use to them." It is a rule of life and so informs them of the will of God and their duty to God and man. As such, it binds them to live in accordance with it. Since it discloses the will of God for human life and actions, it reveals what sin is and so uncovers the sinful inclinations of the human heart. Consequently, believers can use it to examine themselves, to cultivate a hatred for sin, and so to recognize their need for Christ. It demonstrates what sin deserves, both in this life and in the next. Its promises show that God approves obedience and rewards it by grace. Hence, the continued validity of the law, far from undermining grace or perpetuating subservience to the law, is fully compatible with the believer being under grace.

This conclusion is reinforced by 19.7, which denies that "the forementioned uses of the law" are "contrary to the grace of the Gospel, but do sweetly comply with it." The will of God is expressed in his law. The Spirit of God enables the will of man to follow that law freely. Law and gospel are not competitive, but complementary.

The law is developed in exhaustive detail in the Larger Catechism, where the Ten Commandments are expounded in the face of the antinomian threat (LC 91–152). Each commandment is explained in terms of what it teaches and what it forbids, expressed in terms of the context of the day.

One area of interest is the question of the legitimacy of images, in relation to the second commandment. This comes to expression

---

background of English common law, where judges were accustomed to apply statute law and common law to particular situations, while the Court of Chancery functioned as an appeals court and adjudicated in areas where there was no clear application of the law, the Chancellor using *equity* as a distinct principle to inform his judgment.

in LC 109. There was a debate on pictures of the Trinity. A committee was established in S582 — 2.2.45(46) and on the following day, in S583 TU 3.2.45(46), the report was presented by Mr. Whitaker, proposing an addition regarding conduct forbidden by the commandment: "any who shall buy, sell, give or keepe any Images or Pictures of the Trinity or any person thereof—purposely in Reference unto and in esteeme of the said pictures, undefaced." This was debated, but there is no record of what transpired.[12] The proposal said nothing about other images, as neither did LC 109, which proscribed images of Christ or any person of the Trinity for worship, but was silent on images of the saints, presumably because they were not worshiped. The Heidelberg Catechism, 97, allows images of creatures, provided they are not objects of worship or a means of serving God. However, the next question prohibits their use in church.[13]

Christian Liberty (WCF 20)

This chapter should be read, together with the preceding one on the law of God, against the background of the recent repression under Archbishop Laud, on the one hand, and the real threat of the antinomians and sectarians, on the other. WCF 20.1 provides the basis for Christian liberty. This has been purchased for us by Christ under the gospel. It consists of freedom from sin and its consequences, the condemning wrath of God, and the curse of the moral law. In connection with these great gifts, there is also deliverance from the present evil world, sin, and Satan. The edge to all these things has been removed: the *evil* of afflictions, the *sting* of death, the *victory* of the grave, and the consequence of everlasting damnation. Afflictions and death await the Christian believer, but their power has been removed; the bitter impact is no more, for Christ has conquered them. On the positive side, Christian liberty entails freedom to draw near to God, willingly as his children. Now that Christ has obtained redemption,

12. Van Dixhoorn, 6:247–48.

13. For a consideration of images in Orthodoxy and the respective arguments on both sides, see Letham, *Through Western Eyes*, 143–62. However, the Assembly operated against the background of Roman Catholic theology, not Orthodox theology.

all this is evident in clearer measure in the New Testament. Subjection to the ceremonial law has ended, and the Holy Spirit has been given in greater measure.

Morris describes the statement in WCF 20.2, that God alone is the lord of conscience, as "a sublime step in advance of anything that England or Europe had ever known."[14] The liberty Christ has won brings deliverance from bondage to man. He alone has the right to determine what we should believe and how we should act. He alone is Lord of our conscience. We are thus freed from anything that is contrary to his Word. In matters of faith and worship, we are also freed from the obligation to follow commands that are additional to what he has revealed in his Word. In the context of the Laudian repression, this was a powerfully liberating statement. Indeed, Christians are prohibited from yielding their consciences to the whims of man. No one has the right to require blind allegiance. Such demands are contrary, not only to conscience, but to reason. Samuel Rutherford summed it up pithily in his comment: "It is in our power to vow, but not in the churches power to command us to vow."[15] However, the Assembly failed to see the implications of its own teaching and left a bitter legacy for later generations.[16]

WCF 20.3–4 is directed against the sects. On the one hand, Christian liberty is not a license to sin (20.3). Such liberty is deliverance *from* sin, so as to serve Christ in lifelong holiness. It is not a *carte blanche* to ignore God's demands; it sets us free to follow them. In addition, according to 20.4, Christian liberty does not undermine private property or civil government. Sects such as the Levellers had set

---

14. Morris, *Westminster Symbols*, 816.

15. In S264 F 9.8.44; Van Dixhoorn, 5:225.

16. Why did the Assembly fail to achieve the purpose for which it was appointed? Its proposals were dead in the water as soon as the Assembly made them. The Presbyterians had been outmaneuvered by Cromwell, a military genius who was also politically far ahead of his time. The Presbyterians failed to follow through on the logic of their own theology—chapters 20 and 26 of the Confession, on Christian liberty and the communion of the saints. If they had joined forces with the Independents, who controlled the army, to secure the establishment of Presbyterianism, together with liberty of worship for Independents and payment for the soldiers (long overdue), cohesion and stability could have been sustained. It was a failure of political and theological imagination at a time when it was desperately needed. Of this, Cromwell had plenty, but the Presbyterians had little or none. The latter seemed more ready to do a deal with Charles than with the army. The Assembly failed to carry through its own teaching on Christian liberty and paid a heavy political price.

themselves against private wealth. Such ideas were seen as stemming from antinomianism. Christian liberty is joined with the continuing validity of the law of God, described in the previous chapter. Both ecclesiastical and civil authorities have the right to proceed against any who publish such subversive views, since such antinomian egalitarianism was seen as destructive to peace and order. The ongoing preoccupation with the antinomians, their summoning to Parliament for civil action, and the burning of their books stemmed from both theological and practical considerations. Antinomianism was heresy, denying the legitimacy of the law as a rule of life, and it was also subversive, since its consequences threatened civil order.

Religious Worship and the Regulative Principle (WCF 21)

The chapter begins by pointing to the universal recognition by the human race that there is a God who is worthy of our worship and homage. This reflects the teaching at the start of the Confession on general revelation and the light of nature. It follows the thought of Calvin, who argued for a *sensus divinitatis* imprinted on the minds of all people;[17] as he said, "a sense of divinity is by nature engraven on human hearts."[18]

However, sin has estranged man from God. Not all religion is tolerable to God. How is he to be worshiped in an acceptable manner? The answer, the Confession states, is that God alone has the right to determine how people should worship him. Moreover, he has revealed this in Holy Scripture. There is no other way that pleases him. Consequently, true worship is prescribed in Scripture, and he may not be worshiped in any other way. All visible representations of God are thereby outlawed. Human imagination is not to be used to determine how to worship. Human inventions are excluded. Worship is to be based on revelation—not general revelation in creation, but special revelation in Scripture.

Here we note the well-known differences among the Reformed, the Lutherans, and Rome. Rome held that Scripture is to be supple-

17. Helm, *John Calvin's Ideas*, 218–45.
18. Calvin, *Institutes*, 1.4.4.

mented by unwritten traditions—the written books and the unwritten traditions. These the church received and venerated "with an equal affection of piety and reverence."[19] Lutheranism and High Church Anglicanism of the Laudian variety considered that proper worship may consist of anything not forbidden by Scripture. Therefore, established customs were a legitimate part of the church's worship. In contrast, the Reformed churches held that worship is to be determined by God, and its basis and content are to be found in Scripture. Worship is to be in accordance with what Scripture requires; that alone is to be our guide. In contrast with the position that what is not forbidden by Scripture is permissible, the Reformed held that only what Scripture prescribes is permissible.

This principle has to be understood in conjunction with the Assembly's doctrine of Scripture. In chapter 1, the Assembly states that the whole counsel of God either is set down explicitly in Scripture or by good and necessary consequence can be deduced from Scripture. Hence, the Assembly does not reduce the Bible to a manual of commands, whereby worship is to be shaped by explicit commands of Scripture, for which chapter and verse are required. As Kelly rightly says, from this "one can logically deduce some proper element of worship through 'good and necessary consequence,'" and so "it has been the general Puritan position that a valid inference from Scripture is just as binding as a specific statement."[20]

We need to appreciate how the regulative principle functioned in the historical context of the Assembly. The Elizabethan settlement and its aftermath put it in perspective. The focus of these statements cannot be understood apart from the draconian legislation that governed worship in the Church of England, whether it was observed more in the breach or not. The Act for the Uniformity of Common Prayer (1559), which restored the Book of Common Prayer of 1552, specified:

19. See A. E. McGrath, ed., *The Christian Theology Reader* (3rd ed.; Oxford: Blackwell, 2007), 10; D. Kelly, "The Puritan Regulative Principle and Contemporary Worship," in *Westminster Confession into the 21st Century* (ed. Duncan), 2:63–98, esp. 65. Kelly gives a good account of the issues and difficulties in implementing the regulative principle. See also J. M. Frame, "Some Questions about the Regulative Principle," *WTJ* 54 (1992): 357–66.
20. Kelly, "Puritan Regulative Principle," 2:77.

And further be it Enacted by the Queen's Highness, with the assent of the Lords and Commons in this Parliament assembled, and by the Authority of the same, That all and singular Ministers, in any Cathedral, or Parish-Church, or other place, within this Realm of *England, Wales*, or Marches of the same . . . shall . . . be bounden to say and use the Mattens, Evensong, Celebration of the Lord's Supper, and Administration of each of the Sacraments, and all their common and open Prayer, in such order and form as is mentioned in the said Book.

If any minister refuse to use the book in such order and form,

or shall wilfully, or obstinately . . . use any other Rite, Ceremony, Order, Form, or Manner of celebrating of the Lord's Supper, openly or privily, or Mattens, Evensong, Administration of the Sacraments . . . than is . . . set forth in the said Book . . . or shall preach, declare or speak anything in the derogation . . . of the said Book . . . and shall be thereof lawfully convicted, according to the laws of this Realm, by verdict of twelve men, or by his own confession . . . shall lose and forfeit . . . all his Spiritual Benefices, or Promotions, coming or arising in one whole Year next after his Conviction.

He would also face imprisonment for six months without bail or mainprise. On a second offense, "after his conviction eftsoons offend" and following lawful conviction, the penalty was imprisonment for one year and deprivation of all spiritual promotions. On a third offense, "then the Person so offending, and convicted the third time, shall be deprived *ipso facto* of all his Spiritual Promotions, and also shall suffer imprisonment during his life." If the offender had no spiritual benefices, on his first offense there would be imprisonment for one year, and on a second offense, life imprisonment.

If any person whatsoever writes or says anything against the Book or should interrupt a vicar in services of the Book, the first offense was punishable by fine of 100 marks, the second offense by 400 marks, and on a third offense the offender shall "forfeit to our Sovereign Lady, the Queen, all his Goods and Chattels, and shall suffer Imprisonment during his life." Power to hear such cases was to rest with the mayors, bailiffs, and other officers of cities, boroughs, and towns-corporate, and archbishops and bishops had full powers to investigate and punish.[21]

Until Laud, these sanctions were observed mostly in the breach. As one striking example, the bishop of Ely, Richard Cox, used the leading Puritan, Richard Greenham, vicar of Dry Drayton from 1571 to 1591, who did not observe all the niceties of the Book—and had at one point written in support of Thomas Cartwright, the early Presbyterian—as his chief investigator of heretical teaching in his diocese.[22] Since Puritanism was predominantly a movement among the emerging middle class, local magistrates in areas of Puritan influence were themselves likely to be Puritan sympathizers. It is with the accession of Charles I and the rise of Laud that these measures began to be implemented in earnest and the crisis erupted.

In this context, the focus of WCF 21.1 is more immediately liberating than restricting. Bound in its worship to the direction of the Word of God alone, the church is freed from the dictates of man, whether these are contrary to the Word or simply additional to it. The yoke of imposition is lifted. The church is free from the dictatorial impositions of man and free to worship God, not as man himself may want, but as God requires, whether by express statements in Scripture or by good and necessary consequence from it. In this sense, WCF 21.1 must be read in conjunction with the entire section (chapters 19–24) of which it is a central part, dealing with law and liberty, church and state.[23]

When we reflect on the drastic imposition of the Book of Common Prayer by the Elizabethan settlement and its aftermath, we

21. *The Book of Common Prayer and Administration of the Sacraments and other Rites and Ceremonies of the Church according to the Use of the Church of England* (Oxford: Oxford University Press, n.d.), vii–x.

22. E. J. Carlson, "'Practical Divinity': Richard Greenham's Ministry in Elizabethan England," in *Religion and the English People 1500–1640: New Voices, New Perspectives* (ed. E. J. Carlson; Kirksville, MO: Thomas Jefferson University Press, 1998), 147–93.

23. Kelly discusses whether the regulative principle is found in Scripture in "Puritan Regulative Principle," 2:80ff. If an explicit command of Scripture were needed for every worship practice, this would pose a problem, since there is no explicit statement in the Bible to the effect that only that can be done in the worship of the church that the Bible specifically commands. The problem is resolved if the whole teaching of the Assembly on Scripture is considered. In that case, since good and necessary consequence is part of the whole counsel of God for his glory, our salvation, faith, and life, church worship is to be shaped by the sense of Scripture—its entailments as well as its commands—and so an explicit proof text is not required.

see why the Assembly produced a directory of worship giving free-dom to individual ministers to conduct worship services within the boundaries of the regulative principle of Scripture. It was the binding legal requirement, imposed by the crown, with penalties attached, that was the real nub of the problem with the liturgy for Puritan minds. While opposing the legal imposition of set liturgies, the Assembly was not abandoning liturgies as such. The Directory for the Publick Worship of God contains a range of model prayers to be used in the regular service, at the start, before the sermon, after the sermon, before and after baptism, during and after com-munion, at the solemnization of marriage, in visiting the sick, and at public solemn fasting.[24] Even John Owen, a few years too young to have been appointed to the Assembly, when writing on liturgies, stressed that he was not opposed to them or to the Book of Com-mon Prayer, but to their imposition by law, with the forbidding of the slightest deviation from the set words.[25] The standard practice of the Reformed churches had been to have a liturgy with set prayers; the problem for the divines was the rigid imposition and the repressive, punitive sanctions for failure to comply.[26]

24. "The Directory for the Publick Worship of God," in *The Confession of Faith, the Larger and Shorter Catechisms with the Scripture Proofs at Large Together with the Sum of Saving Knowledge* (Applecross: Publications Committee of the Free Presbyterian Church of Scotland, 1970), 375–92.

25. John Owen, "A Discourse Concerning Liturgies, and Their Imposition" (1662), in *Works of John Owen*, 15:33, where he states, "I do not in especial intend the liturgy now in use in England, any further than to make it an instance of such imposed liturgies, whereof we treat." He adds, "Nor, secondly, do I oppose the directive part of this liturgy as to the reading of Scripture . . . nor the composition of forms of prayer suitable to the nature of the institutions to which they relate, so they be not imposed on the administrators of them to be read precisely as prescribed. But, thirdly, this is that alone which I shall speak unto,—the composing of forms of prayer in the worship of God . . . to be used by the ministers of the churches, in all public assemblies, by a precise reading of the words prescribed unto them, with commands for the reading of other things, which they are not to omit, upon the penalty contained in the sanc-tion of the whole service and the several parts of it." The problem for Owen and his friends, he explains, was that this imposition was accompanied by a restriction on preaching. Later he refers to "the prescription of the liturgy, to be used as prescribed" (15:47), and to "the precise reading and pronouncing of the words set down therein, without alteration, diminution, or addi-tion" (15:49). Kelly is wrong when he writes that Owen was "against all set liturgies" ("Puritan Regulative Principle," 2:74).

26. See further on the practice of the Reformed churches, Old, *Patristic Roots*; H. O. Old, *The Shaping of the Reformed Baptismal Rite in the Sixteenth Century* (Grand Rapids: Eerdmans, 1992); I. J. Hesselink, *On Being Reformed: Distinctive Characteristics and Common Misunderstand-ings* (Ann Arbor: Servant Books, 1983), 21–30.

During the debates on the preface of the Directory, there was a conflict of sorts between George Gillespie and many members of the Assembly over the Book of Common Prayer. Gillespie claimed that there was gold amid the dross in the Prayer Book, adding that "this book cannot be buried with honour, but as 'the buriall of the uncircumcised.'" Some parts of it complied with the Mass and had received the approval of the papal nuncio.[27] However, Cornelius Burgess was quick to reply that no aspersions should be cast on any person or thing unless there is demonstrably sin. Herle asked, "Doth this booke comply with the masse booke because some things in it are taken out of the masse booke? Shall we pluck downe our churches because a complyance with Judaisme?" Gillespie retorted that the pope had given his approval through his nuncio to these elements in the Prayer Book. Moreover, churches have a necessary use; the Prayer Book is not a necessity. The matter in hand was referred back to the committee on the grounds that its proposals would "reflect upon the honour of all the clergy of England."[28] When the committee had first introduced the Directory, in S226 F 24.5.44, its spokesman, Stephen Marshall, had pointed out that "if noe formed prayers made but every one left to his owne will—soe many raw & unexperienced ministers as would make the ordinances of God ridiculous."[29]

The Assembly might have been better advised to reverse the order of the first two sections of WCF 21. As it stands, the chapter begins with a statement of the regulative principle and follows with a statement that worship is directed to the Trinity. This follows the order of the first two chapters: first Scripture, second God. However, the regulative principle stands here somewhat isolated, without theological context, as effectively a self-evident principle. If the order were reversed, the chapter would begin by affirming that true worship is worship of God the Father, the Son, and the Holy Spirit. The question would then arise as to where the will of the Holy Spirit is to be sought, and how we can worship in the Spirit, to which the regulative principle would be the answer. Since Scripture is breathed out by the Spirit (WCF 1.4), worship in the Spirit is conformed to the will of the Spirit in Holy

27. In S314 TH 31.10.44 (Van Dixhoorn, 5:441–42).
28. Ibid., 5:442–44.
29. Ibid., 5:133.

Scripture. All else is at odds with the mind of the Holy Spirit and so is not part of the acceptable way of worshiping him.

Sections 21.3 and 21.4 both focus on prayer with thanksgiving, as one special part of religious worship. This method of stating an element of worship, but balancing it with the appropriate way it is to be undertaken, is a feature of this chapter. The divines had an eye on the response of the worshipers. This, after all, is a crucial part of worship. It stands in contrast with a purely superficial formality, such as might be associated with a ritualistic attitude to the worship of the church—the kind of thing that had been encountered in the Laudian repression.

Prayer is a universal responsibility, the Confession states. All people are under obligation to pray to God. This opens up the point that the nonelect are without excuse for their failure to give God thanks, as Paul comments in Romans 1. However, while prayer is required by God of all people, not all prayer is acceptable to God. Acceptable prayer is Trinitarian. It is offered in the name of the Son and by the help of the Holy Spirit; the implication here is that it is directed to the Father. Since Christ is the one mediator between God and men, and he is the only way to the Father, prayer can only be made in his name. Moreover, acceptable prayer is made according with his will, which chapter 1 has already said is found in Holy Scripture. It is to be made in faith, with understanding, reverence, humility, love, patience, and perseverance. In other words, prayer that is acceptable to God is specifically Christian and Trinitarian. In contrast with Rome's use of Latin, public prayer is to be in a known language.

As to the content of prayer, 21.4 is clear. It can be made for all things lawful. This includes those things promised in Scripture and other things that are compatible with Scripture and its entailments. Intercession can be made for all sorts of people, but they must either be alive either at the time or at some stage in the future. Prayers for the dead, sanctioned by Rome, are impermissible. The implied point here is that the destiny of the dead is already unchangeably fixed. Contrary to the Roman doctrine of purgatory, there is nothing that the prayers or intercessions of the living can do to alter the circumstances of those who have already died. The elect are safe in union with Christ; unbelievers await the judgment. Additionally, prayer is not to be offered for those of whom it may be known that they have sinned the sin unto death (1 John 5:16). Since the identity of this sin had always been something of a conundrum, it is unlikely that it can be known exactly what the Assembly had in mind.

Attention turns to other parts of ordinary religious worship in 21.5. First comes the reading of the Scriptures with godly fear. The Confession has already declared that the Bible's origin is from God, so that the order here is an important one. The Scriptures are to be received with godly fear precisely because they are the voice of God in human language. Closely connected to that is the sound preaching and conscionable hearing of the Word in obedience to God. Behind this lie the words of the Second Helvetic Confession, 1, which states that where the Word of God is proclaimed by preachers lawfully called, there the Word of God is actually and truly heard.[30] Then comes the singing of psalms with grace in the heart. We note again the balance between the content—the psalms—and the worshiper, who is to have grace in his or her heart. The due administration and worthy receiving of the sacraments instituted by Christ refers to baptism and the Lord's Supper and implicitly negates the five sacraments of Rome denied by Protestants.

We will consider much of this in the chapter on the church and the sacraments. However, one point arises here that has been discussed at length in subsequent years. When the Confession refers to the singing of psalms, it is unquestioned that the divines had in mind the Psalms of David. However, did they believe that only the Psalms should be sung in the worship of the church? Or were they simply reflecting the staple diet of the Church of England at the time? In short, is their reference to the singing of psalms prescriptive or merely descriptive? If the former, what did the Assembly mean by "psalms"?

Nick Needham has presented a considerable amount of evidence to establish that the Assembly did not restrict itself to the Psalms of David when it mentioned "psalms" here in the Confession.[31] Of course, it regarded the Psalter as the backbone of the singing of the church. There was much debate on the production of a suitable

30. See Schaff, *Creeds*, 3:237–38, 831–32; Old, *Patristic Roots*, 194–95.
31. N. Needham, "Westminster and Worship: Psalms, Hymns? and Musical Instruments?" in *Westminster Confession into the 21st Century* (ed. Duncan), 2:223–306.

Psalter. That is a given that needs little support on our part. However, most of Needham's article is an examination of the practice of the Reformed churches of the sixteenth and seventeenth centuries—in particular, whether they allowed in principle for songs other than the Psalms to be sung in the worship of the church. Needham presents comprehensive evidence to show the widespread acceptance of songs other than the Davidic Psalms, although he stresses that the latter provided the main diet of the Reformed church's worship in song. He concludes that "there is abundant evidence that in 17th century English, the word 'psalm' often meant simply a religious song."[32] The verb *psallo* meant "to pluck or twang," referring to a song sung to stringed musical accompaniment.[33] He unearths evidence from Richard Baxter, Zwingli and Bullinger, Calvin, and the French, German, and Dutch Reformed churches, concluding that "the pattern of sung worship in the Continental Reformed Churches, then, does not fit into an exclusive psalmodist framework."[34] The English Protestants in Geneva were not opposed to singing other scriptural passages in worship, while the standard English Psalter by Sternhold and Hopkins contained a considerably greater number of non-Davidic songs and was definitive until 1696.[35] While in Scotland exclusive psalmody was the rule, that does not prove the Scots were opposed in principle to non-Davidic compositions.[36] Indeed, before the Assembly the Scots used the *Gloria Patri*, but were required to desist by the Puritans.[37] Thus, Needham considers "the weight of evidence decisively favours interpreting Confession 21.5 as referring to a broader category of song than the Davidic psalter."[38] On the other hand, the Assembly is silent about instrumental worship and does not support it.[39] He points out that Parliament decreed on 9 May 1644 that all ecclesiastical organs be destroyed, a move in keeping with the Reformed churches' belief that instrumental worship belonged

32. Ibid., 249.
33. Ibid., 250–51.
34. Ibid., 252–60.
35. Ibid., 260–63.
36. Ibid., 274.
37. Ibid., 279.
38. Ibid., 280.
39. Ibid., 291.

to the Mosaic covenant and had been supplanted by the coming of Christ.[40] In contrast with this, it is noteworthy that the *Annotations*, in the passage correctly cited by Needham, refer "psalms, hymns, and spiritual songs" to three different things, with *psalm* explained as a song plucked with stringed instruments!

Section 21.5 also refers to worship on special occasions and includes religious oaths, vows, solemn fastings, and thanksgivings in this category. These are to be used in their special times and seasons, and are not expected to take place on a regular basis. The Puritans were fond of fastings and thanksgivings, and there were plenty of both during the Assembly. The times called for them, with the political situation so uncertain.

In 21.6 the divines assert that the place of worship has been relativized under the gospel. Religious worship is not made acceptable by the place toward which it is directed; there is no special significance to the East, contrary to the practice of Rome or Laudian Anglicanism in praying toward it. On the positive front, God can be worshiped anywhere and everywhere, provided worship is in spirit and in truth.[41] He is to be worshiped daily in private families,[42] daily in secret by individuals,[43] and corporately and more solemnly in public assemblies.[44] These latter gatherings of the church are to be frequented regularly. The reason for this is seen in what follows in WCF 27–29. It is there that the means of grace are found: the ministry of the Word and the sacraments.

While place is no longer principially relevant to religious worship, time still is. In 21.7, it is asserted that the Sabbath is to be kept holy to God. This is a moral and perpetual commandment of God. From creation to the resurrection of Christ, it was the last day of the week. As a creation ordinance, it is binding on all

40. Ibid.

41. While there is no concrete evidence that the Assembly meant this itself, the Greek Fathers understood the phrase "in spirit and in truth" in John 4:21–24 to refer to the Holy Spirit and to Jesus Christ, who is the truth. See my book, *The Holy Trinity*, 412–17.

42. The proof texts are Jer. 10:25; Deut. 6:6–7; Job 1:5; 2 Sam. 6:18–20; 1 Peter 3:7; Acts 10:2.

43. The proof texts are Matt. 6:6; Eph. 6:18.

44. The proof texts are Isa. 56:6–7; Heb. 10:25; Prov. 1:20–21, 24; 8:34; Acts 13:42; Luke 4:16; Acts 2:42.

people everywhere and at all times. At the resurrection of Christ, the day was changed to the first day of the week, the Lord's Day. This continues in force until the end of the world. How is this day to be observed? Section 21.8 outlines the answer. It is to be kept holy to the Lord. Beforehand, our hearts are to be prepared and our common affairs set in order. The day itself is to be a holy rest from our own works and thoughts about our worldly occupations. Instead, we are to be taken up the whole time in the public and private exercises of God's worship and in duties of necessity and mercy.

Barth criticizes the divines for neglecting the biblical teaching on the eternal Sabbath rest.[45] His comments are in order. The letter to the Hebrews makes it clear that the ultimate orientation of the Sabbath is to heaven (Heb. 4:9–10). The Greek fathers consistently saw the unending nature of the seventh day in Genesis 2 as pointing to the resurrection and the life of the world to come, in which we will share by grace in the eternal rest of God. Mention of this would have made this section more complete and given it the future orientation that Scripture gives it. Moreover, the Assembly presents an apparent nature-grace dualism here. Worldly employments are to be forgotten on the Lord's Day. There is a sense in which this is a necessary element of religious worship: to cast from ourselves distracting thoughts that would hamper our worship of God. However, the reality may be different. It is probable that the Assembly was resisting commercial activity on the Sabbath, for there is plenty of evidence that in their respective ministries on the Sabbath they addressed biblical principles about commercial life. This is a case where the language of the mid-seventeenth century can be easily misunderstood at a distance of several centuries.[46] Since the earth is the Lord's and all things are his, Christians need to develop an appreciation of how the gospel impinges on our "worldly employments and recreations." These cannot be kept as hermetically sealed compartments unaffected by the claims of God.

45. Barth, *Reformed Confessions*, 145.
46. I am grateful to Sherman Isbell for this suggestion.

310

Lawful Oaths and Vows (WCF 22; LC 111–14)

This chapter may appear rather arcane to modern readers, but we should recall that, according to the Assembly, a lawful oath is part of religious worship used at special times and seasons (22.1; see 21.5). The chapter counters the Anabaptists' refusal to take oaths in court. Section 22.2 states that oaths are to be sworn only in the name of God. It is a breach of the third commandment to take an oath in the name of the Trinity insincerely. It breaks the first commandment if it is done in another name.

In 22.3, the boundaries of oaths are mapped out. The oath-taker should consider the weightiness of the matter, be persuaded of the truth concerning which the oath is taken, and do so only for a good and just reason. If such occasions occur, it is a sin to refuse an oath. An oath is binding (22.4).

The same stipulations apply also to vows (22.5). These are to be made to God alone, voluntarily, in faith and out of duty, with thankfulness (22.6). They may not be made contrary to the Word of God, or on matters not in one's own power to perform. The popish vows of celibacy, poverty, and obedience are sinful snares (22.7).

Civil Government (WCF 23; LC 123–33)

The area of civil government was of immense concern to the Assembly, at a time when the nation was at war with itself, and in view of its subservient relationship to Parliament.

WCF 23.1 sets out the broad principles of civil government. God has ordained government. He is the supreme governor as Lord and King of the whole world. Human rulers are under his authority and accountable to him. They are given the task of ruling over the people; there is no hint here of "government of the people, by the people." The first task of civil rulers is to promote the glory of the triune God. Then comes their responsibility to promote the common good. These prime functions cut right across the common human desire for power in order to enhance the well-being of the ruler. God has given civil rulers the power of the sword. Force may legitimately be used, but God has given it expressly in order to defend the good and to punish evildoers, to promote his glory and to effect the common good—and for no other reason.

Against this background, it is lawful for Christians to accept office in civil government, according to 23.2. This was contrary to the teachings of the Anabaptists and separatist sects. Since government is an ordinance of God, it is a legitimate undertaking for Christians. Their responsibility, as that of all rulers, is to maintain piety, justice, and peace "according to the wholesome laws of each commonwealth." This involves the protection of the Christian church, but makes allowances for the differences that may exist from one body politic to another. In addition, they may lawfully wage war on just and necessary occasion; here the just war theory from Aquinas is in view. In the case of the current hostilities, Parliament was waging war against the king; in the eyes of the Assembly, it was both just and necessary. It was necessary for self-defense. It was just because of the previous usurpation of ecclesiastical power by Laud and the perceived popish influence on the king himself. It was both just and necessary in view of English constitutional developments reaching back to the Magna Carta.

The civil authorities have limits imposed on them by God, according to 23.3. The civil magistrate has no right to administer the Word and sacraments or to exercise church discipline. There is a clear distinction between civil and ecclesiastical government. This was contrary to the Erastians and to the Henrician settlement, whereby the functions of the church were effectively governed by the reigning monarch. However, it was also contrary to the insistence of Parliament that discipline be a state function. This was a sore area, a bone of contention between the Assembly and Parliament. Many feared that the location of disciplinary power in the church would undermine the unity and cohesion of the nation by rendering asunder what they believed God had joined together. While few of its members held to Erastian views, the Assembly itself was an Erastian body in the sense that its powers and functions were entirely circumscribed by Parliament. This was a radical proposal for the times.

However, the civil ruler has the duty to ensure that unity, peace, and truth prevail in the church. He is responsible to ensure that corruption and abuses do not enter it or are removed if found to be present. He must suppress heresy. He must satisfy himself that the ordinances of God are observed in proper order. To do this, he may call synods, he may attend them himself, and he may ensure that their proceedings are in accordance with the mind of God in Holy Scripture. It was axiomatic for the Assembly that the civil ruler was not a neutral umpire, but had a role in promoting the true religion. While the Assembly recognized a distinction between the government of the church and the government of the nation, it nevertheless equally maintained that there is to be a close connection between them. This was a burning issue, with huge uncertainty about the future pressing hard.[47]

Finally, in 23.4, the Assembly discusses the responsibilities of the people toward their rulers. They are to pray for them, to honor them, to pay tribute, and to obey their lawful commands. Unbelieving magistrates have the same rights as others; just as the sacraments are not nullified by lack of piety in the one who administers them (WCF 27.3), so is civil government not set at naught by an unbelieving ruler. However, papal claims are rejected out of hand. The pope has no civil jurisdiction, nor has he any lawful power over ecclesiastical persons, to deprive any of life or dominions under any pretense, including heresy.

Marriage and Divorce (WCF 24; LC 137–39)

WCF 24.1 expounds the nature of marriage and the principle of monogamy. Marriage is between one man and one woman. Therefore, polygamy and polyandry are both unlawful. In 24.2, the purpose of marriage is explained. It was ordained by God for the mutual help of both husband and wife, for the increase of mankind with a legitimate issue, for the increase of the church with a holy seed, and for the preventing of uncleanness. As a creation ordinance it serves civil ends, but since God's covenant is administered along household lines, it

47. Here the difference from the American situation is obvious. The Assembly did not entertain the idea that civil government should be neutral. Its responsibility was to uphold and maintain the Reformed faith. At the same time, the church had the sole right to minister the Word, dispense the sacraments, and exercise church discipline. The divines upheld the establishment of the true religion. The vast majority of the Westminster divines were neither Erastian nor separatist in their thinking.

also functions as the arena within which his redemptive purposes are chiefly worked out. The purposes listed here are identical to those in the Form of the Solemnization of Matrimony in the Book of Common Prayer, although in different order.

As to who may marry, WCF 24.3 allows all who are able to give their judgment and consent. However, it is not to be undertaken "within the degrees of consanguinity and affinity forbidden by the Word," as specified in Leviticus 18. Moreover, Christians may only marry other Christians. Further, Reformed Christians should not marry infidels, papists, or other idolaters, the notoriously wicked or heretics.

Excursus 5: Who Are "Papists"?

Another area of detail for which the English context is vital for understanding is the question of "papists"—whom those who profess the Reformed religion are not to marry. This was, if anything, more a political term. Papists were those in league with France and Spain, plotting to overthrow the Protestant faith and install a king on the throne who would renew allegiance to Rome, contrary to English independence.

This is only the second Reformed confession to comment on marriage, and the first to mention anything about marrying papists. Neither the French Confession, drawn up under the editorial direction of Calvin (1559), the Scots Confession written by Knox (1560), the Belgic Confession (1561), the Heidelberg Catechism (1563), the Second Helvetic Confession (1566), nor the Canons of Dort (1619) say anything about marriage. The Thirty-Nine Articles (1562, 1571) have a chapter on the marriage of priests (article 32). It states that bishops, priests, and deacons are not bound to abstain from marriage. "Therefore it is lawfull also for them, as for all other Christian men, to mary at ther owne discretion." The Articles place responsibility for marriage entirely in the hands of the one marrying, and do not make it a matter of ecclesiastical jurisdiction. The relevant place in the Westminster Confession states:

> It is lawful for all sorts of persons to marry. . . . Yet is it the duty of Christians to marry only in the Lord. And therefore such as profess the true reformed religion should not marry with infidels, papists, or other idolaters: neither should such as are godly be unequally yoked, by marrying with such as are notoriously wicked in their life, or maintain damnable heresies. (WCF 24.3)

314

This statement of the Confession is necessarily dependent on historical context. A statement such as this was not regarded, and could not have been regarded, by the Assembly as applicable and binding at all times and in all places.

To grasp this point, we recall that the gospel was first brought to England by the papacy. In 597, Pope Gregory the Great sent Augustine of Canterbury to England to convert the Angles and thereafter gave him constant support, once ordering him to continue with the mission despite his fearful desire to withdraw. This was in line with Gregory's lifelong devotion to the missionary enterprise of the church. So the Confession's statement could not apply to the entire time from 597 to 1532/3, during which the English church was nominally under the authority of Rome and owed ecclesiastical allegiance to the pope, and when all Christians were papists; otherwise, Christian marriage could not have occurred during this period! Therefore, the Assembly did not see this as a universally applicable principle, but instead one dependent on historical context.

In this connection, political and theological elements were inseparably intermingled. To us this may not be self-evident. The Confession's language seems to cite religious rather than political factors as debarring marriage. However, the theological and the political were inextricably tangled in mid-seventeenth-century England.

After Henry VIII's break with Rome in the 1530s, the Roman Catholic Church did not exist legally in England. The entire English church was now independent of Rome under the headship of the king. While various individuals were still loyal to Rome (often aristocrats who practiced the Roman rite in secret), the Roman church as such did not exist. Roman Catholics could not travel more than five miles from their home under penalty of imprisonment. They were banned from Parliament and from university education until well into the nineteenth century. If a Roman priest was found, he was to be executed—not for heresy, but for treason.

Papists, moreover, were seen as enemy sympathizers—in collusion with France or Spain—aiming to overthrow the government and the Protestant system. Two crucial events in the decades before Westminster embedded themselves deep in the national psyche, with consequences still evident today. First, in 1588 the Spanish Armada set sail in a failed attempt to invade England and restore the country to the papacy. Second, in 1605 the Gunpowder Plot was discovered. Led by Robert Catesby, assisted by a mercenary soldier named Guido Fawkes and others, the plan was to blow up the king and both Houses of Parliament by gunpowder stored in a Westminster cellar and then bring a Roman Catholic to the throne. The plot's discovery was hailed as a merciful act of divine providence. To this day, Guy Fawkes night (5 November) is one of the landmark dates on the English calendar. In July 1988, beacons were lit across Britain commemorating the four hundredth anniversary of the deliverance from the Armada. These monumental events, of towering significance, were seen as instigated from outside the country and were directly linked in the public mind with the papacy. Affairs of church and state were inseparable.

In the light of these factors, stringent penalties were exacted from any with connections to the Roman Church. The Act of Succession prohibited a Roman Catholic from occupying the throne (it is still in force). Priests "who acknowledged the supremacy of the Pope were liable to the penalties of high treason."[48] As Christopher Hill says,

> The tolerance of even a Cromwell or a Milton did not extend to Papists. For this the reasons were largely political. Papists were regarded as agents of a foreign power. They had solidly supported Charles in the Civil War. . . . Hostility to Papists was not a monopoly of the Puritans. In 1640 a group of condemned men in Newgate gaol had conscientious scruples about being hanged unless seven condemned priests whom the King was trying to save were hanged with them. The Parliamentarians also refused toleration to "Prelatists," for similar political reasons.[49]

Again,

> The heretics burnt in Mary's reign had been popularised as the victims of Spain by Foxe's Book of Martyrs . . . The tortures of the Spanish Inquisition, the Netherlands Revolt, the Massacre of St. Bartholomew in France, the Spanish Armada, the Gunpowder Plot, all had been skilfully exploited to build up a picture of cruel Papists striving to dominate the world, and of God's Englishmen bravely thwarting them.[50]

Following Charles I's accession to the throne in 1625, his marriage to Princess Henrietta Maria of France shortly after, and William Laud's appointment to Canterbury in 1633, the Puritans feared a deep-laid plan to restore Roman Catholicism. Queen Henrietta Maria was a practicing Catholic with her own priests, Masses, and chapel. Arminianism was effectively popery. These fears were exacerbated by Laud's drive for uniformity of worship.

48. Ashley, *England in the Seventeenth Century*, 32.
49. C. Hill, *The Century of Revolution 1603–1714* (New York: W. W. Norton, 1961), 172–73.
50. Ibid., 57.

The Westminster Assembly was not based upon any assumptions of separation of church and state. These may seem axiomatic in many modern cultures, especially that of the United States; it was not so for the Assembly. In turn, "papists" were persons who combined ecclesiastical and political concerns. Believers were not to marry them because they were idolaters—note the allusion to both 1 and 2 Corinthians—and a threat to civil order.

However, there are boundaries within which marriage is not only impermissible, but cannot constitute marriage at all, even if it is sanctioned by human authority. These limits are spelled out in 24.4. No union can occur "within the degrees of consanguinity or affinity forbidden by the Word." Reference is made to Leviticus 18; 1 Corinthians 5:1; and Amos 2:7. Such unions are incestuous. They can never be made lawful. The parties are not, nor can they be, husband and wife. Moreover, the degrees apply to the kindred of the other party as well.

Section 24.5 deals with grounds for terminating an engagement or a marriage. In the first place, premarital adultery and fornication are legitimate reasons to end a premarital contract. Here the divines refer to Matthew 1:18–20, where Joseph decided to divorce Mary on the grounds that she was pregnant. The cultural contexts of first-century Israel and seventeenth-century England were, of course, quite different from our own, since a premarital contract was regarded as binding, rather than simply as a declaration of intention to marry. After marriage has occurred, the Confession continues, if one party commits adultery, the marriage can legitimately be ended by divorce. Behind this lies the civil legislation of the Mosaic covenant, according to which an adulterer was to be stoned to death. In this sense, an adulterous marriage partner was judicially dead, so the other party to the marriage could not only effect a divorce, but also proceed to marry someone else. The Assembly produced proof texts from Matthew 5:31–32; 19:9; and Romans 7:2–3.

The legitimate grounds for divorce are the focus of section 24.6. Here it is denied that there are any further grounds for divorce other than those listed, despite the tendency of sinful human beings to search for reasons to justify ending marriages. Adultery has already been mentioned. In addition to this, willful desertion is a basis for divorce. However, it is "such wilful desertion as can no way be remedied by the Church, or civil magistrate." Hence, concerted attempts to avert such a result are required before a divorce can be given. Moreover, these attempts must be both public and orderly. A thorough attempt is to be made to get to the root of the problem and to seek correction. Additionally, the parties seeking divorce on these grounds are not to be permitted to pursue the matter independently of the civil and ecclesiastical authorities. This "public and orderly course of proceeding" requires careful investigation of the case for both adultery and willful desertion, so as to ascertain whether these things have in fact occurred.[51]

It is noteworthy that the Assembly rejected a number of proposals relating to this chapter. In S682 M 3.8.46, the proposal that "persons before they marry ought to be able to performe necessary marriadge dutyes, and to make a good choyse" was not carried. Neither was the proposal that "children under parents Government ought to have their parents consent to their marriage, yet soe as they be not forced against their owne liking."[52] This does not necessarily mean that the majority of divines opposed such sentiments; the point is that they did not think it prudent to place them in a confession of faith. Along these lines, in S703 TH 10.9.46pm, the proposal that the chapter should include the statement that "death doth soe fully dissolve[s] the bond of marriage that the surviving party may marry another" was waived.[53] In all probability, the clause was considered superfluous.

51. Behind this, it may be surmised that there is an implicit rebuke to the Independents, for by the nature of independent church government it is hardly possible for "an orderly course" to be followed.
52. Van Dixhoorn, 6:335.
53. Ibid., 6:353.

14

Church and Sacraments

And we believe in one holy, catholic, and apostolic church;
we confess one baptism for the forgiveness of sins.

WCF 25–31; LC 60–65, 153–96

In both the Confession and the Larger Catechism, the church is considered in connection with the *ordo salutis* and the work of Christ. In the Larger Catechism, there is a distinction between the visible church (all who profess the true religion and their children) and the invisible church (the whole number of the elect). Not all in the visible church will be saved, since their profession of faith may be spurious and they may abandon it. However, the visible church enjoys God's protection and preservation against all enemies. In it, the saints have communion with one another and there are found the ordinary means of salvation, while in and through it the gospel is heard (LC 60–63). The invisible church—the elect, present and future—enjoys union and communion with Christ in grace, now in this life and in glory, in the future eternal kingdom (LC 64–65). We noted the significance of union with Christ in our discussion of the *ordo salutis*.[1]

Elsewhere I have argued that this stress on the church as the place where salvation is to be found is at the heart of the historic Christian faith. It is seen in the Apostles' Creed ("I believe in the holy catholic

---

1. Cf. also WCF 25.1–2.

church, the communion of saints, the forgiveness of sins"). These phrases are expanded in the Niceno-Constantinopolitan Creed ("and in one holy, catholic, and apostolic Church; we confess one baptism for the forgiveness of sins"), where the phrase "one baptism for the forgiveness of sins" indicates that the more cryptic "the forgiveness of sins" in the Apostles' Creed refers to baptism—and thus to the sacraments in general. Calvin, I have argued, follows this line of thought in his *Institutes*, where church and sacraments are the particular focus of Book 4. He refers approvingly to Cyprian's comment that one cannot have God for his Father who does not have the church for his mother. However, post-eighteenth-century evangelicalism moved into new territory, focusing on the individual and his or her personal faith, in abstraction from the church.[2] The validity of the historic tradition is that even if a person becomes a Christian seemingly in isolation merely by reading the Bible, it is the gospel message penned by the apostles and prophets in the Bible that brings him to faith—and the apostles and prophets were the foundation of the church.

Here we note the important statement in SC 88: "The outward and ordinary means whereby Christ communicateth to us the benefits of redemption, are his ordinances, especially the word, sacraments, and prayer; all which are made effectual to the elect for salvation."[3] These are found nowhere else than in the church. For all its flaws—there was then no properly constituted church in England!—it is there we hear the gospel and are nurtured in our faith.

Behind the Word as a means of grace lies the classic statement of the Second Helvetic Confession, 1: "Wherefore when this Word of God is now preached in the church by preachers lawfully called, we believe that the very Word of God is preached, and received of the faithful." Its marginal note adds: "The preaching of the Word of God is the Word of God."[4] Preaching was one of the main features, if not *the* main feature, of English Puritanism. One of the main causes of contention with the Laudian establishment was the restriction placed on preaching. Since preaching is a means of

2. See Letham and Macleod, "Is Evangelicalism Christian?"
3. See LC 154.
4. Schaff, *Creeds*, 3:237, 832.

320

grace, its restriction effectively diminished the opportunities for the grace of God to run freely in England.[5]

Anthony Tuckney argues that the preaching of the Word of God is the ordinary means of conversion. However, it is not the efficient cause of salvation, as if it had power in itself to bring sinners to faith. Rather, it is the ordinary mode, means, occasion, and condition through which faith is engendered. This is because conversion does not always follow preaching; the parable of the sower demonstrates that. The external word preached is powerless of itself (*destitutum*) without the internal operation of the Holy Spirit.[6]

The Church

WCF 25 iterates and expands on this theme. It distinguishes between the visible church of believers and their children[7] and the invisible church, composed of the elect of all ages and places. It stresses that outside the visible church "there is no ordinary possibility of salvation." It identifies the church with the kingdom of the Lord Jesus Christ. To the visible church "the ministry, oracles, and ordinances of God, for the gathering and perfecting of the saints, in this life, to the end of the world" have been committed. This is so, despite the fact that these churches are only "more or less pure" and that even the purest churches "are subject both to mixture and error." The efficacy of the Word, sacraments, and prayer is therefore not due to the church itself, nor to the relative level of its purity; it depends entirely on the presence of Christ and the Holy Spirit, according to his promise.

Some churches have degenerated, the Confession states, so as to become no churches of Christ, but synagogues of Satan (WCF 25.5). In view is the Church of Rome and probably also the Church of England under Laud. However, we should hesitate before regarding this as a blanket condemnation of the Roman Church. The Assembly accepted baptism in the name of the Trinity. If a person had been

---

5. See LC 155–60.

6. Tuckney, *Praelectiones theologicae*, 258–62.

7. In contrast with various types of Baptists, who claimed that the church is restricted to believers only.

baptized in the Roman Church, he was not to be rebaptized.[8] In this, Rome possessed one of the marks of the church and so could not be said to be no church of Christ at all. Moreover, the Assembly debates were full of references, not merely to the Fathers, but to a range of medieval Roman theologians, cited as authorities on particular points. The vigorous defense of the Reformation against Rome found in the Thirty-Nine Articles was, of course, assumed. The threats from France and Spain seen in the Armada, the Gunpowder Plot, and the feared "popish plot," were real. The more immediate pressures from Laud were still fresh in mind, although Laud was on record as being as consistently opposed to Rome as was the Assembly. What is probably foremost in mind is seen in WCF 25.6, where the papal claims are robustly rejected: "There is no other head of the Church but the Lord Jesus Christ. Nor can the Pope of Rome, in any sense, be head thereof: but is that Antichrist, that man of sin, and son of perdition, that exalteth himself, in the Church, against Christ and all that is called God."[9]

The Communion of Saints

Union and communion with Christ is the heart of salvation, according to the Larger Catechism. It comes to expression in the various elements of the *ordo salutis*, and is evident both in grace and, most fully, in glory. Here it is the foundation of the communion that the saints have with one another. This is explicit in WCF 26.1: union with Christ in grace and glory, as it is unfolded in LC 66–90, entails union with one another in love. For all the earlier hesitation on the three creeds, this chapter is an expansion and description of the phrase "the communion of saints" in the Apostles' Creed. Indeed, the doctrine of the creeds comes fully to expression in the Assembly's doctrine, even if the creeds themselves were not explicitly republished or reaffirmed.

8. See below, on WCF 28.6. In addition, see R. Letham, "Baptism in the Writings of the Reformers," *SBET* 7/2 (1989): 21–44. Martin Bucer, in *Quid de baptismate infantium* (Strasbourg, 1533), A. viii,b, for one, argued strongly that baptism does not belong to any particular church, but to God the Trinity, in accordance with the baptismal formula.

9. This statement should be seen in the light of the extensive outpouring of literature that claimed that the return of Christ was near.

The connection between union with Christ and love for all who are united to him is evident in WCF 26.2. This extends to practical matters, including the relief of material needs, as well as ministry and communion in the worship of God and "other spiritual services." There are two strong denials in WCF 26.3. First, union with Christ does not mean that the saints are equal to Christ, nor does it involve participation in his deity. Some of the extreme sectarians had asserted this to be so. The divines' denial is in harmony with the teaching of the Eastern church, stretching back to Athanasius, on deification—a doctrine that did not mean that the saints become divine, but rather that they are transformed by the Holy Spirit into the image of God throughout this life, with its fulfillment in the eternal kingdom.[10] The second denial is directed against sects such as the Levellers, who wanted private property abolished. The communion that the saints enjoy with each other does not erode or destroy the integrity of the individual, and in particular his or her property. This is an outflow of the doctrine of the Trinity: there is unity (and union), but in diversity.

This chapter of the Confession is a serious challenge to the church in all ages. The Assembly recognizes that the communion the church enjoys in Christ extends to all who call on the name of the Lord Jesus, whether they are in full agreement on every point of doctrine or not. Indeed, that love and union on the human level reflects the union that the saints have in Christ. A breach in the church entails questions concerning the reality of the relationship with Christ. This is a forgotten chapter, and its neglect bespeaks a guilty collective conscience.

The Sacraments (WCF 27; LC 161–64)

T. F. Torrance bemoans what he calls the Westminster Assembly's depreciation of the evangelical character of the sacraments as taught by the Reformation and the older Scottish tradition. He cites George Gillespie, who held the sacraments to be only confirming ordinances, not converting ordinances. Thus, Torrance says, the divines understood them in the popular Latin sense of oaths taken by enlisted

10. See Letham, *Through Western Eyes*, 253–63; N. Russell, *The Doctrine of Deification in the Greek Patristic Tradition* (Oxford: Oxford University Press, 2004).

soldiers, rather than as mysteries or signs and seals, which Robert Bruce affirmed.[11] Torrance takes Gillespie as representative of the whole Assembly, when he was not a member of it. Moreover, the chapter on the Lord's Supper in the Westminster Confession affirms that the faithful feed on Christ—which is not merely akin to a soldier's oath, but is more in line with a mystery. Again, Torrance says that baptism not only is a sign and seal of grace, but also exhibits it and is the instrumental cause of the Holy Spirit's conferring of it.[12] But this is clearly stated in the chapter on the sacraments. There grace is said to be "exhibited" in or by the sacraments (WCF 27.3)—and, as Wright argues, the verb had a stronger meaning then than it does now. Moreover, this grace exhibited in or by the sacraments is "conferred" by the Holy Spirit.[13] The sacraments are efficacious, but this conferral of grace is not due to any power they have in themselves. It does not depend on the faith or Christian life of the minister who dispenses them; it cannot even be negated if he is ungodly. If this were so, the sacraments would fluctuate in their validity from week to week or place to place. No, the grace conferred comes from the Holy Spirit and the word of institution, and behind that the promise of God (WCF 27.3). The sacraments belong to Christ.

Therefore, the sacraments are not bare signs. They are not merely symbolic, although there is symbolism aplenty. They are not to be reduced to the horizontal dimension of relationships among members of the church, as emblems of commitment to one another. The promise of God undergirds them, the activity of the Holy Spirit pervades them, and the grace of God is given in and through them. They are the ordinary way in which Christ communicates to us the benefits of salvation. The prime benefit of salvation is Christ himself. Salvation consists in union and communion with Christ in grace and glory (LC 65–90). In the sacraments, union and communion

11. See Robert Bruce, *The Mystery of the Lord's Supper: Sermons on the Sacrament Preached in the Kirk of Edinburgh by Robert Bruce in A.D. 1589* (trans. and ed. T. F. Torrance; London: James Clarke, 1958).

12. T. F. Torrance, *Scottish Theology*, 146.

13. I am grateful to Robert B. Strimple for drawing my attention to the vital distinction between the sacraments *exhibiting* the grace of God and the Holy Spirit *conferring* this grace through the sacraments. It is the difference between the efficient cause of grace (the Holy Spirit) and the instrumental cause (the sacraments).

with Christ are not only symbolized, but also exhibited visibly to our eyes and conferred by the Holy Spirit according to the promise of God. In them we encounter the Holy Trinity.

Baptism

The Assembly's discussions of baptism occurred in connection with both the Confession and the Directory for the Publick Worship of God. These debates are of great interest, are recorded in great detail, and so will occupy us to a great extent. A grasp of the general tenor of discussion is needed in order to understand what the Assembly intended to say. Much debate concerned practical administrative matters. However, the theological meat had to do with baptism's efficacy and how it relates to elect infants. This point has been lost for most modern Christians. Conservative Protestants have distanced themselves from the remotest connection with the Roman Catholic doctrine of baptism and, since the nineteenth century, from High Church Anglican sacramentalism too. In doing so, they have left themselves with a truncated sacramental theology in which the signs have been reduced to symbols. The classic Reformed sacramental theology has been largely lost.

Should Baptism Be Administered in the Congregation or in Private?

During debates on the Directory for the Publick Worship of God, in S256 TH 11.7.44, there was extended discussion on whether the sacrament of baptism was to be administered in the church or in the home. There were proponents of both positions, while many argued that the place of administration was inconsequential. Some pointed to biblical precedents, where it could not be established that particular baptisms were carried out in the presence of a congregation. Others connected baptism with the administration of the keys (discipline), arguing for its being done in the church. Moreover, it was thought, if baptism were administered in the home, the superstitious idea of the urgent and immediate necessity of baptism, akin to the teaching of Rome, might be promoted. In the Middle Ages, baptism was regarded as necessary for salvation, so infants were baptized right away, irrespective of location. In reaction to Rome, in some places hardly a child was brought to the church for baptism. According to Calamy, in London none had been baptized in the church for two or three years.[14] The eventual conclusion, in the Directory, was that baptism was not to be administered privately, but in the presence of the congregation, with the font located where everyone could see it. This was in line with Augustine's description of the sacraments as "visible words of God."

In this debate, as Wright points out, there was an astonishing omission: no one suggested the connection between the sacraments and the Word, an axiom of Reformed theology. It was a case of not seeing the forest for the trees. The debate was threatened by a quest for precise scriptural guidance, at the expense of theological connections.[15]

Are the Children Only of Godly Parents to Be Baptized?

The debate on the subjects of baptism, in S257 F 12.7.44, aroused the concern of continental Reformed churches,[16] due to the Assembly's focus on the parents, taken out of the context of an ongoing covenantal line. Guilielmus Apollonius, a minister at Middelburg writing to the Assembly on behalf of the Wallachrian Classis and expressing this and other misgivings, referred to the Reformed custom of baptizing infants even if their parents are ungodly, provided they come from a Christian stock. This practice was based on the belief that the nation is federally holy. Apollonius cited Calvin, Walaeus, and the Leiden Synopsis in support. In addition, he referred to the promise of God in the Abrahamic covenant that he would be the God of Abraham and his seed *throughout their generations*, which underlay the whole Reformed doctrine of the covenant of grace, and baptism in particular.[17] We noted how Apollonius's book was received with unanimous thanks—a highly unusual event—and when he was in

14. D. F. Wright, "Baptism at the Westminster Assembly," in *Westminster Confession into the 21st Century* (ed. Duncan), 1:176.
15. Ibid., 176–77. See Van Dixhoorn, 5:195–200.
16. Van Dixhoorn, 5:200–201.
17. Apollonius, *A consideration of certaine controversies*, 84–89.

England in the summer of 1645, he was invited to the Assembly to receive public recognition from the prolocutor.[18]

This question, as Apollonius remarked, had been addressed by Calvin. In reply to a letter from John Knox, asking whether it was legitimate to baptize the children of idolaters and excommunicates before the parents had testified to their repentance, Calvin replied, in a letter dated 7 November 1559, with the unanimous backing of the Company of Pastors of Geneva, strongly asserting its legitimacy. He affirmed that "God's promise comprehends not only the offspring of every believer in the first line of descent, but extends to thousands of generations." Baptism derives its force and efficacy from God's promise, which cannot be set aside by the superstitions of popery. It is therefore "unjust, when God, three hundred years ago or more, has thought them worthy of adoption, that the subsequent impiety of some of their progenitors should interrupt the course of heavenly grace." It is necessary in such cases that sponsors should be found to bring them up in the principles of pious religion, "but we see no reason for rejecting any child for whom a due pledge has been given."[19]

Again, the Leiden Synopsis (1625) had addressed the same question and answered identically. Adults who profess faith and infants who are born to faithful covenant parents ought to be baptized. On the other hand, the children of Mohammedans, Jews, and others who are outside the covenant are to be excluded from the sacrament.[20] However, the Synopsis continues, neither do we exclude from baptism those infants who are born from Christian stock, although their parents are ungodly, since that cannot invalidate the covenant or the efficacy of baptism. Moreover, in the new covenant the sons shall not bear the iniquity of the fathers, as is taught in Ezekiel 18.[21]

18. Carruthers, *Everyday Work*, 71.
19. John Calvin, "Letter DXLIX to John Knox," in *Selected Works of John Calvin: Tracts and Letters* (ed. H. Beveridge; repr., Grand Rapids: Baker, 1983), 7:74–75.
20. Polyander et al., *Synopsis purioris theologiae*, 655–57.
21. "Qui ex Christiana stirpe & baptizatis parentibus nati sunt, etsi ipsorum parentes per vitam improbam, aut fidem imputam foederis in Baptismo obsignati efficaciam adversus se irritam reddant; si ab iisdem parentibus aut eorum propinquis, sub quorum potestate sunt, iuxta ordinem in Ecclesiis nostris consuetum Baptismo offeruntur; quia sub novo foedere filius non fert iniquitatem Patris, & Deus nihilominus manet eiusmodi liberorum Deus." Ibid., 657–58.

In contrast, in the debate, Gataker was concerned that the draft Directory did not specify any commitment on the part of the father. Wilkinson referred to the case of those who moved to a new area to obtain work; what shall be done in this case? Calamy's comments indicate a flexibility in determining who should be baptized (in S301 TH 10.10.44): "The latitude of the judgements of many divines will baptize many children whose parents are not members."[22] It is clear that with Westminster, there is a definite restriction to the children of a believing parent or parents. There is a narrowing of the basis for infant baptism, although it was not an entirely novel development.[23]

Baptism and Remission of Sins

In S258–59 M 15.7.44 and TU 16.7.44, Woodcock was concerned with a lack of clarity in the proposed words "the water signifyes the bloud of Christ doing away the gult of sin." Gouge, in support, said the main thing in baptism is the blood of Christ. Burgess argued that either there is no sign at all of the blood in baptism or else water must be the sign, for the Holy Spirit applies the blood of Christ. Rayner pointed out that remission of sins is often signified by washing. On the other hand, Marshall thought that what answers to water is the Holy Ghost, according to Titus 3: "The gift of the Spirit is set out by water. I know nowhere in Scripture where water refers to the blood of Christ." To this, Gillespie countered by referring to two texts (Acts 2:38; Luke 3:3) where sealing in baptism is expressly connected with water. Moreover, he continued, water signifies washing—both remission and regeneration. Besides, there is more evidence for water signifying the blood of Christ than the Spirit. Titus does not mention baptism—it is connected to baptism by analogy.

George Walker took a middle position: some arguments point to the blood of Christ, others to the Spirit; it is clear that both are involved. Rutherford supported the connection between water and

22. Van Dixhoorn, 5:390.

23. That the practice was not new is clear from the French Confession, 35, which says that the children of believing parents should be baptized. I am here describing Reformed practice and debate in and up to the time of the Westminster Assembly, rather than expounding my own theological beliefs as such.

the remission of sins. It is undeniable, he argued, that remission of sins is the proper fruit sealed in baptism. In turn, there must be some sign conferring this fruit—and all interpreters expound it of baptism [referring to Ephesians 5:25–26]. For Herle, Christ is not divided; his blood has both faculties. Marshall reentered the debate, affirming that pardon of sin and justification are fully exhibited in baptism. The Spirit applies all those benefits to us; the question is to what water refers. Seaman thought it referred to both, but especially the blood of Christ, since it is by his blood that the Spirit is procured. Eventually on motion it was resolved: "signifying the washing away of the guilt of sin by the blood of Christ."[24]

What Does Paul Mean in 1 Corinthians 7:14 in Calling the Children of a Believing Parent Holy?

In the next session, S259 TU 16.7.44, the divines debated the proposed words "they are Christians & holy" in relation to infants presented for baptism.[25] A lengthy dispute pertained to what Paul had in mind. Are those baptized holy in reality or are they to be considered holy merely in federal terms, by being in a covenantal relationship with God, which may or may not involve the regenerating presence of the Holy Spirit?

Thomas Goodwin claimed that the holiness in view is such that if they die they will be saved. He was uncertain whether they have the holiness of election or regeneration, but he thought they have the Holy Ghost. In short, Goodwin thought that those baptized are to be regarded as really holy, rather than simply federally holy.

Lazarus Seaman countered by pointing out that this is to make a different ground for baptism. Goodwin replied by denying that infants are actually saved, but affirming that we are to judge them so. This was too much for Stephen Marshall, who said that Goodwin was wrong: our judgment of charity must not determine whom we admit to the sacrament. We have no warrant to judge that they are saved. It is sufficient that the infants of believing parents are federally holy. Rutherford agreed, pointing out that real and federal holiness

24. Van Dixhoorn, 5:201–3.
25. Ibid., 5:204–7, where the comments that follow are all to be found.

are different. The Lord has election and reprobation among infants; if they are in a state of salvation, how can any be lost?

To this barrage of opposition, Goodwin insisted that the question is not about the reality (whether or not the infant is regenerate) but "how I am to judge of them. I cannot judge that all are holy & saved, I judge so of this child & that child." Marshall pointed to a clear mistake in Goodwin's interpretation and application: the minister is to judge and believe that they are holy with the holiness Paul speaks of, not with any real holiness. While for Goodwin, the holiness in 1 Corinthians 7:14 is the holiness of salvation, Marshall's rebuttal was that saving holiness infallibly saves. His underlying assumption was that since not all who are baptized will be saved, Paul cannot be referring to saving holiness. Goodwin did not give up. He agreed that an infallible judgment about an infant's salvation was impossible, but what Paul had in view was a judgment compatible with the promise—an indefinite faith grounded on an indefinite promise.

Vines countered Goodwin by denying that the text had anything to do with the judgment of the minister about the child. It applied to each and every child in relation to the parents from whom they proceed. The holiness must be present in each one who comes into the category described in the text. If the infants were really holy, there would be a passing down of such holiness from the parents, and so they would be born regenerate and really holy. Moreover, whatever the kind of holiness intended in the text, it is altogether different from the judgment of the minister. Walker then underlined the distinction between federal and real holiness—many are called holy who are yet wicked and profane. Seaman pointed out that "federall holnesse is the true ground of administration of sacraments."

Goodwin returned to the debate to state that it is not a holiness by traduction, but only by way of designation. Palmer put the text in its proper context. Paul, he said, is not speaking of what we are to judge, but of a case of conscience, whether if one parent is an unbeliever that makes the child unclean. The apostle says no—the child is holy. He speaks of the state of such children, and so it must be a universal proposition and so we are bound to believe it of each and every one. For his part, Goodwin pointed out that Palmer's argument would also apply in 1 Corinthians 7:14 to the unbelieving spouse; holiness in the Old Testament refers to the judgment passed on them, and so it is a universal proposition.

The Directory eventually concluded that the children of believers are Christians and federally holy before baptism, and therefore that they are to be baptized. Goodwin's argument for the real holiness of the infants aroused great concern. It appeared either to mean that all infants would certainly be saved, or to undermine election and reprobation. In the end, the exegesis of the passage was left unresolved.[26]

Baptism and Regeneration

Much discussion centered on the relationship between baptism and regeneration. This is a connection that conservative Protestants tend to deny or ignore, but was a commonplace in the classic Reformed period. On the one hand, Westminster did not share the Roman Catholic belief that the sacraments are efficacious *ex opere operato* (by the fact of being performed), but neither did they sympathize at all with the Anabaptist view that they were merely symbolic.

In the debates on the Directory for the Publick Worship of God, in S260 F 19.7.44, the Assembly considered the proposed words "joyne the inward baptisme with the outward baptisme." Except for Gataker, there was consistent agreement on the connection between baptism and regeneration. Vines thought that we pray that the ordinance be effectual to its use. However, Gataker wanted to know what biblical evidence there was for baptism being an instrument of regeneration, since the general teaching of Reformed divines was that only the Word brings grace. Calamy felt it surprising that anyone should exclude the Spirit from the time of baptism. Whitaker agreed with Vines on the need for prayer that baptism be effectual: "I conceive we may pray & should pray that God would at time give them the inward washing. We are said to be baptized into Christ. The child is as capable of the working of the spirit in baptisme as afterwards." Palmer agreed, not knowing how we should pray otherwise. Seaman was content with the proposed wording. Herle thought the word "instrument" is of great and dangerous use in the context. Gataker preferred "that as the child

---

26. Wright, "Baptism at the Westminster Assembly," 181.

is baptized outwardly with water, soe he may be baptized inwardly by his spirit." Palmer affirmed: "We doe it in the name of God, not only by his command, but as his Instruments, he baptizeth. If he doe it, he doth it inwardly as well as outwardly."[27]

Later, in S566 M 5.1.45(46), when the chapter on baptism was being considered, the proposed clause concerning "the grace of God bestowed sometime before" was debated.[28] Whitaker professed his inability to find how baptism conferred grace, while recognizing that "our divines do hold it" and that, when opposing the papists, they say it is more than a sign and a seal. He referred to Chamier, who said the grace signified is exhibited; "so it is in the French Confession; it doth *efficaciter donare*. It does not do so *ex opere operato*." He produced other arguments in support. First, what Scripture attributes to baptism we are to ascribe. Baptism is an ordinance to effect those ends, "an ordinance of ingrafting into Christ & of our spirituall regeneration & new birth." We are baptized for the remission of sins. Baptism saves— it is a saving ordinance, the sign accompanied by the thing signified; and without grace none of these things can be. Second, if the Word instrumentally confers grace, so does baptism. Third, since the Eucharist is a sacrament of our spiritual growth, in the same proportion it holds with baptism. "That which a minister is bound to pray for, that he is bound to beleive."

Palmer was skeptical of Whitaker's argument. Baptism differs from the Word and the Eucharist, he maintained, in both of which the recipients are regarded as having grace already; this is not so with baptism. However, it is not a naked sign—there is a union in the sacrament, for whatever is promised in the word is granted by participation in the sign.[29] Whitaker was not to be deflected from his case: "The scripture speaks more about conferring then it doth either of signing and sealing." Wright notes that the word "exhibit" was stronger in meaning than it is in modern English, being closer to "convey."[30] In earlier debates (see S302 F 11.10.44), Dr. Smith had averred "that baptism

27. Van Dixhoorn, 5:208–10.

28. Ibid., 6:235–57, in which the record of the following debate is to be found.

29. Wright finds Palmer difficult to follow here. Wright, "Baptism at the Westminster Assembly," 167.

30. Ibid., 168.

saves sacramentally is noe such incongruous speech."[31] Wright agrees that "the Westminster divines viewed baptism as the instrument and occasion of regeneration by the Spirit, of the remission of sins, of ingrafting into Christ (cf. 28.1). The Confession teaches baptismal regeneration."[32] While the Catechisms speak only of baptism as a "sign and seal," the Directory's model prayer goes much further. Wright calls this the Confession's "vigorous primary affirmation."[33] In it, the minister declares of the children baptized that "they are Christians, and federally holy before baptism, and therefore are they baptized."[34] This is accompanied by prayer that the Lord "would receive the infant now baptized, and solemnly entered into the household of faith, into his fatherly tuition and defence, and remember him with the favour that he sheweth to his people," and that he would "make his baptism effectual to him."[35]

Excursus 6: The Reformed Doctrine of Baptism to 1643

Before the Assembly convened, two prominent Westminster divines wrote important treatises on baptism, addressing the connection between baptism and regeneration in detail. Cornelius Burgess, in his *Baptismall regeneration of elect infants* (1629),[36] cites the Bible, the Fathers (Cyprian, Gregory of Nazianzus, Athanasius, Chrysostom, Jerome, Ambrose, Augustine), the Reformed confessions, and an array of Reformed theologians (Vermigli, Zanchius, Musculus, Junius, Bucer, Calvin, Pareus, Danaeus, Chamier) and English divines (Ames, Jewel, Whitaker, Fulke, Davenant, White, Featley, Hooker, Thomas Rogers, Thomas Taylor, and Aynsworth) in support of his view. He refers to the Second Helvetic Confession, the Scots Confession, the French Confession, the Belgic Confession, and the Heidelberg Catechism. Burgess's argument is that regeneration is twofold.

31. Van Dixhoorn, 5:395.
32. Wright, "Baptism at the Westminster Assembly," 169.
33. Ibid., 170.
34. "The Directory for the Publick Worship of God," in *The Confession of Faith, the Larger and Shorter Catechisms with the Scripture Proofs at Large Together with the Sum of Saving Knowledge* (Applecross: Publications Committee of the Free Presbyterian Church of Scotland, 1970), 383.
35. Ibid., 384.
36. Cornelius Burgess, *Baptismall regeneration of elect infants, professed by the Church of England, according to the Scriptures, the primitive Church, the present Reformed Churches, and many particular divines apart* (Oxford: I. L. for Henry Curteyn, 1629) [STC 632.01].

There is an infusion of grace by the Holy Spirit at the baptism of elect persons, including elect infants, while actual regeneration, which produces faith, occurs at effectual calling.

Daniel Featley, in *A Second parallel together with a writ of error served against the appealer* (1626), is in broad agreement with Burgess, saying that "the inward grace ordinarily accompany the outward signe, and we ought to beleeve, by the iudgement of Charity, that all who are baptised are truly regenerate." He also acknowledges, as Burgess does, that all who are baptized are not actually regenerate by the judgment of precise and infallible truth. "This is not alwaies," as the fathers speak, but those who are not so regenerated are not elected.[37]

For both Burgess and Featley, all elect persons are regenerate in the initial sense at baptism and in the actual sense at effectual calling. On the other hand, nonelect persons are not regenerate in the initial sense at baptism, nor are they in the actual sense either. However, since we do not know who the elect are, we are by the judgment of charity to judge that all who are baptized are regenerate at baptism in the initial sense.[38]

The Reformed confessions are clear on the connection between baptism and regeneration. While they consistently oppose the Roman Catholic doctrine of *ex opere operato*, which asserts that the sacraments are efficacious by the fact of their use, they are equally severe on those who would reduce baptism and the Lord's Supper to mere symbols.

The Tetrapolitan Confession, drawn up by Martin Bucer in 1530, asserts that baptism "is the washing of regeneration, that it washes away sins and saves us."[39] The First Helvetic Confession of 1536, composed by a committee consisting of Bullinger, Grynaeus, Myconius, Jud, and Menander, assisted by Bucer and Capito, maintained that the sacraments are efficacious; they are not empty signs, but consist of the sign and the substance. "For in baptism the water is the sign, but the substance and spiritual thing is rebirth and admission into the people of God." All sanctifying power is to be ascribed to God alone. Baptism "is a bath of regeneration which the Lord offers and presents to his elect with a visible sign through the ministry of the Church."[40] Both of these early Reformed statements clearly allude to Titus 3:5.

37. Daniel Featley, *A second parallel together with a writ of error served against the appealer* (London: Robert Milbourne, 1626) [STC 834.09], 90.

38. On the relationship between baptism and regeneration, see also Featley, *The dippers dipt* [Wing 2245:15]. Featley talks of baptism as the laver of regeneration (10–11), which was common currency in the debates at Westminster. See also Polyander et al., *Synopsis purioris theologiae*, 653.

39. Cochrane, *Reformed Confessions*, 74.

40. Ibid., 107–8.

A quarter of a century elapsed before the French Confession was drawn up in 1559, following a draft by Calvin. Chapters 34–38 refer to the sacraments. Chapter 35 states that although we are baptized only once, the gain that it symbolizes to us reaches over our whole life and to our death. In chapter 37, we read that "in the Lord's Supper, as well as in baptism, God gives us really and in fact that which he there sets forth to us; and that consequently with these signs is given the true possession and enjoyment of that which they present to us" (*Dieu nous donne réellement et par effet ce qu'il y figure. Et partant, nous joignons avec les signes la vraie possession et jouissance de ce qui nous est là présenté*). The next chapter speaks of the water of baptism testifying to us in truth the inward cleansing of our souls in the blood of Jesus Christ by the efficacy of his Spirit.[41] The Confession makes a close connection between the sign and the reality: the Holy Spirit gives the reality to which the sign testifies. This is a connection, not an identity. By baptism, we are ingrafted into the body of Christ, so as to be washed and cleansed by his blood and renewed in purity of life by his Holy Spirit. The washing and renewal are consequent to baptism and depend on the Spirit, not the water. Baptism is "a sacrament of faith and penitence" (*un sacrament de foi et de pénitence*), according to article 35; it is rendered efficacious by the Holy Spirit through faith.

Questions 69–73 of the Heidelberg Catechism are notable:

Q. 69: How is it signified and sealed unto thee in holy Baptism that thou hast part in the one sacrifice of Christ on the cross? A: . . . that Christ has appointed this outward washing with water, and has joined therewith this promise, that I am washed with his blood and Spirit from the pollution of my soul, that is, from all my sins, as certainly as I am washed outwardly with water whereby commonly the filthiness of the body is taken away.

Q. 70: What is it to be washed with the blood and Spirit of Christ? A: It is to have the forgiveness of sins from God, through grace . . . and also to be renewed by the Holy Ghost, and sanctified to be members of Christ. . . .

Q. 72: Is the outward washing of water itself the washing away of sins? A: No; for only the blood of Jesus Christ and the Holy Spirit cleanse us from all sin.

Q. 73: Why, then, doth the Holy Ghost call Baptism the washing of regeneration and the washing away of sins? A: . . . to teach us that as the filthiness of the body is taken away by water, so our sins are also taken away by the blood and Spirit of Christ . . . [and] by this divine pledge and token he may assure us that we are as really washed from our sins spiritually as our bodies are washed with water.[42]

41. Ibid., 156–57.
42. Schaff, *Creeds*, 3:329–31.

Here the sign (washing with water) and the reality (cleansing from sin and regeneration) are paralleled, rather than directly conjoined.

The Belgic Confession (1561) points in article 33 to the sacraments as "visible signs and seals of an inward and invisible thing, by means whereof God worketh in us by the power of the Holy Ghost . . . the signs are not in vain or insignificant, so as to deceive us." This is so because Jesus Christ is the true object presented by them, without whom they would be of no moment (*signes et sceaux visibles de la chose intérieure et invisible, moyennant lesquels Dieu opère en nous par le vertu du Saint-Esprit. Les signes donc ne sont pas vains et vides pour nous tromper et décevoir*).[43] Article 34, on baptism, states that the sacrament "signifies that as water washes away the filth of the body . . . so the blood of Christ, by the power of the Holy Ghost, internally sprinkles the soul, cleanses it from its sins, and regenerates us from children of wrath unto children of God" (*nous significant par cela que comme l'eau lave les ordures du corps . . . ainsi le sang de Christ par le Saint-Esprit, fait le même intérieurement en l'âme, l'arrosant et nettoyant de ses péchés et nous régénérant d'enfants de colère en enfants de Dieu*). "Therefore the ministers administer the sacrament, that which is visible, but our Lord gives what is signified by the sacrament, namely, the gifts and invisible grace; washing, cleansing, and purging our souls of all filth and unrighteousness; renewing our hearts and filling them with all comfort; giving unto us a true assurance of his fatherly goodness; putting on us the new man, and putting off the old man with all his deeds. Neither does baptism avail us only at the time of baptism but also through the whole course of our lives" (*Et toutefois ce baptême ne profite pas seulement quand l'eau est sur nous, et que nous la recevons, mais profite tout le temps ne nostre vie*).[44]

The Scots Confession, composed by John Knox in 1560, in article 21, asserts that the sacraments are instituted to "seill in their hearts the assurance of his promise, and of that most blessed conjunction, union, and societie, quhilk the elect have with their head Christ Jesus. And this we utterlie damne the vanitie of thay that affirme Sacramentes to be nathing ellis bot naked and baire signes. No, wee assuredlie beleeve that be Baptisme we ar ingrafted in Christ Jesus, to be made partakers of his justice, be quhilk our sinnes ar covered and remitted."[45]

The Thirty-Nine Articles of the Church of England (1563, 1571), in article 25, "Of the Sacraments," maintains that they are not only badges

---

43. Cochrane, *Reformed Confessions*, 213.
44. Ibid., 214.
45. Schaff, *Creeds*, 3:467–70.

and tokens of Christian men's profession, but "certaine sure witnesses and effectuall signes of grace and Gods good wyll towardes vs, by the which he doth worke invisiblie in vs, and doth not only quicken, but also strengthen and confirme our fayth in hym." According to article 26, the unworthiness of ministers does not hinder the effect of the sacraments, since they belong to Christ. Thus baptism, says article 27, is "a signe of regeneration or newe byrth, whereby as by an instrument, they that receaue baptisme rightly, are grafted into the Church: the promises of the forgeuenesse of sinne, and of our adoption to be the sonnes of God, by the holy ghost, are visibly signed and sealed: fayth is confyrmed: and grace increased by vertue of prayer vnto God."

The Second Helvetic Confession (1562, 1566), drawn up by Bullinger and the most widely accepted of all Reformed symbols, discusses baptism in chapter 30. Inwardly we are regenerated, purified, and renewed by God through the Holy Spirit; outwardly we receive the assurance of the greatest gifts in the water, by which also those gifts are represented, and, as it were, set before our eyes to behold.[46]

A later work, demonstrative of mainstream Reformed opinion shortly after the Synod of Dort, is the Leiden Synopsis, composed by four leading Dutch theologians in support of the Canons of Dort, and first published in 1625. Here, citing Titus 3:5, baptism is said to seal remission of sins and regeneration.[47] There is a connection between the outward sign and the washing away of sins (Rev. 1:5; 1 Cor. 6:11; Eph. 5:27; Titus 3:5), a sacramental union between the sign and the thing signified (*in unione illa sacramentali, quae est inter signum & rem signatum*). This is a relative conjunction—the *signum* and the *res*—and it is set before the eyes on condition of faith (*sub conditione fidei*). Christ by his Spirit unites us with himself; no creature is capable of this. Thus, God appeals both to our ears and to our eyes.[48] The Synopsis rejects Rome's doctrine of *ex opere operato*, and also that of the Lutherans— the ubiquitarians—who tie regeneration to baptism. On the other hand, it opposes those who distinguish between adult and infant baptism, granting that adult baptism is a sign and seal of regeneration, but thinking that infant baptism is an instrument of regeneration just begun *(signum & signaculum regenerationis acceptae esse concedant, sed infantium Baptismum instrumentum regenerationis inchoandae esse velint)*. This distinction is nowhere found in Scripture, since baptism is of one kind. This seems to be aimed against views

---

46. Cochrane, *Reformed Confessions*, 282.
47. Polyander et al., *Synopsis purioris theologiae*, 644–47.
48. Ibid., 648–49.

later expressed by both Burgess and Featley.[49] The efficacy of baptism is not tied to the time of administration. Faith and repentance are necessary, as is love. When a seed is sown, it does not germinate at the same moment; it is dependent on rain and heat. So neither the word nor the sacrament is effective at the moment of administration, but at the time when the blessing of the Holy Spirit comes. *(Efficaciam ergo Baptismi non alligamus ad momentum illud, quo aqua externa corpus tingitur.)* In infants of the covenant *semen et spiritum fidei ac resipiscentiae statuendam esse, contendimus; quam in adultis, in quibus actualis fidei & resipiscentiae professio est necessaria. Deinde, quemadmodum semen in terram conjectum, non semper eodem momento incrementa sumit, sed quando pluvia aut calor coelitus supervenit; ita nec verbum, nec Sacramenti signum semper primo sui momento est efficax, sed eo demum tempore, cum Spiritus sancti benedictio accedit.*[50]

The external power of baptism is as a seal. By this we mean two things. *Primo, certiorationem gratiae promissae, & a causa principali collatae aut conferendae. Secundo, eiusdem confirmationem & augmentum.* The promise, however, is joined to a condition of faith and repentance, so the grace is not sealed except to those who believe and repent. However, baptism is more than a sign and seal, for it exhibits and confers the promised *res*, due to the promise of God and the life-giving Spirit. *(Sacramentum, sicuti & reliqua, etiam esse rei promissae exhibitivum, quia in legitimo & digno huius Sacramenti usu haec quae promittuntur, per Spiritum sancti fidelibus non tantum offeruntur, sed etiam reipsa exhibentur & conferuntur: quum Deus sit verax in obsignatione suarum promissionum, & Sacramenta nostra non sunt appendices occidentis literae sed vivificantis spiritus.)*[51] It is in reality the laver of regeneration *(est lavacrum regenerationis)*, which has perpetual efficacy.[52]

We have already noted the position of the Synopsis on the subjects of baptism. No special time for it is prescribed—this is a matter of church order. However, it is to be joined with the preaching of the Word, whether in public or private *(sive in locus publicus fuerit, sive privatorum domus).*[53] Apart from times of persecution, it is better done in public.

In summary, the Reformed confessions teach a conjunction between the sign (baptism in water in the name of the Trinity) and the reality (the grace given in Christ, regeneration, cleansing from sin, and so on). From this, it is legitimate for the one to be described in terms of the other; this

49. Ibid., 650.
50. Ibid., 651.
51. Ibid., 652.
52. Ibid., 653–54.
53. Ibid., 659.

is found in Scripture itself in such expressions as "baptism saves" (1 Peter 3:21). The divines repeatedly refer to baptism as "the laver of regeneration." However, at the same time there is also a distinction between the sign and the reality. Baptism is not salvation; it signifies and exhibits salvation by the grace of God in Christ. The power of baptism resides not in the water but in the Holy Spirit, who applies God's grace to his elect people in his own time. He is sovereign; salvation is by grace. The reality is distinct from the sign, yet the sign cannot be detached from the reality, for the two go together. As the Belgic Confession puts it, "The ministers dispense the sacrament . . . the Lord gives what is signified."[54]

Is Dipping a Legitimate Mode of Baptism?[55]

Three sessions, S261 M 22.7.44 through S263 TH 8.8.44, were occupied by discussion of the lawfulness of dipping (immersion) as a mode of baptism.[56] The Assembly was divided right down the middle. In S261 M 22.7.44, Nye argued that dipping should not be excluded; if there is a ground for it, it should be put in the text to that effect. Both Woodcock and Tuckney thought that dipping, like sprinkling, was covered by "washing," which the word *baptidzo* signified. Jeremiah Burroughs, supporting Nye, wondered how sprinkling could remind us of burial with Christ. Woodcock's rejoinder was that if the mode should represent burial, how could this be done with dying? Chambers, referring to the baptism of the Philippian jailor in Acts 16:33, claimed that the apostles must have baptized by sprinkling, since the whole household could not have been baptized in the house by dipping. Gataker, however, thought Chambers's argument not proved; it is neither impossible nor improbable that they could have been baptized by dipping—especially since *baptidzo* means "to wash by dipping."

54. My translation, article 34; see Schaff, *Creeds*, 3:426; Cochrane, *Reformed Confessions*, 214. The original reads, "Les Ministres nous donnent de leur part le Sacrement et ce qui est visible; mais notre Seigneur donne ce qui est signifié par le Sacrement."

55. On the debates in the Reformed churches on the mode of baptism—immersion, pouring, or sprinkling—see Old, *Shaping of the Reformed Baptismal Rite*, 264–82. See also Letham, "Baptism in the Writings of the Reformers." On immersion or dipping as the mode of baptism, see Martin Bucer, *In epistolam d. Pauli ad Romanos* (Basel, 1562), 321; Calvin, *Institutes*, 4.15.19; Vermigli, *In epistolam S. Pauli apostoli ad Romanos commentarii doctissimi*, 199; J. C. McLelland, *The Visible Words of God: An Exposition of the Sacramental Theology of Peter Martyr Vermigli A.D. 1500–1562* (Edinburgh: Oliver and Boyd, 1957), 140.

56. For the following debate, see Van Dixhoorn, 5:201–10.

Moreover, if the apostles sometimes used sprinkling, this would not exclude dipping at other times, since both John's and Jesus' disciples washed by dipping. Ley agreed that dipping should not be omitted, but he reminded the Assembly that in early times there was no lack of baptism by sprinkling. If we were to say that dipping is necessary, we would be promoting Anabaptism.

Seaman insisted that the question was whether Christ instituted sprinkling or dipping—or both. If the word means "dipping," he could see no warrant for sprinkling. Moreover, if it has that meaning in the institution of Christ, then it must be administered that way now. There must be an analogy with the thing signified. Walker asked how 5,000 people could be dipped in one day. What must we dip—the whole person or some part? Hoyle referred to 2 Kings 3, where the pouring out of water on Elijah's hands signifies washing. Arrowsmith argued that there are many places in Scripture where the word does *not* mean "washing by dipping"—the washing of hands and tables, baptizing with the Holy Ghost, Israel being baptized into Moses—so how can these passages require immersion in water? The cloud might have dropped on the Israelite heads, but this would be closer to sprinkling than dipping. Gataker reminded everyone that the debate was not about the necessity of dipping, but since the word means "to dip," there was no reason to exclude it. But Rutherford said that all divines recognize that the word means "to wash"; the particulars are therefore either dipping or sprinkling. However, he saw no ground or warrant or at least necessity for dipping. Gillespie acknowledged that if the proper meaning was "dipping," it would follow that we do not baptize except we wash by dipping. Palmer argued from Mark 7:4, referring to Bucer, that *baptidzo* means "pouring." For Woodcock, the word meant "washing."

In S262W 7.8.44, the divines debated the proposition "agreeable to the Institution of Christ." An unnamed participant set forth the case that there are "3 wayes [of baptizing]: *aspersio, perfusio*, powring water over the whole body as in Muscovy, & I have heard it used in Spaine. This may have ground that the Holy Ghost is said to be powred out. 3. Dipping, I thinke, was commonly used in the primitive church. For the lawfullnesse of all 3, I make noe question."[57] Marshall

---

57. Van Dixhoorn, 5:214.

pleaded with the Assembly not to limit baptism to one particular mode. Temple disagreed. Against the argument that the child must be dipped, with sprinkling used only in case of weakness, he replied that there was no cogent argument that there ever was dipping. Marshall agreed that to restrict baptism to dipping would lead to great inconveniences. Seaman confessed that he had been very favorable to dipping, but now questioned whether there was any ground for it, as the Anabaptists contended. Nye affirmed that no one was advocating dipping as the Anabaptists did, but suggested a mean between these two positions. Rutherford disputed the claim that the Word of God says nothing about it. All grant that baptism by sprinkling is lawful; then something is determined in the Word of God concerning it. The question is about dipping. Coleman commented that baptism was practiced long before the time of Christ. Proselytes "went in up to the necke, & the party to be baptized did dip himselfe all over. The Hebrew word is for dipping, 3 Act. 18, they went into the water."[58] This assertion met a riposte from Lightfoot, citing Rabbi Solomon to the effect that proselyte baptism was not by dipping, but sprinkling. Rutherford also denied that the Jews dipped. In Hebrews 9, the Book of the Covenant was sprinkled. In Acts 8, both Philip and the eunuch went down into the water; the word must apply to both, so if dipping is meant, then Philip was dipped also. Seaman acknowledged that there were great differences in the use of the word, both transitively and intransitively. Bridge felt that the mode most agreeable to apostolic practice was pouring. Marshall brought the Assembly back to the point: the debate did not require a proof that dipping was essential, but that it must be only by sprinkling. Gillespie held that the debate concerned a matter of practice, not of necessity. Marshall responded: "I desire such a way as may not determine mens practise to one."[59] Palmer insisted that those whom John baptized were dipped because of the words *hypo tou*—"under him."

Eventually, "the question twice put: 25 for Affir: 24 for neg.; 24 for affirmative, 25 for the negative."[60] According to Lightfoot, "There

58. Ibid., 5:215.
59. Ibid., 5:217.
60. Ibid., 5:218.

grew a great heat upon it: and when we had done all, we concluded upon nothing in it."[61]

The following day, in S263 TH 8.8.44, the question was put again for the third time. It was resolved that the proposition be debated further. A motion was passed agreeing to the lawfulness of sprinkling. Another motion was proposed to debate the lawfulness of dipping, reopening the previous debate. Gataker stated that this debate would arouse a great deal of prejudice. Henderson remarked that the question is whether there be any warrant from the institution or apostolic example. Gataker said that if the Assembly agreed there was apostolic authorization for dipping, people will then ask about the biblical basis for sprinkling. Walker argued that there is no ground in Scripture for dipping, as there is for sprinkling. Nye pointed out that it was unnecessary to discuss whether there was any warrant for dipping: "We do not say that anything *de modo* is *ex institutione*. We do not say of sprinkling that it is *de institutione*."[62] Lightfoot suggested that the question could be on the sufficiency of dipping rather than its lawfulness. Gillespie argued that the question is not whether dipping be *ex institutione Christi* but whether the lawfulness of dipping can be proved from Scripture. For Nye, washing is lawful, and so whatever is washing is permissible, whether it be dipping, sprinkling, or pouring. Palmer begged the Assembly: let's stop the debate—we are getting nowhere. Walker affirmed that dipping may be lawfully used, but there was insufficient ground to commend it in a directory, while there was sufficient ground for sprinkling. Herle had the last recorded word, with the striking comment that "if you conclude against it [dipping], you condemne the reformed churches that practise it. Those that incline most to popery are all for sprinkling." The vote was taken, for the third time. The Assembly resolved that dipping was lawful.

An interesting note on this occurs in the *Annotations*, where on Romans 6:4 ("buried with him in baptism") we read: "In this phrase the Apostle seemeth to allude to the ancient manner of Baptisme, which was, to dip the parties baptized, and as it were to bury them under the water for a while, and then to draw them out

---

61. Lightfoot's journal, in *The Whole Works of the Rev. John Lightfoot* (ed. J. R. Pitman; London: Hatch and Son, 1824), 13:300.
62. Van Dixhoorn, 5:219.

of it, and lift them up, to represent the buriall of our old man, and our resurrection to newnesse of life."[63]

Should the Parents of an Infant to Be Baptized Be Required to Make a Profession of Faith?

On the question whether the parents of an infant to be baptized should be required to make a profession of faith, the debate was spread over four sessions—S300 W 9.10.44 through S303 M 14.10.44—and the Assembly was evenly divided for and against.[64] Again, a similar division occurred over whether such a profession should take the form of questions and answers. Throughout this debate, there was great stress on conformity with other Reformed churches.[65] The Assembly voted 28–16 to include a parental affirmation of faith by affirmative answers to creedal questions, but Parliament deleted the section in early 1645.[66]

Arguments in favor of professions of faith were based on their use in the Reformed churches, on the precedents from the ancient church, and on the example of the Philippian jailor (Acts 16:30–33). However, it was difficult to find much support from the Bible; no such profession was required before circumcision, it placed members of the church on the same ground as nonmembers, and it implied that federal holiness was not the basis for baptism. It was seen by some as a concession to the Anabaptists.[67]

The Teaching of the Assembly on Baptism

T. F. Torrance criticizes the Assembly for regarding baptism as a sign and seal of the covenant of grace, calling for the fulfillment of conditions, rather than a sacrament of the fatherhood of God.[68] This stems from the shape of Torrance's own theology, with

63. *Annotations*, on Romans 6:4.
64. It had also been discussed in S257 F 12.7.44 and S258 M 15.7.44.
65. Van Dixhoorn, 5:385–99.
66. Journals of the House of Commons, IV, 70; Journals of the House of Lords, VII, 264, cited by Wright, "Baptism at the Westminster Assembly," 171.
67. The *Annotations* reflect something of this in the comments on 1 Peter 3:20 ("baptism saves"), which is interpreted to mean that the confession of faith saves.
68. T. F. Torrance, *Scottish Theology*, 148.

its apparently universalist undertones. The point he misses is that salvation has already been seen in part as adoption, by which the elect are brought into the family of God, who is now their Father. Moreover, Torrance consistently ignores the Larger Catechism, where the whole *ordo salutis* and its outworking, including the church and the sacraments, is understood as union and communion with Christ in grace and glory.

For the Assembly, baptism admits the person baptized into the visible church, whether the one baptized is an adult professing faith or an infant. There was some debate as to whether the infant became a member of the covenant through baptism or whether he or she was to be baptized because of being in the covenant already. The drift of the argument on 1 Corinthians 7:14 was that the holiness in view was federal or covenantal due to the relationship with the godly parent, and that the infant was already in God's covenant.

However, baptism is more than an admission into the visible church. It is also a sign and seal of the covenant of grace. It is a sign because it is a sacrament, and so points to what is signified. It seals because it is a mark of ownership, for Christ has taken the one baptized as his own. The covenant of grace, of which baptism is a sign and seal, consists of ingrafting into Christ; the one baptized is a member of Christ and thus of his body, the church. This ingrafting into Christ includes regeneration, remission of sins, and sanctification. Thus, at the very start, in WCF 28.1 (and also in LC 165), baptism is brought directly into connection with the whole of salvation, from regeneration to sanctification. It signifies these things and it seals them. It is more than admission to the visible church. It is certainly more than a symbolic representation.

In WCF 28.2, baptism is said to be administered by means of water in the name of the Father, the Son, and the Holy Spirit. Baptism is Trinitarian. It belongs to God, not to the church, which simply administers it in the name of the Holy Trinity. This identifies baptism with the historic Christian church, including the Church of Rome and the Orthodox. It was one of the reasons why the Reformers resisted the Anabaptists so strongly and why the Assembly did not want to be identified in any way with their successors. These latter rejected the baptism of infants, whether by

Rome or the Church of England. In so doing, they were rejecting the sacrament conducted on behalf of the Trinity.

Moreover, baptism is only to be administered "by a minister of the Gospel, lawfully called thereunto." On the one hand, this rules out baptism by midwives, as practiced by Rome, when the life of the newborn child was in jeopardy. On the other, it also undercuts the sects, whose ministers were not lawfully called in the eyes of Parliament or the Assembly. The rationale for this restriction lies in the integral connection between the Word and the sacrament in Reformed theology. The sacrament is given its identity by the Word. The word of institution was necessary for a sacrament to be a sacrament. Hence, the one administering the sacrament had to be one capable of preaching the Word. Therefore, lawful calling by the church and ordination to the gospel ministry were essential in order to dispense the sacraments.

WCF 28.3 reflects the debate on dipping. Dipping is not necessary for baptism, since pouring and sprinkling are lawful modes of administration. This statement restricts itself to denying the Anabaptist claim that immersion was indispensable. The divines say this is not so. However, it does not rule out dipping. It is permissible, as well as sprinkling and pouring.

WCF 28.4 notes that the subjects of baptism are believers, together with the infants of one, or both, believing parents. In this, the Anabaptist denial of infant baptism is rejected. However, it is a restriction of the subjects of baptism in comparison with the general practice of the Reformed churches of the time. LC 166 adds that infants descending from a believing parent are in the covenant and so are to be baptized, thereby indicating again that the divines concluded that covenant membership preceded baptism, rather than being occasioned by it.

WCF 28.5, in opposition to Rome, denies the necessity of baptism for salvation. However, as Moore argues, the first clause—"Although it be a great sin to contemn or neglect this ordinance"—was probably directed against antipaedobaptists who failed to present their infant children for baptism. There are no complimentary references in the minutes to antipaedobaptists. They are uniformly described as "anabaptists" and invariably linked with antinomians.[69] In relation to the Roman error, we should recognize that it allowed the possibility of a "baptism of desire," where a person could be saved who, for reasons outside his control, could not be baptized before his death, provided that he desired baptism. However, the divines here oppose the more representative Roman claim for baptism, as an instrumental cause of salvation, having efficacy *ex opere operato*, by the fact of its being performed.

This latter point is challenged more directly in WCF 28.6. Baptism is efficacious for salvation, the Confession insists. However, this needs qualification. It is not to be understood in a temporal sense, as if at the moment of baptism the person baptized is regenerated and saved; there is no such temporal connection. Baptism is efficacious in uniting a person with Christ, regenerating and sanctifying him "in [God's] appointed time." Moreover, baptism is not efficacious for everyone who receives it. It is not automatic. It is effective for God's elect, "to such (whether of age or infants) as that grace belongeth unto." Since the Holy Spirit makes baptism efficacious as a means of grace, it is beyond the power of the church or its ministry to do this, nor does it happen automatically.

It is in this same section that the heart of the Assembly's view of baptism appears most clearly. Allowing for the above caveats, "the grace promised is not only offered, *but really exhibited, and conferred, by the Holy Ghost*" (italics added). It is not the case that baptism simply offers or demonstrates the grace of God, which is then received by the one baptized. Nor is it merely the fact that baptism is a visible demonstration of the gospel, setting forth washing from sins, death, and resurrection to newness of life. It is, of course, both of these things. However, it is something more. In baptism, the promised grace—regeneration, remission of sins, sanctification, and above all union with Christ—is *conferred* by the Holy Spirit. We have seen how this differs from the doctrine of the Church of Rome. Union with Christ, regeneration, cleansing from sin, and sanctification of the elect people of God is achieved through baptism by the Holy Spirit

69. J. D. Moore, "The Westminster Confession of Faith and the Sin of Neglecting Baptism," *WTJ* 69 (2007): 63–86.

"in God's own time." This is not by any power of the sacrament itself; *the Holy Spirit* confers grace; the efficacy is entirely his. Moreover, the Spirit can work as and how he pleases, so baptism is not absolutely indispensable for salvation. However, anomalous situations aside, God's promises of grace in Christ are dispensed by the Holy Spirit *through* baptism, as long as we bear in mind the divines' caveat that this is so in inseparable conjunction with the Word.[70] The connection is neither automatic nor temporal, but theological. The focus of LC 167 on improving our baptism—"all our life long"—corresponds on our side, in terms of our responsibility, to the side of divine efficacy. The Spirit works through means, in his own time, and so we are to work under his enabling throughout our life in response.

For these reasons, baptism can be administered only once. Christ died once for all on the cross; his atonement can be neither repeated nor prolonged. He rose from the dead but once, never again to die. If baptism were repeatable, it would question the finality of the work of Christ. That is why the Reformers resisted so strongly demands to rebaptize those who had received baptism as infants, including those like themselves who had been baptized in the Roman Church.[71] On the validity of Roman Catholic baptism, the French Confession (1559), drafted by Calvin, was particularly clear in article 28. While it condemned the papal assemblies, since the pure Word of God had been banished from them and the sacraments corrupted, "nevertheless, as some trace of the Church is left in the papacy, *and the virtue and substance of baptism remain,* and as the efficacy of baptism does not depend upon the person who administers it, we confess that those baptized in it do not need a second baptism. But, on account of its corruptions, we can not present children to be baptized in it without incurring pollution" (italics added).[72] The divines were well aware of this common position, and there is no evidence that they abandoned it. For the Assembly, if a person were to submit a second time to the baptismal rite, only one thing could happen—he would get wet.

---

70. This is not the theology of baptism commonly held today in conservative Protestant circles, or even in many Reformed and Presbyterian churches. Yet so integral to Reformed theology is its sacramentalism that claims to being Reformed must be challenged that lack this vital element.

71. See Letham, "Baptism in the Writings of the Reformers."

72. Schaff, *Creeds*, 3:376.

The Lord's Supper

Here, the position of the Assembly has often been taken for granted or ignored, with the result that important teachings of this chapter have virtually been forgotten. WCF 29.1 reads:

> Our Lord Jesus, in the night wherein He was betrayed, instituted the sacrament of His body and blood, called the Lord's Supper, to be observed in His Church, unto the end of the world, for the perpetual remembrance of the sacrifice of Himself in His death; the sealing all benefits thereof unto true believers, their spiritual nourishment and growth in Him, their further engagement in and to all duties which they owe unto Him; and, to be a bond and pledge of their communion with Him, and with each other, as members of His mystical body.

This first section recounts the founding of the Lord's Supper by Jesus and the purposes for which he gave it. There are five discernible reasons for it. First, it is a permanent memorial of his sacrificial death. This is an indisputable part of the sacrament, even though it is not the only part. LC 168 adds that Christ's death is "shewed forth" in the Supper. The second purpose is "the sealing all benefits [of His death] unto true believers." The benefits of Christ's death encompass the whole of redemption. The previous chapters in the Confession have listed the fruits of Christ's passion. Included are effectual calling, justification, adoption, sanctification, saving faith, repentance, good works, perseverance, and assurance (chapters 10–18). The Lord's Supper seals these benefits, affirming them and assuring us of their truth and reality. In the 1640s, a seal was something that authenticated or confirmed something, or attested a promise, often of a covenant.[73] Third, the Supper provides for true believers' "spiritual nourishment and growth in Him." Entailed here is feeding and sustenance, akin to the physical feeding that sustains our bodily lives. Not only is the Supper the occasion of our succor, but it also enables us to grow in union with Christ, as LC 168 stresses. Fourth, it engages true believers "in and to all duties which they owe unto

73. See *The Oxford English Dictionary*.

Him," which is also reiterated in LC 168. It impels us to obedience. On the one hand, the focus on the love of Christ, seen in his freely giving himself to the cross, moves us to follow him more faithfully. At the same time, the nourishment and consequent growth in Christ that we enjoy elicits an answering response on our part, given by the Holy Spirit, of thankful love and willing obedience. Fifth, the Lord's Supper is for true believers "a bond and pledge of their communion with Him, and with each other, as members of His mystical body." As LC 168 puts it, they "have their union and communion with him confirmed." Here the Confession points further toward union and communion with Christ, at the same time stressing that this union also has inseparable horizontal connections. We have communion with Christ, and at the same time, and as a direct corollary, communion with the other members of the body of Christ here on earth. Head and members are indissolubly united.

WCF 29.2 continues:

In this sacrament, Christ is not offered up to His Father; nor any real sacrifice made at all, for remission of sins of the quick or dead; but only a commemoration of that one offering up of Himself, by Himself, upon the cross, once for all: and a spiritual oblation of all possible praise unto God, for the same: so that the popish sacrifice of the mass (as they call it) is most abominably injurious to Christ's one, only sacrifice, the alone propitiation for all the sins of His elect.

The Confession here targets the Church of Rome. It distances itself radically from the dogma of the Mass. In particular, the priestly view of the church and its ministry that underlies Roman Catholic sacramentalism receives short shrift. "Christ is not offered up to His Father; nor any real sacrifice made"—in short, the minister is not a priest, and the Supper is not a sacrifice. Christ's offering is neither extended, repeated, nor prolonged. It was offered once for all, since it was perfect and complete for our redemption. Thus, in this sense the Supper is a memorial of a completed act, an act that took place "upon the cross, once for all." We are reminded here of the wonderful statement in article 31 of the Thirty-Nine Articles of the Church of England (1563, 1571): "The offering of Christ once made is that perfect redemption, propitiation and satisfaction . . . and there is none other satisfaction for man, but that alone."[74]

On the other hand, the Lord's Supper *is* a sacrifice of a kind—a spiritual sacrifice of praise to God, as Hebrews 13:15–16 puts it. We might even say ourselves that the reality on which it is founded is the one sacrifice of Christ on the cross, and so, in communion with him, we share in that perfect sacrifice. The problem with the Roman position lies in the sacrificial view of church and ministry and the consequent implication (even if official Roman Catholic dogma tries hard to maintain the once-for-all nature of the cross[75]) of a priestly, bloodless repetition. The outcome, the Confession states, is injurious to the perception of the work of Christ—exceedingly injurious, abominably injurious. The Confession can have no truck with the Mass, but its statements both here and later, while strong, are measured and have a certain restraint.

WCF 29.3 reads (see also LC 169):

> The Lord Jesus hath, in this ordinance, appointed His ministers
> to declare His word of institution to the people; to pray, and bless
> the elements of bread and wine, and thereby to set them apart
> from a common to an holy use; and to take and break the bread,
> to take the cup, and (they communicating also themselves) to give
> both to the communicants; but to none who are not then present
> in the congregation.

Here is spelled out the task of the minister and what he actually does. The minister is given this role by the Lord Jesus himself, and so he is appointed by the Lord whose supper it is and who has exclusive rights to determine what may and may not be done. He has appointed ministers and no one else to administer the sacraments (see 27.4) because the Word governs the sacrament, and thus a minister of the Word alone is authorized to preside. Thus, the very first thing—the matter of the utmost importance—is that his ministers "declare His word of institution to the people." This constitutes the sacrament—it is

---

74. Schaff, *Creeds*, 3:507.
75. See *The Catechism of the Catholic Church* (London: Geoffrey Chapman, 1994), 306–9.

a necessary condition for the Lord's Supper to be. Without a minister declaring the word of institution, there is no sacrament. Entailed in this is that private instances of the Eucharist, in which a loose aggregation of believers participate without "a minister of the Word lawfully ordained," are not instances of the Lord's Supper at all.

Second, the minister is "to pray, and bless the elements of bread and wine." Note, he does not effect a change of substance. They remain bread and wine. On the other hand, they are now set apart for a holy use. While we must not worship them and have no need to reserve them, we should still treat them respectfully and dispose of them appropriately, for they have been dedicated to a sacred purpose. We recall here that the giving of thanks at this point gives to the Supper the name of Eucharist.[76]

Third, the minister is "to take and break the bread" in the sight of the people. This entails a single loaf, in conformity with the practice of the early church (1 Cor. 10:16–17). The first name for the sacrament was "the breaking of bread." Here is why Augustine could call the sacrament a "visible word of God," for the breaking of the bread graphically portrays the breaking of Christ's body on the cross to deliver us from sin. The fraction thus takes place in the sight of the people.

Fourth and similarly, the minister takes the cup. Again, there is to be one cup, just as there is one loaf. The church, as one body for Christ, is not divided into one hundred or more fragments. He gives the cup to the laity, unlike Rome, for there is no fear in Protestantism of the blood of Christ spilling on the ground, since the wine remains simply wine.

Finally, the Confession warns against private instances of the Lord's Supper. This is a sacrament of the church, the body of Christ. It is decisively *not* to be understood as an individual, private, spiritual experience. It is corporate first, and individual only within that clearly understood and defined context.[77]

76. In addition, we note that the elements appointed by the Lord Jesus are "bread and wine," and that the right to determine these rests with him alone, and not with the temperance movement of the nineteenth century. While Jesus changed the water into wine, the temperance movement changed the wine into grape juice concentrate. No one has any right to change the elements of the Lord's Supper, any more than water may be replaced in baptism by orange juice. To do this is to usurp the authority of Christ.

77. On the problems of individualism in the Western world and its effect on the Christian church, see my book *The Work of Christ* and also my article "Is Evangelicalism Christian?"

The Confession goes on to say (29.4):

Private masses, or receiving this sacrament by a priest, or any other, alone; as likewise, the denial of the cup to the people, worshipping the elements, the lifting them up, or carrying them about, for adoration, and the reserving them for any pretended religious use; are all contrary to the nature of this sacrament, and to the institution of Christ.

This section reinforces the teaching of the last. The errors of Rome receive further assault. Private Masses, the denial of the cup to the laity, and the worshiping and reserving of the elements are all contrary to the sacrament and Christ's institution. All these errors are due to the fundamental error of transubstantiation. If that were true, these should follow, but it is not true. This explains the balanced and judicious attack on Rome. These are contrary to what Christ ordered. But the language of the Confession is restrained. The veneration of the host is the point at issue, flowing from the change of substance that Rome considers to take place. It is this latter point (the change of substance) that is the source of the problem. The Confession does not oppose lifting the elements so that the people may see them, for this is an essential part of the sacrament as Christ appointed it.

Section 29.5 reads:

The outward elements in this sacrament, duly set apart to the uses ordained by Christ, have such relation to Him crucified, as that, truly, yet sacramentally only, they are sometimes called by the name of the things they represent, to wit, the body and blood of Christ; albeit, in substance and nature, they still remain truly and only bread and wine, as they were before.

This section considers the relation between the signs and the reality. Once consecrated, the bread and wine have an exceedingly close relation to Christ. They remain bread and wine and do not change their substance. Nevertheless, due to the sacramental relation, they can be called the body and blood of Christ.

---

including the rejoinder by Donald Macleod and my surrejoinder. See also Bruce, *Mystery of the Lord's Supper*, 108.

Section 29.6 continues to discuss the substance of the elements:

> That doctrine which maintains a change of the substance of bread
> and wine, into the substance of Christ's body and blood (commonly
> called transubstantiation) by consecration of a priest, or by any other
> way, is repugnant, not to Scripture alone, but even to common sense,
> and reason; overthroweth the nature of the sacrament, and hath been,
> and is, the cause of manifold superstitions; yea, of gross idolatries.

At last the Confession gets to grips with the root of its opposition
to the Roman Catholic doctrine, the teaching on transubstantiation. It
is repugnant, not only to Scripture, but to reason and common sense.
It overthrows the sacrament. We saw how the Confession regarded
it as "abominably injurious" to the one sacrifice of Christ. Transubstantiation itself is "the cause of manifold superstitions; yea, of gross
idolatries." The point is that these superstitions, idolatries, and injuries
result from the belief in transubstantiation. The Assembly sees that this
is the root problem and that the superstitions flow from here. Once
this dogma is accepted, idolatries follow. Thus the real problem is the
dogma. The Confession deals with it by pointing to its departure from
Scripture and indicating that it is rationally unsupportable.

The Confession next explains how the sacrament is received in
faith (29.7; see LC 170):

> Worthy receivers, outwardly partaking of the visible elements, in this
> sacrament, do then also, inwardly by faith, really and indeed, yet
> not carnally and corporally but spiritually, receive, and feed upon,
> Christ crucified, and all benefits of His death: the body and blood of
> Christ being then, not corporally or carnally, in, with, or under the
> bread and wine; yet, as really, but spiritually, present to the faith of
> believers in that ordinance, as the elements themselves are to their
> outward senses.

This, to my mind, is the single most significant part of the chapter and the one most neglected. It speaks of what happens in the
Lord's Supper when "worthy receivers," or true believers, receive
the outward elements. It is full of negative statements distancing it
from the Lutheran teaching, and is encumbered by a succession of

clauses piled on top of one another. The entire section is, in fact, only one sentence.

First, we note the negatives. The Confession deals less vehemently with the Lutheran doctrine, since it is less injurious than the Roman Catholic. However, it is clearly opposed. True believers do not feed on Christ "carnally and corporally," for the body and blood of Christ are "not corporally or carnally, in, with, or under the bread and wine." Consubstantiation is rejected. Christ is not present physically. It is important to see what this section rejects, so we can detach it from the convoluted language and then move on to see what the Confession affirms.

Second, the positive affirmation is clear. True believers "inwardly by faith, really and indeed . . . spiritually, receive, and feed upon, Christ crucified, and all benefits of His death." The reason for this is that "the body and blood of Christ [are] . . . as really, but spiritually, present to the faith of believers . . . as the elements themselves are to the outward senses." The main coordinate verbs of the whole are "receive and feed upon." True believers receive and feed upon Christ, as surely as they eat the outward elements. Christ is the key, for this is *the Lord's* Supper. This section teaches the same as Calvin, that there is a true feeding on Christ in the Eucharist, not in a physical manner, but by the Holy Spirit. This a real and a true feeding, a communion that sustains and nourishes us and so brings about our growth in union with Christ.

WCF 29.8 concludes:

> Although ignorant and wicked men receive the outward elements in this sacrament; yet, they receive not the thing signified thereby; but, by their unworthy coming thereunto, are guilty of the body and blood of the Lord, to their own damnation. Wherefore, all ignorant and ungodly persons, as they are unfit to enjoy communion with Him, so are they unworthy of the Lord's table; and cannot, without great sin against Christ, while they remain such, partake of these holy mysteries, or be admitted thereunto.

The final section of the chapter discusses who may receive the Lord's Supper. First of all, it distinguishes between those who receive the elements and those who receive Christ. It is sadly possible to eat and drink bread and wine only. Since transubstantiation is rejected, it is possible to have the sign but not the reality. Since faith is necessary to feed on Christ (here are echoes of John 6), those without faith or godliness do not receive Christ at all, even though they may receive the sacrament. Moreover, they are guilty of the body and blood of Christ and so are liable to damnation. They sin against Christ by participating. They cannot be admitted to the table.

These people are described as "ignorant" and "wicked." This implies that knowledge and piety are necessary. True believers, or worthy receivers, are those who have faith and who are able to examine themselves concerning their knowledge, faith, and repentance (SC 97). Those who are "found to be ignorant or scandalous," whom the church authorities may after due process have determined to lack saving faith or to be living an ungodly life, are to be kept from the Lord's Supper (LC 173). Since the Confession and Catechisms all regard baptism as the sacrament of initiation, coming before the Lord's Supper, a strong implication is that any who have not been baptized lack the knowledge requisite for participation in the Supper too.[78]

The Larger Catechism expounds the positive side of this matter in LC 171–72, 174–75. Before receiving the Supper, the faithful are to examine themselves of their being in Christ, of their sins, of their faith and its fruits, of their desires after Christ, and of their obedience, renewing these graces "by serious meditation, and fervent

78. In the *Annotations*, there is a clear difference between the annotators of John's gospel and those of 1 Corinthians. John 6:52–53 is interpreted as spiritual feeding on Christ himself, without obvious reference to the Lord's Supper. Our souls are nourished with the body and blood of Christ, as our bodies with meat and drink—seemingly a spiritualist view. However, the notes on 1 Corinthians 11:20 refer to "the holy Eucharist, the Banquet wherein we are fed with the body and blood of Christ, as S. Augustine in his 118 Epistle, and S. Cyprian in his Tract *de Coena Domini* rightly expound the Text." In the same context, on 1 Corinthians 11:23, the Supper is a bond of union, while in verse 25 it is a sign and seal (but not exhibiting or conveying grace—this is not denied, but neither is it mentioned). Earlier, commenting on 1 Corinthians 10:3, the *Annotations* say that the believers at the time of the exodus "by faith in the eating and drinking of them laid hold upon Christs body and blood the true spirituall food of our soules" since, with reference to the next verse, Christ "streamed forth the true water of life and spirituall drink to all his Church." This was figurative and sacramental; by institution and covenant, God has joined with it the real, but spiritual, enjoying of Christ. Hence, the annotator of verse 16 refers to "the sacrament thereof accompanyed with the effect and spirituall realitie, by the operation of the holy Ghost: or, a signe and pledge of the spirituall communion which we have together, who by faith participate in the body and blood of Christ."

355

prayer" (LC 171). This is a call to serious introspection; it may have encouraged the lack of assurance later common in Scottish Presbyterianism. On the other hand, it is hardly out of harmony with the similar call to self-examination in the Book of Common Prayer of the Church of England, nor in the spiritual disciplines used in the Orthodox Church.

In fact, LC 172 immediately answers the potential question about lack of assurance. Those who doubt whether they are in Christ, and are duly affected by the matter, and desire to be in Christ and to depart from sin, "may and ought to come to the Lord's supper, that [they] may be further strengthened." The divines were aware of the pastoral dangers lurking in LC 171 and immediately balanced the call to self-examination by affirming the grace of God for those more sensitive to the nagging accusations of doubt. Perhaps this answer was neglected in later years, when the problems of assurance arose.

The Catechism also addresses what to do during and after the Supper. In LC 174, it is said that while the sacrament is administered, the people are to wait upon God "with all holy reverence and attention . . . diligently observe the sacramental elements and actions, heedfully discern the Lord's body, and affectionately meditate on his death and sufferings." This, it is affirmed, will stimulate their graces—judging themselves for their sins, hungering and thirsting for Christ, feeding on him by faith, receiving of his fullness, trusting in his merits, rejoicing in his love, giving thanks for his grace, and renewing their covenant with God and love for all the saints. There is missing from this the point that, since believers feed on Christ, he is risen and ascended. The focus should be as much on his ascension as on his death, although the latter must by no means be sidestepped. This reflects the fact that the Lord's Supper is also the Eucharist, the giving of thanks. Balancing the death with the ascension would further offset any misapplication of the introspective self-examination required by LC 171. After the Supper, Christians should reflect on how they have conducted themselves in it, according to LC 175.

T. F. Torrance asserts that there is no indication of the import of the resurrection and ascension of Christ in the Assembly's consideration of the Supper. This was a vital matter that impacted the early church, Calvin, and the older Scottish tradition.[79] While we have hinted that this is a surprising omission, we should recall that the crucial point of the whole chapter in the Confession is that the faithful "receive and feed upon Christ," which presupposes his resurrection and ascension. Communion with Christ is communion with the risen and ascended one. LC 51–55 expounds the resurrection, ascension, and heavenly session in great detail. In the following questions, 66–90, it unfolds salvation as "union and communion with Christ in grace and glory." The Lord's Supper is directly connected with the living Christ in LC 168, while LC 170 is given over to a discussion of how the faithful "do therein feed upon the body and blood of Christ." Torrance constructs his arguments only by eliminating important evidence that contradicts him. On the other hand, the focus of the Larger Catechism can be criticized for an imbalance that may well have encouraged the sacrament to be treated more as a funeral than a joyful thanksgiving and communion.

Church Censures (WCF 30)

A major point of contention with which the Assembly had to deal was the legitimacy of a government in the church separate from the state. Episcopalians objected to this. It also met with considerable reserve from Parliament, whose servant the Assembly was. To many Members of Parliament, it seemed to jeopardize the stability of the body politic by positing a center of power additional to the existing authorities. Those who favored a continuation of the Erastian arrangements argued that the power of excommunication had to be wielded by the civil authority or else the unity of the nation would be undermined. This was, of course, especially pertinent at a time of civil war, when the fabric of society and government had already been torn asunder.

The Assembly itself was, as we have seen, a *de facto* Erastian body. However, the majority of the divines clearly saw a biblical mandate for a government of the church distinct from the civil authority, wielding the power of disciplinary sanctions, despite what Parliament might say

---

79. T. F. Torrance, *Scottish Theology*, 150.

or fear. Yet, according to WCF 23.3, the civil magistrate has the right to call synods, so there is no clear break between church and state. This follows the historic line of the church in both East and West.[80]

Synods and Councils (WCF 31)

Barth stresses the Reformed distinction between synods and councils on the one hand and Scripture on the other: "For the Reformed, that which is given and revealed by the Holy Spirit can only be the Holy Scriptures themselves."[81] Because of this, "the Reformed confessions essentially could not have the character of final words, as did the Lutheran." After rehearsing the revisions and replacements of a range of Reformed confessions, Barth refers to the Westminster Confession, "which has in turn been constantly edited and worked on up to the modern day."[82]

This chapter asserts the limits of church authority. It can simply declare the teaching of the Word of God. Scripture alone has the right to bind the conscience, since it is from God; no human court has that authority. Its decisions and edicts must simply reflect the teaching of Scripture, no more, no less (31.3). Even the greatest theologians and the most learned councils may err; the ecumenical councils are not exempt from this judgment. On the other hand, the Bible cannot err. Therefore, church synods cannot be made the rule of faith or practice. They can declare the teaching of the Word of God and exercise discipline over the church in accordance with the Word of God, but they cannot require a person to do this or that other than what the Word may specify. To contravene the Word of God is sin; to reject an edict of the church authorities is only sin if it has the support of Holy Scripture, for verdicts of ecclesiastical authorities made in their own name have no binding force whatever.

80. The later American developments, in which this position was changed and a clear separation between church and state was introduced, are a break from the historic position of the church. No consideration will be given here to whether such changes were or are biblically or theologically sustainable, since this book is simply an analysis of the Westminster Assembly's theology.

81. Barth, *Reformed Confessions*, 19.

82. Ibid., 26.

Neither the Westminster Confession nor the Catechisms prescribe a specific form of church government. However, the Form of Presbyterial Church-Government is clear on the matter. Yet the Assembly allowed for Independents to voice their views and made every attempt to accommodate them, while various shades of Presbyterians, both principial and pragmatic, found representation. While its membership included a number of convinced Episcopalians, its Form of Presbyterial Church-Government makes no mention of diocesan bishops.[83]

---

83. The Root and Branch Petition was successful, at least at this point. Episcopacy was to be restored in 1660.

15

Death, Resurrection, and Judgment

*We look for the resurrection of the dead
and the life of the world to come.*

After Death (WCF 32; LC 84–86)

Death is the wages of sin (LC 84), and so it is appointed to all
to die, since all have sinned (WCF 6.6; LC 28). From this the righteous are not exempt. However, for them the sting of death has been
removed; death for them is the prelude to sharing the glory of God,
and so it is an experience of God's love, freeing them from the sin
and misery of a fallen world. Moreover, they will be delivered from
death at the last day, and it is in anticipation of that great event that
they undergo this solemn experience (LC 85).

In WCF 32.1, the Assembly considers what happens in death
to all people without exception. While the body returns to dust and
sees corruption, the soul neither dies nor sleeps, since it is immortal
and returns to God. This, of course, is classic Christian teaching.
It has often been attacked on the ground that it appears to imply
the Platonic idea of the immortality of the soul. This accusation is
mistaken. The Platonic idea is that the soul is eternal and has no
beginning, being intrinsically immortal. In the Christian view, the
soul is created by God and so has a beginning and is subject to time.
Moreover, God gives it immortality; this is not something intrinsic

to its nature. Aside from this question, death is a fearful thing, disrupting and dissolving the psychosomatic unity that is at the heart of what it means to be human.

The Confession then turns to consider how the righteous experience death. Their souls, on death, are made perfect in holiness. They are received into the highest heavens and see the face of God in light and glory, while they await the redemption of the body at the resurrection. This echoes the Niceno-Constantinopolitan Creed, with its affirmation that "we look for the resurrection of the dead and the life of the world to come." On the one hand, the reality of death is felt keenly, for we shall be "away from the body" (2 Cor. 5:8–9). On the other hand, we shall be "at home with the Lord," shall see the face of God, shall be safe in Christ, and shall be freed from all sin. Our bodies will "rest in [our] graves as in [our] beds" (LC 86). This is because even in death and corruption our bodies remain united to Christ. There is no greater affirmation of triumph in the whole of Scripture than the declaration that believers are dead "in Christ." At the point when "death's mightiest powers have done their worst" and utterly expended their force, we remain unshakably in union with Christ. This follows from the fact that Christ, in his humiliation, remained under the power of death until the third day, but saw no corruption, for death could not hold him—and the righteous are united to him in his death, burial, and resurrection. Hence, the Holy Spirit pronounces blessing on those who die in the Lord from the time of Christ's resurrection onward (Rev. 14:13). We will be made "capable of further communion with Christ in glory" (LC 85), not by a process of purgation, as the Roman Church holds, but by the freedom from sin and the heightened communion with Christ of which the intermediate state consists. Indeed, LC 86 presents the condition of the righteous immediately after death as "the commencement of communion in glory with Christ."

The souls of the wicked, however, are cast into hell immediately upon death. There they are in torments and utter darkness. They are kept there, awaiting not the life of the world to come, but the final judgment. Their bodies will be "kept in their graves, as in their prisons" (LC 86). The contrast between the righteous resting in their beds and the wicked kept in their prisons is striking. These are the only two possibilities after death. There is no intermediate situation between these two—this is an emphatic denial of the Roman Catholic doctrine of purgatory. It is also clearly a rejection of the Anabaptist and sectarian notion of soul sleep. The states of blessedness and torment require consciousness.

The Resurrection of the Dead (WCF 32; LC 87)

Here again, the Assembly distinguishes between what will happen to all people and what differentiates the righteous from the wicked. At the last day, those who are alive will be changed. They will not undergo resurrection, since they will not have died. However, they will be transformed (WCF 32.2; LC 87). The dead will be both resurrected and changed, but their bodies will be the selfsame ones as those they had when alive. To what stage of their previous life these bodies will conform we are not told and can only speculate. However, these bodies will have different qualities. Moreover, the psychosomatic unity essential to the integrity of human nature will have been restored. The Assembly, in WCF 32.2, in addressing what will happen to human beings in general, appears to grant the wicked the same participation in the resurrection as the righteous. However, the biblical evidence establishes that the elect will be glorified and changed in the resurrection, but this prospect does not seem to be granted to the wicked. The situation is clarified in LC 87, which affirms that the just—by virtue of the resurrection of Christ, their head—will, by the Holy Spirit, "be raised in power, spiritual, incorruptible, and made like to his glorious body," while the bodies of the wicked "shall be raised up in dishonour by him, as an offended judge." There the difference is as clear as it is obscure in the Confession.

In WCF 32.3, the condition of the unjust is made more explicit. By the power of Christ, they will be raised to dishonor. However, the bodies of the just will be raised by Christ's Spirit to honor and conformed to Christ's glorious body.

362

The Last Judgment (WCF 33; LC 88–90)

Immediately after the general resurrection comes the final judgment. No one knows when these things will be. Our ignorance here is a call to prayer and watchfulness, rather than speculation (LC 88). God has appointed this day, and so its coming is absolutely certain (WCF 33.1).

According to WCF 33.1, at the judgment God will judge the world in righteousness by Jesus Christ, to whom the Father has given all power and dominion. The apostate angels and all human beings will be judged before Christ's tribunal. Humans will be judged in accordance with what they have done, in thought, word, and deed. They will receive a just retribution on the basis of their actions during their lifetime on earth.

The ultimate purpose of the judgment is to manifest God's glory, as is declared in 33.2.

The glory of God's mercy and justice will be evident in the eternal salvation of the elect and the damnation of the reprobate, respectively. Notable here is the description of the reprobate as those "who are wicked and disobedient." The responsibility for their damnation rests squarely on their own shoulders, due to their conduct during their lives. Moreover, their damnation is just; it displays the glory of God's justice and is given "according to what they have done in the body" (33.1). The righteous will go into everlasting life, to receive the fullness of joy and refreshing from the presence of the Lord. The wicked, who do not know the Lord, will be punished with everlasting destruction from his presence. Their wicked rejection of the Lord and their ignorance of him will issue in everlasting separation from his presence, a just outcome in accordance with their life on earth. Their torments will be eternal, and their destruction everlasting. LC 89 stresses that this sentence is to be based "upon clear evidence, and full conviction of their own consciences," so that what is pronounced against them is a "just sentence." It is based on the objective basis of their lives and is matched by their own recognition of its justice. The ensuing punishment will be in the company of the devil and all his angels and will consist of "unspeakable torments." Beyond this the Assembly does not presume to go.

There is no reference to hell in the Shorter Catechism. Nor had Calvin mentioned it in his Geneva Catechism,[1] which followed the Apostles' Creed, from which it is also absent. When asked why this was missing, Calvin answers that it is not part of the confession of our faith.[2] Of the major Reformed confessions, only the Belgic Confession mentions hell and everlasting punishment.[3] There is a difference here; the church "looks for the resurrection of the dead and the life of the world to come," but does not look with such keen anticipation for hell and everlasting torment. This is an example of something that, although true, may not necessarily be part of a confessional document.[4]

WCF 33.3 reminds us that the time of the judgment is unknown to us. Christ's purpose in this is to keep us from "carnal security," so that we may always be watchful. We will then look for that day, as the Niceno-Constantinopolitan Creed confesses.

Millennial Themes

There is no discussion of millennial theories in these chapters, or in the Assembly's documents as a whole. This is despite the eruption of millennial views at the time and the common belief that the Antichrist was now present. The Arminian premillennialist Joseph Mede was highly regarded by many at the Assembly.[5] However, the discussion in the Confession of the parousia, resurrection, and final judgment together as one points to an amillennial commitment. LC 88 indicates that the judgment will follow immediately upon the res-

1. "M: Why, then, is there mention only of eternal life and not of hell? C: Since nothing is held by faith except what contributes to the consolation of the souls of the pious. Hence there are here recalled the rewards which the Lord has prepared for his servants. Therefore it is not added what fate may await the impious whom we know to be outcasts from the Kingdom of God." John Calvin, "The Catechism of the Church of Geneva," in *Calvin: Theological Treatises* (trans. J. K. S. Reid; Philadelphia: Westminster Press, 1954), 104.

2. Mitchell, *Westminster Assembly*, 450.

3. Belgic Confession, 37, in Cochrane, *Reformed Confessions*, 218–19.

4. A good case can be made that belief in everlasting punishment is a litmus test of the health of the Christian church. The gospel is set against the backcloth of sin, the wrath of God, and condemnation of the wicked. If this is unclear, so will be the message of the gospel. There is a need to distinguish between what is true and vital and must be preached, and what may or must go into a confession.

5. Jue, "Active Obedience of Christ," 105–6.

urrection. Historic premillennialism is definitely not represented in the documents. However, perspectives such as this are not explicitly outlawed, although the Assembly had every opportunity to do so. On the other hand, there are hints of postmillennialism in LC 191. In praying the request in the Lord's Prayer, "Thy kingdom come," we are asking God that the Jews would be called and the fullness of the Gentiles brought in. Romans 11:25–26 is cited as a proof text. There were many at the time who held that Paul envisaged in that passage a widespread turning of Jews to Christ, followed by a worldwide reviving of the church. For instance, the *Annotations*, on Romans 11:15–16, argue that Paul refers to the assumption of the Jews into the church, while on Romans 11:25 they state that the reference to the salvation of "all Israel" is to "the last conversion of the Jews," which is "clearly set forth in the gospel." The theme continues in the comments on verse 26. There was a significant group of theologians and exegetes who understood Romans 11 to refer to a future widespread conversion of the Jews and their incorporation into the church before the parousia. Yet even if this is in view in the Larger Catechism, its presence is decidedly muted. There is no trace of similar sentiments in the Confession or in the Shorter Catechism, and the *Annotations* are not an official production of the Assembly as such.

Indeed, comments on matters such as these are noticeable by their absence. The eschatological commitments are reserved for the key points—death, the intermediate state, the resurrection, and by implication the parousia, the final judgment, and heaven and hell. Underlying this reticence is the fact that the Assembly was charged with producing documents for the reformed Church of England and the churches in the other two kingdoms. This was not an occasion for speculation or for the exclusion of views that came within the ambit of the Assembly's generic Calvinism.

Derek Thomas points to a few eschatological comments in addition to the central themes.[6] WCF 25.6 calls the pope the Antichrist—a claim that has been heavily criticized down the years since. It indicates that many in the Assembly anticipated that the eschatological events

---

6. D. W. Thomas, "The Eschatology of the Westminster Confession and Assembly," in *The Westminster Confession into the 21st Century* (ed. Duncan), 2:307–79.

were close at hand and that they were in the final battle before the consummation of history. This was a common thought in the midst of the ferment of the time: the virtual collapse of organized society in England, together with the devastation of the Thirty Years' War on the continent. On a different tack, purgatory and soul sleep are, by implication although not by name, ruled out by the stress on the blessedness of the just after death and before the resurrection. Annihilation, a belief of the Socinians, is also excluded by the everlasting punishment of the wicked. Apart from these comments, the divines show great reserve, not being prepared to put into confessional documents ideas less than central to the great themes of God's glory and our salvation, faith, and life. As Thomas comments,

> Knowing how divisive the issue of eschatology can be . . . the divines chose their words carefully, making no reference whatsoever to issues of major division and misunderstanding (e.g., the millennium), and choosing a formula of expression that comprehensively included several traditions (e.g., the calling of the Jews), as well as denouncing views that were clearly opposed to biblical teaching (e.g., the doctrines of soul sleep and annihilation). In its criticism of premillennial views, Westminster is a model of gentleness.[7]

The Life of the World to Come

LC 90 focuses on what shall be done to the righteous at the day of judgment. We shall be openly acknowledged and acquitted at the tribunal of Christ. We will join with Christ in judging the reprobate angels and human beings. This comment alone, reflecting the words of Paul in 1 Corinthians 6:2–3 cited in the proof text, gives the lie to the claim that Calvinism has a low view of humanity. Quite the reverse is true: united with Christ, we shall share with him in his kingly rule!

The life of the world to come consists in perfect and full union and communion with Christ in glory, "in the immediate vision and fruition of God the Father, of our Lord Jesus Christ, and of the Holy Spirit to all eternity." We will be received into heaven. We will be

7. Ibid., 2:378–79.

fully and forever freed from all sin and misery. We will be filled with inconceivable joys, perfectly holy and happy in body and soul. These things, which are more than eye has seen or ear has heard (1 Cor. 2:9), are what God has prepared for those who love him. Ultimately, salvation, faith, and life go far beyond the great gifts of the gospel such as justification and sanctification. In unimpeded and unsullied union with Christ, we shall come to full and unclouded knowledge of, and communion with, the Holy Trinity. Freed from sin, transformed into his image, glorified in both body and soul, we shall see him as he is.[8] Now we know in part; then we shall know, even as we are known. Then will come to pass the purpose for which God made us—we will glorify him and enjoy him forever (SC 1).

---

8. Glorification in Reformed theology corresponds to deification in Eastern theology. Neither robs us of our humanity, any more than the hypostatic union robs Christ of his; we were made for union with the Son of God. I have written elsewhere on this theme. See Letham, *The Holy Trinity*, 458–78; Letham, *Through Western Eyes*, 253–63. It will be a prominent theme in my forthcoming book, *Union with Christ* (Phillipsburg, NJ: P&R). A fruitful area for research, hitherto unexplored, is the interaction of Reformed theologians in the early seventeenth century (before the Assembly) with Cyril Lucar (1583–1638), the Calvinist patriarch of Constantinople. He was influenced by the Reformed and published a Calvinistic confession of faith, referring explicitly to predestination and justification by faith; was there any reciprocal feedback? We know that Owen had copies of Palamas in his personal library, and that he, many at the Assembly, and Calvin before them, cited the Greek fathers. There is scope for at least a doctoral thesis here.

Bibliography

Apollonius, Guilielmus. *A consideration of certaine controversies at this time agitated in the Kingdome of England, concerning the government of the Church of God, written at the command and appointment of the Walachrian Classis. And Sent from the Wallachrian Churches, to the Synod at London. Octob. 16. 1644.* London: G. M. for Tho. Underhill, 1645.

Armstrong, Brian G. *Calvinism and the Amyraut Heresy: Protestant Scholasticism and Humanism in Seventeenth-Century France.* Madison: University of Wisconsin Press, 1969.

Ashley, Maurice. *England in the Seventeenth Century.* London: Penguin, 1967.

Atkinson, Nigel. *Richard Hooker and the Authority of Scripture, Tradition and Reason: Reformed Theologian of the Church of England?* Carlisle: Paternoster, 1997.

Baillie, Robert. *The Letters and Journals of Robert Baillie: Principal of the University of Glasgow 1637–1652.* Edited by David Laing. 3 vols. Edinburgh: Robert Ogle, 1841.

Ball, John. *A Treatise of the Covenant of Grace.* London: Simeon Ash, 1645.

Barker, William S. *Puritan Profiles: 54 Influential Puritans at the Time When the Westminster Confession of Faith Was Written.* Fearn: Mentor, 1996.

Barth, Karl. *Church Dogmatics.* Edited by G. W. Bromiley and T. F. Torrance. 14 vols. Edinburgh: T. & T. Clark, 1956–77.

———. *The Theology of the Reformed Confessions.* Translated by Darrell L. Guder. Louisville: Westminster John Knox Press, 2002.

Berkouwer, G. C. *Divine Election.* Grand Rapids: Eerdmans, 1960.

Bernard, G. W. *The King's Reformation: Henry VIII and the Remaking of the English Church.* New Haven: Yale University Press, 2005.

The Book of Common Prayer. Oxford: Oxford University Press, n.d.

Bracton, Thomas. *Bracton on the Laws and Customs of England*. Edited by Samuel E. Thorne. Cambridge, MA: Harvard University Press, 1968.

Bray, Gerald, ed. *The Anglican Canons 1529–1947*. Church of England Record Society, 6. Woodbridge: The Boydell Press, Church of England Record Society, in conjunction with the Ecclesiastical Law Society, 1998.

Bruce, Alexander Balmain. *The Humiliation of Christ in Its Physical, Ethical, and Official Aspects*. Edinburgh: T. & T. Clark, 1905.

Bruce, Robert. *The Mystery of the Lord's Supper: Sermons on the Sacrament Preached in the Kirk of Edinburgh by Robert Bruce in A.D. 1589*. London: James Clarke, 1958.

Bucanus, Guilielmus. *Institutiones theologiae seu locorum communium Christianae religionis*. [Geneva:] Ioannes & Isaias lePreux, 1604.

Bucer, Martin. *Metaphrasis et enarrationes in perpetuae epistolarum d. Pauli apostoli: Tomus Primus*. Strasbourg, 1536.

Bullinger, Henry. *The Decades of Henry Bullinger*. Edited by Thomas Harding. Parker Society. Cambridge: University Press, 1850.

Burgess, Cornelius. *Baptismall regeneration of elect infants, professed by the Church of England, according to the Scriptures, the primitive Church, the present Reformed Churches, and many particular divines apart*. Oxford: I. L. for Henry Curteyn, 1629.

Calvin, John. *Institutes of the Christian Religion*. Translated by Ford Lewis Battles. Edited by John T. McNeill. 2 vols. Philadelphia: Westminster Press, 1960.

————. "Letter DXLIX to John Knox." In *Selected Works of John Calvin: Tracts and Letters*, edited by Henry Beveridge and Jules Bonnet. 7 vols. Volume 7: *Letters, Part 4: 1559–1564*, 73–76. Reprint, Grand Rapids: Baker, 1983.

Carlson, Erik Josef. "'Practical Divinity': Richard Greenham's Ministry in Elizabethan England." In *Religion and the English People 1500–1640: New Voices, New Perspectives*, edited by Erik Josef Carlson, 147–93. Kirksville, MO: Thomas Jefferson University Press, 1998.

Carruthers, S. W. *The Everyday Work of the Westminster Assembly*. Edited by J. Ligon Duncan III. Greenville, SC: Reformed Academic Press, 1994.

Certain Learned Divines. *Annotations upon all the books of the Old and New Testament, wherein the text is explained, doubts resolved, Scriptures parallelled and various readings observed by the joynt-labour of certain learned Divines, thereunto appointed, and therein employed, as is expressed in the Preface*. London: John Legatt and John Raworth, 1645.

Cochrane, Arthur C. *Reformed Confessions of the 16th Century.* London: SCM, 1966.

Davies, Julian. *The Caroline Captivity of the Church: Charles I and the Remoulding of Anglicanism 1625–1641.* Oxford: Clarendon Press, 1992.

De Witt, John R. *Jus Divinum: The Westminster Assembly and the Divine Right of Church Government.* Kampen: J. H. Kok, 1969.

Duffield, G. E. *John Calvin.* Appleford: Sutton Courtenay Press, 1966.

Duncan, J. Ligon III, ed. *The Westminster Confession into the 21st Century: Essays in Remembrance of the 350th Anniversary of the Westminster Assembly.* 2 vols. Fearn: Mentor, 2003–5.

Eaton, John. *The honey-combe of free justification by Christ alone collected out of the meere authorities of Scripture and common and unanimous consent of the faithfull interpreters and dispensers of Gods mysteries upon the same, especially as they expresse the excellency of free justification.* London: Robert Lancaster, 1642.

Featley, Daniel. *The dippers dipt, or the anabaptists duck'd and plung'd over head and eares, at a disputation in Southwark.* London: Nicholas Bourne and Richard Royston, 1645.

————. *A second parallel together with a writ of error served against the appealer.* London: Robert Milbourne, 1626.

Fenner, Dudley. *Sacra theologia, sive veritas quae secundum pietatem.* Geneva, 1585.

Fesko, J. V. *Diversity Within the Reformed Tradition: Supra- and Infralapsarianism in Calvin, Dort, and Westminster.* Greenville, SC: Reformed Academic Press, 2003.

————. "The Westminster Confession and Lapsarianism: Calvin and the Divines." In *The Westminster Confession into the 21st Century: Essays in Remembrance of the 350th Anniversary of the Westminster Assembly,* edited by J. Ligon Duncan III, 2:477–525. 2 vols. Fearn: Mentor, 2003–5.

Frame, John M. "Some Questions about the Regulative Principle." *WTJ* 54 (1992): 357–66.

Fraser, Antonia. *Cromwell: The Lord Protector.* New York: Dell, 1973.

Gerstner, John H. *A Guide: The Westminster Confession of Faith: Commentary.* Signal Mountain, TN: Summertown Texts, 1992.

Godfrey, W. Robert. "Tensions Within International Calvinism: The Debate on the Atonement at the Synod of Dort." Ph.D. dissertation, Stanford University, 1974.

Goodwin, Thomas. *The Works of Thomas Goodwin.* Edited by John C. Miller and Robert Halley. Edinburgh: James Nichol, 1861–66.

Graham, Michael. "The Civil Sword and the Scottish Kirk, 1560–1600." In *Later Calvinism: International Perspectives*, edited by W. Fred Graham, 237–48. Kirksville, MO: Sixteenth Century Journal Publishers, 1994.

Green, J. R. *Short History of the English People.* New York, 1877.

Ha, Polly. "English Presbyterianism c. 1590–1640." Ph.D. thesis, Cambridge University, 2006.

Helm, Paul. *John Calvin's Ideas.* Oxford: Oxford University Press, 2004.

Heron, Alasdair I. C., ed. *The Westminster Confession in the Church Today.* Edinburgh: Saint Andrews Press, 1982.

Hetherington, William Maxwell. *History of the Westminster Assembly of Divines.* Reprint, Edmonton: Still Waters Revival Books, 1993.

Hill, Christopher. *The Century of Revolution 1603–1714.* New York: W. W. Norton, 1961.

_____. *Society and Puritanism in Pre-Revolutionary England.* London: Secker and Warburg, 1964.

Hillerbrand, Hans J., ed. *Oxford Encyclopedia of the Reformation.* 4 vols. Oxford: Oxford University Press, 1996.

Hodge, A. A. *The Confession of Faith: A Handbook of Christian Doctrine Expounding the Westminster Confession.* Reprint, London: Banner of Truth, 1961.

_____. *Outlines of Theology.* Reprint, Grand Rapids: Eerdmans, 1972.

Hughes, Christopher. *On a Complex Theory of a Simple God: An Investigation in Aquinas' Philosophical Theology.* Ithaca: Cornell University Press, 1989.

Hughes, Philip Edgcumbe. *The Theology of the English Reformers.* Grand Rapids: Eerdmans, 1965.

Jue, Jeffrey. "The Active Obedience of Christ and the Theology of the Westminster Standards: A Historical Investigation." In *Justified in Christ: God's Plan for Us in Justification*, edited by K. Scott Oliphint, 99–130. Fearn: Mentor, 2007.

Junius, Franciscus. *Opera theologica.* Geneva, 1607.

Keep, David J. "Henry Bullinger and the Elizabethan Church." Ph.D. thesis, University of Sheffield, 1970.

Kelly, Douglas. "The Puritan Regulative Principle and Contemporary Worship." In *The Westminster Confession into the 21st Century: Essays in Remembrance of the 350th Anniversary of the Westminster Assembly*, edited by J. Ligon Duncan III, 2:63–98. 2 vols. Fearn: Mentor, 2003–5.

Kendall, R. T. *Calvin and English Calvinism to 1649*. Oxford: Oxford University Press, 1979.

Kickel, Walter. *Vernunft und Offenbarung bei Theodor Beza: Zum Problem der Verhältnisses von Theologie, Philosophie und Staat*. Beiträge zur Geschichte und Lehre der Reformierten Kirche. Neukirchen-Vluyn: Neukirchener Verlag des Erziehungsvereins, 1967.

Kirby, W. Torrance. *Richard Hooker's Doctrine of the Royal Supremacy*. Leiden: E. J. Brill, 1990.

Kirk, J. R. Daniel. "The Sufficiency of the Cross (1): The Crucifixion as Jesus' Act of Obedience." *SBET* 24 (2006): 36–64.

Kline, Meredith G. *By Oath Consigned: A Reinterpretation of the Covenant Signs of Circumcision and Baptism*. Grand Rapids: Eerdmans, 1968.

_____. "Covenant Theology Under Attack." *New Horizons in the Orthodox Presbyterian Church* 15.2 (February 1994): 3–5. Available at www.opc.org/new_horizons/Kline_cov_theo.html as of 24 July 2008.

Lane, Anthony N. S. *John Calvin: Student of the Church Fathers*. Grand Rapids: Baker, 1999.

_____. *Justification by Faith in Catholic-Protestant Dialogue: An Evangelical Assessment*. London: T. & T. Clark, 2002.

Lang, August, ed. *Der Heidelberger Katechismus und vier verwandte Katechismen*. Leipzig: Deichert, 1967.

Leith, John H. *Assembly at Westminster: Reformed Theology in the Making*. Richmond: John Knox Press, 1973.

Letham, Robert. "Amandus Polanus: A Neglected Theologian?" *SCJ* 21 (1990): 463-76.

_____. *Assurance in Theological Context: Reformed Dogmatics 1523–1619*. Rutherford Studies in Historical Theology. Edinburgh: Rutherford House, forthcoming.

_____. "Baptism in the Writings of the Reformers." *SBET* 7/2 (Autumn 1989): 21–44.

_____. "The Foedus Operum: Some Factors Accounting for Its Development." *SCJ* 14 (1983): 63–76.

_____. *The Holy Trinity: In Scripture, History, Theology, and Worship*. Phillipsburg, NJ: P&R, 2004.

_____. "'In the Space of Six Days': The Days of Creation from Origen to the Westminster Assembly." *WTJ* 61 (1999): 149–74.

_____. *The Lord's Supper: Eternal Word in Broken Bread*. Phillipsburg, NJ: P&R, 2001.

_____. "Saving Faith and Assurance in Reformed Theology: Zwingli to the Synod of Dort." 2 vols. Ph.D. thesis, University of Aberdeen, 1979.

_____. *Through Western Eyes: Eastern Orthodoxy: A Reformed Perspective*. Fearn: Mentor, 2007.

_____. *The Work of Christ*. Leicester: Inter-Varsity Press, 1993.

_____ and Donald Macleod. "Is Evangelicalism Christian?" *EQ* 67/1 (1995): 3–33.

Lightfoot, John. *The Whole Works of the Rev. John Lightfoot*. Edited by J. R. Pitman. London: Hatch and Son, 1824.

Lillback, Peter A. *The Binding of God: Calvin's Role in the Development of Covenant Theology*. Grand Rapids: Baker Academic, 2001.

MacCulloch, Diarmaid. *Thomas Cranmer: A Life*. New Haven: Yale University Press, 1996.

Masson, David. *The Life of John Milton*. London: Macmillan, 1873.

McGrath, Alister E. *A Life of John Calvin: A Study in the Shaping of Western Culture*. Oxford: Basil Blackwell, 1990.

Milne, Garnet H. *The Westminster Confession of Faith and the Cessation of Special Revelation: The Majority Puritan Viewpoint on Whether Extra-Biblical Prophecy Is Still Possible*. Carlisle: Paternoster, 2007.

Milton, Anthony, ed. *The British Delegation and the Synod of Dort (1618–1619)*. The Church of England Record Society, 13. [Woodbridge:] Boydell Press, 2005.

_____. *Catholic and Reformed: The Roman and Protestant Churches in English Protestant Thought 1600–1640*. Cambridge: Cambridge University Press, 1995.

Mitchell, Alexander F. *The Westminster Assembly: Its History and Standards: Being the Baird Lectures for 1882*. Philadelphia: Presbyterian Board of Publication and Sabbath-School Work, 1897.

Mitchell, Alex. F., and John Struthers, eds. *Minutes of the Sessions of the Westminster Assembly of Divines While Engaged in Preparing the Directory for Church Government, Confession of Faith and Catechisms (November 1644 to March 1649): From Transcripts of the Originals Procured by a Committee of the General Assembly of the Church of Scotland*. Edinburgh: William Blackwood and Sons, 1874.

Moore, Jonathan D. *English Hypothetical Universalism: John Preston and the Softening of Reformed Theology*. Grand Rapids: Eerdmans, 2007.

————. "The Westminster Confession of Faith and the Sin of Neglecting Baptism." *WTJ* 69 (2007): 63–86.

Morrill, John. "The Religious Context of the English Civil War." *Transactions of the Royal Historical Society* 34 (1984): 155–78.

Morris, Edward D. *Theology of the Westminster Symbols: A Commentary Historical, Doctrinal, Practical on the Confession of Faith and Catechisms, and the Related Formularies of Presbyterian Churches*. Columbus: Champlin, 1900.

Muller, Richard A. *After Calvin: Studies in the Development of a Theological Tradition*. Oxford: Oxford University Press, 2003.

————. *Christ and the Decree: Christology and Predestination in Reformed Theology from Calvin to Perkins*. Durham, NC: Labyrinth, 1986.

————. "Either Expressly Set Down . . . or by Good and Necessary Consequence: Exegesis and Formulations in the Annotations and the Confession." Conference paper presented at Westminster Assembly 2004. Philadelphia: Westminster Theological Seminary, 2004.

————. *God, Creation, and Providence in the Thought of Jacob Arminius: Sources and Directions of Scholastic Protestantism in the Era of Early Orthodoxy*. Grand Rapids: Baker, 1991.

————. "Inspired by God . . . Kept Pure in All Ages: The Doctrine of Scripture in the Westminster Confession." Paper presented at Westminster Assembly 2004. Philadelphia: Westminster Theological Seminary, 2004.

————. *Post-Reformation Reformed Dogmatics: The Rise and Development of Reformed Orthodoxy, ca. 1520 to ca. 1725*. 4 vols. 2nd ed. of vols. 1–2. Grand Rapids: Baker, 2003.

————. "Scholasticism in Calvin: A Question of Relation and Disjunction." In *Calvinus Sincerioris Religionis Vindex = Calvin as Protector of the Purer Religion*, edited by Wilhelm H. Neuser, 247–65. Kirksville, MO: Sixteenth Century Journal Publishers, 1997.

————. *The Unaccommodated Calvin: Studies in the Foundation of a Theological Tradition*. New York: Oxford University Press, 2000.

Musculus, Wolfgang. *In Epistolam d. apostoli Pauli ad Romanos, commentarii*. Basel: Sebastian Henricpetri, 1555?

————. *In Genesim Mosis commentarii plenissimi*. Basel: Sebastain Henricpetri, 1554?

————. *Loci communes theologiae sacrae*. Basel: Sebastian Henricpetri, [n.d.].

Needham, Nick. "Westminster and Worship: Psalms, Hymns? and Musical Instruments?" In *The Westminster Confession into the 21st Century: Essays in Remembrance of the 350th Anniversary of the Westminster Assembly*, edited by J. Ligon Duncan III, 2:223–306. 2 vols. Fearn: Mentor, 2005.

Neuser, Wilhelm H., ed. *Calvinus Sincerioris Religionis Vindex = Calvin as Protector of the Purer Religion*. Kirksville, MO: Sixteenth Century Journal Publishers, 1997.

Newman, John Henry. *An Essay on the Development of Christian Doctrine*. Notre Dame, IN: University of Notre Dame Press, 1989.

Norris, Robert M. "The Thirty-Nine Articles at the Westminster Assembly." Ph.D. thesis, University of St. Andrews, 1977.

Oden, Thomas C. *The Word of Life: Systematic Theology*. 2 vols. New York: Harper & Row, 1989.

Old, Hughes Oliphant. *The Patristic Roots of Reformed Worship*. Zürich: Theologischer Verlag, 1975.

————. *The Shaping of the Reformed Baptismal Rite in the Sixteenth Century*. Grand Rapids: Eerdmans, 1992.

Olevian, Caspar. *De substantia foederis gratuiti inter Deum et electos*. Geneva, 1585.

Owen, John. *The Works of John Owen*. Edited by William H. Goold. 24 vols. London: Johnstone & Hunter, 1850–55. (Volumes 18–24 are Owen's *An Exposition of the Epistle to the Hebrews*.)

Owen, Paul. "Calvin and Catholic Trinitarianism: An Examination of Robert Reymond's Understanding of the Trinity and His Appeal to John Calvin." *CTJ* 35 (2000): 262–81.

Paul, Robert S. *Assembly of the Lord: Politics and Religion in the Westminster Assembly*. Edinburgh: T. & T. Clark, 1983.

Perkins, William. *The Workes of that famous and worthie minister of Christ, in the Universitie of Cambridge, Mr. W. Perkins*. [Cambridge:] Iohn Legate, 1608.

Pettegree, Andrew. "The Reception of Calvinism in Britain." In *Calvinus Sincerioris Religionis Vindex = Calvin as the Protector of the Purer Religion*, edited by Wilhelm H. Neuser, 267–89. Kirksville, MO: Sixteenth Century Journal Publishers, 1997.

Piscator, Johannes. *De iustificatione hominis coram Deo*. Leiden: Andreas Clouquius, 1609.

_____. *Analysis logica Epistolarum Pauli ad Romanos, Corinthios, Ephesios, Philippenses, Colossenses, Thessalonicenses*. London: George Bishop, 1591.

Platt, John. "Eirenical Anglicans at the Synod of Dort." In *Reform and Reformation: England and the Continent c1500–c1750*, edited by D. Baker, 221–43. Oxford: Blackwell, 1979.

Polanus, Amandus. *Partitiones theologiae*. Basel, 1607.

_____. *Partitiones theologiae*. 2nd ed. Basel, 1590.

_____. *Syntagma theologiae Christianae*. Basel, 1609; Geneva: Petri Auberti, 1612.

Polanyi, Michael. *Personal Knowledge*. Chicago: University of Chicago Press, 1958.

_____. *The Tacit Dimension*. Chicago: University of Chicago Press, 1958.

Polyander, Johannes, et al. *Synopsis purioris theologiae, disputationibus quinquaginta duabus comprehensa*. Leiden: Ex officina Elzeverianus, 1625.

Porter, H. C. *Reformation and Reaction in Tudor Cambridge*. Cambridge: University Press, 1958.

Reid, J. K. S. "The Office of Christ in Predestination." *SJT* 1 (1948): 1–12.

Reymond, Robert L. *A New Systematic Theology of the Christian Faith*. New York: Nelson, 1998.

Robertson, O. Palmer. "The Holy Spirit in the Westminster Confession." In *The Westminster Confession into the 21st Century: Essays in Remembrance of the 350th Anniversary of the Westminster Assembly*, edited by J. Ligon Duncan III, 1:57–99. 2 vols. Fearn: Mentor, 2003–5.

Rogers, Jack B. *Scripture in the Westminster Confession*. Grand Rapids: Eerdmans, 1967.

_____ and Donald K. McKim. *The Authority and Interpretation of the Bible: An Historical Approach*. San Francisco: Harper and Row, 1979.

Rogers, Thomas. *The English creede, consenting with the true, auncient, catholique, and apostolique Church in al the points, and articles of religion, which everie Christian is to knowe and beleeve that would be saved*. London: Iohn VVindet (first part) and Robert Walde-grave (second part) for Andrew Maunsel, 1585, 1587.

_____. *The faith, doctrine, and religion professed & protected in the Realme of England, and Dominions of the same: expressed in 39 Articles concordablie agreed upon by the Reverend Bishops, and Clergie of this Kingdome, at two severall meetings, or convocations of theirs, in the yeare of our Lord, 1562, and*

1604: The said Articles analised into propositions, and the propositions prooved to be agreeable both to the written Word of God, and to the extant Confessions of all the neighbour Churches, Christianlie Reformed. [Cambridge:] Iohn Legatt, Printer to the Vniversitie of Cambridge, 1607.

Rollock, Robert. *In epistolam S. Pauli apostoli ad Romanos.* Geneva: Franc. lePreux, 1596.

————. *Tractatus de vocatione efficaci.* Edinburgh: Robert Waldegrave, 1597.

————. *A treatise of God's effectual calling.* Translated by Henry Holland. London: Felix Kyngston, 1603.

Rolston, Holmes, III. *John Calvin Versus the Westminster Confession.* Richmond: John Knox Press, 1972.

Schaff, Philip. *The Creeds of Christendom.* 3 vols. Reprint, Grand Rapids: Baker, 1966.

Shaw, Robert. *Exposition of the Westminster Confession of Faith.* Reprint, Fearn: Christian Focus, 2003.

Skinner, Quentin. "Meaning and Understanding in the History of Ideas." In *Visions of Politics,* vol. 1: *On Method,* 57–89. Cambridge: Cambridge University Press, 2002.

Spear, Wayne R. "William Whitaker and the Westminster Doctrine of Scripture." *RTJ* 7 (1991): 38–48.

————. "Word and Spirit in the Westminster Confession." In *The Westminster Confession into the 21st Century: Essays in Remembrance of the 350th Anniversary of the Westminster Assembly,* edited by J. Ligon Duncan III, 1:39–56. 2 vols. Fearn: Mentor, 2003–5.

Spinks, Bryan D. *Two Faces of Elizabethan Anglican Theology: Sacraments and Salvation in the Thought of William Perkins and Richard Hooker.* Lanham, MD: Scarecrow Press, 1999.

Thomas, Derek W. H. "The Eschatology of the Westminster Confession and Assembly." In *The Westminster Confession into the 21st Century: Essays in Remembrance of the 350th Anniversary of the Westminster Assembly,* edited by J. Ligon Duncan III, 2:307–79. 2 vols. Fearn: Mentor, 2003–5.

Torrance, James B. "Covenant or Contract? A Study of the Background of Worship in Seventeenth-Century Scotland." *SJT* 23 (1970): 51–76.

Torrance, Thomas F. *Scottish Theology: From John Knox to John McLeod Campbell.* Edinburgh: T. & T. Clark, 1996.

378

Troxel, A. Craig. "Amyraut 'at' the Assembly: The Westminster Confession of Faith and the Extent of the Atonement." *Presbyterion* 22/1 (1996): 43–55.

_____ and Peter J. Wallace. "Men in Combat over the Civil Law: 'General Equity' in WCF 19.4." *WTJ* 64 (2002): 307–18.

Trueman, Carl R. *The Claims of Truth: John Owen's Trinitarian Theology*. Carlisle: Paternoster, 1998.

_____. *Luther's Legacy: Salvation and the English Reformers 1525–1556*. Oxford: Clarendon Press, 1994.

_____ and R. Scott Clark, eds. *Protestant Scholasticism: Essays in Reassessment*. Carlisle: Paternoster, 1999.

Trumper, Tim J. R. "Covenant Theology and Constructive Calvinism." *WTJ* 64 (2002): 387–404.

_____. "A Fresh Exposition of Adoption: II. Some Implications." *SBET* 23 (2005): 194–215.

_____. "The Metaphorical Import of Adoption: A Plea for Realisation. I: The Adoption Metaphor in Biblical Usage." *SBET* 14 (1996): 129–45.

_____. "The Metaphorical Import of Adoption: A Plea for Realisation. II: The Adoption Metaphor in Theological Usage." *SBET* 15 (1997): 98–115.

Tuckney, Anthony. *None but Christ, or a Sermon on Acts 4.12 preached at St. Maries in Cambridge, on the Commencement Sabbath, July 4. 1652*. London: John Rothwell and S. Gellibrand, 1654.

_____. *Praelectiones theologicae, nec non determinationes quaestionum variarum insignium in Scholis Academicis Cantabrigiensibus habitae; quibus accedunt exercitia pro gradibus capassendis*. Amsterdam: Ex officina Stephani Smart, impensis Jonathanis Robinsonii, & Georgii Wells, Bibliopolarum Londinensium, 1679.

Turretin, Francis. *Institutes of Elenctic Theology*. Edited by James T. Dennison. 3 vols. Phillipsburg, NJ: P&R, 1992.

Tyacke, Nicholas. "Anglican Attitudes: Some Recent Writings on English Religious History, from the Reformation to the Civil War." *JBS* 35 (1996): 139–67.

_____. *Anti-Calvinists: The Rise of English Arminianism, c. 1590–1640*. Oxford: Oxford University Press, 1987.

Van Dixhoorn, Chad B. "Anglicans, Anarchists, and the Westminster Assembly: The Making of a Pulpit Theology." Th.M. thesis, Westminster Theological Seminary, 2000.

_____. "New Taxonomies of the Westminster Assembly (1643–1652): The Creedal Controversy as Case Study." *RRR* 6 (2004): 82–106.

_____. "Reforming the Reformation: Theological Debate at the Westminster Assembly 1643–1652." 7 vols. Ph.D. thesis, Cambridge University, 2004.

_____. "Westminster Assembly (act. 1643-52)." *Oxford Dictionary of National Biography*, online edition. http://www.oxforddnb.com/view/theme/92780, accessed 22 April 2008.

Vermigli, Pietro Martire. *The common places of the most famous and renowned doctor Peter Martyr, divided into foure principall parts.* Translated by Anthonie Marten. London: Henrie Denham, Thomas Chard, William Broome, and Andrew Maunsell, 1583.

_____. *In epistolam S. Pauli apostoli ad Romanos commentarii doctissimi.* Basel: Petrum Pernam, 1558.

Vos, Johannes G. *The Westminster Larger Catechism: A Commentary.* Edited by G. I. Williamson. Phillipsburg, NJ: P&R, 2002.

Warfield, Benjamin Breckinridge. *The Westminster Assembly and Its Work.* New York: Oxford University Press, 1934.

Weber, Hans Emil. *Reformation, Orthodoxie und Rationalismus.* Gütersloh: C. Bertlesmann, 1937–51.

Weinandy, Thomas G. *Does God Suffer?* Notre Dame, IN: University of Notre Dame Press, 2000.

Wenger, Thomas L. "The New Perspective on Calvin: Responding to Recent Calvin Interpretations." *JETS* 50 (2007): 311–28.

Williamson, G. I. *The Westminster Confession of Faith for Study Classes.* Philadelphia: Presbyterian and Reformed, 1964.

Index of the Westminster Standards

164—77
165—77, 170, 173, 344
166—249, 345
167—170, 347
168—78, 348–49, 357
168–77—151
169—350
170—78, 173, 353,
    357
171—356
171–72—355
172—356
173—355

174—356
174–75—355
175—356
178—170
178–96—151
186–96—151
191—365

Westminster Shorter Catechism

1—134, 138, 244, 367
2—134
4—159

5—168
6—168
9–10—188
13–19—188
16—205
20—188
21–28—188
24—153
29–38—188
42—282
88—143, 185, 276, 278,
    320
97—355

Index of Subjects and Names

385

on reprobation, 185
on revelation, 125–26, 127
on Scripture, 120–21, 129, 131, 133, 139, 142, 146, 149
Wars of Religion, 29
Watts, Isaac, 183n32
Weber, Hans Emil, 58, 101, 103
Weinandy, T. G., 162n9
Wendelius, 121
western Catholic tradition, and Westminster Assembly, 94–98
Westminster Assembly
  as advisory body to Parliament, 34–35
  biblical exegesis of, 104, 105, 261
  chronology of, 42
  composition of, 31–34
  and continental Reformed churches, 85–93, 157
  diversity of views at, 33
  doctrinal mandate of, 30–31, 105
  documents as compromise

documents, 103, 111–17
English context, 6, 41, 47–48, 50–51
as Erastian body, 35, 312
failure to achieve ends in England, 44, 47
missionary awareness of, 109, 234
and Western Catholic tradition, 94–98
Whitaker, Jeremiah, 176, 298, 331, 332, 333
Whitaker, William, 53, 93, 121, 122
White, John, 333
Whitgift, John, 17, 20, 53, 69, 86, 209
whole counsel of God, 18n23, 138–39, 141, 154, 158, 301, 303n23
"whole obedience" of Christ, 39, 113–14, 252, 257–61, 263
Wilberforce, William, 5
Wilkinson, Henry, 95, 179, 181n28, 265, 328
Willis, E. D., 162n9
will of God, 182

Wilson, Thomas, 257
Wishart, George, 160
Witte, J., 162n9
Woodcock, Francis, 254, 255, 258, 259, 328, 339, 340
Word and sacraments, 326, 345
Word and Spirit, 152–53
"worldly employments and recreations," 310
works of supererogation, 70, 74, 95, 282
world to come, 310, 366–67
worship, 152, 170, 300–310
wrath of God, 298
Wren, Matthew, 20, 26, 51
Wright, D. F., 324, 326, 332–33

Young, Thomas, 96

Zanchius, Jerome, 333
Zealand, 89
Zurich, 89, 90
Zwingli, Ulrich, 102, 128, 207, 227, 308

Robert Letham (M.A.R., Th.M., Westminster Theological Seminary; Ph.D., University of Aberdeen) is the senior tutor in systematic and historical theology at the Wales Evangelical School of Theology. Previously, he was senior minister of Emmanuel Orthodox Presbyterian Church, Wilmington, Delaware. He has taught at London Bible College, is adjunct professor of systematic theology at Westminster Theological Seminary, Philadelphia, and is visiting professor at Reformed Theological Seminary.

Dr. Letham is the author of *The Holy Trinity: In Scripture, History, Theology, and Worship* (winner of the Evangelical Christian Publishers Association's Gold Medallion Award), *The Work of Christ, Reformed Dogmatics 1523–1619, Through Western Eyes,* and *The Lord's Supper.*